CRITICAL
THEORY
AND
SOCIETY

CRITICAL
THEORY
AND
SOCIETY

A READER

EDITED AND WITH AN INTRODUCTION BY
STEPHEN ERIC BRONNER AND
DOUGLAS MACKAY KELLNER

ROUTLEDGE

NEW YORK   LONDON

Published in 1989 by

Routledge
An imprint of Routledge, Chapman and Hall, Inc.
29 West 35 Street
New York, NY 10001

Published in Great Britain by

Routledge
11 New Fetter Lane
London EC4P 4EE

Printed in the United States of America

Library of Congress Cataloging in Publication Data

Critical theory and society : a reader / edited and with an
  introduction by Stephen Eric Bonner and Douglas Mackay Kellner.
      p.   cm.
    Includes bibliographical references.
    ISBN 0-415-90040-9   ISBN 0-415-90041-7 (pbk.)
    1. Critical theory.   2. Frankfurt school of sociology.
  I. Bronner, Stephen Eric, 1949–   . II. Kellner, Douglas, 1943–
HM24.C76   1989
301'.01—dc20   89-10558
                                                        CIP

British Library Cataloguing in Publication Data also available

Contents

Acknowledgments

There are a number of people to whom we would like to express our gratitude for their encouragement, comments, and support. They include Bob Antonio, Steve Best, Judith Burton, Mark Ritter, Ann Sweeny, and Marianne Stewart. Special thanks are also due to Diana Owen and Victoria Irmiere, as well as to our translators, Micheline Ishay, Mark Ritter, and Peter Wagner. Renee Gibson, Liz Hiles, Patricia Gehle, Kristy Bartlett, Susan Tims, and Lori DeRick provided invaluable help in producing the manuscript. Rainer Funk, the literary executor of the Erich Fromm Archives, provided permission to include some untranslated essays, and Suhrkamp Verlag, Fischer Verlag, Transaction Press, Beacon Press, Harcourt, Brace & Jovanovich, Holt Rinehart and Winston, and W. W. Norton were cooperative in providing permission to reprint the texts for this reader. Thanks are also due to *Arguments, New German Critique, Salmagundi, Canadian Journal of Social and Political Theory,* and *Telos,* all of which have sought to develop the legacy of critical theory. Finally, without the support and aid of our editor, Maureen MacGrogan, this book would not have been possible.

Introduction

Stephen Eric Bronner and
Douglas MacKay Kellner

Critical Theory and Society: A Reader provides a selection of particularly important essays by members of the Institute for Social Research. Founded in 1923 in Frankfurt, Germany, it became the first formally unaffiliated Marxist-oriented institute in Europe. Under its most influential director, Max Horkheimer, its members attempted to revise both the Marxian critique of capitalism and the theory of revolution in order to confront those new social and political conditions which had evolved since Marx's death. In the process a "critical theory" of society emerged to deal with those aspects of social reality which Marx and his orthodox followers neglected or downplayed.

The term *critical theory* itself was only coined in 1937, after the majority of the Institute's members had already emigrated to the United States following the triumph of Hitler. The concept was initially a type of code which, while differentiating its adherents from prevailing forms of orthodoxy, also tended to veil their radical commitments in an environment that was hostile to anything remotely associated with Marxism. But the term stuck and soon was used to encompass and define the general theory of contemporary society associated with Max Horkheimer, Herbert Marcuse, T. W. Adorno, Leo Lowenthal, and Frederick Pollock—as well as with Jürgen Habermas and others who later undertook to continue the tradition.

We have assembled this reader in the belief that critical theory can promote important developments in social theory today. Growing dissatisfaction with the academic division of labor and the dominant views in the various disciplines have led to increased interest in both theoretical and political alternatives. Critical theory offers a multidisciplinary approach to society which combines perspectives drawn from political economy,

1

sociology, cultural theory, philosophy, anthropology, and history. It thus overcomes the fragmentation endemic to established academic disciplines in order to address issues of broader interest.

An antidote to the frequently noncritical quantitative approaches within contemporary social science, critical theory also provides a potentially more useful and politically relevant alternative than currently fashionable approaches like existentialism and phenomenology, poststructuralism and postmodernism, as well as the various versions of humanist idealism which are periodically recycled and repackaged. By contrast, critical theory maintains a nondogmatic perspective which is sustained by an interest in emancipation from all forms of oppression, as well as by a commitment to freedom, happiness, and a rational ordering of society. Eschewing divisions between the humanities and the social sciences, it thus sets forth a normative social theory that seeks a connection with empirical analyses of the contemporary world.

Fundamentally inspired by the dialectical tradition of Hegel and Marx, critical theory is intrinsically open to development and revision. Inherently self-critical, it offers a well-articulated standpoint for thematizing social reality—unlike the current postmodern theories which attack all forms of thought in an undifferentiated manner. Against all relativistic and nihilistic excesses, critical theory seeks an emancipatory alternative to the existing order.

The diversity of interests and insights among critical theorists made the choice of texts for this book particularly difficult. Our selection was guided by an attempt to emphasize the most characteristic theorists and themes within the tradition. We also sought to balance the historical importance of any given text with its contemporary relevance. Finally, without sacrificing intellectual quality, we tried to choose texts which were somewhat less esoteric than some for which the critical theorists are infamous.

This reader focuses, for the most part, on the "inner circle" of the first generation of critical theorists, which consisted of Horkheimer, Adorno, Marcuse, Lowenthal, Pollock, and Erich Fromm. Yet we have also included texts by Siegfried Kracauer and Walter Benjamin, who were to varying degrees associated with critical theory, as well as selections from Jürgen Habermas, who is clearly the most significant member of the second generation. Unfortunately, space constraints forced us to omit texts by contemporary critical theorists such as Oskar Negt, Alfred Schmidt, Claus Offe, and Albrecht Wellmer. We also could not include works by such significant members of the Institute as Karl Wittfogel, Franz Neumann, Otto Kirchheimer, Franz Borkenau, and Henryk Grossmann, as well as related theorists like Karl Korsch and Ernst Bloch, who were occasionally supported by the Institute or—in Korsch's case—published by its journal.

This volume has been designed both to provide an introduction to critical theory and to inspire the advanced student. The selections have been organized into five sections which, we believe, highlight the most significant aspects of critical theory. Part I opens with some key texts which set forth the original program and research agenda of the Institute for Social Research. This section, like the others, contains important texts which have been translated into English for the first time and which should provide an informative introduction to the program and scope of the original enterprise. Part II is constructed around the theory of society which the Institute sought to develop, while Part III attempts to elaborate the cultural criticism and critique of mass culture for which its members have become justly famous. Part IV contains provocative contributions to their project for a new social psychology, while Part V advances certain "critical visions" which attempt to link critical theory with politics and provide perspectives for future inquiry within the framework of this tradition.

Each section is organized chronologically, and many of the essays comment on previous positions set forth within the Institute. Yet even when they address similar issues, it will become apparent that sharp differences existed between members of the Institute. In fact, critical theory is not a single doctrine or unified worldview. Instead, it is a set of basic insights and perspectives which undermine existing "truths" even as they foster the need for a theory of society that remains to be completed. In this spirit, while not systematically evaluating the positions set forth in each essay, our introduction will attempt to illuminate the socio-historical matrix wherein critical theory evolved and indicate the relevance of basic issues addressed with respect to the project as a whole.

Our first section contains essays concerning The Institute for Social Research and its original program. When the Institute was founded in 1923, the "heroic" period of the Russian Revolution as well as the proletarian revolts which followed World War I had come to an end. The Weimar Republic, established following the abdication of Kaiser Wilhelm II, was initially threatened by uprisings from the left and the right. By 1923, however, the period of revolutionary upsurge had waned and intense discussion had begun concerning the "failure of the revolution" and "the crisis of Marxism." Many members of the Institute maintained ties with the various parties of the Left and—under the leadership of the Austrian Marxist Carl Grünberg—developed a research program centering around the character of the labor movement, the capitalist economy, the new experiments with planning in the Soviet Union, as well as those "subjective" conditions which subverted a proletarian victory in Germany. During the period of Grünberg's tenure, a rather orthodox Marxism permeated the Institute and was carried over, to a greater or lesser degree, in many of the writings from the thirties. Nevertheless, a shift in direction took place when Max Horkheimer became director in 1930, following Grünberg's retirement due to a stroke.

The son of a German industrialist, a philosopher by training, Horkheimer was also interested in sociology as well as a wide range of other academic pursuits. It was under his leadership that the Institute developed the project for which it would become internationally renowned. A highly effective academic entrepreneur, he gathered around him many individuals who would eventually achieve fame in a variety of disciplines. Under Horkheimer's direction, the Institute undertook to develop a theory of society, and it is fitting that the first selection in our volume should be Horkheimer's previously untranslated inaugural lecture "The State of Social Philosophy and the Tasks of an Institute for Social Research." Here, Horkheimer defines the tasks of the Institute and sets forth the multidisciplinary program which would characterize it. Presenting the Institute's position against more mainstream conceptions of social theory and science, Horkheimer calls for a multidisciplinary integration of philosophy with the sciences in the hope of providing a theoretical instrument for transforming politics, society, the economy, and everyday contemporary life.

One of the distinguishing features—and novelties—of the new approach was its attempt to develop a critical social psychology. For this task, the Institute appointed a Freudian psychoanalyst, Erich Fromm, who would become one of the most widely read social theorists of the postwar era with works like *Escape from Freedom* and *The Sane Society*. Our second selection is accordingly the first English translation of a 1929 lecture by Fromm entitled "Psychoanalysis and Sociology," which clearly sketches the attempt to combine sociology and psychology in a new theoretical framework. Though he never did develop a theory of the manifold mediations which exist between the individual and society—in the manner of, say, Jean-Paul Sartre—Fromm, along with Siegfried Bernfeld and Wilhelm Reich, became one of the first to undertake a Marx-Freud synthesis in order to analyze the ways in which social conditions constituted the psyche and psychological factors affected social life.

The Institute's members published the results of their research in a journal, the *Zeitschrift für Sozialforschung,* which served as their public platform. In keeping with the Institute's general project, its key members usually read and discussed each others' work so that the edited and published version often reflected the spirit of a collaborative enterprise. The first issue of the journal illustrated the Institute's approach to the various disciplines. It contained articles by Fromm on psychology, by Henryk Grossmann and Pollock on economics, and by Adorno on music, as well as a host of others. From this issue, we decided to include Leo Lowenthal's essay "On Sociology of Literature" and Horkheimer's "Notes on Science and the Crisis." Both of these articles argue that application of the Marxian historical materialist approach to the relevant disciplines provides the best starting point for inquiry and research.

Lowenthal, who would become an important critic of literature and mass culture at the University of California at Berkeley, argues against dominant idealist and philological positions. Instead, he favors an approach which interprets texts and determines the meaning of cultural objects within their social and historical context. Refusing to study literature as a self-contained object, Lowenthal was unable to provide either an explanation for literary transcendence or normative aesthetic criteria in the manner of Lukàcs. Nevertheless, he became a pioneer in the development of the sociology of literature—as well as a member of Horkheimer's "inner circle" who played a key role in managing Institute affairs.

Horkheimer himself tended to publish the key programmatic statements of the Institute. "Notes on Science and the Crisis" is one of those pieces which addresses a particular historical situation and its impact on the Institute's research agenda. The "crisis" refers to the world economic depression of 1929, whose persistence was producing ever more massive unemployment as well as social and political instability. In his article, Horkheimer explains how science and technology are potentially emancipatory forces of production even as they are fettered by the irrationality of the capitalist economic system. The implicit presupposition is that a more rational form of social organization would use science and technology to dramatically improve human life. It was only in their later work that members of the Institute would assume a more critical stance on the role of science, technology, and the notion of progress with which both bourgeois society and "actually existing socialism" (Rudolf Bahro) identified.

Even initially, however, the Institute's theorists believed that only by calling the most basic assumptions into question would it become possible to provide an adequate critical theory of society. In a 1937 essay, "Philosophy and Critical Theory," Herbert Marcuse pointed to the importance of critical rationalism for the Institute's theoretical enterprise. Indeed, along with Horkheimer's classic "Traditional and critical theory," this essay contains one of the most comprehensive programmatic statements of the Institute's attempts to synthesize philosophy, the sciences, and a radical political perspective.

Where traditional social sciences based on positivist assumptions wish to exclude normative concerns from social scientific inquiry, and banish them to the realm of metaphysics or obscurantism, Marcuse highlights the importance of concepts such as reason, freedom, and happiness for critical theory. Recognizing the need for empirical research, though ultimately unable to define its role within the new project, Marcuse emphasizes that speculative reason is the yardstick with which to measure the degree of social rationality or irrationality inherent in any given form of social or political organization.

Despite his inability to specify institutions by which an emancipated order might reproduce itself, Marcuse is aware that freedom is not license and that a rational ordering of society will universally expand the opportunities for the exercise of individual autonomy. Such notions are crucial to the tradition of philosophical idealism which Marcuse wants to link with a materialist heritage whose importance derives from its concrete emphasis on individual happiness and well-being. A materialist stance suggests that freedom, happiness, and reason are not spiritual features of the individual. Instead, they are concrete potentialities for satisfaction that demand realization. It is this commitment to the "good life" which critical theory places at the forefront, and then uses to call existing repressive conditions into question. Thus, according to the new standpoint, a materialist project of social reconstruction requires a foundation in critical rationalism which alone can forward the utopian projection of a free society.

This utopian commitment of critical theory points to the fervent desire of its proponents for an emancipatory alternative during a period when the Great Depression was spreading throughout the capitalist world and fascism was threatening to engulf Europe. In this vein, it is impossible to overestimate the importance of fascism for the development of critical theory. Since most of the Institute's members were Jews and Marxists, the Nazis quickly forced them into exile. In 1934, after numerous complications, its headquarters were finally moved from Frankfurt to Columbia University, in New York, which offered office space and institutional support. Upon coming to the United States the Institute's members began their inquiry into the roots of the fascism and the manner in which socializing institutions—especially the family—induced individuals to accept even the most irrational forms of social and political authority. It was also while in exile at Columbia University that the Institute's members developed their particular style of "ideology critique" which analyzes the social interests ideologies serve by exposing their historical roots and assumptions, no less than the distortions and mystifications which they perpetuate. Indeed, this was the time when the Institute began to programmatically form its conception of critical social theory.

Part II is entitled "Fragments of a Theory of Society" because, in reality, the Institute never produced that comprehensive theory of society which its members sought. While they provided elements for a theory of the transition from market/entrepreneurial to new forms of state and monopoly capitalism, their positions on these developments were quite diverse and their various insights never coalesced into a coherent theory. Consequently, though these fragments provide some of critical theory's most important contributions, the failure to articulate a more fully developed social theory points to the limitations of the original program sketched out by Horkheimer.

The section opens with the first English translation of Horkheimer's essay "The Jews and Europe." Written in 1938, as Hitler was preparing for war, it prefigures many of the basic concerns which would later define critical theory even as it shows how a certain orthodox Marxism remained part of the original project. Consistent with the general thinking of the Institute's members, the essay views fascism as an outgrowth of capitalism moving from its liberal to its monopoly stage; thus, in an oft-quoted passage, Horkheimer writes: "Whoever is not willing to talk about capitalism should also keep quiet about fascism."

Although the topic nominally involves European Jewry, Horkheimer basically interprets anti-Semitism in terms of its usefulness for monopoly capitalism. In considering it as a mere ideological facade for the elimination of an entire sphere of circulation, defined by small banks and the vestiges of a market, Horkheimer grossly underestimates the centrality of anti-Semitism to the Nazi project—a flawed interpretation that later Institute studies would rectify. The essay, however, also reflects Horkheimer's deep despair over a future in which he foresaw mass-mobilized groups submitting to new forms of totalitarian domination.

All of the Institute members were in agreement that fascism had emerged from a capitalism in crisis and that it evidenced a new form of the capitalist state. Still, there were sharp arguments within the Institute over whether the new fascist state was basically independent of the economy or merely a tool of monopoly capitalist interests. Franz Neumann, perhaps the most prominent scholar in the Institute, published the classic *Behemoth* (1941), which argued that fascism was a form of totalitarian state capitalism. Neumann had been a famous labor lawyer in Weimar Germany, as well as an important member of the German Social Democratic party. In his widely discussed book, he stressed the continuing primacy of the economy over the state in the fascist era. Against him, the Institute economist Frederick Pollock argued for "the primacy of the political" and claimed that the state was assuming power over the economy in the current era of fascism and welfare-state capitalism.

The interested reader might consult Neumann's *Behemoth* and contrast it with Pollock's article "State Capitalism," which is included in the present volume. Pollock's article is historically important insofar as it presents an interpretation of fascism shared by Horkheimer and others within the Institute. In fact, it established a framework for the Institute's later analysis of the new relations between the state and the economy during the postwar era. Pollock claims that state capitalism—in both its "democratic" and "totalitarian" forms—produces a "command economy" exhibiting a "primacy of the political" whereby the state comes to manage the economy. Against Neumann, Pollock maintained that "the profit motive is superseded by the power motive." Indeed, the Institute members would never agree whether economic or political imperatives were primary for the new fascist state.

Building on the Austrian Social Democrat Rudolf's Hilferding's *Finance Capital* (1910), Pollock's essay laid the foundation for later claims regarding the integration of the economy, the state, and the public sphere. It also maintained that capitalism had discovered new strategies to avoid economic crisis and provided the basis for the burgeoning belief that capitalism could henceforth stabilize itself and prevent the realization of socialism. Thus, it raised new doubts concerning the revolutionary role of the working class which was so central to the classical Marxian theory.

For Marx, the industrial proletariat was to serve as the agent of socialist revolution. Bearing the burden of industrial production, the working class was seen as the logical subject of revolution due to its crucial position in the production process and its potential for growth and organization in highly centralized and large-scale industries. The Marxian theory of revolution also predicted severe capitalist economic crisis which would lead the working class to revolt against conditions of poverty where it had "nothing to lose but its chains." Even as capitalism was undergoing one of its most intense crises in the 1930s, however, the powerful parties and unions of the European working classes were defeated by the forces of fascism. Indeed, following that defeat, the prospects for socialist revolution looked ever bleaker to the Institute theorists.

As a consequence, they increasingly distanced themselves from the traditional Marxist position which claimed that socialist revolution was inevitable and that historical progress would necessarily lead from capitalism to socialism. Henceforth, the critical theorists' relation to Marxism would become more ambivalent and complex. Thus, where individuals like Horkheimer would eventually abandon Marxism altogether for a form of mystical irrationalism derived from Schopenhauer and Nietzsche, Marcuse and others would continue to develop their own particular versions of the Marxian theory.

After World War II, the Institute theorists began their widely discussed analyses of working class integration within contemporary capitalist societies. According to many of the critical theorists, new forms of technology, new modes of organizing production, new configurations of class, and new methods of social control were producing a "one-dimensional" society without opposition. It also seemed that new forms of political, social, and especially cultural conformity were becoming institutionalized. This development of a "totally administered society" led Adorno and Horkheimer to proclaim "the end of the individual" and to stress the importance of preserving subjectivity in order to fulfill the goals of liberalism and socialism alike. The eradication of subjectivity, they believed, was a betrayal of the promise of modernity, which was itself predicated on the belief that the augmentation of science and technology would improve human control over nature and produce more freedom, individuality, and happiness. Instead, the critical theorists argued, the institutions and practices of "advanced industrial society" were apparently producing ever greater conformity and social domination. Thus in his highly esoteric *Negative Dialectics* and *Aesthetic Theory*, Adorno attempted to resurrect a repressed subjectivity against mass society and its philosophical expressions like existentialism and positivism.

Still, it was ultimately Marcuse who provided the most comprehensive formulation of this position in *One-Dimensional Man*. In his now-classic analysis, advanced industrial society integrates and absorbs all forces of opposition so that the "subjective" conditions for conflict between classes, as well as between the individual and society, vanish at the very time that the "objective" reality of exploitation and injustice intensifies. That argument would perhaps come to define the idea of the Institute more than any other, and so we include here an article by Marcuse, "From Ontology to Technology: Fundamental Tendencies of Industrial Society"—translated from French into English for the first time—which provides a sketch for *One-Dimensional Man*. In this essay, Marcuse analyzes the new forms of social control in "one-dimensional society" and the diminution of the "other dimension" of social critique, rebellion, and utopian thinking which present alternatives to the existing order.

Marcuse describes a universe in which technology and scientific rationality produce a new world of thought and behavior. Where thought had previously functioned to provide alternatives to the existing society, in the new technological universe, it exists merely to make the prevailing system more efficient and raise technical means over normative ends. Indeed, precisely because moral and critical ends lose their force, the dominant modes of thinking analyzed by Marcuse make individuals adapt to the existing order rather than foster their capacities for critical judgment.

One of the key Institute positions was that the "culture industries" were now playing an increasingly important role in managing consciousness and obscuring social conflict. First sketched in Adorno and Horkheimer's *Dialectic of Enlightenment*, written during the early 1940s and published in 1947, this standpoint became an essential component of critical theory and inaugurated a new discourse about the role of mass communication and culture in the constitution of contemporary societies. According to Adorno and Horkheimer, the culture industries were organs of mass deception which manipulated individuals into accepting the current organization of society. In their view, the culture industries were therefore engaging in sophisticated forms of ideological indoctrination, using "entertainment" to sugar-coat the ideological content of oppression while eroding cultural standards in order to quell any forms of expression which might contest the given order.

This critique of the culture industries appears in an article by Adorno, arguably the most brilliant and multitalented of all the Institute's members, entitled "The Culture Industry Reconsidered." He argues that "mass culture" is not a "popular culture" rising from the experiences and concerns of the people, but rather a form of administered culture imposed from above. The theorists of the Frankfurt School were among the first to provide a critical approach to mass culture, and this article summarizes many of their insights regarding the new socio-cultural forms by which neocapitalist societies legitimate and reproduce themselves.

In this vein, Jürgen Habermas, a student of Adorno and Horkheimer, carried through a ground-breaking historical and theoretical investigation of the transition from liberal democratic societies of the eighteenth and nineteenth centuries to modern capitalism. Where in an earlier stage of capitalist society, the individual developed his ideas in a free "public sphere" which protected him from the state, advanced industrial society has redefined that sphere in terms of an artificially induced public opinion which binds the individual to the existing order and undermines his critical capacities. The study was published in German as *Structural Change of the Public Sphere (Strukturwandel der Öffentlichkeit),* and we include here a translation of the German encyclopaedia article "The Public Sphere," which summarizes Habermas's position.

This essay provides both a historical sketch of the transition to our current media-dominated society and a normative model for a more democratic public sphere. It is also important because the concept of a "public sphere" would animate Habermas's later philosophical endeavors, including his attempt to elaborate a theory and practice of "undistorted" communication, as well as his attempt to reinvigorate democratic life by bringing normative social judgments to bear on putatively technical forms of decision-making by elites. Such free and unrestrained communication would foster public debate, as well as the democratization of everyday life and the promulgation of generalizable interests necessary to ascertain and institutionalize "the common good."

The distance between Habermas's work and that of the first generation of critical theorists points to the increasing heterogeneity of the Frankfurt

School and the significant differences within critical theory. While Adorno and Horkheimer became increasingly critical of the Enlightenment tradition and the project of modernity with which it was connected, Habermas eventually came to the defense of both the Enlightenment and modernity itself. The collaboration of Adorno and Horkheimer during the early 1940s, in fact, marked a distinctive shift in the development of critical theory. Surrendering attempts to develop a Marxian theory of society oriented toward radical social transformation, they became concerned with how modernity was rooted in forms of domination which went back to the Greeks. *Dialectic of Enlightenment* thus represents a shift away from interdisciplinary social theory to philosophy and cultural criticism, around which much of critical theory would center during the next two decades.

The growing fragmentation of critical theory, which would culminate in the break-up of the Institute, was in part a result of the historical situation. During World War II, Marcuse, Lowenthal, Neumann, and others went to Washington to work for the U.S. government in the struggle against fascism, while Adorno and Horkheimer moved to California, where they pursued their theoretical endeavors. After the war they returned, with Pollock, to Germany while the others remained in the United States. Henceforth, the differences between the one-time colleagues would multiply and a variety of positions would eventually emerge among those who had participated in the original Institute.

Critical theorists are perhaps most celebrated for their cultural criticism and critique of mass culture. The third section of our reader therefore provides some key examples of this crucial dimension within their theory. It opens with a fascinating article by Siegfried Kracauer, "The Mass Ornament." Kracauer was a close friend of Adorno and intimate with other members of the Institute—though he was never formally affiliated. After a brief career as an architect, he became a well-known writer and cultural critic in Weimar Germany. In the United States, he would become famous for his outstanding works of film criticism, which include *From Caligari to Hitler* and *Theory of Film*.

"The Mass Ornament" was written for the *Frankfurter Zeitung* and later appeared as the title essay in an important collection of Kracauer's work. First published in 1927, it presents a model of cultural criticism which stands in direct relation to the cultural concerns of the Institute. The critical theorists shared Kracauer's conviction that typical artifacts of mass culture and other surface manifestations of a society can disclose its basic traits as well as the most important historical trends of an epoch. Through a close analysis of the "Tiller Girls"—a popular revue of dancing girls who were featured in movies, newsreels, and variety shows during the 1920s—

Kracauer uncovers some basic features of contemporary capitalist society. He argues that the geometric patterns and highly orchestrated movements reflect the massification of audiences before spectacles of the "distraction factories"—Kracauer's term for the culture industries.

Kracauer's study seeks to provide a physiognomy of the emerging mass society following World War I. At the same time, it anticipates the emergence of totalitarianism by portraying the ways in which masses can be mobilized and manipulated through mass culture. Although the article is extremely dense and quite difficult, we believe that its richness and suggestiveness justify the intellectual efforts its comprehension requires. Indeed, to the extent that the essay develops the art of deciphering important social insights from obscure and offbeat phenomena, an encounter with it might even yield surprising new insights into such social phenomena as movies, massification, capitalism, mythologies, and fairy tales.

In a similar vein, T. W. Adorno's "Lyric Poetry and Society" extends the sociological approach to literature outlined in the earlier article by Leo Lowenthal. Adorno argues that even in lyric poetry, seemingly the most ethereal mode of high culture, social tendencies are evident. He acutely notes that approaches which interpret poetry as one of the most sublime escapes from the cares of everyday life themselves point to an oppressive organization of society which requires transcendence. The article reveals how culture can provide sources of critical knowledge, and attests to the Institute's concern for a subjectivity threatened by the modern world. Through a close reading of poems by German poets like Goethe, Rilke, Mörike, and Stefan George, Adorno demonstrates how social insights can be unearthed from the form, rhythm, and images of lyric poetry as well as from its content. Adorno's article therefore also embodies critical theory's claim that authentic art provides both a form of opposition to the established society and a utopian mode of reconciliation with nature. Indeed, as their hopes for revolutionary political change diminished, Adorno and Marcuse in particular celebrated the "aesthetic dimension" as a domain of emancipatory experience that posed one against and beyond established consciousness.

In general, critical theorists prized the modernist avant-garde over the exponents of realism. Walter Benjamin's "Surrealism" reveals that commitment to the avant-garde, but also the potential importance of such movements to political revolution—which sharply distinguishes his position from that of Adorno. Benjamin was radicalized through his relationships with the maverick Marxist Ernst Bloch and a Russian revolutionary named Asja Lacis. He also became close to the Marxist playwright Bertolt Brecht, whose theater he championed as a model of revolutionary art. Benjamin never officially joined the Institute, but he received a small stipend which helped finance his studies in Paris during the early years of the fascist epoch. Long a devotee of French culture, Benjamin believed that surrealism retained great revolutionary potential by virtue of its "profane illumination" of everyday life and its intoxicating experiences of break, rupture, and ecstasy.

Benjamin opens his article by reflecting on the origins and nature of surrealism and attempting to illuminate the movement through discussing some of its most important advocates such as André Breton. In general, Benjamin believed that certain kinds of art provided a virtually mystical "revelation" of truths and insights concerning social life which are hidden from the everyday consciousness—a position which he shared with Adorno and Kracauer. Nevertheless, in contrast to Adorno, who rigidly separated art from radical politics, Benjamin believed that certain experiences which broke with everyday consciousness and routine could promote revolutionary awareness and action. It is for this reason that Benjamin wanted to illuminate and appropriate the energies of surrealism for the revolutionary movement of the day.

"Surrealism" is typical of Benjamin's frequent willingness to judge different types of art in terms of their revolutionary potential or lack of it. Unlike other critical theorists, for instance, he advanced a profound belief in film's ability to promote socially critical consciousness—at least under the proper circumstances. More than that, however, this piece evidences the most radical expression of critical theory's revolutionary message. Anticipating the "situationist" attempt to transform everyday life and the values of individual experience, as well as the cultural politics of the 1960s, it praises "surrealism" for rebelling against the "inner poverty" of the individual and exploding the verities of "normal" perception from a standpoint which manifests the "intoxication" of the revolution.

In "Historical Perspectives on Popular Culture," Leo Lowenthal provides a clear contextualization of the Institute's theory of mass culture. Attacking the uncritical empirical approaches to culture and society that were particularly dominant in the United States, he sharply contrasts them to the historical and critical approaches of the Institute. Situating present debates over the nature and value of popular culture in the contrasting attitudes toward leisure of Pascal and Montaigne, Lowenthal shows how the former believed that popular entertainment distracted individuals from their religious vocation. Montaigne, by contrast, maintained that modern life required a certain amount of relaxation and diversion which popular culture could provide—and which thus made it beneficial for individuals and society. Stripping Pascal's critique of mass culture of its religious overtones, Lowenthal defends a critical approach to the study of mass culture. The article concludes with a concise summary of the approaches to popular culture developed by the Institute, and suggestions concerning how they can be utilized to provide more adequate analyses.

The attack on conformity and the culture industry, however, has its blindspots and limitations. In "Perennial Fashion—Jazz" Adorno provides one of the most controversial and sharply criticized attacks on mass culture produced by the critical theorists. Whereas many people believe that American jazz creates a type of rebellious, nonconformist musical experience, Adorno argues that it actually reveals the conformist tendencies shared by all forms of fashion and the culture industry. For Adorno, rather than providing a fresh and innovative musical idiom, jazz merely exhibits "incessantly repeated formulae" and accelerates the trends toward standardization, commercialization, and reification implicit in all mass culture. Thus, in Adorno's view, jazz is "utterly impoverished" while its fans joyfully experience nothing more than "psychological regression."

Adorno's uncompromising critique raises the much-debated issue of the cultural elitism which allegedly informed the Institute's perceptions of mass culture. Indeed, there is no doubt that the "inner circle" was composed of highly cultured European intellectuals and radicals who found life in the United States extremely distasteful. Clearly, they blamed mass culture for making the working classes blind to their own exploitation, and thus for creating obstacles to radical social change. Despite their biases, however, it was nonetheless the critical theorists who provided the first set of sustained and systematic insights into the important new roles that mass communications and culture were playing in contemporary societies. It was precisely their status as European exiles which enabled them to gain insights into the ideological nature and social functions of mass culture, which were missed by American theorists and radicals, who simply took mass culture for granted as a fact of social life, and so overlooked its increasingly important social functions.

By the same token, their status as exiles also caused the critical theorists to ignore certain key aspects of American life, such as the continuation of political and cultural struggle during that difficult period, and the contradictions within mass culture which frequently exhibit socially critical elements. By assuming that the transformation of an artwork into a commodity destroys its emancipatory function, many critical theorists reached the conclusion that popular culture had no emancipatory potential whatsoever. That is why most of them have traditionally been so emphatic in maintaining the division between "high" and "low" (or mass) culture. Even so, they never provided categories for differentiating among cultural artifacts or the diverse purposes which they can serve.

Against this view it is preferable to perceive culture as a contested terrain with potentially subversive elements. Still, the aesthetic theories of the Frankfurt School contain many valuable aspects, and their analyses of cultural texts are among their major contributions. The commitment to aesthetics was genuine. Indeed, both Adorno and Marcuse sincerely

believed that only the aesthetic realm could preserve a subjectivity threatened by the very structure of advanced industrial society.

The freedom and autonomy of the individual was always a central
concern of the Institute, and the attempt by Erich Fromm to synthesize
Marx and Freud in terms of a critical social psychology was obviously
meant to compensate for the neglect of consciousness and the "subjective"
factor in orthodox Marxism. In a 1931 article titled "Politics and Psychoanalysis," Fromm argues for the relevance of psychoanalytic perspectives
to revolutionary politics, claiming that psychoanalysis provides a theory
which can help explain mass behavior and political events as well as
the actions of an individual. While suggesting how the socio-economic
analysis of events typical of Marxism can be combined with psychoanalytic explanation, he argues against interpretations which claim that the
two theories are incompatible. Indeed, Fromm believes that they can work
together to explain the ways that instinctual drives and psychic attitudes
can be mobilized to support political movements and leaders.

Fromm's essay was written when the Nazis were seizing power in
Germany. The Institute responded by attempting to provide an explanation
of the appeal and power of fascism. One of the distinguishing aspects of
their analysis was their discussion of how psychological dispositions
toward authoritarianism nurtured submission to fascist domination. In a
collective work published in 1936, *Studies in Authority and the Family,*
the Institute members explored some of the ways that the patriarchal
family engendered authoritarian traits which would predispose individuals
to embrace fascism. In fact, the Institute became involved in a number of
such studies which sought to analyze how various established institutions
and ideologies promote the development of personalities susceptible to
manipulation and authoritarian domination.

After the defeat of fascism, in conjunction with a Berkeley research
group, Adorno and other members of the Institute for Social Research
undertook a collective inquiry of the psychological propensities toward
authoritarianism in the United States. The result was a major work, *The
Authoritarian Personality,* from which we include the introduction. Here
Adorno and his colleagues outline the project of their social research, as
well as the basic assumptions and methods utilized in the study. There is
no doubt that the undertaking itself was motivated by the fear that a new
character type, the authoritarian personality, was emerging. In a manner
somewhat inconsistent with the Institute's position on mass culture, however, the authors conclude that education might prevent a duplication of
the European experience.

The researchers devised an elaborate set of questionnaires, which were sent to 2,099 respondents, along with a set of interpretive techniques to determine a potentially fascist mind-set from the answers tabulated. The answers were classified to correlate individuals on an A-S (anti-Semitism) scale, an E (enthnocentrism) scale, a PEC (political-economic conservativism) scale, and an F (potentially fascist) scale. Interviews were then conducted with a large number of individuals who registered both the highest and lowest scores on the fascist potential scale to draw further conclusions about the behavior and personality structure of the authoritarian personality.

Questionnaire and interview results were tabulated, analyzed, and published in the various studies that comprise *The Authoritarian Personality*. The study disclosed a surprising degree of anti-Semitic prejudice in the United States and an alarming number of people who scored high on the scale which measured the extent of authoritarian potential in individuals. *The Authoritarian Personality* was widely read and discussed, and remains to this day a classic example of critical group research which combines interviews, psychological depth analysis, and socio-economic data with a critical perspective.

Setting forth a different view, Herbert Marcuse, in a lecture entitled "The Obsolescence of the Freudian Concept of Man," claimed that the sort of psychological configuration analyzed by Freud—whereby individuals submit to mass leaders—is now obsolete. Marcuse maintains that the Freudian concept of man presupposes an individual ego that stands in conflict with the demands of society, as represented by the superego, and that individuals will identify with leaders who emerge as surrogate father figures to alleviate guilt and anxiety. This Freudian model, however, also assumes that the family is the basic institution of socialization and that individuals develop their personalities in conflict with their fathers while still identifying with patriarchal images and roles. Against this model, Marcuse claims that cultural institutions are currently socializing individuals directly, and so replacing the family as the dominant instrument of socialization.

In Marcuse's view, the mass media, school, sports, and peer groups are coming to directly manage ego-development. A new form of socialization tends to eliminate the conflict between individual and society built into the Freudian model—thereby producing massive social conformity and weak egos. As a consequence, Marcuse claims that in contemporary industrial society individuals ever more surely identify with society itself—with the entire apparatus of production, consumption, and entertainment. A submission to authority therefore takes place which engenders psychological regression into herdlike conformity, a weakening of mental faculties, and an unthinking acceptance of whatever is offered by mass society, from television to the nuclear arms race. Thus, for Marcuse, a critical social psychology becomes another way to explain the creation of one-dimensional society.

While all critical theorists agreed upon the importance of developing a radical social psychology—and the need to synthesize Marx and Freud—there were significant differences among the Institute's members on the nature of psychoanalysis and the role it should play. To demonstrate this, we conclude our section on critical theory and psychology with a selection from Erich Fromm's "Crisis of Psychoanalysis." Fromm, who was a practicing analyst, claims that a crisis has resulted from the transformation of Freud's critical categories like the unconscious into instruments of conformity and adjustment. In this essay, written long after his break with the Institute, Fromm attacks Marcuse's use of Freudian theory and vividly demonstrates the profound differences within the tradition of critical theory.

Although the full story of Fromm's break with the Institute has yet to be told, increasingly bitter polemics broke out between him and his former colleagues. The split initially surfaced in public in 1955 with the publication of Marcuse's *Eros and Civilization,* which attacked Fromm as a neo-Freudian revisionist whose theory was putatively conformist and idealist. Fromm countered with a sharp critique of Marcuse, who, in turn, riposted with a defense of his position in the pages of *Dissent* magazine. In "The Crisis of Psychoanalysis," however, Fromm spells out his criticisms in detail, claiming that Marcuse fails to understand some of Freud's key concepts and that the former's ideal of a "non-repressive society" is "an infantile paradise where all work is play and where there is no serious conflict or tragedy."

There is an argument to be made that both Fromm and Marcuse misrepresent the other's position in their polemics, and the reader is strongly advised to read their main works themselves. But there are also clear differences between Marcuse's "meta-psychological" use of Freud to create a theory of instinctual liberation and a nonrepressive civilization, and Fromm's more modest clinical use of Freud's psychological insights. For Marcuse, the unconscious provides integral images of happiness and liberation which allow for a critique of existing society. Nevertheless, both Marcuse and Fromm see libidinal energies as a source of opposition to the existing order and privilege subjectivity as an emancipatory force.

Against the trends toward conformity, massification, and submission, the critical theorists all advocate strengthening the ego and developing critical individualism. This psychological emphasis comes to shape their politics and points to both their contributions and limitations. But although such emphasis on the emancipatory role of the individual psyche can help foster individual rebellion, it can also simply reproduce the egotistical values of advanced industrial society. In fact, the critical theorists neither developed an adequate theory of social change nor achieved that unity of theory and practice which they so frequently championed.

The Frankfurt School's political perspectives tended to be rather abstract, and its members never based their critique of advanced industrial society on any positive theory of revolution. But they did produce a set of what might be termed "critical visions" regarding the mutable character of history, society, and the future. In this concluding section, we have selected texts which articulate some of these perspectives. In one way or another, all of them point to the legacy of critical theory and the impetus it might offer to future social inquiry with an emancipatory intent.

In his controversial and paradoxical "Theses on the Philosophy of History," Walter Benjamin seeks to confront the triumph of fascism as well as what he considers the atavistic assumptions of an orthodox Marxism which maintains that the capitalist transition to socialism, and then to a superior communist order, is somehow "inevitable." Opposed to all unilinear conceptions of progress, while aware of the contemporary barriers to emancipatory change, Benjamin proposes the need to remember and compensate for the evils and suffering of the past. This recollection of past suffering is what he believes will provide an inspiration for struggle against oppression in the present. It is therefore "the image of enslaved ancestors rather than that of liberated grandchildren" which offers the best impetus to continue the quest for emancipation. To move forward, it is therefore necessary to look backwards so that an emancipated future ultimately comes to rest on a philosophical reappropriation of the past.

Writing in 1940, as the Nazi war machine blitzed through Europe, Benjamin saw modernity as an unending catastrophe and thus viewed more optimistic theories of history with contempt. Providing a considerably more critical perspective on Western culture than Marcuse in "Philosophy and Critical Theory," Benjamin claimed that even high culture was often merely the ideological cloak for barbarism, and that it was always the victors—however barbaric—who wrote history and established systems of thought to legitimate their systems of oppression. Shortly after publishing these theses, Benjamin himself was forced to flee the Nazi occupation of France, and committed suicide on the Spanish border when it appeared that he would be captured by the fascists. Ironically that action spurred the Spanish border officials to allow the rest of Benjamin's group to escape into freedom.

By this time, Horkheimer and his associates were already established in New York. His "Notes on Institute Activities" sketches some of the defining features of critical theory in the new context as well as its relevance for contemporary research and politics. The validity of its concepts is, first, determined by their ability to comprehend historical processes and the trends for social transformation. In this vein, Horkheimer describes the inductive character of critical theory and how it presents society as a system in which every part should be interpreted from the standpoint of the whole. At the same time, however, he maintains that critical theory also projects alternatives to the existing society by engaging in what the Frankfurt School theorists call "immanent critique"—a method which judges society by the very norms of freedom and happiness which it professes to accept.

Although Adorno would later make some very different and more subjectivist assumptions in *Negative Dialectics,* this perspective is further articulated in his 1963 article "Society." Revealing how Critical Theory retains a positive relation to the Marxian heritage, Adorno argues that the very concept of "society" is historical in nature, and that it should not be used simply to denote abstract relations of individuals to one another. Instead, "the specifically social" refers to "the imbalance of institutions over human beings." "Society" thus refers to the system of social organization and the ways that social institutions, roles, practices, and the organization of the economy come to dominate the activity of human beings in specific historical constellations. Following Marxian arguments, Adorno can therefore claim that society is the living background for every empirical occurrence and that the capitalist market system imposes commodity and exchange relations on every individual act—even as it fuels an overriding rationalization process which provides an apparatus of social control. Against those who argue that the Marxian concept of class is no longer relevant to social processes, Adorno insists that we still live in a world fundamentally organized around class relations and characterized by class struggle. Thus, even as particular members of the Frankfurt School like Horkheimer were turning sharply to the right and away from Marxism, a connection to that old tradition and the Institute's standpoint before World War II continued to exist.

Of all the critical theorists, it was probably Herbert Marcuse who most systematically attempted to relate theory to politics and consistently contrasted critical perspectives on the current social order with those of an emancipated future. In "Liberation from the Affluent Society," he sketches what in retrospect emerges as a vision of liberation which articulates many New Left perspectives of the 1960's. The address begins by asserting the importance of those radical cultural currents which seemed to constitute a "great refusal" of the competitive, materialistic, and bellicose values of advanced industrial society. It is important to remember that Marcuse's utopian rationalism exerted a powerful influence in the sixties. During that time, even while believing that the working class remained the sine qua non for revolutionary transformation, Marcuse was one of the prime exponents of what became known as "the marginal groups theory," which suggested that the catalysts for radical action by workers would be those groups least integrated into the given order—students, racial minorities, women, etc. This argument anticipated militant movements and struggles in France and Italy , even though the reaction which was gathering force in the 1970s began to make Marcuse ever more skeptical about the "proletariat"—a skepticism central to his 1978 article "The Reification of the Proletariat," which we have also included.

During the 1970s, Marcuse continued to believe that a linkage between critical theory and the new social movements was possible. It was in this period that he desperately searched for a revolutionary agent to replace the industrial proletariat. Putting aside the undifferentiated and radical indictment of a liberal advanced industrial society central to his and the Institute's earlier work, Marcuse stressed the importance of democratic struggles and political reforms. Supporting McGovern in the 1972 presidential election, he continued his support for national liberation struggles in the third world, and even looked to the "Eurocommunist" parties— which were tactically seeking to separate themselves from Brezhnev's Soviet Union in Spain, France, and Italy—for a radical response to contemporary capitalist societies. Yet, in "The Reification of the Proletariat," which was published shortly before his death in 1979, Marcuse also analyzed the "right turn" which would come to characterize the prevailing political climate of the 1980s. Although Marcuse is doubtful that the traditional industrial "proletariat" continues to be the main force of revolution in advanced capitalist countries, he somewhat uncritically believes that a growing working class with expanding consciousness and political awareness will provide a new base for radical social change in contemporary society even as he points to a set of emerging social movements as catalysts for a new era. Though he has nothing to say about the matter of political organization, Marcuse correctly insists that revising Marxism and critical theory in the light of new conditions does not constitute a betrayal. Yet the article also points to how far from their earlier socialist revolutionary perspectives the critical theorists had traveled. Indeed, the Frankfurt School never developed adequate criteria to judge the political potential of different movements in different historical epochs and, with few exceptions, stood apart from the major political controversies of the postwar era.

While Marcuse gained world renown as the defender of the New Left in the 1960's, it is Habermas who developed the most consistent political position following the decline of the student movement of the sixties. Throughout his publications in the 1980s, he has defended the democratic and rationalist heritage of the Enlightenment and reinterpreted critical theory accordingly. In the process, he has intervened in some of the most important debates within German intellectual circles, ranging from attempts by arch-conservatives like Ernst Nolte to turn their backs on the Nazi past in the "historians' controversy," to those of postmodernists who have sought to foster a pseudo-radical spirit of nihilistic relativism. Our reader thus closes with a selection from Habermas's "The Tasks of a Critical Theory of Society," which forms part of the conclusion to his two-volume *Theory of Communicative Action* (1981).

In this selection, Habermas explores the central themes of critical theory after World War II, and then indicates some unfinished tasks for the contemporary era. These include the need to analyze 1) the new mechanisms of political integration within post-liberal societies; 2) the forms of familial socialization and ego-development; 3) the role of mass media and mass culture; and 4) the potential for crisis and the contemporary possibilities for protest especially with respect to the "new social movements" which have assumed such political importance.

Whether these are actually *the* crucial issues remains open to question. After all, Habermas concentrates exclusively on the reproductive mechanisms of advanced industrial society. Missing are those concerns which directly relate to the production process itself and its corresponding logic of accumulation. Though his emphasis on the role of new social movements is laudatory, the issue of class cannot be ignored. It is thus important to address particularism and promote inter-group unity in order to confront the obstacles which have been erected against extending democracy and civic responsibility in the modern state. Then too, since the world of the future is becoming ever more surely defined by multinationals, new technologies, and a new trans-national economy, critical social theorists should advance the need for new cosmopolitan values and international institutions which constrict the arbitrary use of power. A reconstruction of critical theory is necessary to meet these concerns. A new generation thus has new challenges to confront in reinvigorating and repoliticizing that notion of emancipation which inspired critical theory in the first place.

Part I

The Institute For Social Research and its Original Program

1

The State of Contemporary Social Philosophy and the Tasks of an Institute for Social Research

Max Horkheimer

Although social philosophy is the focus of general philosophical concern, it is in no better shape today than most philosophical, indeed most fundamentally intellectual, efforts. One is unable to find a substantive conception of social philosophy that could be considered everywhere as binding. Given the present situation in the sciences, in which the traditional boundaries between disciplines are in question and we do not yet know where they might be drawn in the future, the attempt to give ultimate definitions for academic domains seems rather untimely. Nevertheless, one can reduce the general views of social philosophy to one brief idea. According to it, the final goal of social philosophy is the philosophical interpretation of human fate—insofar as humans are not mere individuals but members of a community. Social philosophy must therefore primarily concern itself with those phenomena that can be interpreted only in the context of the social existence of humans, such as the state, law, economy, religion: in short, with all of the material and spiritual culture of humanity as such.

Social philosophy, thus understood, became in the history of classical German Idealism the decisive philosophical task. Its most brilliant achievements are in turn the most powerful aspects of Hegel's system. To be sure, even before Hegel, philosophy attempted to understand socio-philosophical phenomena: Kant's main works contain the philosophical theories of science, law, art, and religion. But this kind of social philosophy was grounded in a philosophy of the individual: those realms of being were to be seen as the designs of the autonomous individual. Kant made the total unity of the rational subject into the sole source of all constitutive principles for each cultural sphere. The being and the structure of culture were to be derived solely from the dynamic of the individual, from the

Translated by Peter Wagner

basic activities of a spontaneous ego. In terms of Kant's philosophy, we certainly should not equate the autonomous subject with an empirical human being. Nevertheless, we certainly are able to investigate all aspects of cultural creativity in the temperament of each individual rational being. All-encompassing structures of being that belong to a supra-personal whole, and are only discoverable within a social totality to which we would have to subject ourselves, do not exist; their assertion would be dogmatic, and any action directed towards them would have to be grounded heteronomically. The moral individual as seen in the *Metaphysical Foundations of Jurisprudence* is thus an individual "subjected to no other laws than those that it has (either alone or at least together with others) established for itself."[1]

The German Idealism connected with Kant developed the interconnection between autonomous reason and empirical being. The tension between a finite human being and the ego as infinite obligation can, however, still be discerned—in Fichte's first philosophy of the self-reflecting mind. The eternal ought, the instruction to satisfy our human destiny, flows from the depths of subjectivity. The medium of philosophy is here still self-reflection. But Hegel has freed this self-reflection from the chains of introspection, and referred the question of our own being, the question of the autonomous culture-creating subject, to the labor of history—through which it gives itself objective form.

For Hegel, the structure of objective spirit [*Geist*], which realizes in history the cultural artifacts of the absolute spirit (i.e., art, religion, philosophy), is not discerned any longer from a critical analysis of personality [*Personlichkeit*], but rather from universal dialectical logic. The development and the works of the objective spirit are not arrived at by the free decisions of a subject, but by the spirit of the dominant peoples that succeed each other on the battlefields of history. The destiny of the particular fulfills itself in the fate of the universal. The essence, the substantial content, of the individual is not revealed in personal actions but in the life of the totality to which it belongs. Thus, Hegel's Idealism has become in its constitutive parts social philosophy: the philosophical understanding of the collective whole, in which we live and which serves as the foundation for all creations of absolute culture, is now simultaneously knowledge of the meaning of our own being, its true worth and contents.

Let me remain for a moment with this Hegelian conception! From its dissolution and the impossibility of recreating it in thought without falling behind the present state of knowledge, one is in principle able to explicate the present state of social philosophy. Hegel assigned the realization of the goal of Reason to the objective spirit, in the last instance to the world-spirit. The development of this spirit is shown in the conflict of the "concrete ideas," the "spirit of the peoples," out of which "as signs and ornaments of its grandeur" the world-historical kingdoms emerge in necessary sequence.[2] This development happens regardless of whether individuals in their historical actions know of it and will it; the development has its own law. Nevertheless, as with the French Enlightenment and English liberalism, Hegel does accept the drives and passions of human beings as real motive powers. Even the great men are driven to their actions by their own ends. They "have formed purposes to satisfy themselves, not others."[3] Yet they are in their world "its clear-sighted ones; *their* deeds, *their* words are the best of that time."[4] Nothing, however, has happened in history without "interest on the part of the actors."[5] The interests of the great men as well as those of the masses are of course used "cunningly" by the rational law of development to its own end. And as Hegel explains past history only indirectly with that law, but directly with competing interests, so does he explain the life-process of modern society. While himself referring to the liberal economists Smith, Say, and Ricardo, he shows how out of the "medley of arbitrariness,"[6] which is created by the striving of individuals to satisfy their needs and wants, the totality is maintained. "In bourgeois society," he writes in the *Philosophy of Right,* "each member is his own end, everything else is nothing to him. But except in contact with others he cannot attain the whole compass of his ends, and therefore these others are means to the end of the particular member. A particular end, however, assumes the form of universality through this relation to other people, and it is attained in the simultaneous attainment of the welfare of others."[7] Thus, and only thus, can the state exist according to Hegel: it is directly determined by the conflict of interest in society.

But if history and the state are created eternally out of the "medley of arbitrariness," if therefore the historian has to deal with a chain of pain and death, of stupidity and baseness, and if finite being perishes in indescribable agony and history can be seen in Hegel's term as the "slaughter-bench at which the happiness of peoples, the wisdom of states, and the virtue of individuals are being sacrificed,"[8] then philosophy transcends the viewpoint of the empirical observer. Because "what is called reality," he teaches in the *Philosophy of History,* "is seen by philosophy only as something rotten, which seems to exist but is not real in and for itself. This insight, one might say, is consolation against the conception of absolute disaster, the madness of all that which has come to pass. Consolation, however, is only a substitute for the misfortune that should never have happened, and makes its home in the finite world. Philosophy is therefore not a consolation; it is more: it reconciles, it transfigures, a reality that appears to be unjust, making it appear rational. It exhibits it as such, shows it to be grounded in the idea itself, as that with which reason is supposed to be satisfied."[9] The "transfiguration" of which Hegel speaks is precisely attained by that theory according to which the true essence of human beings does not exist in mere inwardness and the actual fate of finite individuals, but asserts itself in the lives of peoples and is realized in the state. With the thought that the material essence, the idea, is preserved in world history, the destruction of the individual seems to carry no philosophical weight. In this regard, the philosopher is able to declare: "The particular is for the most part of too trifling value as compared with the general: individuals are sacrificed and abandoned. The idea pays the price of existence and of transitoriness, not from itself, but from the passions of individuals."[10] Only insofar as the individual partakes in the totality as a living being—or better, only insofar as the totality lives within the individual—is the individual endowed with reality. For the life of the totality is the life of the spirit. The totality at its most determined is the state. It "does not exist for its citizens; one might say it is the end and they are its means."[11]

According to Hegel, the finite individual being can attain the conceptual consciousness of its freedom within the state only through idealist speculative thinking. He essentially saw in this mediating function the achievement of his philosophy, and thus of philosophy as such. Philosophy is to him identical with the transfiguration of the real "that appears unjust." When the esteem of his system had waned in Germany around the middle of the last century, a future-oriented, individualistic society believing in progress replaced the metaphysics of the objective spirit with an unmediated belief in the prestabilized harmony of individual interests. It seemed as if what was needed to mediate between the empirical existence of the individual and the consciousness of its freedom in the social totality was not philosophy, but steady progress in the positive sciences, technology, and industry. But as the disappointment in that belief grew, a scorned metaphysics took its revenge. Deserted by the philosophical conviction that the divine idea existing within the totality is its true reality, the individual experienced the world as "medley of arbitrariness" and itself as the mere "price of existence and transitoriness." The sober glance directed towards the particular and the immediate was no longer capable of discerning "the cunning of Reason" behind the surface of warring individual wills, perpetual need, the indignities of the everyday world, and the terror of history. And so Hegel's greatest enemy, Schopenhauer, saw the dawn of his antihistorical, pessimistic, and consolatory philosophy.

The conviction that each and every one by virtue of his association with a historical unity and its own characteristic laws, which forms the dialectic of world history, partakes of the eternal life of the spirit—this notion ensuring the salvation of the individual from the infamous chain of becoming and perishing—disappeared with objective idealism. The suffering and the death of individuals threatened to appear in their naked meaninglessness—the last fact of an age enthralled by facts. With the deepening of the contradiction in the principle of individualistic life-form (that is, the contradiction between the unbroken progress of the happiness of the individuals within a given social context on the one hand, and the prospects of their actual situation on the other), philosophy, and especially social philosophy, was called more and more urgently to play again the role that Hegel had assigned to it. And social philosophy has heeded that call.

The cautious theory of Marburg neo-Kantianism states that a human being is not just an individual, but a being that stands "in various pluralities . . . in rank and file" and that "only in unity" can fulfill "the circles of its being,"[12] while the philosophical teachings of the present maintain that the meaning of existence, as in Hegel, fulfills itself only within meta-personal units of history such as class, state, or nation. From Hermann Cohen to Othmar Spann, philosophy has brought forth varying shades of socio-philosophical systems in the last few years. Even recent attempts at grounding moral and legal philosophy anew, in contradistinction to positivism, virtually have only one point in common, namely, the striving to find above and beyond the ground of actual incidents a higher realm of being or, at least, a higher realm of norms or ethics with its own characteristic laws in which finite human beings partake, but which cannot itself be reduced to natural incidences. Indeed, they too form a transition to a new philosophy of an objective spirit. While even Kelsen's individualistic and relativistic theory of law carries these features, one can find them in a higher degree in the formalistic value philosophy of the southwestern neo-Kantian school (as well as in Adolf Reinach's phenomenological theory): the essence of the structures of law—for example, the essence of private property, the essence of promise, the essence of the legal claim—can each be seen in its own "objective manifestation." Scheler's material ethics of value, his teaching of the being-in-itself of values, has made recently in the work of its most important representative, Nicolai Hartmann, the conscious connection to the philosophy of the objective spirit. The theory of the spirit of peoples had again been proclaimed by Scheler himself even before the publication of Hartmann's ethics.[13]

All of these projects of contemporary social philosophy seem to provide individual human beings with access into a supra-personal sphere that is more invested with being, more meaningful, more substantial than their own existence. They therefore accomplish the task of transfiguration prescribed by Hegel. Further, in Heidegger's *Sein und Zeit*—the only modern philosophical work that radically rejects social philosophy and that discovers real being only in the interior of individually existing human beings—care [*Sorge*] is the focal point. This philosophy of individual human existence is in its simple contents not transfiguration in Hegel's sense. Human existence is in it only a being-unto-death, a sheer finitude. It is a melancholy philosophy. If it is acceptable at this point to put the matter bluntly, one might say that today social philosophy meets the desire of a life hindered in its own individual pursuit of happiness with a new statement of meaning. Social philosophy appears to be part of the philosophical and religious efforts to plant the hopeless individual existence back into the womb, or to put it, in Sombart's term, in the "golden ground" of meaningful totalities.

But, ladies and gentlemen, having confronted this situation of social philosophy, let us now turn to delineate its deficiency. Social philosophy today, as we have seen, has taken a generally polemical stand against positivism. Positivism, it is charged, sees only the particular and in the realm of society thus sees only the individual and the relations between individuals; all is exhausted by facts. That there are facts that can be ascertained by means of analytical science, philosophy does not dispute. But philosophy posits against these facts more or less constructively, more or less in its own philosophizing, ideas, essences, totalities, independent spheres of objective spirit, units of meaning, spirit of peoples that it considers to be "more original" or even "genuine" elements of being. The discovery of certain unprovable metaphysical presuppositions within positivism is taken by philosophy as constituting lawful ground for raising the metaphysical stakes. So it happens that against the school of Vilfredo Pareto, for example—a school that, because of its positivist understanding of reality, has to deny the existence of class, nation, humanity—various standpoints, from which these entities are posited, are offered as a "different world view," a "different metaphysics," or a "different consciousness," without ever making a binding commitment possible. There are, one might say, different conceptions of reality, which make it possible to investigate what kind of genesis they had, to which sensibility of life and to which social group they belong, without providing an objectively grounded priority.

It is precisely in this dilemma of social philosophy, which speaks of its subject, the cultural life of humanity, in terms of professions of faith, and which sees the differences between the social theories of Auguste Comte, Karl Marx, Max Weber, and Max Scheler as different acts of faith, rather than distinguishing them in terms of true/false or, as of now, problematic theories—precisely in this dilemma do we perceive the deficiency that has to be overcome. To be sure, the simultaneous existence and validity of varying conceptions of reality signify the contemporary intellectual situation at large, but this variety addresses a plethora of scientific areas and spheres of life; it does not concern one and the same conceptual field.

The constitutive categories of philology and those of physics might thus diverge so far that it seems difficult to harmonize them; but within physics, indeed within the sciences of inorganic nature in general, there is no such tendency to construct noncompatible concepts of reality: the opposite is rather the case. Here, the concrete scientific investigation of the empirical subject matter proves to be a corrective.

At this point one might interject the view that social philosophy is not a scientific discipline, that it is materialist sociology whose subject matter involves distinct forms of socialization. As a discipline it investigates the various concrete ways in which people live together, all forms of associations: from the family to economic groups, and from political associations to the state and to humanity. In it, one might find objective determinations on the same level as in political economy. But sociology has nothing to say either about the degree of reality or about the value of those phenomena. All that is the province of social philosophy; and for these essential questions as it deals with them there are final pronouncements, but no universally binding, true statements which are an integral part of large-scale investigations.

This view presupposes a conception of philosophy that is no longer tenable. However one might want to draw the boundaries between the particular disciplines of sociology and social philosophy, which, I believe, would necessitate a high degree of arbitrariness, one thing is certain: If socio-philosophical thought about the relationship of the individual to society, the meaning of culture, the formation of communities, or the overall status of social life—in short, about the great, principal questions—should be left behind as the sediment in the reservoir of social scientific problems after those problems that can be advanced in concrete investigations have been drained off, then social philosophy can still perform a social function (e.g., that of transfiguration), but its intellectual fruitfulness would be destroyed. The relationship between the philosophical and the empirical disciplines should not be conceptualized as if it were philosophy that treated the essential problems, constructing theories that cannot be attacked by the empirical sciences, its own conceptions of reality and systems embracing the totality, while in contrast empirical science comes out of its long, boring studies fragmented into a thousand individual questions, in order only to end up in the chaos of specialization. This view, according to which the empirical scientist has to regard philosophy as a beautiful yet scientifically fruitless enterprise, and the philosopher in contrast emancipates himself from the empirical scientist because the former assumes that he cannot wait for the latter in his far-reaching quest, is presently being superseded by the thought of an ongoing dialectical permeation and evolution of philosophical theory and empirical-scientific praxis. In this regard, the relations between the philosophy of nature and the natural sciences present us with good examples. Chaotic specialization is not being superseded by bad syntheses of specialized research results, nor is the impartiality of empirical research secured through the attempt to eliminate the theoretical elements with it. Rather, chaotic specialization is overcome by the fact that philosophy is able to inject spiritual impulses into empirical research through its own theoretical intention towards the whole, the essential, while being open enough to be itself influenced and transformed by the developments in concrete research.

The correction of the deficiency in the situation of social philosophy hinted at above seems to us to lie neither in a profession of faith of a more or less constructive interpretation of cultural life, nor in positing a new meaning for society, state, law, and what have you. Today, on the contrary, and I am surely not alone in this opinion, all depends on organizing research around current philosophical problematics which, in turn, philosophers, sociologists, political economists, historians, and psychologists engage by joining enduring research groups in order to do together what in other areas one is able to do alone in the laboratory and what all true scientists have always done: namely, to pursue their philosophical questions directed at the big picture with the finest scientific methods, to transform and to make more precise these questions as the work progresses, to find new methods, and yet never lose sight of the whole. In this way, no positive or negative answers to philosophical questions can be given. Instead, the philosophical questions themselves are dialectically integrated into the empirical scientific process; that is to say, their answers are to be found in the progress of substantive knowledge which also effects the form. This approach to the science of society cannot be mastered by one person alone—given the vast subject matter as well as the variety of indispensable scientific methods whose assistance is called for. Despite the gigantic effort on his part, even Max Scheler has failed in this regard.

Given this situation, one has to view the transformation of the chair of this university for the directorship of the Institute for Social Research into a chair for social philosophy and its relocation to the Department of Philosophy as highly legitimate. Carl Grunberg held this chair as a lecturer in political economy in the Department of Political Science. With the new, difficult, and decisive task of employing a grand empirical scientific apparatus in the service of social philosophy, with my appointment I have felt the immeasurable gap separating a great scientist whose name is mentioned with great respect and thankfulness all over the world wherever work in his discipline is being done, from the young, unknown man who was designated as his successor. His long illness belongs to those senseless facts in the life of individuals that put philosophical transfiguration to shame. According to his own deeply rooted and precisely defined interests, as determined by the historical school of political economy, he emphasized first and foremost the history of the labor movement. In doing so, his all-encompassing knowledge of the relevant sources in the world has made possible the acquisition of archival material and especially of a unique special library now containing approximately fifty thousand volumes; this library is now being put to good use, not just by students at our university, but also by many scholars in and outside of Germany. The series of writings from the Institute, edited by him, contains only works that have been recognized by relevant authorities of diverse political viewpoints as exceptional scientific achievements.

Having set myself the task of directing the work of the Institute towards a new goal following the prolonged illness of its director, I am able to draw not only on the experience of its associates and its collected library treasures, but on the Institute's charter, defined in an important way by its director. According to this charter, the director, designated by the minister, is independent "with respect both to the educational administration and the founders" to the point where there exists, as Grunberg used to say, in place of a council charter "the dictatorship of the director." Because of it, it will be possible for me to use what has been created by him in order to erect with my colleagues, at least on a small scale, a dictatorship of the planned work over the coexistence of philosophical construction and empirical research in the theory of society. As a philosopher in the sense of my teacher, Hans Cornelius, I accepted the call to direct this research institute in order to pursue this possibility, which is equally important to philosophy and empirical science, and not to make factual research into the auxiliary of philosophy.

But now some of you would like to know details about how these conceptions could be implemented, how one might conceive of their working in practice. Within the time allotted to me, I cannot address this issue adequately enough to give you an example of how it is possible to implement what has been said. It is not an example picked at random, fancied for this particular occasion, but one that gives the stated methodological conviction a concrete problematic which will become, in a short while, the trajectory of the collective work in the Institute.

There is one question around which the discussion of society has started to crystallize itself ever more clearly, in social philosophy, narrowly understood, as well as in the circles of sociology. It is not just a fashionable question, but one which presents an actualized version of some of the most ancient and important philosophical problems: the question of the connection between the economic life of society, the psychological development of its individuals and the changes within specific areas of culture to which belong not only the intellectual legacy of the sciences, art and religion, but also law, customs, fashion, public opinion, sports, entertainments, lifestyles, and so on. The intention to study these three processes presents merely an updated version by way of contemporary methodologies and the present state of our knowledge, of the ancient question as to the relation of particular existence and universal reason, of the real and the idea, of life and spirit—adapted to a new problematic.

Mostly, however, one reflects either metaphysically on the above theme, as in Scheler's "Sociology of Knowledge," or one states, more or less dogmatically, some general thesis on it; that is to say, one usually picks one of the theses advanced in history in a simplified fashion and, remaining dogmatically abstract, battles it out with all the other theses. Thus, one can find the following pronouncement: that economy and spirit are the respective expressions of one and the same essence: this amounts to a bad Spinozism. Or one can find the following: ideas, "spiritual" contents, force themselves into history and determine the actions of humans, so that they become primary while material life remains merely derivative; world and history have their source in the spirit: this would amount to an abstract, badly understood Hegel. Or one finds the contrary belief: the economy, material being, is the only true reality; the human psyche as well as law, art, and philosophy are purely derivative and mere reflections of it; this would be an abstract and therefore badly understood Marx. Besides the fact that these theses naively posit an uncritical, outdated separation of spirit and reality, a separation that is not dialectically sublated, those kinds of statements, if they are taken seriously in their abstractness, are ultimately devoid of any type of verification procedures: all can indiscriminately claim for themselves to present the truth. These dogmatic convictions are spared the scientific difficulties of the problem, if only because they consciously or unconsciously take the total identity of ideational and material processes for granted—not caring for, or even ignoring, the complex role of the psychic mediations.

The issue is seen quite differently if we pose the question more precisely in the following manner: In a definite time frame and in some particular countries, what relations can we delineate between a particular social group and the role of this group in the economy, the changes in the psychical structure of its members, and the thoughts and institutions created by it which influence it as a whole through the social totality? Then the possibility of real research projects that will be conducted in the Institute can come into view. At first, we would like to direct them towards a very important and particular social group in Germany, skilled labor and white-collar employees, and continue after that with the corresponding segments in the other highly developed European countries.

There is little time left to give a necessarily summary and insufficient overview of the most important paths that the full members of the Institute will have to follow in close-knit fashion to initially gather the empirical material with which the relations in question can be studied. At the top of the list is obviously the interpretation of the published statistics, the reports of organizations and political associations, the material of public corporations, and so on. This can happen only in connection with the ongoing analysis of the overall economic situation. Furthermore, it is necessary to investigate sociologically and psychologically the press and literature for the value of their pronouncements on the situation of the groups in question, but also because of literature's categorical structure, which enables it to influence the members of these groups. Especially important is then the development of a variety of survey methods. Questionnaires, amongst others, can be integrated into our research in manifold ways and can be of good service, if one always keeps in mind that inductive conclusions derived through them alone are always prematurely drawn. The essential purpose of questionnaires in our case is twofold: first, they should stimulate the research and keep it in touch with reality; second, they can be used to check knowledge gained by other means and thereby preempt errors. For the design of these questionnaires American social research has done important preliminary work which we will assimilate and advance for our own purposes. Also, we will have to use expert opinions on a grander scale. Where it is possible to advance particular aspects of problems by as yet unrecorded experiences of competent evaluators, one should try to include them wherever one might find them. Most times that will mean using the experience of practitioners for the sciences. A special task, moreover, is the collection and interpretation of documents that cannot be found in books. To that end, namely to employ scientifically the extremely rich sociological archives of the International Labor Bureau in Geneva, we will create a branch of the Institute there. Mr. Albert Thomas, the director of the International Labor Organization, has welcomed our plan and assured us, in a most pleasant manner, of his support. One has to add to all these paths, naturally, the methodological study of all published and forthcoming scientific treatises on the subject.

Each of these methods alone is completely insufficient, but perhaps all together, through years of patient and extended research, they might bear fruit for the general problematic. This can only be the case, in turn, if the members of the Institute constantly refer to the material and form their opinions not according to their own preferences, but according to the demands of the subject; if they refrain from all terms of transfiguration— and, finally, if we can preserve the unified intention to oppose both dogmatic ossification and descent into the technical-empirical.

I conclude. It has only been possible for me to delineate from all the tasks of the Institute the collective research work whose implementation will be the focus of the years to come. Besides that, the independent research of the individual members in the areas of theoretical economics, economic history, and the history of the labor movement should equally

2

Psychoanalysis and Sociology

Erich Fromm

The problem of the relations between psychoanalysis and sociology, about which I will speak in the Institute's courses, has two sides. The first is the application of psychoanalysis to sociology, the second that of sociology to psychoanalysis. Of course, it is not possible even to list in a few minutes all the problems and themes that result from both sides. Therefore, I shall merely attempt to make a few fundamental remarks about the principles which seem to apply to the scientific treatment of psychoanalytic-sociological problems.

The application of psychoanalysis to sociology must definitely guard against the mistake of wanting to give psychoanalytic answers where economic, technical, or political facts provide the real and sufficient explanation of sociological questions. On the other hand, the psychoanalyst must emphasize that the subject of sociology, society, in reality consists of individuals, and that it is these human beings, rather than an abstract society as such, whose actions, thoughts, and feelings are the object of sociological research. Human beings do not have one "individual psyche," which functions when a person performs as an individual and so becomes the object of psychoanalysis, contrasted to a completely separate "mass psyche" with all sorts of mass instincts, as well as vague feelings of community and solidarity, which springs into action whenever a person performs as part of mass, and for which the sociologist creates some makeshift concepts for psychoanalytical facts unknown to him. There aren't two minds within a person's head, but only one, in which the same mechanisms and laws apply whether a person performs as an individual or people appear as a society, class, community, or what have you. What

---

Translated by Mark Ritter

psychoanalysis can bring to sociology is the knowledge—though still imperfect—of the human psychic apparatus, which is a determinant of social development alongside technical, economic, and financial factors, and deserves no less consideration than the other factors mentioned. The common task of both sciences is to investigate in what way and to what extent the psychic apparatus of the human being causally affects or determines the development or organization of society.

Let me mention here only one essential concrete problem. It is necessary to investigate what role the instinctual and the unconscious play in the organization and development of society and in individual social facts, and to what extent the changes in mankind's psychological structure, in the sense of a growing ego-organization and thus a rational ability to cope with the instinctual and natural, is a sociologically relevant factor.

Now the other side of the problem: the application of sociological approaches to psychoanalysis. However important it may be to point out to sociologists the banal fact that society consists of living people and that psychology is one of the factors affecting social development, it is equally important that psychology not underestimate the fact that the individual person in reality exists only as a socialized person. Psychoanalysis, in contrast to some other schools of psychology, can claim that it has understood this fact from the beginning. Indeed, the recognition that there is no *homo psychologicus,* no psychological Robinson Crusoe, is one of the foundations of its theory. Psychoanalysis is predominantly oriented to questions of genesis; it devotes its special interest to human childhood, and it teaches us to interpret a very essential part of the development of the human psychological apparatus on the basis of people's attachment to mother, father, siblings, in short to the family, and thus to society. Psychoanalysis interprets the development of individuals precisely in terms of their relationship to their closest and most intimate surroundings; it considers the psychological apparatus as formed most decisively by these relationships.

Certainly, this is only a beginning, and from it a series of further important problems result, which have so far scarcely been attacked; for instance, the question of to what extent the family is itself the product of a particular social system, and how a socially conditioned change in the family as such might influence the development of the psychic apparatus of the individual. Or there is the question of what influence the growth of technology—i.e., an ever increasing gratification, or a decreasing deprivation, of the instincts—has on the psyche of the individual.

The classification from which we proceed, into problems that result from the application of psychoanalysis to sociology and of sociology to psychoanalysis, is of course only a crude one, which corresponds to practical needs. In keeping with the reciprocal interaction of person and society, there are a whole series of further problems. Some of the most important ones are precisely those where it is impossible to apply one method to the other, but where a set of facts, which are equally psychological and social in character, can be investigated by both methods and can be understood only by employing both perspectives. It is just such a problem of how much certain concerns of psychology, which are simultaneously sociological, such as religion, depend on the material development of mankind in their appearance and decline, that constitutes the subject of the latest book by Freud.

There Freud advances the idea that religion is the psychic correlative to mankind's helplessness in the face of nature. From there he opens a perspective onto a problem which may be considered one of the most important psychologic-sociological questions: What connections exist between the social, especially the economic-technical, development of humanity, and the development of the psychic apparatus, especially the ego-organization, of the human being? In short, he raises the question of the developmental history of the psyche. Psychoanalysis has so far asked and answered this question only for the individual. Freud in his latest book has extended this genetic inquiry to the psychic development of society, and has thus given important guidance to future psychoanalytic-sociological work.

In summary, I would like to say: Psychoanalysis, which interprets the human being as a socialized being, and the psychic apparatus as essentially developed and determined through the relationship of the individual to society, must consider it a duty to participate in the investigation of sociological problems to the extent the human being or his/her psyche plays any part at all. In this effort, one may quote the words, not of a psychologist, but of (Karl Marx) the greatest sociologist of all: "History does nothing, it possesses no immense wealth, it fights no battles. It is instead the human being, the real living person, who does everything, who owns everything, and who fights all battles."

3

On Sociology of Literature

Leo Lowenthal

History of literature is in a unique way subject to the difficulties which arise with every historical effort. Not only is it implicated in all theoretical discussions concerning the conceptual meaning and material structure of history, but, in addition, its object of study falls into the realm of numerous scientific disciplines. Over and beyond the techniques involved in the critical analysis of sources, numerous disciplines step forward with a variety of claims, among them philosophy, aesthetics, psychology, pedagogy, philology, and even statistics. When we turn to day-to-day practice, however, we find that literary studies have become scientific jetsam. Everybody, from the "naive reader" to the presumably legitimate teacher with special expertise, is prepared to launch interpretations of literary texts in the most arbitrary and capricious ways. Knowledge of a language, combined with the conviction that an adequate technical terminology can be dispensed with, are considered sufficient prerequisites to engage in such ventures. On the other hand, academics have thusfar not developed methods of research and analysis which would do justice to the complexity of their object of study. This is not a wholesale indictment of every single specialized work; rather, what I am concerned with here are the prevailing principles underlying today's study of literary history and literary criticism.

Virtually all of the scholars who contributed to the collection of essays *Die Philosophie der Literaturwissenschaft*[1] [The philosophy of literary studies] are in agreement that a "scientific" approach to the history of literature would lead nowhere. Not only do they believe—and rightly so—that each literary work contains some nonrational elements, they also consider any rational approach inadequate with regard to the very nature of the object under investigation. Consequently, the study of literature as

---

Translated by Susanne Hoppmann-Lowenthal

it was founded in the nineteenth century is condemned and rejected as "historical pragmatism,"[2] as "historicizing psychologism,"[3] and as "positivistic method."[4] Certainly, Hermann Hettner's or Wilhelm Scherer's works lack absolute validity; indeed, they would never have claimed it. But all attempts to deal with literature which profess to a scholarly character have to draw critically on the scientific methods of the nineteenth century.

Isolation and simplification of a literary historical object is admittedly achieved in an exceedingly sublime process. Author and work become abstracted from the matrix of historical circumstances, and molded into a kind of predictable coalescence from which the diverse manifold of details and dimensions has been drained. Through this reification they acquire a dignity and worthiness which no other cultural phenomenon can boast. "In the history of literature acts and actors are 'givens,' whereas in world history we are presented with more or less falsified accounts of mostly shady dealings by rarely identifiable dealers."[5] True dignity is reserved for such historical phenomena which are a manifestation of the mind, or may be perceived at least as existing in a unique domain.[6] Of course, only when an object of investigation is not considered part of inner and outer nature and its variable conditions, but instead has to be ontologically conceived as a creation of a higher kind, do positivistic methods prove fundamentally insufficient. With the confidence of a philosophical instinct, the concept of structure introduced by Dilthey, which was based on historical contextuality, is abandoned and replaced by the concept of the organic "that clearly, unambiguously and decisively characterizes the spiritual as the individualization in history determined by unity of meaning."[7] Ambiguous terms such as *work, form,* and *content* proclaim a metaphysically grounded unity of author and work, transcending and negating all diversity. This radical estrangement from historical reality finds its purest expressions in concepts such as "classicism" and "romanticism" which are not only relegated to history, but also metaphysically transfigured. "Like the superordinate concept of eternity, both the concept of perfection and that of infinity are derived from historical and psychological experience as well as from philosophical knowledge."[8]

This rigid and in itself irrational stance on the part of those representing literary scholarship today presumes its legitimation in the fact that the "methods of the natural sciences" analyze their object into bits and pieces, and when attempting to define its "vital poetic soul," these methods cannot help but miss entirely its "secret."[9] The significance of these statements is hard to grasp. For nobody has ever demonstrated why, and to what extent, an object would be harmed or distorted by a rational approach. Any study of a phenomenon can be mindful of its wholeness, its Gestalt, while being conscious of a selective methodology. Admittedly, such an analysis will only yield the elements of a mosaic whose sum never represents the whole. But where on earth does scientific analysis exhaust itself in nothing but a summation of fractured parts? And are the methods of the natural sciences exclusively atomistic in nature? Certainly not, and neither do methods of literary analysis have to be, if they are inappropriate to a specific task. On their journey into the vagaries of metaphysics, the literary scholars also appropriated the concept of law. However, rather than to identify law with order and regularity which can be submitted to scrutiny and observation, the concept, from the start, is burdened with a troublesome new and vague meaning. Instead of the search for regularity there appears a "unity of meanings," and the "artistic personality" and the "poetic work"[10] are identified, among others, as the major problems of literary studies, problems which seem to be resolved before they have been investigated. Yet, *personality* and *work* belong to those conceptual constructs which thwart any theoretical effort precisely because they are opaque and finite.

Inasmuch as these fashionable literary scholars point to the pitfalls involved in seeking to understand the relationship of author and work through, for instance, mere philological data analysis, I have no quarrel with this antipositivistic attitude. But precisely when it comes to an evaluation of a work of art and its qualitative aspects, an understanding of its intrinsic merit and its authenticity—questions so much at the center of the concerns of these scholars—their methods reveal their utter inadequacy. The question of whether and to what extent the literary artist consciously applies conventions of form, can only be explored by rational means. But the metaphysical mystification so prevalent in contemporary literary studies impedes any sober reflection and scholarship. Its tasks are not only historical in nature; I would like to refer to Dilthey's concept of *Verstehen* [understanding] and its particular emphasis on the relationship between the author and his work. Admittedly, the demystification of investigative approaches to literature cannot be achieved by means of a formal poetics alone. What is needed above all is a psychology of art, i.e., a study of the psychological interaction between artist, artistic creation, and reception. What is not needed, however, is a psychology that places the "great work of art" in a mystical relationship "with the people," and that finds the "personal biography of the author . . . interesting and necessary, but unessential with regard to the act of artistic creation."[11]

In contrast to the vague declamatory statements so characteristic of Jungian psychology, the classical Freudian model of psychoanalysis has already made important theoretical contributions to a psychology of art. Some of its proponents have discussed central questions of literature, particularly those dealing with the psychic conditions under which great works of art originate, specifically the origins and structure of artistic imagination, and, last but not least, the question of the relationship between the artistic work and its reception, which so far has been ignored or at least insufficiently explored.[12] Admittedly, some of these psychoanalytic propositions are not yet polished and refined enough and remain somewhat schematic. But to reject the assistance of scientific psychology in the study of art and literature does not provide protection from "a barbarian assault of conquerors,"[13] as one contemporary literary mandarin put it, but rather is a "barbarian" argument itself!

Coupled with the condemnation of "historicizing psychologism," which cannot explore the secret of the "authentic poetic soul,"[14] is the repudiation of accepted historical methodology and particularly of any theory of historical causality, in short, what in modern literary scholarship is anathematized as "positivistic materialism."[15] But as in the case of psychology, the trendsetters take liberties: modern literary scholarship has no qualms and even consistently makes use of grand historical categories such as "folk, society, humanity,"[16] or the "pluralistic, aspiring" and the "spiritualizing, articulating experience."[17] There is mention of "associations of essence and fate," of "perfection and infinity" as a "conceptual basis" of "historical experience."[18] But, while the phraseology of the "age of Homer, Pericles, Augustus, Dante, Goethe"[19] is acceptable, any historically and sociologically oriented theoretical approach will meet with scorn and contempt when it attempts to understand literature as a social phenomenon in combination with the positivistic and materialistic methods which evolved out of the historical scholarship of the nineteenth century. The bluntly stated objective is "the abandonment of the descriptive vantage point of positivism and the return to a commitment to the metaphysical character of the *Geisteswissenschaften* [humanities]."[20] We shall see that such "abandonment" is demanded with even greater determination once the theory of historical materialism replaces traditional historical description. Even the boundary between scholarship and demagoguery is obscured when the antihistorical transfiguration of a work of art has to be maintained: "Historical pragmatism may perhaps conclude that syphilis led to the disappearance of Minnesang and its polygamous convention, or that the currency reform of 1923 gave rise to Expressionism. . . . The essence of Minnesang and Expressionism remains unaffected by such findings. The question here is not why is it but what is it? The 'why' would simply lead to an infinite regress: Why at the end of the Middle Ages was lues spread, why at the beginning of 1924 was the Reichsmark introduced, and so on until the egg of Leda."[21] This kind of rhetoric makes a caricature of any legitimate scholarly inquiry. By no means do causal questions require infinite regress; clearly stated, they can be precisely answered, even if new questions might be posed by this answer. An investigation of the reasons for Goethe's move to Weimar does not require an investigation of the history of urban development in Germany!

Considering the current situation of literary scholarship as sketched in the preceding outline, its precarious relationship to psychology, history, and social science, the arbitrariness in the selection of its categories, the artificial isolation and the scientific alienation of its object, one might agree with a modern literary historian who, dissatisfied with the "metaphysicalization" that has invaded his discipline, calls for the return to strict scientific standards, a passionate devotion to material, a deep concern for pure knowledge; in short, a new "appreciation of knowledge and learning."[22] If Franz Schultz, however, simultaneously rejects any overarching theory,[23] he does not have the courage of his own convictions. In fact, it is possible to conceive of a theoretical approach to literature which remains faithful to "knowledge and learning" and interprets literary works historically and sociologically, avoiding the pitfalls of either descriptive positivism or mere metaphysical speculation.

Such concern with the historical and sociological dimensions of literature requires a theory of history and society. This is not to say that one is limited to vague theorizing about the relationships between literature and society in general, nor that it is necessary to speak in generalities about social conditions which are required for the emergence of literature. Rather, the historical explanation of literature has to address the extent to which particular social structures find expression in individual literary works and what function these works perform in society. Man is involved in specific relations of production throughout his history. These relations present themselves socially as classes in struggle with each other, and the development of their relationship forms the real basis for the various cultural spheres. The specific structure of production, i.e., the economy, is the independent explanatory variable not only for the legal forms of property and organization of state and government but, at the same time, for the shape and quality of human life in each historical epoch. It is illusionary to assume an autonomy of the social superstructure, and this is not altered through the use of a scientific terminology claiming such autonomy. As long as literary history is exclusively conceived as *Geistesgeschichte,* it will remain powerless to make cogent statements, even though in practice the talent and sensibilities of a literary historian may have produced something of interest. A genuine, explanatory history of literature must proceed on materialistic principles. That is to say, it must investigate the economic structures as they present themselves in literature, as well as the impact which the materialistically interpreted work of art has in the economically determined society.

Such a demand, along with the social theory which it presupposes, has a dogmatic ring unless it specifies its problematic. This has been achieved to a large extent in the fields of economics and political history, but even in the area of literary studies fledgling attempts have been made. Worthy of mention are Franz Mehring's[24] essays on literary history which, sometimes using a simplified and popular, sometimes a narrowly defined political approach, have for the first time attempted to apply the theory of historical materialism to literature. But as in the case of the aforementioned psychological studies, the work of Mehring and other scholars of his persuasion has either been ignored or even ridiculed by literary historians. A sociologist of culture recently referred to "such a conceptual framework not only as unsociological or incompatible with scientific sociology," but also comparable to a "a parasitic plant" that "draws off the healthy sap of a tree."[25]

The materialistic explanation of history cannot afford to proceed in the simplifying and isolating manner so characteristic for the academic establishment of literary history, interpretation, and criticism. Contrary to common assertions, this theory neither postulates that culture in its entirety can be explained in terms of economic relations, nor that specific cultural or psychological phenomena are nothing but reflections of the social substructure. Rather, a materialistic theory places its emphasis on mediation: the mediating processes between a mode of production and the modes of cultural life including literature. Psychology must be considered as one of the principal mediating processes, particularly in the field of literary studies, since it describes the psychic processes by means of which the cultural functions of a work of art reproduce the structures of the societal base. Inasmuch as the basis of each society in history can be seen as the relationship between ruling and ruled classes and is, in fact, a metabolic process between society and nature, literature—like all other cultural phenomena—will make this relationship transparent. For that reason the concept of ideology will be decisive for the social explanation of all phenomena of the superstructure from legal institutions to the arts. Ideology is false consciousness of social contradictions and attempts to replace them with the illusions of social harmony. Indeed, literary studies are largely an investigation of ideologies.

The often-voiced criticism that the theory of historical materialism lacks methodological refinement and possesses a crude conceptual apparatus can easily be countered: the proponents of this theory have never avoided the discussion of its flaws. Its findings and results have always been open to the scrutiny of other scholars, as well as to possible theoretical changes prompted by new experiences in social reality. Historical materialism has certainly not taken refuge in quasi-ontological imagery which, seductive and enchanting as it might be, connotes a spurious philosophy of knowledge. As long as a theory does not consider itself finite but rather continuously sustained and possibly altered by new and different experiences, the frequent accusation that historical materialism ultimately contains an element of faith seems of little consequence.

The following examples are intended to illustrate the application of historical materialism to literary studies and will address questions of form, motif, and content.

Beginning with the issue of *form,* I should like to consider the problem of the encyclopedic novel as it exists in Balzac's *Comédie humaine* or in Zola's *Les Rougon-Macquart*. Both seek to represent, through their all-encompassing narratives, the society of their time in its entirety with all its living and dead inventory, occupations, and forms of state, passions, and domestic furnishings. Their aim appears anchored in the bourgeois-rationalist belief that, in principle, it is possible to possess the world through thought and to dominate it through intellectual appropriation. In the case of Balzac, this rationalism is mediated by his adherence to a mercantilist model of the economy which supposedly allows government to regulate society in an orderly fashion—a Balzac anachronism rooted in his peculiar psychological infatuation with the ancien régime. In the case of Zola, however, one faces a critical orientation toward the capitalist mode of production and the hope of remedying its deficiencies through a critical analysis of the society it conditions. The breadth of each of these cyclic novels reveals just as much about the author and his place in class society as it does about the theoretical and moral position he adopts toward the social structure of his time.

Social meanings present themselves in more specific issues as well. The same literary form, for instance, can have a completely different social meaning in different contexts. One example would be the emphasis on dialogue and the resulting limitation of the narrative voice or commentative inserts in the text. The works of Gutzkow and Spielhagen and the impressionist writers are paradigmatic for this style. Gutzkow was probably the first to introduce into German literature the modern bourgeois dialogue. The history of the dialogue in narrative texts is that of a development from a tradition of stiff conventions to the spontaneous, open conversational technique of the present. The dialogue is in reality the criterion of the varying degrees of psychological astuteness which the freely competing members of capitalist society, at least in its liberal epoch, are able to demonstrate. Those who are more adroit and possess superior insight into the response mechanisms of their interlocutors also have superior chances of economic success, so long as the situation is not controlled by crude power relations which would make any discussion impossible in the first place. The function of the conversational form in the literature of the Junges Deutschland [young Germany: the liberal intelligentsia of the 1830s and 1840s], which was almost entirely oblivious of its social context, is only indirectly identifiable, and in Spielhagen appears burdened by a kind of theory. The epic narrative insert has been reduced to a minimum, creating the impression that the author's arrangement of events has been dictated by the demands of reality, i.e., the verbalized interactions of the novel's characters, and that he has drastically reduced authorial interference through actions, events, and incidents as well as their authorial interpretation. Beginning with the later Fontane and Sudermann up until Arthur Schnitzler's last novellas, the impressionist novella makes extensive use of the uncommented dialogue. But this "renunciation of the privileges of the interpreting and supplementing narrator"[26] has one meaning and function in Spielhagen and another in the German impressionists.

Spielhagen's technique is based on the conviction that through the conversations of people social reality becomes transparent to the reflective reader, who then will discover their underlying theory about human and societal relations. A bourgeois idealist, Spielhagen believes in the power of the objective mind which materializes in the articulated thoughts of men so that the free exchange of dialogue can leave no doubt as to the substantive convictions of the author. In contrast, the ascetic absence of commentary characteristic for the impressionists is an expression of the self-criticism that liberal bourgeois society pronounced on itself since the beginning of the twentieth century. The inability to formulate a theory of society, the increasing insecurity, if not helplessness, of the German middle class, resulted in fact in a mentality of relativism, a loss of confidence in the subjective mind which believed in the possibility of universally applicable knowledge. While Gutzkow's groping increments in dialogue reflect the economic gropings of a liberal bourgeoisie in Germany in the first stages of upward mobility, and while the novelistic technique of Spielhagen celebrates its social victory, the impressionist style reflects its crisis: it either hides this crisis with an ideological film or admits to it through pointless conversations which lead nowhere.

Other class relationships reveal themselves when one compares the technique of the narrative frame in the novellas of Theodor Storm and C. F. Meyer. This literary device fulfills radically opposed functions in the work of these authors. Storm assumes a posture of resignation, of renunciatory retrospection. He is the weary, petty bourgeois pensioner whose world has collapsed, a world in which he could hope to engage in affairs of social importance. Time has run out; the only sustenance the present still offers are "framed," idealized remembrances of the past. Memory is capable of recovering only those fragments of the past that do not immediately bear on the gloomy present and therefore do not have to be repressed. In the case of Meyer, on the other hand, the narrative frames of his novellas quite literally serve as the magnificent frames of a glorious painting, and as such function as indicators of the worthiness of the image they enclose and are meant to separate the unique, which is all that matters, from the indifferent diversity of appearances. The same stylistic device which in Storm's worlds symbolizes the modest, the small and the waning, is used by Meyer as the symbol of vital reality. While the petty bourgeois soul of Storm quietly mourns, Meyer thrusts his characters into a world that corresponds to the feudal daydreams of the German upper classes in the 1870s.

As a final example of the sociological implications in problems of form, I shall briefly consider the use of pictorial imagery. For Lessing the aesthetician, the pictorial has no place in literary arts. For Meyer it is a favorite artistic device. The progress of humanity in historical time and the development of mankind are the important issues for Lessing, who was a firm believer in the future. He was an early champion of a rising bourgeois society which saw in the tensions and resolutions of a drama the paradigm for the conflicts and possible resolutions in society. Meyer is the heir to the dramatic traditions, but the surviving victors are now limited to the members of the upper class. Where Lessing is a dramatist, Meyer has become a sculptor. Where the former animates, the latter in fact halts the motion of progress. If for Lessing art expresses a universalist morality binding for all men, a morality which transcends individual idiosyncracies, it is for Meyer the extraordinary and the unique in selected individuals that finds expression in art. Magnificently framed, the infinite diversity of reality is condensed into the great moments of great individuals and eternalized as in a painting, transcending time and place. This ideological position mirrors precisely the self-image of the dominant strata of the bourgeoisie in the last third of the nineteenth century, for which the social world is but an opportunity for the development of the great personality, in short, the social elite. Its members stand aloof from trivial everyday cares and live surrounded by significant people, great ideals, and important affairs which all reflect and confirm their uniqueness.

A motif that likewise serves to glorify economic power positions is the motif of boredom in the novels of Stendhal. Boredom is as fatal as death for "the happy few" who alone are entitled to read his books and for whom alone he chooses to write. These happy few, far removed from the consequences of an economically limited existence, are entitled to pursue their happiness according to their own autonomous morality. Just as Stendhal is the supreme novelist of the bourgeois aristocracy in the age of Napoleon, so Gustav Freytag sings the praise of the German mid-nineteenth century bourgeoisie, which he transfigures by denying any

knowledge of the contradictions that are evident in the division, organization, and remuneration of labor. Inasmuch as Freytag applies an undifferentiated concept of "work" to the equally undifferentiated concept of "the
people" (two concepts Stendhal would have never used), he successfully
overlooked, in a literal sense, the antagonistic social order with its competing and feuding classes. Ideology comes to the fore at the very beginning
of his major work *Soll und Haben* [Debit and credit], which has as its
motto the words of Julian Schmidt: "The novel ought to look for the
German people where they are at their virtuous best, that is, at work."

I should like to touch upon the death motif as it is struck repeatedly
in Mörike's *Maler Nolten* [Painter Nolten] and Meyer's *Jürg Jenatsch*.
Mörike's world is that of the *Biedermeier*, of the honest man, the not yet
politically emancipated bourgeois in the period of the *Vormärz*, i.e., the
period between the Congress of Vienna and the, in fact, abortive revolutions of 1848–49. In his novels, the death motif may be interpreted as a
harbinger of the political defeat of the bourgeoisie in his generation. The
motifs of transience, fate, and death serve as ideological metaphors for
the political impotence of the middle class in his time, of which he himself
was a prototype. By contrast, in the stories of Meyer, death takes on the
aspect of a highly intensified moment in the fullness of life. When Lucretia
kills Jürg Jenatsch, this deed also marks the beginning of her own physical
destruction. What is in fact a violent double murder is presented as the
expression of heroic lifestyles. Only Jürg and Lucretia are worthy of one
another; they represent a rare and perfect balance of character and fate;
only by virtue of this singular congruity do these two have the right to
eliminate each other. The solidarity of the international ruling minority
proves itself unto death.

Finally, turning to *content,* I once more refer to Freytag and Meyer.
Both wrote historical novels and short stories. Freytag's collected works
might be called the textbook of the conformist middle class, exhorting the
virtues and perils of its members. The study of history is not seen as an
occasion for intellectual enjoyment for its own sake, but rather for its
pedagogical value. Either for the purpose of warning or emulation, it
contains the history of individuals and groups intended to teach future
generations lessons of social competence which might help them avoid
the dubious fate of the aristocracy or the sordid fate of the lower classes.
If this stance toward history is a manifestation of the self-image of a
bourgeoisie struggling for its existence with tenacious diligence, then,
by contrast, Meyer's selective approach to history may be dubbed a
"historicism of the upper bourgeoisie." When history is constituted ran-
domly from disjointed events, the abundance of historical phenomena is
forced into a dim twilight and the chain of diachronic experiences itself has
no significance at all. There is no continuum of events of any interpretable

character, be it causal, theological, or otherwise teleological in nature. Political, economic, cultural changes carry no weight, and the flow of history is in itself without importance. The historian turns spectator, taking pleasure in observing the singular like a magnificent drama. Thus, the category of play penetrates real history as much as historical research to the extent that history's diversity and complexity are reduced to a puppet theater of heroes whose lives and activities are reconstituted for the playful enjoyment of the spectator-interpreter. An upper-class bourgeois likes his favorite historian to be an aesthete.

Another example for the exploration of the content is the question of politics. In Gottfried Keller we find an almost bold disregard for economic realities, but considerable emphasis is placed on the political sphere, whether in the occasional caricaturization of armchair politics or in the informed and competent conversations with the burgher in the *Fähnlein der sieben Aufrechten* [The seven upright] on topics of general import. To identify politics as the supreme, if not exclusive, arena for the confrontation and final settlement of public affairs, is characteristic for social groups which, on the one hand, experience themselves as economically secure, but whose social mobility, on the other hand, is limited. All through the nineteenth century the middle class is inclined to look at politics as a resource for arbitration between competing groups and individuals, as, literally, a "middle" way. This notion of the middle station, incidentally, was already fervently glorified in the fictional and pamphlet literature read by the English middle class in the eighteenth century. In the case of Stendhal, politics does not function as an ideological device; rather, consciously or not, he acts as spokesman for the upper class of his time, who considered political dealings part of economic transactions and conflicts, and governments nothing more than business partners of big business itself.

It has always been of great interest to me why a task as important as the study of the reception of literature among various social groups has been so utterly neglected, even though a vast pool of research material is available in journals and newspapers, in letters and memoirs. A materialistic history of literature, unhampered by the anxious protection of the literary arts by its self-styled guardians and without fear of getting stranded in a quagmire of routine philology or mindless data collection, is well prepared to tackle this task.

Notes

1. Emil Ermatinger, ed., *Die Philosophie der Literaturwissenschaft* (Berlin, 1930).
2. Herbert Cysarz, "Das Periodenprinzip in der Literaturwissenschaft" (The principle of periodization in literary studies), in Ermatinger, *Die Philosophie*, p. 110.
3. D. H. Sarnetzki, "Literaturwissenschaft, Dichtung, Kritik des Tages" (Literary study, literary work, contemporary criticism), in Ermatinger, *Die Philosophie*, p. 454.

4. Ermatinger, *Die Philosophie*, passim.

5. Cysarz, op. cit.

6. See Werner Ziegenfuss, "Kunst" (Art), in *Handwörterbuch der Soziologie* (Encyclopedia of sociology), (Berlin,1931), p. 311.

7. Emil Ermatinger, "Das Gesetz in der Literaturwissenschaft" (Law in literary study), in *Die Philosophie*, p. 352.

8. Fritz Strich, *Deutsche Klassik und Romantik* (German classicism and romanticism), (Munich, 1924), p. 7.

9. Sarnetzki, op. cit.

10. Ermatinger, op. cit., p. 363f.

11. C. G. Jung, *Psychologie und Dichtung* (Psychology and literature), quoted in Walter Musch, *Psychoanalyse und Literaturwissenschaft* (Psychoanalysis and literary study), (Berlin, 1930), p. 330.

12. See the important publication of Hanns Sachs, *Gemeinsame Tagträume* (Shared daydreams), (Leipzig, 1924), esp. pt. 1.

13. Musch, *Psychoanalyse*, p. 15.

14. Sarnetzki, op. cit.

15. Ibid.

16. Ziegenfuss, op. cit., p. 337.

17. Herbert Cysarz, *Erfahrung und Idee* (Experience and ideal), (Vienna and Leipzig, 1922), p. 6f.

18. Strich, op. cit.

19. Friedrich Gundolf, *Shakespeare* (Berlin, 1928), vol. 1, p. 10.

20. Ermatinger, op. cit., p. 352.

21. Cysarz, op. cit., p. 110.

22. Franz Schultz, *Das Schicksal der deutschen Literaturgeschichte* (The fate of German literary history), (Frankfurt, 1928), p. 138.

23. Ibid., p. 141ff.

24. Franz Mehring, *Schriften und Aufsätze* (Writings and essays), vol. 1 (Berlin, 1929); vol. 2, *Über Literaturgeschichte* (On literary history), (Berlin, 1929); *Die Lessinglegende* (The Lessing legend), (Berlin, 1926).

25. Ziegenfuss, op. cit., p. 330f.

26. Oskar Walzel, *Die Deutsche Literatur von Goethes Tod bis zur Gegenwart* (German literature from Goethe's death to the present), (Berlin, 1918), p. 664.

4

Notes on Science and the Crisis

Max Horkheimer

1.   In the Marxist theory of society, science is regarded as one of man's productive powers. In varying ways it has made the modern industrial system possible: as condition of the general flexibility of mind which has developed along with science over recent centuries; as a store of information on nature and the human world, which in the more developed countries is possessed even by people in the lower social classes; and, not least, as part of the intellectual equipment of the researcher, whose discoveries decisively affect the forms of social life. Insofar as science is available as a means of creating social values, that is, insofar as it takes shape in methods of production, it constitutes a means of production.

2.   The fact that science contributes to the social life-process as a productive power and a means of production in no way legitimates a pragmatist theory of knowledge. The fruitfulness of knowledge indeed plays a role in its claim to truth, but the fruitfulness in question is to be understood as intrinsic to the science and not as usefulness for ulterior purposes. The test of the truth of a judgment is something different from the test of its importance for human life. It is not for social interests to decide what is or is not true; the criteria for truth have developed, rather, in connection with progress at the theoretical level. Science itself admittedly changes in the course of history, but this fact can never stand as an argument for other criteria of truth than those which are appropriate to the state of knowledge at a given level of development. Even though science is subject to the dynamisms of history, it may not be deprived of its own proper character and misinterpreted for utilitarian ends. Of course, the reasons which justify rejecting the pragmatist theory of knowledge and

Translated by Matthew J. O'Connell

relativism in general, do not lead to a positivist separation of truth and action. On the one hand, neither the direction and methods of theory nor its object, reality itself, is independent of man, and, on the other hand, science is a factor in the historical process. The separation of theory and action is itself a historical phenomenon.

3.   In the general economic crisis, science proves to be one of the numerous elements within a social wealth which is not fulfilling its function. This wealth is immensely greater today than in previous eras. The world now has more raw materials, machines, and skilled workers, and better methods of production than ever before, but they are not profiting mankind as they ought. Society in its present form is unable to make effective use of the powers it has developed and the wealth it has amassed. Scientific knowledge in this respect shares the fate of other productive forces and means of production: its application is sharply disproportionate to its high level of development and to the real needs of mankind. Such a situation hinders the further development, qualitative and quantitative, of science itself. As the course of earlier crises warns us, economic balance will be restored only at the cost of great destruction of human and material resources.

4.   One way of hiding the real causes of the present crisis is to assign responsibility for it to precisely those forces which are working for the betterment of the human situation, and this means, above all, rational, scientific thinking. The attempt is being made to subordinate the more intense cultivation of such thinking by individuals to the development of the "psychic" and to discredit critical reason as a decisive factor except for its professional application in industry. The view is abroad that reason is a useful instrument only for purposes of everyday life, but must fall silent in the face of the great problems and give way to the more substantial powers of the soul. The result is the avoidance of any theoretical consideration of society as a whole. The struggle of contemporary metaphysics against scientism is in part a reflection of these broader social tendencies.

5.   Science in the prewar years had in fact a number of limitations. These were due, however, not to an exaggeration of its rational character but to restrictions on it which were themselves conditioned by the increasing rigidification of the social situation. The task of describing facts without respect for nonscientific considerations and of establishing the patterns of relations between them was originally formulated as a partial goal of bourgeois emancipation in its critical struggle against scholastic restrictions upon research. But by the second half of the nineteenth century this definition had already lost its progressive character and showed itself to be, on the contrary, a limiting of scientific activity to the description, classification, and generalization of phenomena, with no care to distinguish the unimportant from the essential. In the measure that concern for

a better society, which still dominated the Enlightenment, gave way to the attempt to prove that present-day society should be permanent, a deadening and disorganizing factor entered science. The result of science, at least in part, may have been usefully applied in industry, but science evaded its responsibility when faced with the problem of the social process as a whole. Yet this was the foremost problem of all even before the war, as ever more intense crises and resultant social conflicts succeeded one another. Scientific method was oriented to being and not to becoming, and the form of society at the time was regarded as a mechanism which ran in an unvarying fashion. The mechanism might be disturbed for a shorter or longer period, but in any event it did not require a different scientific approach than did the explanation of any complicated piece of machinery. Yet social reality, the development of men acting in history, has a structure. To grasp it requires a theoretical delineation of profoundly transformative processes which revolutionize all cultural relationships. The structure is not to be mastered by simply recording events as they occur, which was the method practiced in old-style natural science. The refusal of science to handle in an appropriate way the problems connected with the social process has led to superficiality in method and content, and this superficiality, in turn, has found expression in the neglect of dynamic relationships between the various areas with which science deals, while also affecting in quite varied ways the practice of the disciplines. Connected with this narrowing of scientific purview is the fact that a set of unexplicated, rigid, and fetishistic concepts can continue to play a role, when the real need is to throw light on them by relating them to the dynamic movement of events. Some examples: the concept of the self-contained consciousness as the supposed generator of science; the person and his world-positing reason; the eternal natural law, dominating all events, the unchanging relationship of subject and object; the rigid distinction between mind and nature, soul and body, and other categorical formulations. The root of this deficiency, however, is not in science itself but in the social conditions which hinder its development and are at loggerheads with the rational elements immanent in science.

6.   Since around the turn of the century scientists and philosophers have pointed out the insufficiencies and unsuitability of purely mechanistic methods. The criticism has led to discussion of the principles involved in the main foundations on which research rests, so that today we may speak of a crisis within science. This inner crisis is now added to the external dissatisfaction with science as a means of production which has not been able to meet expectations in alleviating the general need. Modern physics has in large measure overcome within its own field the deficiencies of the traditional method and has revised its critical foundations. It is to the credit of postwar metaphysics, especially that of Max Scheler, that it has

once again turned the attention of science as a whole to numerous neglected areas and prepared the way at many points for a method less hindered by conventional narrowness of outlook. Above all, the description of important psychic phenomena, the delineation of social types, and the founding of a sociology of knowledge have had fruitful results. Yet, leaving aside the fact that essays in metaphysics almost always presented as concrete reality something called "life," that is, a mythical essence, and not real, living society in its historical development, such essays in the last analysis did not stimulate science but were simply negative towards it. Instead of pointing out and finally breaking through the limitations science had put upon itself by its narrow concentration on classification, metaphysics identified the very inadequate science of former times with rationality as such; it denied even judgmental thinking and abandoned itself to arbitrarily chosen objects and to a method cut completely loose from science. A philosophical anthropology arose which, in its independence, absolutized certain characteristics of man; to critical reason it opposed an intuition which rejected all restraining scientific criteria and trusted unquestioningly in its own clarity of vision. Metaphysics thereby turned its back on the causes of the social crisis and even downgraded the means of investigating it. It introduced a new confusion of its own by hypostatizing isolated, abstractly conceived man and thereby belittling the importance of a theoretical comprehension of social processes.

7. Not only metaphysics but the science it criticizes is ideological, insofar as the latter retains a form which hinders it in discovering the real causes of the crisis. To say it is ideological is not to say that its practitioners are not concerned with pure truth. Every human way of acting which hides the true nature of society, built as it is on antagonisms, is ideological, and the claim that philosophical, moral, and religious acts of faith, scientific theories, legal maxims, and cultural institutions have this function is not an attack on the character of those who originate them but only states the objective role such realities play in society. Views valid in themselves and theoretical and aesthetic works of undeniably high quality can in certain circumstances operate ideologically, while many illusions, on the contrary, are not a form of ideology. The occurrence of ideology in the members of a society necessarily depends on their place in economic life; only when relationships have so far developed and conflicts of interest have reached such an intensity that even the average eye can penetrate beyond appearances to what is really going on, does a conscious ideological apparatus in the full sense usually make its appearance. As an existing society is increasingly endangered by its internal tensions, the energies spent in maintaining an ideology grow greater and finally the weapons are readied for supporting it with violence. The more the Roman Empire was threatened by explosive inner forces, the more brutally did the Caesars

try to revitalize the old cult of the state and to restore the lost sense of unity. The ages which followed the Christian persecutions and the fall of the empire supply many other frightful examples of the same recurring pattern. In the science of such periods the ideological dimension usually comes to light less in its false judgments than in its lack of clarity, its perplexity, its obscure language, its manner of posing problems, its methods, the direction of its research, and, above all, in what it closes its eyes to.

8. At the present time, scientific effort mirrors an economy filled with contradictions. The economy is in large measure dominated by monopolies, and yet on the world scale it is disorganized and chaotic, richer than ever yet unable to eliminate human wretchedness. Science, too, shows a double contradiction. First, science accepts as a principle that its every step has a critical basis, yet the most important step of all, the setting of tasks, lacks a theoretical grounding and seems to be taken arbitrarily. Second, science has to do with a knowledge of comprehensive relationships; yet, it has no realistic grasp of that comprehensive relationship upon which its own existence and the direction of its work depend, namely, society. The two contradictions are closely connected. The process of casting light on the social life-process in its totality brings with it the discovery of the law which holds sway in the apparent arbitrariness of the scientific and other endeavors. For science, too, is determined in the scope and direction of its work not by its own tendencies alone but, in the last analysis, by the necessities of social life as well. Despite this law, a wasteful dispersal of intellectual energies has characterized the course of science over the last century, and philosophers of the period have repeatedly criticized science on this score. But the situation cannot be changed by purely theoretical insight, any more than the ideological function of science can be. Only a change in the real conditions for science within the historical process can win such a victory.

9. The view that cultural disorder is connected with economic relationships and with the conflicts of interest that arise out of them says nothing about the relative reality and importance of material and intellectual values. It does contradict, of course, the idealist thesis that the world is the product and expression of an absolute mind, for it refuses to consider mind as separable from historical being and independent of it. But we can regard idealism as essentially consisting not in such a questionable metaphysics but in the effort to develop effectively the intellectual capabilities of man. If so, the materialist thesis of the nonindependence of the ideal order corresponds better to such a conception of classical German philosophy than does a great part of modern metaphysics. For the effort to grasp the social causes of the stunting and destruction of human life and effectively to subordinate the economy to man is a more appropriate

task for such striving than is the dogmatic assertion of a priority of the spiritual without heed to the course of history.

10.   Insofar as we can rightly speak of a crisis in science, that crisis is inseparable from the general crisis. The historical process has imposed limitations on science as a productive force, and these show in the various sectors of science, in their content and form, in their subject matter and method. Furthermore, science as a means of production has not been properly applied. Understanding of the crisis of science depends on a correct theory of the present social situation; for science as a social function reflects at present the contradictions with society.

5
Philosophy and Critical Theory
Herbert Marcuse

From the beginning, the Critical Theory of society was constantly involved in philosophical as well as social issues and controversies. At the time of its origin, in the thirties and forties of the nineteenth century, philosophy was the most advanced form of consciousness, and by comparison real conditions in Germany were backward. Criticism of the established order there began as a critique of that consciousness, because otherwise it would have confronted its object at an earlier and less advanced historical stage than that which had already attained reality in countries outside Germany. Once Critical Theory had recognized the responsibility of economic conditions for the totality of the established world and comprehended the social framework in which reality was organized, philosophy became superfluous as an independent scientific discipline dealing with the structure of reality. Furthermore, problems bearing on the potentialities of man and of reason could now be approached from the standpoint of economics.

Philosophy thus appears within the economic concepts of materialist theory, each of which is more than an economic concept of the sort employed by the academic discipline of economics. It is due more to the theory's claim to explain the totality of man and his world in terms of his social being. Yet it would be false on that account to reduce these concepts to philosophical ones. To the contrary, the philosophical contents relevant to the theory are to be educed from the economic structure. They refer to conditions that, when forgotten, threaten the theory as a whole.

In the conviction of its founders, the Critical Theory of society is essentially linked with materialism. This does not mean that it thereby sets itself up as a philosophical system in opposition to other philosophical systems. The theory of society is an economic, not a philosophical,

Translated by Jeremy J. Shapiro

system. There are two basic elements linking materialism to correct social theory: concern with human happiness, and the conviction that it can be attained only through a transformation of the material conditions of existence. The actual course of the transformation and the fundamental measures to be taken in order to arrive at a rational organization of society are prescribed by analysis of economic and political conditions in the given historical situation. The subsequent construction of the new society cannot be the object of theory, for it is to occur as the free creation of the liberated individuals. When Reason has been realized as the rational organization of mankind, philosophy is left without an object. For philosophy, to the extent that it has been, up to the present, more than an occupation or a discipline within the given division of labor, has drawn its life from reason's not yet being reality.

Reason is the fundamental category of philosophical thought, the only one by means of which it has bound itself to human destiny. Philosophy wanted to discover the ultimate and most general grounds of Being. Under the name of reason it conceived the idea of an authentic Being in which all significant antitheses (of subject and object, essence and appearance, thought and being) were reconciled. Connected with this idea was the conviction that what exists is not immediately and already rational but must rather be brought to reason. Reason represents the highest potentiality of man and of existence; the two belong together. For when reason is accorded the status of substance, this means that at its highest level, as authentic reality, the world no longer stands opposed to the rational thought of men as mere material objectivity *(Gegenständlichkeit)*. Rather, it is now comprehended by thought and defined as concept *(Begriff)*. That is, the external, antithetical character of material objectivity is overcome in a process through which the identity of subject and object is established as the rational, conceptual structure that is common to both. In its structure the world is considered accessible to reason, dependent on it, and dominated by it. In this form philosophy is idealism; it subsumes being under thought. But through this first thesis that made philosophy into rationalism and idealism, it became critical philosophy as well. As the given world was bound up with rational thought and, indeed, ontologically dependent on it, all that contradicted reason or was not rational was posited as something that had to be overcome. Reason was established as a critical tribunal. In the philosophy of the bourgeois era, reason took on the form of rational subjectivity. Man, the individual, was to examine and judge everything given by means of the power of his knowledge. Thus, the concept of reason contains the concept of freedom as well. For such examination and judgment would be meaningless if man were not free to act in accordance with his insight and to bring what confronts him into accordance with reason.

> Philosophy teaches us that all properties of mind subsist only through free-
> dom, that all are only means for freedom, and that all seek and produce only
> freedom. To speculative philosophy belongs the knowledge that freedom is
> that alone which is true of mind.[1]

Hegel was only drawing a conclusion from the entire philosophical tradition when he identified reason and freedom. Freedom is the "formal
element" of rationality, the only form in which reason can be.[2]

With the concept of reason as freedom, philosophy seems to reach its
limit. What remains outstanding to the realization of reason is not a
philosophical task. Hegel saw the history of philosophy as having reached
its definitive conclusion at this point. However, this meant for mankind
not a better future but the bad present that this condition perpetuates. Kant
had, of course, written essays on universal history with cosmopolitan
intent, and on perpetual peace. But his transcendental philosophy aroused
the belief that the realization of reason through factual transformation was
unnecessary, since individuals could become rational and free within the
established order. In its basic concepts this philosophy fell prey to the
order of the bourgeois epoch. In a world without reason, reason is only
the semblance of rationality; in a state of general unfreedom, freedom is
only a semblance of being free. This semblance is generated by the
internalization of idealism. Reason and freedom become tasks that the
individual is to fulfill within himself, and he can do so regardless of
external conditions. Freedom does not contradict necessity, but, to the
contrary, necessarily presupposes it. Only he is free who recognizes
the necessary as necessary, thereby overcoming its mere necessity and
elevating it to the sphere of reason. This is equivalent to asserting that a
person born crippled, who cannot be cured at the given state of medical
science, overcomes this necessity when he gives reason and freedom scope
within his crippled existence, i.e., if from the start he always posits his
needs, goals, and actions only as the needs, goals, and actions of a cripple.
Idealist rationalism canceled the given antithesis of freedom and necessity
so that freedom can never trespass upon necessity. Rather, it modestly
sets up house within necessity. Hegel once said that this suspension of
necessity "transfigures necessity into freedom."[3]

Freedom, however, can be the truth of necessity only when necessity
is already true "in itself." Idealist rationalism's attachment to the status
quo is distinguished by its particular conception of the relation of freedom
and necessity. This attachment is the price it had to pay for the truth of
its knowledge. It is already given in the orientation of the subject of
idealist philosophy. This subject is rational only insofar as it is entirely
self-sufficient. All that is "other" is alien and external to this subject and
as such primarily suspect. For something to be true, it must be certain.

For it to be certain, it must be posited by the subject as its own achievement. This holds equally for the *fundamentum inconcussum* of Descartes and the synthetic a priori judgments of Kant. Self-sufficiency and independence of all that is other and alien are the sole guarantee of the subject's freedom. What is not dependent on any other person or thing, what possesses itself, is free. Having excludes the other. Relating to the other in such a way that the subject really reaches and is united with it (or him) counts as loss and dependence. When Hegel ascribed to reason, as authentic reality, movement that "remains within itself," he could invoke Aristotle. From the beginning, philosophy was sure that the highest mode of being was being-within-itself *(Beisichselbstsein)*.

This identity in the determination of authentic reality points to a deeper identify: property. Something is authentic when it is self-reliant, can preserve itself, and is not dependent on anything else. For idealism, this sort of being is attained when the subject has the world so that it cannot be deprived of it—that is, disposes of it omnipresently—and so that it appropriates it to the extent that in all otherness the subject is only with itself. However, the freedom attained by Descartes' *ego cogito,* Leibniz's monad, Kant's transcendental ego, Fichte's subject of original activity, and Hegel's world-spirit is not the freedom of pleasurable possession with which the Aristotelian God moved in his own happiness. It is rather the freedom of interminable, arduous labor. In the form that it assumed as authentic Being in modern philosophy, reason has to produce itself and its reality continuously in recalcitrant material. It exists only in this process. What reason is to accomplish is neither more nor less than the constitution of the world for the ego. Reason is supposed to create the universality and community in which the rational subject participates with other rational subjects. It is the basis of the possibility that, beyond the encounter of merely self-sufficient monads, a common life develops in a common world. But even this achievement does not lead beyond what already exists. It changes nothing. For the constitution of the world has always been effected prior to the actual action of the individual; thus, he can never take his most authentic achievement into his own hands. The same characteristic agitation, which fears really taking what is and making something else out of it, prevails in all aspects of this rationalism. Development is proclaimed, but true development is "not a transformation, or becoming something else."[4] For at its conclusion it arrives at nothing that did not already exist "in itself" at the beginning. The absense of concrete development appeared to this philosophy as the greatest benefit. Precisely at its maturest stage, the inner stasis of all its apparently so dynamic concepts become manifest.

Undoubtedly, all these characteristics make idealist rationalism a bourgeois philosophy. And yet, merely on account of the single concept of reason, it is more than ideology, and in devoting oneself to it one does more than struggle against ideology. The concept of ideology has meaning only when oriented to the interest of theory in the transformation of the social structure. Neither a sociological nor a philosophical but rather a political concept, it considers a doctrine in relation not to the social conditions of its truth or to an absolute truth but rather to the interest of transformation.[5] Countless philosophical doctrines are mere ideology and, as illusions about socially relevant factors, readily integrate themselves into the general apparatus of domination. Idealist rationalism does not belong to this class, precisely to the extent that it is really idealistic. The conception of the domination of Being by reason is, after all, not only a postulate of idealism. With a sure instinct, the authoritarian state has fought classical idealism. Rationalism saw into important features of bourgeois society: the abstract ego, abstract reason, abstract freedom. To that extent it is correct consciousness. Pure reason was conceived as reason "independent" of all experience. The empirical world appears to make reason dependent; it manifests itself to reason with the character of "for-eignness" *(Fremdartigkeit.)*[6] Limiting reason to "pure" theoretical and practical achievement implies an avowal of bad facticity—but also concern with the right of the individual, with that in him which is more than "economic man," with what is left out of universal social exchange. Idealism tries to keep at least thought in a state of purity. It plays that peculiar double role of opposing both the true materialism of critical social theory and the false materialism of bourgeois practice. In idealism the individual protests the world by making both himself and the world free and rational in the realm of throught. This philosophy is in an essential sense individualistic. However, it comprehends the individual's unique-ness in terms of his self-sufficiency and "property"; all attempts to use the subject, construed in this sense, as the basis for constructing an intersubjective world have a dubious character. The alter ego always could be linked to the ego only in the abstract manner: it remained a problem of pure knowledge or pure ethics. Idealism's purity, too, is equivocal. To be sure, the highest truths of theoretical and of practical reason were to be pure and not based on facticity. But this purity could be saved only on the condition that facticity be left in impurity; the individual is surrendered to its untruth. Nevertheless, concern for the individual long kept idealism from giving its blessing to the sacrifice of the individual to the service of false collectives.

Rationalism's protest and critique remain idealistic and do not extend to the material conditions of existence. Hegel termed philosophy's abiding in the world of thought an "essential determination." Although philosophy reconciles antitheses in reason, it provides a "reconciliation not in reality, but in the world of ideas."[7] The materialist protest and materialist critique originated in the struggle of oppressed groups for better living conditions and remain permanently associated with the actual process of this struggle. Western philosophy had established reason as authentic reality. In the bourgeois epoch the reality of reason became the task that the free individual was to fulfill. The subject was the locus of reason and the source of the process by which objectivity was to become rational. The material conditions of life, however, allotted freedom to reason only in pure thought and pure will. But a social situation has come about in which the realization of reason no longer needs to be restricted to pure thought and will. If reason means shaping life according to men's free decision on the basis of their knowledge, then the demand for reason henceforth means the creation of a social organization in which individuals can collectively regulate their lives in accordance with their needs. With the realization of reason in such a society, philosophy would disappear. It was the task of social theory to demonstrate this possibility and lay the foundation for a transformation of the economic structure. By so doing, it could provide theoretical leadership for those strata which, by virtue of their historical situation, were to bring about the change. The interest of philosophy, concern with man, had found its new form in the interest of critical social theory. There is no philosophy alongside and outside this theory. For the philosophical construction of reason is replaced by the creation of a rational society. The philosophical ideals of a better world and of true Being are incorporated into the practical aim of struggling mankind, where they take on a human form.

What, however, if the development outlined by the theory does not occur? What if the forces that were to bring about the transformation are suppressed and appear to be defeated? Little as the theory's truth is thereby contradicted, it nevertheless appears then in a new light which illuminates new aspects and elements of its object. The new situation gives a new import to many demands and indices of the theory, whose changed function accords it in a more intensive sense the character of "critical theory."[8] Its critique is also directed at the avoidance of its full economic and political demands by many who invoke it. This situtation compels theory anew to a sharper emphasis on its concern with the potentialities of man and with the individual's freedom, happiness, and rights contained in all of its analyses. For the theory, these are exclusively potentialities of the concrete social situation. They become relevant only as economic and political questions and as such bear on human relations in the productive process, the distribution of the product of social labor, and men's active participation in the economic and political administration of the whole. The more elements of the theory become reality—not only as the old order's evolution confirms the theory's predictions, but as the transition to the new order begins—the more urgent becomes the question of what the theory intended as its goal. For here, unlike in philosophical systems, human freedom is no phantom or arbitrary inwardness that leaves everything in the external world as it was. Rather, freedom here means a real potentiality, a social relationship on whose realization human destiny depends. At the given stage of development, the constructive character of Critical Theory emerges anew. From the beginning it did more than simply register and systematize facts. Its impulse came from the force with which it spoke against the facts and confronted bad facticity with its better potentialities. Like philosophy, it opposes making reality into a criterion in the manner of complacent positivism. But unlike philosophy, it always derives its goals only from present tendencies of the social process. Therefore, it has no fear of the utopia that the new order is denounced as being. When truth cannot be realized within the established social order, it always appears to the latter as mere utopia. This transcendence speaks not against, but for its truth. The utopian element was long the only progressive element in philosophy, as in the constructions of the best state and the highest pleasure, of perfect happiness and perpetual peace. The obstinacy that comes from adhering to truth against all appearances has given way in contemporary philosophy to whimsy and uninhibited opportunism. Critical Theory preserves obstinacy as a genuine quality of philosophical thought.

The current situation emphasizes this quality. The reverse suffered by the progressive forces took place at a stage where the economic conditions for transformation were present. The new social situation expressed in the authoritarian state could be easily comprehended and predicted by means of the concepts worked out by the theory. It was not the failure of economic concepts that provided the impetus behind the new emphasis of the theory's claim that the transformation of economic conditions involves the transformation of the entirety of human existence. This claim is directed rather against a distorted interpretation and application of economics that is found in both practice and theoretical discussion. The discussion leads back to the question: In what way is the theory more than economics? From the beginning the critique of political economy established the difference by criticizing the entirety of social existence. In a society whose totality was determined by economic relations to the extent that the uncontrolled economy controlled all human relations, even the noneconomic was contained in the economy. It appears that, if and when this control is removed, the rational organization of society toward which Critical Theory is oriented is more than a new form of economic regulation. The difference lies in the decisive factor, precisely the one that makes the society rational—the subordination of the economy to the individuals' needs. The transformation of society eliminates the original relation of substructure and superstructure. In a rational reality, the labor process should not determine the general existence of men; to the contrary, their needs should determine the labor process. Not that the labor process is regulated in accordance with a plan, but the interest determining the regulation becomes important: it is rational only if this interest is that of the freedom and happiness of the masses. Neglect of this element despoils the theory of one of its essential characteristics. It eradicates from the image of liberated mankind the idea of happiness that was to distinguish it from all previous mankind. Without freedom and happiness in the social relations of men, even the greatest increase of production and the abolition of private property in the means of production remain infected with the old injustice.

Critical Theory has, of course, distinguished among various phases of realization and pointed out the unfreedoms and inequalities with which the new era inevitably will be burdened. Nevertheless, the transformed social existence must be determined by its ultimate goal even at its inception. In its concept of an ultimate goal, Critical Theory did not intend to replace the theological hereafter with a social one—with an ideal that appears in the new order as just another hereafter in virtue of its exclusive opposition to the beginning and its telescoping distance. By defending the endangered and victimized potentialities of man against cowardice and betrayal, Critical Theory is not to be supplemented by a philosophy. It only makes explicit what was always the foundation of its categories: the demand that through the abolition of previously existing material conditions of existence the totality of human relations be liberated. If Critical Theory, amidst today's desperation, indicates that the reality it intends must comprise the freedom and happiness of individuals, it is only following the direction given by its economic concepts. They are constructive concepts, which comprehend not only the given reality but, simultaneously, its abolition and the new reality that is to follow. In the theoretical reconstruction of the social process, the critique of current conditions and the analysis of their tendencies necessarily include future-oriented components. The transformation toward which this process tends and the existence that liberated mankind is to create for itself determine at the outset the establishment and unfolding of the first economic categories. Theory can invoke no facts in confirmation of the theoretical elements that point toward future freedom. From the viewpoint of theory, all that is already attained is given only as something threatened and in the process of disappearing; the given is a positive fact, an element of the coming society, only when it is taken into the theoretical construction as something to be transformed. This construction is neither a supplement to nor an extension of economics. It is economics itself insofar as it deals with contents that transcend the realm of established economic conditions.

Unconditional adherence to its goal, which can be attained only in social struggle, lets theory continually confront the already attained with the not yet attained and newly threatened. The theory's interest in great philosophy is part of the same context of opposition to the established order. But Critical Theory is not concerned with the realization of ideals brought into social struggles from outside. In these struggles it identifies on one side the cause of freedom, and on the other the cause of suppression and barbarism. If the latter seems to win in reality, it might easily appear as though Critical Theory were holding up a philosophical idea against factual development and its scientific analysis. Traditional science was in fact more subject to the powers-that-be than was great philosophy. It was not in science but in philosophy that the traditional theory developed concepts oriented to the potentialities of man lying beyond his factual status. At the end of the *Critique of Pure Reason,* Kant cites the three questions in which "all the interest" of human reason "coalesces": What can I know? What should I do? What may I hope?[9] And in the introduction to his lectures on logic, he adds a fourth question encompassing the first three: What is man?[10] The answer to this question is conceived not as the description of human nature as it is actually found to be, but rather as the demonstration of what are found to be human potentialities. In the bourgeois period, philosophy distorted the meaning of both question and answer by equating human potentialities with those that are real within the established order. That is why they could be potentialities only of pure knowledge and pure will.

The transformation of a given status is not, of course, the business of philosophy. The philosopher can only participate in social struggles insofar as he is not a professional philosopher. This "division of labor," too, results from the modern separation of the mental from the material means of production, and philosophy cannot overcome it. The abstract character of philosophical work in the past and present is rooted in the social conditions of existence. Adhering to the abstractness of philosophy is more appropriate to circumstances and closer to truth than is the pseudo-philosophical concreteness that condescends to social struggles. What is true in philosophical concepts was arrived at by abstracting from the concrete status of man and is true only in such abstraction. Reason, mind, morality, knowledge, and happiness are not only categories of bourgeois philosophy, but concerns of mankind. As such they must be preserved, if not derived anew. When Critical Theory examines the philosophical doctrines in which it was still possible to speak of man, it deals first with the camouflage and misinterpretation that characterized the discussion of man in the bourgeois period.

With this intention, several fundamental concepts of philosophy have been discussed in the journal [*Zeitschrift für Sozialforschung*]: truth and verification, rationalism and irrationalism, the role of logic, metaphysics and positivism, and the concept of essence. These were not merely analyzed sociologically, in order to correlate philosophical dogmas with social loci. Nor were specific philosophical contents "resolved" into social facts. To the extent that philosophy is more than ideology, every such attempt must come to naught. When Critical Theory comes to terms with philosophy, it is interested in the truth content of philosophical concepts and problems. It presupposes that they really contain truth. The enterprise of the sociology of knowledge, to the contrary, is occupied only with the untruths, not the truths of previous philosophy. To be sure, even the highest philosophical categories are connected with social facts, even if only with the most general fact that the struggle of man with nature has not been undertaken by mankind as a free subject, but instead has taken place only in class society. This fact comes to expression in many "ontological differences" established by philosophy. Its traces can perhaps be found even in the very forms of conceptual thought: for example, in the determination of logic as essentially the logic of predication, or judgments about given objects of which predicates are variously asserted or denied. It was dialectical logic that first pointed out the shortcomings of this interpretation of judgment: the "contingency" of predication and the "externality" of the process of judgment, which let the subject of judgment appear "outside" as selfsubsistent and the predicate "inside," as though in our heads.[11] Moreover, it is certainly true that many philosophical concepts are mere "foggy ideas" arising out of the domination of existence by an uncontrolled economy and, accordingly, are to be explained precisely by the material conditions of life.

But in its historical forms philosophy also contains insights into human and objective conditions whose truth points beyond previous society and thus cannot be completely reduced to it. Here belong not only the contents dealt with under such concepts as reason, mind, freedom, morality, universality, and essence, but also important achievements of epistemology, psychology, and logic. Their truth content, which surmounts their social conditioning, presupposes not an eternal consciousness that transcendentally constitutes the individual consciousness of historical subjects, but only those particular historical subjects whose consciousness expresses itself in Critical Theory. It is only with and for this consciousness that the "surpassing" content becomes visible in its real truth. The truth that it recognizes in philosophy is not reducible to existing social conditions. This would be the case only in a form of existence where consciousness is no longer separated from being, enabling the rationality of thought to proceed from the rationality of social existence. Until then truth that is more than the truth of what is can be attained and intended only in opposition to established social relations. To this negative condition, at least, it is subject.

In the past, social relations concealed the meaning of truth. They formed a horizon of untruth that deprived the truth of its meaning. An example is the concept of universal consciousness, which preoccupied German idealism. It contains the problem of the relation of the subject to the totality of society: How can universality as community [*Allgemeinheit*], become the subject without abolishing individuality? The understanding that more than an epistemological or metaphysical problem is at issue here can be gained and evaluated only outside the limits of bourgeois thought. The philosophical solutions with which to resolve the problem are to be found in the history of philosophy. No sociological analysis is necessary in order to understand Kant's theory of transcendental synthesis. It embodies an epistemological truth. The interpretation given to the Kantian position by Critical Theory[12] does not affect the internal philosophical difficulty. By connecting the problem of universality of knowledge with that of society as a universal subject, it does not purport to provide a better philosophical solution. Critical Theory means to show only the specific social conditions at the root of philosophy's inability to pose the problem in a more comprehensive way, and to indicate that any other solution lay beyond that philosophy's boundaries. The untruth inherent in all transcendental treatment of the problem thus comes into philosophy "from outside"; hence, it can be overcome only outside philosophy. "Outside" does not mean that social factors affect consciousness from without as though the latter existed independently. It refers rather to a division within the social whole. Consciousness is "externally" conditioned by social existence to the very extent that in bourgeois society the social conditions of the individual are external to him and, as it were, overwhelm him from without. This externality made possible the abstract freedom of the thinking subject. Consequently, only its abolition would enable abstract freedom to disappear as part of the general transformation of the relationship between social being and consciousness.

If the theory's fundamental conception of the relation of social existence to consciousness is to be followed, this "outside" must be taken into consideration. In previous history there has been no pre-established harmony between correct thought and social being. In the bourgeois period, economic conditions determine philosophical thought insofar as it is the emancipated, self-reliant individual who thinks. In reality, he counts not in the concretion of his potentialities and needs but only in abstraction from his individuality, as the bearer of labor power, i.e., of useful functions in the process of the realization of capital. Correspondingly, he appears in philosophy only as an abstract subject, abstracted from his full humanity. If he pursues the idea of man, he must think in opposition to facticity. Wishing to conceive this idea in its philosophical purity and universality, he must abstract from the present state of affairs. This abstractness, this radical withdrawal from the given, at least clears a path along which the individual in bourgeois society can seek the truth and adhere to what is known. Besides concreteness and facticity, the thinking subject also leaves its misery "outside." But it cannot escape from itself, for it has incorporated the monadic isolation of the bourgeois individual into its premises. The subject thinks within a horizon of untruth that bars the door to real emancipation.

This horizon explains some of the characteristic features of bourgeois philosophy. One of them affects the idea of truth itself and would seem to relativize "sociologically" all its truths from the start: the coupling of truth and certainty. As such, this connection goes all the way back to ancient philosophy. But only in the modern period has it taken on the typical form that truth must prove itself as the guaranteed property of the individual, and that this proof is considered established only if the individual can continually reproduce the truth as his own achievement. The process of knowledge is never terminated, because in every act of cognition the individual must once again re-enact the "production of the world" and the categorical organization of experience. However, the process never gets any further because the restriction of "productive" cognition to the transcendental sphere makes any new form of the world impossible. The construction of the world occurs behind the backs of the individuals; yet it is their work.

The corresponding social factors are clear. The progressive aspects of this construction of the world—namely, the foundation of knowledge on the autonomy of the individual and the idea of cognition as an act and task to be continually re-enacted—are made ineffective by the life-process of bourgeois society. But does this sociological limitation affect the true content of the construction, the essential connection of knowledge, freedom, and practice? Bourgeois society's domination reveals itself not only in the dependence of thought but also in the (abstract) independence of its contents. For this society determines consciousness such that the latter's activity and contents survive in the dimension of abstract reason; abstractness saves its truth. What is true is so only to the extent that it is not the truth about social reality. And just because it is not the latter, because it transcends this reality, it can become a matter for Critical Theory. Sociology that is interested only in the dependent and limited nature of consciousness has nothing to do with truth. Its research, useful in many ways, falsifies the interest and the goal of Critical Theory. In any case, what was linked, in past knowledge, to specific social structures disappears with them. In contrast, Critical Theory concerns itself with preventing the loss of the truths which past knowledge labored to attain.

This is not to assert the existence of eternal truths unfolding in changing historical forms of which they need only to be divested in order for their kernel of truth to be revealed. If reason, freedom, knowledge, and happiness really are transformed from abstract concepts into reality, then they will have as much and as little in common with their previous forms as the association of free men with competitive, commodity-producing society. Of course, to the identity of the basic social structure in previous history certainly corresponds an identity of certain universal truths, whose universal character is an essential component of their truth content. The struggle of authoritarian ideology against abstract universals has clearly exhibited this. That man is a rational being, that this being requires freedom, and that happiness is his highest good are all universal propositions whose progressive impetus derives precisely from their universality. Universality gives them an almost revolutionary character, for they claim that all, and not merely this or that particular person, should be rational, free, and happy. In a society whose reality gives the lie to all these universals, philosophy cannot make them concrete. Under such conditions, adherence to universality is more important than its philosophical destruction.

Critical Theory's interest in the liberation of mankind binds it to certain ancient truths. It is at one with philosophy in maintaining that man can be more than a manipulable subject in the production process of class society. To the extent that philosophy has nevertheless made its peace with man's determination by economic conditions, it has allied itself with repression. That is the bad materialism that underlies the edifice of idealism: the consolation that in the material world everything is in order as it is. (Even when it has not been the personal conviction of the philosopher, this consolation has arisen almost automatically as part of the mode of thought of bourgeois idealism and constitutes its ultimate affinity with its time.) The other premise of this materialism is that the mind is not to make its demands in this world, but is to orient itself toward another realm that does not conflict with the material world. The materialism of bourgeois practice can quite easily come to terms with this attitude. The bad materialism of philosophy is overcome in the materialist theory of society. The latter opposes not only the production relations that gave rise to bad materialism, but every form of production that dominates man instead of being dominated by him: this idealism underlies its materialism. Its constructive concepts, too, have a residue of abstractness as long as the reality toward which they are directed is not yet given. Here, however, abstractness results not from avoiding the status quo, but from orientation toward the future status of man. It cannot be supplanted by another, correct theory of the established order (as idealist abstractness was replaced by the critique of political economy). It cannot be succeeded by a new theory, but only by rational reality itself. The abyss between rational and present reality cannot be bridged by conceptual thought. In order to retain what is not yet present as a goal in the present, fantasy is required. The essential connection of fantasy with philosophy is evident from the function attributed to it by philosophers, especially Aristotle and Kant, under the title of "imagination." Owing to its unique capacity to "intuit" an object, though the latter be not present, and to create something new out of given material of cognition, imagination denotes a considerable degree of independence from the given, of freedom amid a world of unfreedom. In surpassing what is present, it can anticipate the future. It is true that when Kant characterizes this "fundamental faculty of the human soul" as the a priori basis of all knowledge,[13] this restriction to the a priori diverts once again from the future to what is always past. Imagination succumbs to the general degradation of fantasy. To free it for the construction of a more beautiful and happier world remains the prerogative of children and fools. True, in fantasy one can imagine anything. But Critical Theory does not envision an endless horizon of possibilities.

The freedom of imagination disappears to the extent that real freedom becomes a real possibility. The limits of fantasy are thus no longer universal laws of essence (as the last bourgeois theory of knowledge that took seriously the meaning of fantasy so defined them[14]), but technical limits in the strictest sense. They are prescribed by the level of technological development. What Critical Theory is engaged in is not the depiction of a future world, although the response of fantasy to such a challenge would not perhaps be quite as absurd as we are led to believe. If fantasy were set free to answer, with precise reference to already existing technical material, the fundamental philosophical questions asked by Kant, all of sociology would be terrified at the utopian character of its answers. And yet the answers that fantasy could provide would be very close to the truth, certainly closer than those yielded by the rigorous conceptual analyses of philosophical anthropology. For it would determine what man is on the basis of what he really can be tomorrow. In replying to the question What may I hope? it would point less to eternal bliss and inner freedom than to the already possible unfolding and fulfillment of needs and wants. In a situation where such a future is a real possibility, fantasy is an important instrument in the task of continually holding the goal up to view. Fantasy does not relate to the other cognitive faculties as illusion to truth (which in fact, when it plumes itself on being the only truth, can perceive the truth of the future only as illusion). Without fantasy, all philosophical knowledge remains in the grip of the present or the past and severed from the future, which is the only link between philosophy and the real history of mankind.

Strong emphasis on the role of fantasy seems to contradict the rigorously scientific character that Critical Theory has always made a criterion of its concepts. This demand for scientific objectivity has brought materialist theory into unusual accord with idealist rationalism. While the latter could pursue its concern with man only in abstraction from given facts, it attempted to undo this abstractness by associating itself with science. Science never seriously called use-value into question. In their anxiety about scientific objectivity, the Neo-Kantians are at one with Kant, as is Husserl with Descartes. How science was applied, whether its utility and productivity guaranteed its higher truth or were instead signs of general inhumanity—philosophy did not ask itself these questions. It was chiefly interested in the methodology of the sciences. The Critical Theory of society maintained primarily that the only task left for philosophy was elaborating the most general results of the sciences. It, too, took as its basis the viewpoint that science had sufficiently demonstrated its ability to serve the development of the productive forces and to open up new potentialities of a richer existence. But while the alliance between idealist philosophy and science was burdened from the beginning with sins engendered by the dependence of the sciences on established relations of domination, the Critical Theory of society presupposes the disengagement of science from this order. Thus, the fateful fetishism of science is avoided here in principle. But this does not exempt the theory from a constant critique of scientific aims and methods which takes into account every new social situation. Scientific objectivity as such is never a sufficient guarantee of truth, especially in a situation where the truth speaks as strongly against the facts and is as well hidden behind them as today. Scientific predictability does not coincide with the futuristic mode in which the truth exists. Even the development of the productive forces and the evolution of technology know no uninterrupted progression from the old to the new society. For here, too, man himself is to determine progress: not "socialist" man, whose spiritual and moral regeneration is supposed to constitute the basis for planning the planners (a view that overlooks that "socialist" planning presupposes the disappearance of the abstract separation both of the subject from his activity and of the subject as universal from each individual subject), but the association of those men who bring about the transformation. Since what is to become of science and technology depends on them, science and technology cannot serve a priori as a conceptual model for Critical Theory.

Critical Theory is, last but not least, critical of itself and of the social forces that make up its own basis. The philosophical element in the theory is a form of protest against the new "economism," which would isolate the economic struggle and separate the economic from the political sphere. At an early stage, this view was countered with the criticism that the determining factors are the given situation of the entire society, the interrelationships of the various social strata, and relations of political power. The transformation of the economic structure must so reshape the organization of the entire society that, with the abolition of economic antagonisms between groups and individuals, the political sphere becomes to a great extent independent and determines the development of society. With the disappearance of the state, political relations would then become, in a hitherto unknown sense, general human relations: the organization of the administration of social wealth in the interest of liberated mankind.

The materialist theory of society is originally a nineteenth-century theory. Representing its relation to rationalism as one of "inheritance," it conceived this inheritance as it manifested itself in the nineteenth century. Much has changed since then. At that time the theory had comprehended, on the deepest level, the possibility of a coming barbarity, but the latter did not appear to be as imminent as the "conservative" abolition of what the nineteenth century represented: conservative of what the culture of bourgeois society, for all its poverty and injustice, had accomplished nonetheless for the development and happiness of the individual. What had already been achieved and what still remained to be done were clear enough. The entire impetus of the theory came from this interest in the individual, and it was not necessary to discuss it philosophically. The situation of inheritance has changed in the meantime. It is not a part of the nineteenth century but authoritarian barbarity that now separates the previous reality of reason from the form intended by the theory. More and more, the culture that was to have been abolished recedes into the past. Overlaid by an actuality in which the complete sacrifice of the individual has become a pervasive and almost unquestioned fact of life, that culture has vanished to the point where studying and comprehending it is no longer a matter of spiteful pride, but of sorrow. Critical Theory must concern itself to a hitherto unknown extent with the past—precisely insofar as it is concerned with the future.

In a different form, the situation confronting the theory of society in the nineteenth century is being repeated today. Once again, real conditions fall beneath the general level of history. Fettering the productive forces and keeping down the standard of life is characteristic of even the economically most developed countries. The reflection cast by the truth of the future in the philosophy of the past provides indications of factors that point beyond today's anachronistic conditions. Thus, Critical Theory is still linked to these truths. They appear in it as part of a process: that of bringing to consciousness potentialities that have emerged within the maturing historical situation. They are preserved in the economic and political concepts of Critical Theory.

Notes

1. Hegel, *Vorlesungen über die Philosophie der Geschichte*, in *Werke*, 2d ed. (Berlin, 1840–47), IX, p. 22.

Part II

Fragments of a
Theory of Society

6

The Jews and Europe

Max Horkheimer

Whoever wants to explain anti-Semitism must speak of National Socialism. Without a conception of what has happened in Germany, speaking about anti-Semitism in Siam or Africa remains senseless. The new anti-Semitism is the emissary of the totalitarian order, which has developed from the liberal one. One must thus go back to consider the tendencies within capitalism. But it is as if the refugee intellectuals have been robbed not only of their citizenship, but also of their minds. Thinking, the only mode of behavior that would be appropriate for them, has fallen into discredit. The "Jewish-Hegelian jargon," which once carried all the way from London to the German Left and even then had to be translated into the ringing tones of the union functionaries, now seems completely eccentric. With a sigh of relief they throw away the troublesome weapon and turn to neohumanism, to Goethe's personality, to the true Germany and other cultural assets. International solidarity is said to have failed. Because the worldwide revolution did not come to pass, the theoretical conceptions in which it appeared as the salvation from barbarism are now considered worthless. At present, we have really reached the point where the harmony of capitalist society along with the opportunities to reform it have been exposed as the very illusions always denounced by the critique of the free market economy; now, as predicted, the contradictions of technical progress have created a permanent economic crisis, and the descendants of the free entrepreneurs can maintain their positions only by the abolition of bourgeois freedoms; now the literary opponents of totalitarian society praise the very conditions to which they owe their

Translated by Mark Ritter

present existence, and deny the theory which, when there was still time, revealed its secrets.

No one can demand that, in the very countries that have granted them asylum, the emigres put a mirror to the world that has created fascism. But whoever is not willing to talk about capitalism should also keep quiet about fascism. The English hosts today fare better than Frederick the Great did with the acid-tongued Voltaire. No matter if the hymn the intellectuals intone to liberalism often comes too late, because the countries turn totalitarian faster than the books can find publishers; the intellectuals have not abandoned hope that somewhere the reformation of Western capitalism will proceed more mildly than in Germany and that well-recommended foreigners will have a future after all. But the totalitarian order differs from its bourgeois predecessor only in that it has lost its inhibitions. Just as old people sometimes become as evil as they basically always were, at the end of the epoch class rule has taken the form of the "folk community" [*Volksgemeinschaft*]. The theory has destroyed the myth of the harmony of interests [between capital and labor]; it has presented the liberal economic process as the reproduction of power relations by means of free contracts, which are compelled by the inequality of the property. Mediation has now been abolished. Fascism is that truth of modern society which has been realized by the theory from the beginning. Fascism solidifies the extreme class differences which the law of surplus value ultimately produced.

No revision of economic theory is required to understand fascism. Equal and just exchange has driven itself to the point of absurdity, and the totalitarian order is this absurdity. The transition from liberalism has occurred logically enough, and less brutally than from the mercantile system into that of the nineteenth century. The same economic tendencies that create an ever higher productivity of labor through the mechanism of competition have suddenly turned into forces of social disorganization. The pride of liberalism, industry developed technically to the utmost, ruins its own principle because great parts of the population can no longer sell their labor. The reproduction of what exists by the labor market becomes inefficient. Previously the bourgeoisie was decentralized, a many-headed ruler; the expansion of the plant was the condition for every entrepreneur to increase his portion of the social surplus. He needed workers in order to prevail in the competition of the market. In the age of monopolies the investment of more and more new capital no longer promises any great increase in profits. The mass of workers, from whom surplus value flows, diminishes in comparison to the apparatus which it serves. In recent times, industrial production has existed only as a condition for profit, for the expansion of the power of groups and individuals over human labor. Hunger itself provides no reason for the production of consumer goods. To produce for the insolvent demand, for the unemployed masses, would run counter to the laws of economy and religion that hold the order together; no bread without work.

Even the facade betrays the obsolescence of the market economy. The advertising signs in all countries are its monuments. Their expression is ridiculous. They speak to the passers-by as shallow adults do to children or animals, in a falsely familiar slang. The masses, like children, are deluded: they believe that as independent subjects they have the freedom to choose the goods for themselves. But the choice has already largely been dictated. For decades there have been entire spheres of consumption in which only the labels change. The panoply of different qualities in which consumers revel exists only on paper. If advertising was always characteristic of the *faux frais* of the bourgeois commodity economy, still, it formerly performed a positive function as a means of increasing demand. Today the buyer is still paid an ideological reverence which he is not even supposed to believe entirely. He already knows enough to interpret the advertising for the great brand-name products as national slogans that one is not allowed to contradict. The discipline to which advertising appeals comes into its own in the fascist countries. In the posters the people find out what they really are: soldiers. Advertising becomes correct. The strict governmental command which threatens from every wall during totalitarian elections corresponds more exactly to the modern organization of the economy than the monotonously colorful lighting effects in the shopping centers and amusement quarters of the world.

The economic programs of the good European statesmen are illusory. In the final phase of liberalism they want to compensate with government orders for the disintegrating market economy's inability to support the populace. Along with the economically powerful they seek to stimulate the economy so that it will provide everyone with a living, but they forget that the aversion to new investments is no whim. The industrialists have no desire to get their factories going via the indirect means of taxes they must pay to an all-too-impartial government simply to help the bankrupt farmers and other draft animals out of a jam. For their class such a procedure does not pay. No matter how much progovernmental economists may lecture the entrepreneurs that it is for their own benefit, the powerful have a better sense of their interests and have greater goals than a makeshift boomlet with strikes and whatever else belongs to the proletarian class struggle. The statesmen who, after all this, still wish to run liberalism humanely, misunderstand its character. They may represent education and be surrounded by experts, but their efforts are nonetheless absurd: they wish to subordinate to the general populace that class whose particular interests by nature run contrary to the general ones. A government that would make the objects of welfare into subjects of free contracts by garnering the taxes of employers, must fail in the end: otherwise it would involuntarily degenerate from the proxy of the employers into the executive agency of the unemployed, indeed, of the dependent classes in general. Nearly confiscatory taxes, such as the inheritance tax, which are forced not only by the layoffs in industry, but also by the insoluble agriculture crisis, already threaten to make the weak into the "exploiters" of the capitalists. Such a reversal of circumstances will not be permitted in the long run by the employers in any empire. In the parliaments and all of public life, the employers sabotage neoliberal welfare policies. Even if these would help the economy, the employers would remain unreconciled: economic cycles are no longer enough for them. The relations of production prevail against the humanitarian governments. The pioneers from the employers' associations create a new apparatus and their advocates take the social order into their hands; in place of fragmented command over particular factories, there arises the totalitarian rule of particular interests over the entire people. Individuals are subjected to a new discipline which threatens the foundations of the social order. The transformation of the downtrodden jobseeker from the nineteenth century into the solicitous member of a fascist organization recalls in its historical significance the transformation of the medieval master craftsman into the protestant burgher of the Reformation, or of the English village pauper into the modern industrial worker. Considering the fundamental nature of this change, the statesmen pursuing moderate progress appear reactionary.

The labor market is replaced by coerced labor. If over the past decades people went from exchange partners to beggars, objects of welfare, now they become direct objects of domination. In the prefascist stage the unemployed threatened the order. The transition to an economy which would unite the separated elements, which would give the people ownership of the idle machines and the useless grain, seemed unavoidable in Germany, and the world-wide danger of socialism seemed serious. With socialism's enemies stood everyone who had anything to say in the Republic. Governing was carried out by welfare payments, by former imperial civil servants, and by reactionary officers. The trade unions wished to transform themselves from organs of class struggle into state institutions which distribute governmental largesse, inculcate a loyal attitude in the recipients, and participate in social control. Such help, however, was suspect to the powerful. Once German capital had resumed imperialist policies, it dropped the labor bureaucrats, political and trade unions, who had helped it into power. Despite their most honest intentions, the bureaucrats could not measure up to the new conditions. The masses were not activated for the improvement of their own lives, not to eat, but to obey—such is the task of the fascist apparatus. Governing has acquired a new meaning there. Instead of practiced functionaries, imaginative organizers and overseers are needed; they must be well removed from the influence of ideologies of freedom and human dignity. In late capitalism, peoples metamorphose first into welfare recipients and then into followers [*Gefolgschaften*].

Long before the fascist revolution, the unemployed constituted an irresistible temptation for industrialists and agrarians, who wished to organize them for their purposes. As at the beginning of the epoch, uprooted masses are again available, but one cannot force them into manufacturing as one did then; the time of private enterprise is past. The fascist agitator unites his people for the battle against democratic governments. If during the transformation it becomes less and less attractive to invest capital in useful production, then the money is put into the organization of the masses one wishes to wrest away from the prefascist governments. Once that has been accomplished at home, then it is tried internationally. Even in foreign countries the fascist states appear as organizers of power against obstinate governments. Their emissaries prepare the ground for fascist conquests; they are the descendants of the Christian missionaries who preceded the merchants. Today it is not English but German imperialism which strives for expansion.

If fascism in fact follows from the capitalist principle, it is not adapted only to the poor, the "have-not" countries, in contrast to the rich ones. The fact that fascism was initially supported by bankrupt industries concerns its specific development, not its suitability as a universal principle. Already during the time of greatest profitability, heavy industry extorted its share of the class profit by means of its position of economic power. The average profit rate, which applied to it as well, always exceeded the surplus value produced in its own area. Krupp and Thyssen obeyed the principle of competition less than others. Thus, the bankruptcy that the balance eventually revealed showed nothing of the harmony between heavy industry and the needs of the status quo. The fact that the chemical industry was superior in the market to heavy industry in terms of profitability was not socially decisive. In late capitalism the task assigned is to remodel the populace into a combat-ready collective for civil and military purposes, so that it will function in the hands of the newly formed ruling class. Poor profitability thus merely stimulated certain parts of German industry before others to force the development.

The ruling class has changed. Its members are not identical with the owners of capitalist property. The fragmented majority of the shareholders have long since fallen under the leadership of the directors. With the progression of the enterprise from one among many competing economic units to the impregnable position of social power of the modern conglomerate, management gained absolute power. The scope and differentiation of the factories has created a bureaucracy, whose apex pursues its own goals with the capital of the shareholders and, if need be, against them. The same degree of organic conglomeration of capital that limits the economic incentive for further investment allows the directors to put the brakes on production in the course of political machinations, and even to halt it, without being affected much themselves. Directors' salaries at times free themselves from the balance sheets. The high industrial bureaucracy takes the place of the legal owners. It turns out that actual disposition, physical possession, and not nominal ownership are socially decisive.

Juridical form, which actually determined the happiness of individuals, has always been considered a product of ideology. The dispossessed groups in the bourgeoisie cling now to the hypostatized form of private property and denounce fascism as a new Bolshevism, while the latter theoretically hypostatizes a given form of socializing property and in practice cannot stop the monopolization of the production apparatus. It ultimately matters little whether the state takes care of its own by regulating private profits or the salaries of civil servants. The fascist ideology conceals the same relationship as the old harmonizing ideology: domination by a minority on the basis of actual possession of the tools of production. The aspiration for profit today ends in what it always was: striving for social power. The true self of the juridical owner of the means of production confronts him as the fascist commander of battalions of workers. Social dominance, which could not be maintained by economic means, because private property has outlived itself, is continued by directly political means. In the face of this situation, liberalism, even in its decadent form, represents the greatest good for the greatest number, since the amount of misfortune suffered by the majority in the capitalist mother countries is less than that concentrated today upon the persecuted minorities [in totalitarian countries].

Liberalism cannot be re-established. It leaves behind a demoralized proletariat betrayed by its leaders, in which the unemployed form a sort of amorphous class that fairly screams for organization from above, along with farmers, whose methods of production and forms of consciousness have lagged far behind technological development, and finally the generals of industry, the army, and the administration, who agree with each other and embrace the new order.

After the century-long interlude of liberalism, the upper class in the fascist countries has returned to its basic insights. In the twentieth century, the existence of individuals is once again being controlled in all its details. Whether totalitarian repression can persist after the unleashing of productive forces within industrial society cannot be deduced. The economic collapse was predictable, not the revolution. Theory and practice are not directly identical. After the war the question was posed in practical terms.

The German workers possessed the qualifications to rearrange the world. They were defeated. How far fascism reaches its goal will depend on the struggles of the present epoch. The adaptation of individuals to fascism, however, also expresses a certain rationality. After their betrayal by their own bureaucracy since 1914, after the development of the parties into world-spanning machineries for the destruction of spontaneity, after the murder of revolutionaries, the neutrality of workers with respect to the totalitarian order is no sign of idiocy. Remembering the fourteen years [of the Weimar Republic] has more attraction for the intellectuals than for the proletariat. Fascism may have no less to offer them than the Weimar Republic, which brought up fascism.

Totalitarian society may survive economically in the long run. Collapses are not a short-term prospect. Crises were rational signs, the alienated critiques of the market economy, which, though blind, was oriented to needs. In the totalitarian economy, hunger in war and peacetime appears less as a disruption than as a patriotic duty. For fascism as a world system, no economic end is visible. Exploitation no longer reproduces itself aimlessly via the market, but rather in the conscious exercise of power. The categories of political economy—exchange of equivalents, concentration, centralization, falling rate of profit, and so on—still have a tangible validity, except that their consequence, the end of political economy, has been attained. In the fascist countries, economic concentration proceeds rapidly. It has entered, however, into the practice of methodical violence, which seeks to master social antagonisms directly. The economy no longer has any independent dynamism. It loses its power to the economically powerful. The failure of the free market reveals the inability of further progress in the forms of antagonistic society of any kind. Despite the war, fascism can survive, unless the peoples of the world understand that the knowledge and machines they possess must serve their own happiness, rather than the perpetuation of power and injustice. Fascism is retrograde not in comparison to the bankrupt principle of laissez-faire, but in terms of what could be attained.

Even if it had been possible to limit armaments and divide the world, by following the example of the conglomerates (one should recall the efforts at a British-German, and beyond that, a European coal cartel),[1] even then fascism would not have needed to fear for its survival. There are innumerable tasks to be done which would provide food and work and yet not allow individuals to become arrogant. Mandeville, who knew what was needed, already designated the distant goal of fascism at the beginning of capitalism: "We have work for a hundred thousand more paupers than we actually have, work for three or four hundred years to come. In order to make our land useful and well populated everywhere, many rivers would need to be made navigable and many canals built. Many regions would need to be drained and protected for the future against floods. Large expanses of dry soil would have to be made fertile, many square miles of land more accessible and thus more profitable. *Dei laboribus omni vendunt*. There are no difficulties in this area that work and perseverance cannot overcome. The highest mountains can be toppled into the valleys that stand ready to receive them, and bridges can be built in places where we would not dare think of it. . . . It is the state's business to correct social ills, and take on those things first which are most neglected by private persons. Antagonisms are best cured by antagonisms; and since in the case of national failure an example accomplishes more than an order, the government should decide on some great undertaking that would require an immense amount of work for a long period, and thus convince the world that it does nothing without anxious concern for the most distant posterity. This will have a solidifying effect on the wavering spirit and the flighty mind of the people; it will remind us we do not live only for ourselves and will ultimately make people less distrustful, and thus will instill in them greater patriotism and loyal affection for their home soil, which, more than anything else, is necessary for the higher development of a nation.[2]

The terror in which the ruling class now takes refuge has been recommended by authorities ever since Machiavelli. "The wild animal called the people necessarily requires iron leadership: you will be lost immediately if you allow it to become aware of its strength. . . . The ruled individual needs no other virtue than patience and subordination; mind, talents, sciences belong on the side of the government. The greatest misfortune results from the overthrow of these principles. The real authority of the government will cease to exist, if everyone feels called to share in it; the horror of anarchy comes from such extravagance. The only means to avoid these dangers is to tighten the chain as much as possible, to pass the strictest laws, to avoid the enlightenment of the people, above all to resist the fatal freedom of the press, which is the source of all the knowledge that emancipates the people, and finally to terrify them by means of severe and frequent punishments. . . . Do not delude yourself that I understand by 'people' the class one designates as the third estate; certainly not. I call 'people' the venal and corrupt class that, thrown upon our earth like the scum of Nature, is only able to exist in the sweat of its brow."[3] What the National Socialists know was already known a hundred years ago. "One should only assemble people in church or in arms; then they don't think, they only listen and obey."[4] The place of St. Peter's is taken by the Berlin Sport Palace [where Nazi rallies were staged].

Not merely the dark, pessimistic [*dunklen*] philosophers, who are considered inhumane by their ideological descendants, have declared the subordination of the people the precondition for stable conditions; they have only designated the circumstances more clearly than the idealists. The later Kant is not much more convinced of the lower classes' right to freedom than Sade and de Bonald. According to practical reason, the people must obey as if in prison, only with the difference that it also should have its own conscience as warden and overseer, alongside the agents of the regime in power. "The origin of the highest power is for practical purposes inscrutable for the people which is subject to it, i.e., the subject should not practically reason . . . about its origin; for if the subject who had pondered out the ultimate origin were to resist that now prevailing authority, then by the laws of the latter, i.e., with complete justification, he would be punished, destroyed, or (outlawed, *exlex*) expelled."[5] Kant embraces the theory "that whoever is in possession of the supreme ruling and legislating power over a people, must be obeyed, and so juridically-absolutely, that even to research the title to this acquisition in public, that is, to doubt it, in order to resist it in case of some failing, is itself punishable; that it is a categorical imperative: Obey authority that has power over you (in everything which does not contradict the inwardly moral)."[6] But the scholar of Kant knows: the inwardly moral can never protest against an onerous task ordered by the respective authority.

Fascist nationalization, the installation of a terroristic party apparatus alongside the administration, is the opposite of socialization. As usual, the whole functions in the interests of a set group. The command of outside labor by the bureaucracy is now formally the last resort; the command of competing firms is delegated, but the contrasts blur: the owners become bureaucrats and the bureaucrats owners. The concept of the state completely loses its contradiction to the concept of a dominant particularity, it is the apparatus of the ruling clique, a tool of private power, and this is more true the more it is idolized. In Italy as well as in Germany, large public enterprises are being reprivatized. In Italy, electric factories, the monopolies on telephones and life insurance, and other governmental and municipal operations, and in Germany the banks above all, have gone into private hands.[7] Of course, only the powerful profit from that. In the long run the protection of the small businessman proves to be a pure propaganda hoax. The number of corporations which dominate the entire industry grows steadily smaller. Under the surface of the Führer-state a furious battle takes place among interested parties for the spoils. The German and other elites in Europe, which share the intention of keeping the populace in check, would long ago have started an internal and external war without this binding tie. Inside the totalitarian states, this tension is so great that Germany could dissolve overnight into a chaos of gangster battles. From the beginning, the tragic gestures as well as the incessant assurances of a multi-millennial permanence in National Socialist propaganda reflect the intimation of such a frailty. Only because the justified fear of the masses constantly brings them together do the subordinate leaders allow themselves to be integrated and if necessary massacred by the mightiest one. More than was ever the case under capitalism, anarchy is hidden behind the unity and harmony, atomistic private interest behind the planned economy. An equalization occurs which is no less coincidental to human needs than the previous price range of free markets. Despite all the directives, the forces which bring about the distribution of social energies to the various branches of production are as irrational as the mechanisms of the profit economy, which were formerly removed from human power. Freedom is no less a delusion for the leaders than for the businessman; as he depends on the market, they now depend on blind constellations of power. Arms build-ups are dictated to them by the interplay among the groups, by fear of one's own and foreign peoples, by dependence on certain parts of the world of business, just as the expansion of factories is dictated to entrepreneurs in industrial society by social antagonisms, not by the contest of people against nature, which is the only criterion for determining a rational society. The stability of fascism rests on an alliance against the revolution and on the elimination of the economic remedy. The atomistic principle, according to which the success of one person is tied to the misery of the other, has even been intensified today. In the fascist organizations, equality and brotherliness prevail only on the surface. The struggle to rise in the barbarian hierarchy makes one's comrades presumptive opponents. The fact that in a war economy more jobs are available than workers does not abolish the struggle of all against all. Wage differentials in the individual factories, for men and women, for blue-collar and white-collar workers, for various categories of proletarians are crasser than ever. With the abolition of unemployment the isolation of human beings has not been broken. Fear of unemployment is supplanted by fear of the state. Fear atomizes.

The common interest of the exploited is harder than ever to recognize today, when it is stronger than ever. Despite all the crises, at the height of liberalism, the proletariat remained tied to the process of commodity production, the unemployment of the individual passed. The proletarians' labor in industry formed the basis of solidarity, as it was still understood by social democracy. In the time immediately preceding fascism, a great part of the population became permanently unemployed and lost its backbone. The goons from the Technicians' Emergency League [*Technische Nothilfe*, an organization devoted to strike-breaking in the interest of "national security"] showed even the employed German workers their own weakness. In addition, the further the destruction of all spontaneity, conditioned by economic impotence, was driven by the old mass parties, the easier it was for the victims to be captured by the new one. In the new party, as in the old one, collectivism is the ideology of the atomized mass, which is completely the object of dominance. Like work under the dictates of the state, the belief in Führer and community propagated by the state appears to be an escape from a bleak existence. Everyone knows what he has to do and more or less what tomorrow will be like. One is no longer a beggar, and if there is war, one won't die alone. The "folk community" continues the ideology of 1914. National outbursts are the approved substitute for the revolution. Unconsciously, the workers realize the horror of their existence, which they are nevertheless unable to change. Salvation must come from above. Insincere as may be the belief in the insignificance of the individual, the survival of the "folk," or the leaders as personalities, it at least expresses an experience, in contrast to apathetic Christianity. The society is abandoned by the idolized leaders, but not quite as abandoned as it always was by the True God.

Fascism surpasses the conditions before its advent not just negatively, but positively as well. If the life forms of liberal capitalism had an inhibiting function, if idealistic culture had already become a laughing-stock, then their demolition by fascism must also set forces free. The individual is robbed of false securities; the fascist rescue of property, family, and religion scarcely leaves them intact. The masses become powerful instruments and the power of the totalitarian organization, suf-fused by another's will, is superior to the sluggishness of the Reichstag, which was led by the will of the people. The centralization of administra-tion carried out by National Socialism in Germany meets an old bourgeois demand, which was fulfilled elsewhere in the seventeenth century. The democratic trait of the new Germany, the formal abolition of the classes, is rational for the bourgeois. Of course, Richelieu dealt with the feudal lords more energetically than Hitler with the so-called reactionaries. Large landholders still enjoy the well-camouflaged protection of the so-called settlement policy. The successes of fascist foreign policy correspond to its domestic striking power. They authenticate the promises of the regime. The most important reason for the indolence with which fascism is toler-ated by the masses is the sober expectation that it might bully something out of the fragile states all around, something that would benefit even the little man. After the phase of conquests, which to be sure has only begun, National Socialism hopes to give as much as possible to the masses as long as there is no subversion of discipline or the will to sacrifice. In fascism, the number of accidents in factories rises at the same time as the turnover of champagne factories increases, but the certainty that there will continue to be jobs ultimately seems better than democracy. The people are not respected any less under Hitler than under Wilhelm. They will hardly permit a long war.

True, the productive forces are more strongly repressed in fascism than ever before. The invention of artificial materials offers no excuse for the mutilation of human talents, which leads to the annihilation of the humane. But this only continues a process that had already assumed a catastrophic dimension. In the latest phase, the fascist one, the countertendencies also grow stronger. The ideas of nationalism and race are overturned. At bottom, the Germans no longer believe in them. The conflict between liberalism and the totalitarian state no longer runs along national boundaries. Fascism conquers from abroad and from within at the same time. For the first time, the whole world has been pulled into the same political development. India and China are no longer mere peripheral areas, historical entities of a secondary order; now they manifest the same tensions as the advanced capitalist countries.

The lie of justice within modern society, the lie of the reward for achievement, the lie of success as a divine judgment, all the cultural lies that poisoned life, have either become transparent or been abolished. Bureaucracy decides on life and death. It does not shift the responsibility for the failure of individuals to God, as did the old capitalists, but rather to the necessity of the state. The inhumane people who now dispose over lives probably are no more unjust than the market, which was moved only by the will to profit, in selecting who will live and who will die. Fascism has rescued disposition over the means of production for that minority which emerged from the competition as the most determined. It is the up-to-date form. Even where fascism is not in power in Europe, strong social tendencies are at work, which wish to prepare the administrative, legal, and political apparatus for authoritarianism. For reasons of competition alone, the real liberal motive, the capitalists and their supporters are driven to that view. "If the British Government," the Whaley-Eaton Service writes, "is forced to choose between active inflation and totalitarian control of finance and industry, it will take the latter course."[8] Whether people will be content to stay with half-measures and compromises is still undecided.

That is how it is with the Jews. They shed many a tear for the past. That they fared better under liberalism does not guarantee the justice of the latter. Even the French Revolution, which helped the bourgeois economy to victory and gave the Jews equality, was more ambivalent than they dare imagine today. Not ideas but utility are decisive for the bourgeoisie: "It was only decided to bring about the revolutionary changes because people had thought it over. Such thinking was not the province of a few advanced minds; it was a very numerous elite, throughout France, which discussed the causes of the evils and the nature of the remedy."[9] Here, thinking over means calculating. So far as the Revolution overshot the economically desirable goals, things were set right later. People were less concerned with philosophy than with the administration's sluggishness, with provincial and governmental reforms. The bourgeois were always pragmatists; they always kept an eye on their property. For its sake the privileges fell. Even the more radical development, interrupted by the fall of the terrorists, did not point only in the direction of greater freedom. Even then, people were faced with choosing between various forms of dictatorship. Robespierre's and Saint Just's plans envisioned statist elements, a strengthening of the bureaucratic apparatus, similar to the authoritarian systems of the present. The order which set out as the progressive one in 1789 carried the germs of National Socialism from the beginning.

Despite all the fundamental differences between the Committee of Public Safety and the leaders of the Third Reich, which can be confronted with surprising parallels, the practice of both springs from the same political necessity: to preserve control of the means of production for those groups which already own them, so that the others are subject to their direction at work. Political freedom for everyone, equality for the Jews, and all the humane institutions were accepted as means to utilize wealth productively. The democratic institutions fostered the supply of cheap labor, the possibility of planning with assurance, and the spread of free trade. With the changing of circumstances the institutions lost the utilitarian character to which they owed their existence. Rationality which ran counter to the specific commercial conditions at any given stage was also considered eccentric or subversive by the Jewish entrepreneur. This kind of rationality now turns against him. A national morality was immanent to the reality in which the Jews lived their lives, according to which they are now found wanting, the morality of economic power. The same rationality of economic expediency, according to which the defeated competitors have always sunk into the proletariat and been cheated of their lives, has now pronounced judgment on the Jews. Once again a large elite, this time not only throughout France, is discussing "the cause of the evils and the nature of their remedy." The result is bad for the Jews. They are being run over. Others are the most capable today: the leaders of the new order in the economy and the state. The same economic necessity that irrationally created the army of the unemployed has now turned, in the form of carefully considered regulations, against entire minority groups.

The sphere of circulation, which was decisive for the fate of the Jews in a dual fashion, as the site of their livelihood and the foundation of bourgeois democracy, is losing its economic importance. The famous power of money is on the wane today. In liberalism it connected the power of capital to the fulfillment of useful functions. From the growth or loss of finance capital, which accrued to the entrepreneur as the result of every venture, he could see whether and to what extent that venture was useful to the existing society. The judgment of the market on the salability of goods attested to their effect on the progress of general economic life. With the increasing elimination of the market, the importance of money, as the material in which such evidence was given, also diminishes. Needs are not satisfied any more appropriately or justly than they were by the mechanical balancing of variously equipped capital interests. Only now, the verdict of the market on how everyone may live, the verdict over prosperity and misery, hunger and power, is made directly by the ruling economic groups themselves. The anonymity of the market has turned into planning, but instead of the free planning of united humanity, it is the crafty planning of the archenemies of humanity. Previously, the economic fate was not only anonymous, it also took aim at the sinners and the elect without regard to their human particularities; it did people the honor of ignoring them. To that extent it was humane in its inhumanity. In the Führer-state, those who are to live and those who are to die are deliberately designated. The Jews are stripped of power as agents of circulation, because the modern structure of the economy largely puts that whole sphere out of action. They are the first victims of the ruling group that has taken over the canceled function. The governmental manipulation of money, which already has robbery as its necessary function, turns into the brutal manipulation of money's representatives.

The Jews become aware of their despair, at least those who have been victimized. Whoever in England or France is still permitted to curse taxes with the Aryans does not like to see his coreligionists coming across the border; the fascists reckon in advance with that type of embarrassment. The newcomers often have a bad accent or uncouth manners in their new country. This is tolerated in the prominent persons. The others are like Eastern Jews or worse yet—political undesirables. They compromise the established Jews, who feel at home there and in turn get on the nerves of the resident Christians. As if the very concept "at home" in a horrible reality were not a sign of lies and scorn for every single member of Jewry, which has experienced it for millennia; as if the Jews who fancy themselves established anywhere did not know inwardly that the tidy housekeeping from which they now profit could turn against them tomorrow. The newcomers are discomforting in any case. The ideological practice in which people tend to demean the objects of social injustice all over again in their own minds, so as to give the injustice a veneer of rationality— this practice of the ruling classes that has been classical ever since Aristotle, and from which anti-Semitism also lives, is neither Jewish nor gentile; it belongs to every antagonistic society. Whoever fails in this economy may as a rule expect nothing more from those who worship it than the recognition of the economic verdict which has ruined him, anonymously or by name. Probably those affected are not so innocent after all. How should nouveau riche Jews and Aryans abroad, who have always acquiesced in the impoverishment of other social and national groups, in mass poverty in mother countries and colonies, and in the conditions in prisons and insane asylums, how should they come to their senses in the presence of German Jews?

The National Socialist plan to force what remains of the Jews down into the Lumpenproletariat testifies once again how well its authors know the environment. Once the Jews have become shabby, they will no longer even benefit from the fleeting sentiment of bourgeois class solidarity: the outrage that even rich people are no longer safe. Poor Jews are less pitiable. There have to be poor people; they can't change the world. Between the unfulfilled needs of the powerless and the unfulfillable needs of the powerful there exists a preordained harmony. The lower classes must not become too happy, or else they cease to be objects. The rage produced by misery, however, the deep, fervent, secret rage of those dependent in body and soul, becomes active where opportunity presents itself, that is, against the weak and dependent itself. The workers in Germany, schooled in revolutionary teachings, watched the pogroms with disgust; how the populace of other countries would behave is not precisely known. Wherever the emigrating Jews end up, the novelty soon subsides and daily routine takes over. Then the emigres find, despite all the well-wishes of enlightened souls, the callousness of competition and the vague, aimless hate of the crowd, nourished by the sight of them, for more than one reason.

To appeal today to the liberal mentality of the nineteenth century against fascism means appealing to what brought fascism to power. The phrase "make way for the achiever" can be claimed by the victor. He has withstood the national economic competition so well that he can abolish it. Laissez-faire, laissez-aller, he can ask, why shouldn't I do what I want? I am the employer and source of sustenance for no fewer people than any economic champion of the free market countries. I am also ahead in the chemical industry. Proletarians, colonial peoples, and malcontents complain. My God, haven't they always done that?

The hope of the Jews, which attaches itself to the Second World War, is miserable. However it comes out, a seamless militarization will lead the world further into authoritarian-collectivistic ways of life. The German war economy in the First World War was a precursor of modern multiyear plans; the compulsory conscription employed during that war is now a main part of the totalitarian technique. Mobilization brings little that is new, except perhaps the mass grave, to the work battalions assigned to the arms industry, to the construction of more and more new motor highways, subways, and community buildings. The incessant excavation of the earth in peacetime was already a type of trench war. Whether there is a war on remains unclear today, even to the combatants themselves.

The concepts are no longer clearly distinguishable as in the nineteenth century. The resettlement of whole peoples into the bomb shelter is Hitler's triumph, even if he is defeated. Perhaps in the initial fright the Jews will not be noticed, but in the long run they must tremble, along with everyone else, at what is now coming over the Earth.

A large portion of the masses being led against the totalitarian order does not, at bottom, fear fascism. Preserving the status quo is no more sensible a goal for war than for peace. Perhaps after a long war the old economic conditions will be re-established in individual territories for a short time. Then the economic development will repeat itself—fascism did not arise by chance. Since the failure of the market economy, people have faced, once and for all, the choice between freedom and fascist dictatorship. As agents of circulation, the Jews have no future. They will not be able to live as human beings until human beings finally put an end to prehistory.

Anti-Semitism will come to a natural end in the totalitarian order when nothing humane remains, although a few Jews might. The hatred of Jews belongs to the ascendant phase of fascism. At most, anti-Semitism in Germany is a safety valve for the younger members of the SA. It serves to intimidate the populace by showing that the system will stop at nothing. The pogroms are aimed politically more at the spectators than the Jews. Will anyone react? There is nothing more to be gained. The great anti-Semitic propaganda is addressed to foreign countries. Prominent Aryans in business and other areas may express all the outrage they wish, especially if their countries are far from the action; their prospectively fascist masses do not take it very seriously. People can secretly appreciate the cruelty by which they are so outraged. In continents from whose produce all of humanity could live, every beggar fears that the Jewish emigre might deprive him of his living. Reserve armies of the unemployed and the petty bourgeoisie love Hitler all over the world for his anti-Semitism, and the core of the ruling class agrees with that love. By increasing cruelty to the level of absurdity, its horror is mollified. That the offended divine power leaves the evildoers unpunished proves once again that it does not exist at all. In the reproduction of inhumanity, people confirm to themselves that the old humanity and religion along with the entire liberal ideology no longer have any value. Pity is really the last sin.

Even an unnatural end is foreseeable: the leap into freedom. Liberalism contained the elements of a better society. The law still possessed a generality that also applied to the rulers. The state was not directly their instrument. Someone who spoke up independently has not necessarily lost. Of course, such protection existed only in a small part of the world, in those countries to which the others were handed over. Even this fragile justice was limited to a few geographical areas. Anyone who participates in a limited human order must not be surprised if he occasionally falls victim to the limitations himself. One of the greatest bourgeois philosophers stated approvingly: "That some evil or other be done to an innocent man who is not a subject, if it occurs for the common good and without violating any previous agreements, is no violation of the natural law. For all people who are not subjects are either enemies or have ceased through prior agreements to be such. Against enemies, however, who in the view of the state are dangerous to it, one may wage war according to the original natural law; in this case the sword reaches no judgment, nor does the victor distinguish between innocent and guilty with respect to the past, nor does he give any particular consideration to mercy, unless that happens in the interest of his people."[10] Someone who does not belong, who is not protected by treaties, who is not backed up by any power, a stranger, a mere human being, is completely abandoned.

Even in the upright language of the classical economist, the limitation of the bourgeois concept of the human being constantly shows through. "Our goodwill has no limits, it can embrace the endless universe. The administration of the universe, however, the care for the general happiness of all reasonable and intelligent beings, concerns God and not man. . . . The part allotted to man is smaller . . . the care for his own well-being, the happiness of his family, his friends and his country; having the higher in mind never excuses his neglecting his more modest part."[11] The concern for family, country, and nation was a reality in bourgeois society—regard for humanity an ideology. As long as a person is miserable by virtue of the mere organization of this society, however, the identification with it in the name of humanity contains an absurdity. Practical adaptation may be necessary for the individual, but the concealment of the antagonism between the concept of the human being and the capitalist reality deprives thinking of any truth. If the Jews, in an understandable homesickness, glorify the prehistory of the totalitarian state, monopoly capitalism and the Weimar Republic, then the fascists, who always had an open eye for the decrepitude of those conditions, will be vindicated. Even before 1933, today's refugees could be reproached for gentleness with respect to the flaws of bourgeois democracy, flirtation with the forces of reaction, so long as they were not too openly anti-Semitic, arranging themselves in the status quo. The German people, which spasmodically displays its faith in the Führer, has already seen through him better than those who call Hitler a madman and Bismarck a genius.

Nothing can be hoped for from the alliance between the great powers. There can be no relying on the collapse of the totalitarian economy. Fascism sets in place the results of the collapse of capitalism. It is utterly naive to encourage the German workers from abroad to revolution. Someone who can only play at politics should keep away from it. The confusion has become so general that the truth receives more practical dignity the less it eyes self-styled praxis. Theoretical insight is needed and its transmission to those who eventually will lead the way. The optimism of the political appeal arises today from dejection. The fact that the progressive forces have been defeated and fascism can last indefinitely takes away the intellectuals' ability to think. They believe everything that works must also be good, and thus they prove that fascism cannot function. But there are periods in which the status quo in its strength and competence has become evil. The Jews were once proud of abstract monotheism, their rejection of idolatry, their refusal to make something finite an absolute. Their distress today points them back. Disrespect for anything mortal that puffs itself up as a god is the religion of those who cannot resist devoting their life to the preparation of something better, even in the Europe of the Iron Heel.

Notes

1. *Frankfurter Zeitung,* February 2 and March 9, 1939.

2. "Eine Abhandlung über Barmherzigkeit, Armenpflege und Armenschule," in Otto Bobertag and Georg Müller, ed., *Mandevilles Bienenfabel* (Munich, 1914), pp. 283f. and 286f.

3. De Sade, *Histoire de Justine* (Holland, 1797), vol. IV, pp. 275–278.

4. De Bonald, "Pensées sur divers sujets et discours politiques," *Oeuvres* (Paris, 1817), p. 147.

5. Kant, *Die Metaphysik der Sitten,* part I; *Metaphysische Anfangsgründe der Rechttslehre,* part II, section 1 (Akademieausgabe), vol. VI, pp. 318f.

6. Kant, op. cit., p. 371.

7. For Italy, see Perroux, "Economie corporative et système capitaliste," *Revue d'économie politique,* Sept.–Oct. 1933; for Germany, *Frankfurter Zeitung,* July 21, 1936 and Feb. 26, 1937.

8. *Whaley-Eaton Foreign Service,* Letter 1046, May 2, 1939.

9. D. Mornet, *Les origines intellectuelles de la Révolution Française* (Paris, 1933), p. 3.

10. "The Second Part of Commonwealth," *The English Works of Thomas Hobbes* (John Bohn: London, 1839), vol. III, p. 305. See also *The Latin Works of Thomas Hobbes,* p. 228.

11. Adam Smith, *The Theory of Moral Sentiments* (Basel, 1793), pp. 79, 83.

7

State Capitalism:
Its Possibilities and Limitations

Frederick Pollock

Nothing essentially new is intended in this article. Every thought formulated here has found its expression elsewhere. Our aim is to bring widely scattered and often conflicting ideas into a somewhat consistent summary which may form the starting point for a discussion of the workability of state capitalism.

In regard to the method of this study, the following points ought to be emphasized. Whether such a thing as state capitalism exists or can exist is open to serious doubt. It refers here to a model[1] that can be constructed from elements long visible in Europe and, to a certain degree, even in America. Social and economic developments in Europe since the end of the First World War are interpreted as transitional processes transforming private capitalism into state capitalism. The closest approach to the totalitarian form of the latter has been made in National Socialist Germany. Theoretically, the totalitarian form of state capitalism is not the only possible result of the present process of transformation. It is easier, however, to construct a model for it than for the democratic form of state capitalism to which our experience gives us few clues. One of our basic assumptions is that nineteenth-century free trade and free enterprise are on the way out. Their restoration is doomed for similar reasons as was the attempt to restore feudalism in post-Napoleonic France. The totalitarian form of state capitalism is a deadly menace to all values of Western civilization. Those who want to maintain these values must fully understand the possibilities and limitations of the aggressor if their resistance is to meet with success. Furthermore, they must be able to show in what way the democratic values can be maintained under the changing conditions. If our assumption of the approaching end of the era of private capitalism is correct, the most gallant fight to restore it can only lead to a waste of energy and eventually serve as a trail-blazer for totalitarianism.

The Concept of "State Capitalism"

In the rapidly growing literature on the coming social order, the term *state capitalism* is eschewed by most authors and other words stand in its place. "State organized private-property monopoly capitalism," "managerial society," "administrative capitalism," "bureaucratic collectivism," "totalitarian state economy," "status capitalism" "neomercantilism," "economy of force," "state socialism" are a very incomplete set of labels used to identify the same phenomenon. The term *state capitalism* (so runs the argument) is possibly misleading insofar as it could be understood to denote a society wherein the state is the sole owner of all capital, and this is not necessarily meant by those who use it. Nevertheless, it indicates four items better than do all other suggested items: that state capitalism is the successor of private capitalism; that the state assumes important functions of the private capitalist; that profit interests still play a significant role; and that it is not socialism. We define state capitalism in its two most typical varieties, its totalitarian and its democratic forms, as a social order differing on the following points from "private capitalism," from which it stems historically:

1. The market is deposed from its controlling function to coordinate production and distribution. This function has been taken over by a system of direct controls. Freedom of trade, enterprise, and labor are subject to government interference of such a degree that they are practically abolished. With the autonomous market the so-called economic laws disappear.

2. These controls are vested in the state which uses a combination of old and new devices, including a "pseudo-market," for regulating and expanding production and coordinating it with consumption. Full employment of all resources[2] is claimed as the main achievement in the economic field. The state transgresses all the limits drawn from peacetime state activities.

3. Under a totalitarian form of state capitalism, the state is the power instrument of a new ruling group, which has resulted from the merger of the most powerful vested interests, the top-ranking personnel in industrial and business management, the higher strata of the state bureaucracy (including the military), and the leading figures of the victorious party's bureaucracy. Everybody who does not belong to this group is a mere object of domination.

Under a democratic form of state capitalism, the state has the same controlling functions but is itself controlled by the people. It is based on institutions which prevent the bureaucracy from transforming its administrative position into an instrument of power and thus laying the basis for transforming the democratic system into a totalitarian one.

The Heritage of the Market System

We start from the assumption that the hour of state capitalism approaches when the market economy becomes an utterly inadequate instrument for utilizing the available resources. The medium-sized private enterprise and free trade, the basis for the gigantic development of men's productive forces in the nineteenth century, are being gradually destroyed by the offspring of liberalism, private monopolies and government interference. Concentration of economic activity in giant enterprises, with its consequences of rigid prices, self-financing and ever growing concentration, government control of the credit system and foreign trade, quasi-monopoly positions of trade unions with the ensuing rigidity of the labor market, large-scale unemployment of labor and capital, and enormous government expenses to care for the unemployed, are as many symptoms for the decline of the market system. They became characteristic in various degrees for all industrialized countries after the First World War.[3]

The materials collected recently by various government agencies demonstrate how far a similar development has gone in the United States. The disturbances of the market mechanism caused by monopoly have been accentuated by a technical revolution in contemporary farming. A shattering dislocation of the world market since the First World War has blocked the channels of export which were instrumental in overcoming market difficulties during the nineteenth century. The danger involved in this situation has been recognized, and great efforts are being made to solve the problem of creating full employment while freeing the American market system from the forces which strangle it. Analogous developments may reach a point where no measures short of a reorganization of the economic system can prevent the complete disintegration of the social structure. Such a reorganization might take place by a long succession of stopgap measures, many of them contradicting each other, without a preconceived plan, and often very much against the original intentions of their authors. Theoretically, it is possible to construct an integrated model of the new organization which might replace the outworn system, with a promise of achieving two goals: to guarantee full employment and to maintain the basic elements of the old social structure.

If the market system is to be replaced by another organizational form, the new system must perform certain functions which are necessarily connected with the division of labor. In broadest terms, these "necessary"[4] functions fall into three groups: coordination of needs and resources; direction of production; and distribution; implying

1. a way of defining the needs of society in terms of consumer goods, reproduction of plant, machinery, and raw materials, and expansion;[5]
2. allocation of all available resources in such a manner that full employment and "utmost" satisfaction of the recognized needs are attained;
3. coordination and control of all productive processes in order to obtain best performance; and
4. distribution of the social product.

The basic weaknesses of the market system in performing the "necessary" functions have been discussed again and again as its waste and inefficiency increasingly overbalanced its earlier achievements. Criticism was voiced mainly against the shortcomings of the price mechanism in directing production, the contradictory performance of the profit motive which obstructs the use of the available resources, and the murderous mechanics of coordinating the disequilibrated economy, that is, the business cycles with their cumulative processes of destruction. But while before the First World War the market mechanism was still workable, even if it was always far from performing in practice what it was supposed to do theoretically, the intrusion of monopolies with their rigid prices gradually caused the breakdown of the market system in an ever growing sphere.

A New Set of Rules

State capitalism replaces the methods of the market by a new set of rules based upon a combination of old and new means.

1. A general plan gives the direction for production, consumption, saving, and investment. The introduction of the principle of planning into the economic process means that a plan is to be constructed for achieving on a national scale certain chosen ends with all available resources. It does not necessarily imply that all details are planned in advance or that no freedom of choice at all is given to the consumer. But it contrasts sharply with the market system inasmuch as the final word on what needs shall be satisfied, and how, is not left to the anonymous and unreliable poll of the market, carried through *post festum*, but to a conscious decision on ends and means at least in a broad outline and before production starts. The discussion of planning has come to a point where it seems as if the arguments raised against the technical workability of such a general plan

can be refuted.[6] The genuine problem of a planned society does not lie in the economic but in the political sphere, in the principles to be applied in deciding what needs shall have preference, how much time shall be spent for work, how much of the social product shall be consumed and how much used for expansion, etc. Obviously, such decisions cannot be completely arbitrary but are to a wide degree dependent upon the available resources.

2. Prices are no longer allowed to behave as masters of the economic process but are administered in all important sections of it. This follows from the principle of planning and means that in favor of a planned economy the market is deprived of its main function. It does not mean that prices cannot exist any longer, but that if they do they have thoroughly changed their character. Nothing may seem on the surface to have changed, prices are quoted and goods and services paid for in money; the rise and fall of single prices may be quite common. But the relations between prices and cost of production on the one side, and demand and supply on the other, while strictly interconnected in their totality, become disconnected in those cases where they tend to interfere with the general plan. What remains of the market system behaves like its predecessor, but its function has changed from that of a general manager of the economic process into that of a closely controlled tool.[7] In the last decades administered prices have contributed much toward destroying the market automatism without creating new devices for taking over its "necessary" functions. They served to secure monopoly profits at the expense of the nonmonopolistic market prices. Under state capitalism they are used as a supplementary device for incorporating production and consumption into the general plan.

3. The profit interests of both individuals and groups, as well as all other special interests, are to be strictly subordinated to the general plan or whatever stands in its place. To understand the consequences of this principle leads far towards understanding totalitarian striking power. There are two conflicting interpretations of the role of profit interests in Nazi Germany. The one claims that the profit motive still plays the same role as before; the other states that the capitalists have been deprived of their social position and that profit in the old meaning does not exist any longer. We think that both tend to overlook the transformation of such a category as "profit" in modern society. Profit interests may still be very significant in the totalitarian forms of state capitalistic society. But even the most powerful profit interests gradually become subordinate to the general "plan." No state capitalistic government can or will dispense with the profit motive, for two reasons. First, elimination of the profit motive would destroy the character of the entire system, and, second, in many respects the profit motive remains as an efficient incentive. In every case, however, where the interest of single groups or individuals conflicts with

the general plan or whatever serves as its substitute, the individual interest must give way. This is the real meaning of the ideology *Gemeinnutz geht vor Eigennutz*. The interest of the ruling group as a whole is decisive, not the individual interests of those who form the group.[8] The significance of this state capitalist principle can be fully grasped when it is contrasted with recent experiences in countries where private capitalism still prevails and where strong group interests prevent the execution of many urgent tasks necessary for the "common good." This needs no bad will or exceptional greed to explain it. In a system based upon the self-interest of every person, this principle can sometimes be expected to come to the fore in a form that contradicts the optimism of its underlying philosophy. If ever the statement was true that "private vices are public benefits," it could only have been under conditions where the typical economic unit was comparatively small and the free market functioned.

State capitalist policy, which opposed liberalism, has understood that there are narrow limits beyond which the pursuit of private interests cannot be reconciled with efficient general planning, and it has drawn the consequences.[9]

4. In all spheres of state activity (and under state capitalism, that means in all spheres of social life as a whole), guesswork and improvisation give place to the principles of scientific management. This rule is in conformity with state capitalism's basic conception of society as an integrated unit comparable to one of the modern giants in steel, chemical, or motorcar production. Large-scale production requires not only careful general planning but systematic elaboration of all single processes. Every waste or error in preparing materials and machinery and in drafting the elements of production is multiplied numerous times and may endanger the productive process as a whole. The same holds true for society as soon as the previous differentiation between private cost (e.g., wages) and social cost (e.g., unemployment) is replaced by a measurement of the single process in terms of its ability to obtain what the planner considers the most desirable social product. But once this principle of "rationalization" has become mandatory for all public activities, it will be applied in spheres which previously were the sanctuary of guesswork, routine, and muddling through: military preparedness, the conduct of war, behavior towards public opinion, application of the coercive power of the state, foreign trade and foreign policy, etc.[10]

5. Performance of the plan is enforced by state power so that nothing essential is left to the functioning of laws of the market or other economic "laws."[11] This may be interpreted as a supplementary rule which states the principle of treating all economic problems as in the last analysis political ones. Creation of an economic sphere into which the state should not intrude, essential for the era of private capitalism, is radically repudi-

ated. Replacement of the mechanics of laissez-faire by governmental command does not imply the end of private initiative and personal responsibility, which might even be put on a broader basis but will be integrated within the framework of the general plan. During the nonmonopolistic phase of private capitalism, the capitalist (whether an individual or a group of shareholders represented by its manager) had power over his property within the limits of the market laws. Under state capitalism, this power has been transferred to the government which, though still limited by certain "natural" restrictions, is free from the tyranny of an uncontrolled market. The replacement of the economic means by political means as the last guarantee for the reproduction of economic life, changes the character of the whole historic period. It signifies the transition from a predominantly economic to an essentially political era.[12]

Under private capitalism, all social relations are mediated by the market; men meet each other as agents of the exchange process, as buyers or sellers. The source of one's income, the size of one's property are decisive for one's social position. The profit motive keeps the economic mechanism of society moving. Under state capitalism men meet each other as commander or commanded; the extent to which one can command or has to obey depends in the first place upon one's position in the political set-up and only in a secondary way upon the extent of one's property. Labor is appropriated directly instead of by the "roundabout" way of the market. Another aspect of the changed situation under state capitalism is that the profit motive is superseded by the power motive. Obviously, the profit motive is a specific form of the power motive. Under private capitalism, greater profits signify greater power and less dependence upon the commands of others. The difference, however, is not only that the profit motive is a mediated form of the power motive, but that the latter is essentially bound up with the power position of the ruling group while the former pertains to the individual only.

Control of Production

A discussion of the means by which state capitalism could fulfill its program must hew closely to the technical and organizational possibilities available today in all highly industrialized countries. We refer not to any future developments but to the use which could be made here and now of the available resources. If, however, it can be shown that a state capitalist system can carry out more successfully than the market does the "necessary" functions required by the division of labor, it seems reasonable to expect that much greater resources could be made available within a short period. State capitalism must solve the following problems in the sphere of production if a rising social product is to result: create full employment based upon coordination of all productive units; reproduce the existing resources of plant, raw materials, management, and labor on a level adequate to technical progress; and expand the existing plant. All these tasks must be embodied in the general plan. Given this plan, the execution hinges upon the solution of merely technical and administrative tasks instead of on the economic task of producing for an unknown and largely unforeseeable market. Production is for a clearly defined use, not "commodity" production in the meaning of a market system.[13] The experiences piled up by modern giant enterprises and associations of enterprises in carrying through enormous plans make total production control technically possible. Specific means of control include modern statistical and accounting methods, regular reporting of all changes in plant and supply, systematic training of workers for future requirements, rationalization of all technical and administrative processes, and all the other devices developed in the huge modern enterprises and cartels. In addition to these traditional methods which have superseded the occult entrepreneurial art of guessing correctly what the future market demand will be, the state acquires the controlling power implied in complete command over money and credit. The banks are transformed into mere government agencies.[14] Every investment, whether it serves replacement or expansion, is subject to plan, and neither oversaving nor overexpansion, neither an "investment strike" nor *Fehlinvestitionen* can create large-scale disturbances. Errors which are bound to occur can be traced with comparative ease owing to the central position on the planning board. While they may amount to sheer waste, their damaging effects may be minimized by charging them off to the economy as a whole instead of to a single enterprise. Besides the banks, many of the organizations developed by business interests (trade associations, cartels, chambers of commerce, etc.) serve as, or are transformed into, government agencies for the control of production. The rigid control of capital, whether in its monetary form or as plant, machinery, and commodities, fundamentally transforms the quality of private property in the means of production and its owner, the "capitalist." While a good many of the risks (not all of them) borne by the owner under private capitalism might have been eliminated, only so much profit is left to him as the government sees fit to allow. Regulation of prices, limitation of distributed profits, compulsory investment of surplus profits in government bonds or in ventures which the capitalist would not have chosen voluntarily, and, finally, drastic taxation—all these measures converge to the same end, namely, to transform the capitalist into a mere rentier whose income is fixed by government decree as long as his investments are successful but who has no claim to withdraw his capital if no "interests" are paid.

The trend toward the situation described in our model has been widely discussed during recent years. An extreme statement is that of E. F. M. Durbin: "Property in industrial capital has wholly lost the social functions supposed to be grounded in it. It has ceased to be the reward for management, and it has largely ceased to serve as a reward for personal saving. Property in capital has become the functionless claim to a share in the product of industry. The institution is worse than indefensible—it is useless."[15] The same phenomenon is criticized in the following comment: "Emphasis of management today is not upon venture, upon chancetaking as capitalism requires, but is upon price control, market division, avoidance of risk. This may be good short-range policy. But: if business isn't willing to take chances, somebody soon is going to ask why it should enjoy profits, why the management cannot be hired by Government, which is called on to do all the chancetaking, and might want to direct industry."[16]

This trend toward losing his social function as the private owner of capital has found its expression in the stockholder's loss of control over the management. It has culminated so far in the new German legislation on joint-stock companies in which the stockholders are deprived by law of any right to interfere with management.

To sum up, under state capitalism the status of the private capitalist is changed in a threefold way.

1. The entrepreneurial and the capitalist functions, i.e., direction of production and discretion in the investment of one's capital, are separated from each other. Management becomes virtually independent of "capital" without necessarily having an important share in corporate property.

2. The entrepreneurial and capitalist functions are interfered with or taken over by the government.

3. The capitalist (insofar as he is not accepted as entrepreneur on the merits of his managerial qualifications) is reduced to a mere rentier.

Here the question of incentive arises. In private capitalism, the decisive incentives for the capitalist to maintain, expand, and improve production are the profit interest and the permanent threat of economic collapse if the efforts should slacken. The noncapitalists are driven to cooperate efficiently by hunger and their desire for a better life and security. Under state capitalism, both groups lose essential parts of their incentive. What new devices will take over their most "necessary" functions? What will prevent stagnation and even regression in all spheres of state capitalistic society? In relation to the majority of the population, those who neither own nor command the means of production, the answer is simple. The whip of unemployment is replaced by political terror, and the promise of material and ideological rewards continues to incite to the utmost personal effort. The profit motive still plays an important role for capitalists and the managerial bureaucracy, since large compensation is granted for efficient investment and management. Personal initiative is freed from obstructing property interests and systematically encouraged.[17] Within the controlling group, however, the will to political power becomes the center of motivation. Every decision is at bottom oriented to the goal of maintaining and expanding the power of the group as a whole and of each of its members. New industrial empires are being built and old ones expanded with this goal in mind. But we also have here the source of the principle that individual interests must always be subordinated to the common (group) interest. This principle in turn contributes decisively to strengthening governmental control, since only a strong government can integrate conflicting interests while serving the power interests of the whole group.

Control of Distribution

"We have learned how to produce everything in practically unlimited quantities, but we don't know how to distribute the goods." This is the popular formulation to describe the riddle of private capitalism in its latest phase.

Given a general plan and the political power to enforce it, state capitalism finds ample technical means for distributing everything that can be produced with the available resources. The main difficulty of private capitalism is eliminated by the fact that under such capitalism the success of production does not necessarily depend upon finding buyers for the product at profitable prices in an unstable market, but is consciously directed towards satisfying public and private wants which are to a large extent defined in advance. Adjustments which must be made as a result of technical errors in the general plan or unexpected behavior in consumer demands need not lead to losses for the individual producer and even less to economic disaster for him. Losses easily can be pooled by the administration. The means which are available for carrying over the "necessary" distributive function of a competitive market may be conveniently classified into direct allocation (priorities, quotas, etc.) and administered prices. The former applies above all to the distribution of goods to producers, the latter refers mainly to the sphere of consumption. There is, however, no sharp dividing line between the fields of application of the two means.[18] Labor is the outstanding example in which a combination of both methods is applied.

In constructing a rough model of the distributive mechanism under state capitalism, we always have to keep in mind that production and producers' consumption are two aspects of the same process. Since under modern conditions producer and consumer are, as a rule, not the same person, distribution serves as a means of integrating them. The production plan is based on a comparatively arbitrary decision as to how much of the social product is to be available for consumption and how much is to be used for expansion.

All major problems of distribution under state capitalism have been discussed thoroughly in the literature on socialist planning published within the last decade.[19] While all writers in favor of a planned society agree that the tyranny of the market must be abolished, differences of opinion exist on the question of where to draw the limits for the use of a pseudo-market. Some writers recommend that the managers of the social-ized industry should "behave as if under competitive capitalism." They should "play at competition."[20] A model partly constructed on the results of this discussion may be used to illustrate how distribution works under state capitalism. The distribution of goods to producers starts from the following situation:

1. Most productive facilities are privately owned but controlled by the government;
2. Each industry is organized in cartels;
3. Prices react to changes in supply and demand as well as to changes in the cost of structure within the limits permitted by the plan authority and the monopolies;
4. A general plan for the structure of the social product is in existence.

Under these circumstances a system of priorities and quotas will guar-antee the execution of the plan in its broad lines. These allocations cover reproduction of existing resources, expansion (including defense), and the total output of consumers goods, which every industry shall produce. Within each industry a quota system will provide for the distribution according to a more detailed plan or according to expressions of consumer choice. Not much room is left in this set-up for flexible prices. The partial survival of the profit motive will induce manufacturers who are offered higher prices for their products to bid up in turn the prices of their "factors." But the "office of price control" will not permit prices to go higher than is compatible with the general plan. Since all major units of production are under the control of cartels, the propensity to keep prices flexible should not be overestimated. Governmental control will be immensely facilitated by the enormous role of public works necessary to maintain full employment under all circumstances.

Full employment in the strict sense of the word can be achieved in regard to labor only. Due to technological facts, it is not possible in the case of plant and equipment. New plant and new machinery constructed according to the latest technical development require a minimum size of plant, which as a rule leads to temporary overcapacity at the moment of completion. If no ways for using this overcapacity can be found speedily, some idleness of capital will arise. This might happen with entire durable goods industries (e.g., machine tools) if the need for their product is temporarily saturated. Neither this nor other "maladjustments" can produce the cumulative effects so vicious under the free market system,[21] for the capital owner might be compensated for his loss out of pooled profits or public sources, and provision for a constant reserve in planning the labor supply will take care of the displaced workers. Technological unemployment will be handled in a similar way. It has been shown that the opposite case, periodical shortage of capital, can be avoided in a planned society.[22]

Labor under state capitalism is allocated to the different sections of production like other resources. This does not prevent the planning authorities from differentiating wages. On the contrary, premiums in the form of higher real wages can be granted wherever extra efforts are demanded. The slave driver's whip is no workable means for extracting quality products from highly skilled workers who use expensive machinery. This differentiation in wage schedules, however, is not the outcome of market conditions but of the wage administrator's decision. No entrepreneur is allowed to pay higher wages than those fixed by this agency.

With absolute control of wages, the government is in a position to handle the distribution of consumers goods with comparative ease. In cases of severe scarcity, as in wartime, direct allocation of consumers goods might be the only adequate means for their distribution. In such a case consumer choice is very limited but not entirely ruled out.[23] If, however, a somewhat more adequate supply of consumer goods is available, the consumer may be as free or, with the greater purchasing power created by full employment, even more free in his choice under state capitalism than he is now. In order to achieve this goal with the means now at hand, a pseudo-market for consumer goods will be established. The starting point for its operation is a clearly defined relation between purchasing power which will be spent for consumption and the sum of prices of all available consumer goods. Both sums must be equal. In other words, the total income paid out to consumers, minus taxes, compulsory, and voluntary savings, must be the same as the total price of all consumer goods which are for sale. If the "net" consumer income should be higher, a scramble for goods and a bidding up of prices would result (under our definition that net income excludes savings). If it should be lower, only part of the products could be distributed. The first step toward distributing the consumer goods is therefore to make the net income of all consumers in a given period equivalent to the sum of consumer goods output as decided by the general plan and the available inventory. This first step will prove insufficient for two reasons:

1. The consumers' voluntary savings may deviate from the plan—they may save either more or less than was expected in calculating the equilibrium. Both cases may be remedied by the use of the market laws of demand and supply, which will create inflationary or deflationary price movements to "clear the market"—if the price controlling agencies permit it.

2. The consumers' choices may deviate from the calculations of the planners—they may prefer some products and reject others. Here again the old market mechanism may be allowed to come into play to enforce higher prices for goods in greater demand and to lower prices where and as long as an oversupply exists. A system of subsidies and surtaxes will eliminate serious losses as well as surplus profits which could disturb the functioning of the plan. The distributive agency may completely "over-rule" the consumers' choice for all practical purposes by fixing prices either extremely high or disproportionately low. So far the price mechanism obeys the same laws as in the free market system. The difference becomes manifest in the effects which changing prices exercise on production. The price signals influence production only insofar as is compatible with the general plan and the established public policy on consumption. Price movements serve as a most valuable instrument for announcing differences between consumers' preferences and the production plan. They cannot, however, compel the planning authority to follow these manifestations of consumers' will in the same way they compel every nonmonopolistic producer in a free market.[24] Under private capitalism, the monopolist, in resisting the market signals, disrupts the whole market system at the expense of all nonmonopolistic market parties. Under state capitalism the disconnection between price and production can do no harm because the function of coordinating production and consumption has been transferred from the market to the plan authority. Much attention has been given to the question of how consumers' choice can be calculated in advance. No "God-like" qualities are required for the planning board. It has been shown[25] that freedom of consumers' choice actually exists only to a very limited degree. In studying large numbers of consumers, it becomes evident that size of income, tradition, and propaganda are considerably leveling down all individual preference schedules. The experiences of large manufacturing and distributing concerns as well as of cartels contribute a most valuable supplement to the special literature on planning.

Economic Limitations of State Capitalism

In raising the question of economic limitations, we point to those which may restrict the arbitrariness of the decisions in state capitalism as contrasted with other social structures in which they may not appear. We are not concerned with limitations that apply to every social set-up, e.g., those which result from the necessity to reproduce the given resources and to maintain full employment and optimum efficiency. The first and most frequent objection against the economic workability of a state capitalistic system is that it is good only in a scarcity economy, especially for periods of war preparedness and war. For a scarcity economy, so runs the argument, most of the economic difficulties against which private capitalism struggles do not exist. Overproduction and overinvestment need not be feared, and all products, however inefficiently produced, and however bad their quality, find a ready demand. As soon as the temporary emergency has passed, however, and a greater supply becomes available in all fields, state capitalism will prove utterly inadequate for securing the best use of available resources, for avoiding bottlenecks in one product and overproduction in others, and for providing the consumers with what they may demand at the lowest possible cost. Even if all means of production are under governmental control, efficient planning is possible only under conditions of emergency. The argument advanced for this view can be boiled down to the following:[26] In a planned economy costs cannot be accounted for, the free choice of the consumers must be disregarded, the motives for efficient production and distribution disappear, and as a result a planned economy must under modern conditions be much less productive than a market economy.

We think that anyone who seriously studies the modern literature on planning must come to the conclusion that, whatever his objections to the social consequences of planning, these arguments against its economic efficiency no longer hold. All technical means for efficient planning, including the expansion of production in accordance with consumer wants and the most advanced technical possibilities, and taking into account the cost in public health, personal risks, unemployment (never adequately calculated in the cost sheet of private enterprise)—all these technical means are available today.

Another counterargument holds that as soon as state capitalism turns from concentrating upon armaments to a genuine peace economy, its only alternative, if it wants to avoid unemployment, is to spend a very substantial part of the national income for the construction of modern "pyramids," or to raise considerably the standard of living. No economic causes exist which could prevent a state capitalistic government from doing so. The obstacles are of a political nature and will be dealt with later.

A third argument points in the opposite direction. It objects that state capitalism necessarily leads to a standstill in technics or even a regress. Investments will slow down and technical progress cease if the market laws are put out of operation. As long as competitive armament continues, the contrary will probably be true. Besides the profit motive, the vital interests of the controlling group will stimulate both investment and technical progress. In the effort to maintain and extend its power, the controlling group will come into conflict with foreign interests, and its success will depend upon its military force. This, however, will be a function of the technical efficiency. Any slackening in the speed of technical progress might lead to military inferiority and to destruction.[27] Only after all possible enemies have disappeared, because the whole world will be controlled by one totalitarian state, will the problem of technological progress and capital expansion come to the fore.

Are there, one may ask, no economic limitations at all to the existence and expansion of state capitalism? With its rise, will a utopia emerge in which all economic wants can easily be fulfilled if political factors don't interfere? Did not the liberal theory also believe it had proved that the market system will guarantee its constituents the full use of all resources if not interfered with? And did it not become apparent later that inherent forces prevented the market system from functioning and ushered in growing interference by private monopolies and the government? Forewarned as we are, we are unable to discover any inherent economic forces, "economic laws" of the old or a new type, which could prevent the functioning of state capitalism.[28] Government control of production and distribution furnishes the means for eliminating the economic causes of depressions, cumulative destructive processes, and unemployment of capital and labor. We may even say that under state capitalism economics as a social science has lost its object. Economic problems in the old sense no longer exist when the coordination of all economic activities is effected by conscious plan instead of by the natural laws of the market. Where the economist formerly racked his brain to solve the puzzle of the exchange process, he meets, under state capitalism, with mere problems of administration. There are indeed limitations to state capitalism, but they derive from natural conditions as well as from the very structure of the society which state capitalism seeks to perpetuate.

Natural and Other Noneconomic Limitations

1. To be fully workable, state capitalism needs an adequate supply of raw material, plans, and labor of all kinds (technicians, administrators, skilled and unskilled labor) characteristic for a highly industrialized country.[29] Without a plentiful supply of raw materials and the outfit in machinery and skill of a modern industrial society, great waste must accompany state capitalistic intervention, possibly greater than under a market economy. For the first limitation, inadequate supply of raw materials, a typical

example is offered by Nazi Germany. The enormous machinery which had to be built to compensate for the insufficiency of the raw material basis—too small to cope with the armament program—and the difficulties for the producer in obtaining raw materials and, in consequence, new machinery,[30] cannot be attributed to the system itself, but to the fact that one of its main prerequisites was lacking from the very beginning.

On the other hand, many of the Soviet Russian economic failures may be traced back to the lack of both raw materials and adequate development of the productive forces. Lack of trained technicians, skilled workers, and the qualities known as work discipline, all of which are plentiful only in highly industrialized countries, goes a long way in explaining the slow progress of rearming, reorganizing the transportation system, and raising or even maintaining the standard of living in Soviet Russia. But even here a government-controlled economic system has shown the power to survive under conditions where a system of free enterprise would have collapsed completely. Government-controlled foreign trade and the development of an industry for ersatz materials may overcome the limitations of a too narrow basis of raw materials. Filling the gap between a fully industrialized and a chiefly agricultural economy is a much more painful and drawn-out process.

2. Differences in vital interests will crop up in the group or groups controlling the state. They can stem from different positions within the administration, different programs for maintaining or expanding power, or the struggle for the monopoly of control. Unless adequate provisions are made for overcoming these differences, bad compromises and continuous struggle will arise.

3. Conflicting interests within the ruling class might thwart the construction of a general plan embodying the optimum of all available resources for achieving consistent chosen ends. The choice of the ends itself represents a major problem as long as no common will has been established. In our discussion we started always from the assumption "given a general plan." This means a plan for certain ends which must be chosen from among a variety of possible ones.

Once the minimum requirements for consumption, replacement, and expansion are fulfilled, the planners have a great deal of leeway. If their decisions do not converge into a consistent program, no general plan for the optimum use and development of the given productive forces can be drafted.

4. Conflicting interests, however, do not operate in the ruling group only. Since totalitarian state capitalism is the expression of an antagonistic society at its worst, the will to dominate from above and the counterpressure from below cut deeply into the psuedo-liberty of the state capitalist planners. The planning board, while vested with all the technical means

for directing the whole economic process, is itself an arena of struggle among social forces beyond its control. It will be seen that planning in an antagonistic society is only in a technical sense the same tool as that used by a society in which harmony of interests has been established. Political considerations interfere at every step with the construction and execution of an optimum plan. The following paragraphs will offer some examples.

How will expansion of production and technical progress be motivated and fear of aggression or objects for new conquest have vanished? Will not the dreaded technological standstill make its appearance under such conditions, thus spoiling all chances of reducing the drudgery of labor while raising the standard of living?[31] A case could be made out for the view that a new set of motivations will arise under totalitarian state capitalism which will combine the drive for power over men with the will to power over nature and counteract the development toward a static economy. But this is such a distant perspective that we may leave the question open, the more so since under totalitarian capitalism there are serious reasons to keep the productive forces static.

Under a state capitalistic set-up, will the general standard of living rise beyond narrow limits if the expansion program permits? This question can be answered in the affirmative for the democratic form of state capitalism only. For its authoritarian counterpart, however, the problem is different. The ruling minority in a totalitarian state maintains its power not only by terror and atomization but by controlling the means of production and keeping the dominated majority in complete spiritual dependence. The masses have no chance of questioning the durability and justification of the existing order; the virtues of war are developed and all "effeminacy," all longing for individual happiness, is rooted out. A rise in the standard of living might dangerously counteract such a policy. It would imply more leisure time, more professional skill, more opportunity for critical thinking, out of which a revolutionary spirit might develop. It is a wide spread error that the most dangerous revolutions are instigated by the most miserable strata of society. The revolutionary craving for liberty and justice found its most fertile breeding ground not among the paupers but among individuals and groups who were themselves in a relatively better position. The ruling group in totalitarian state capitalism might therefore decide that from the point of view of its own security a low general standard of living and long, drudging working hours are desirable. An armament race and the excitement over threat of foreign "aggression" seem to be appropriate means for keeping the standard of living low and the war virtues high while maintaining full employment and promoting technical progress. Such a constellation, however, would furnish a striking example for a political limitation of productivity.

The highly speculative question might be permitted: What would happen if totalitarian state capitalism were embodied in a unified world state in which the threat of aggression had disappeared for good? Even public works of undreamed scope could not prevent the general standard of living from rising under conditions of full employment. In such a case the most clever devices of ideological mass domination and the grimmest terror are unlikely to uphold for a long period a minority dictatorship which can no longer claim itself to be necessary to maintain production and to protect the people from foreign aggression. If our assumption is correct that totalitarian state capitalism will not tolerate a high standard of living for the masses and cannot survive mass unemployment, the consequence seems to be that it cannot endure in a peace economy. As long as one national state capitalism has not conquered the whole earth, however, there will always be ample opportunities to spend most of the productive excess capacity (excess over the requirements for a minimum standard of living) for ever-increasing and technically more perfect armaments.

Why can the policy of aggression not come to a standstill before one state has conquered the entire world? Even after a totalitarian state has acquired full autarchy within its own territory, "preparedness" and foreign wars must be on at a rapid pace in order to protect against aggression from outside and revolution from within. A democratic state capitalism, while safe from within, is menaced by totalitarian aggression and must arm to the teeth and be ready to fight until all totalitarian states have been transformed into democracies. In the last century it became evident that a society based on slave labor could not exist side by side with one organized on the principle of free labor. The same holds true in our day for democratic and totalitarian societies.

Control of the State under State Capitalism

If state capitalism is a workable system, superior in terms of productivity to private capitalism under conditions of monopolistic market disruption, what are the political implications? If the state becomes the omnipotent comptroller of all human activities, the question "who controls the comptroller" embraces the problem of whether state capitalism opens a new way to freedom or leads to the complete loss of it as far as the overwhelming majority is concerned. Between the two extreme forms of state capitalism, the totalitarian and the democratic, numerous others are thinkable. Everything depends upon which social groups in the last analysis direct the decisions of a government whose power has in all matters—"economic" as well as "noneconomic"—never been surpassed in modern history. The following is intended as a rough sketch of the social structure under totalitarian state capitalism.

1. The government is controlled by, and composed of, a new ruling

class. We have defined this new class as an amalgamation of the key bureaucrats in business, state, and party, allied with the remaining vested interests.[32] We have already mentioned that inherited or acquired wealth may still play a role in opening a way to this ruling group, but that it is not essential for participating in the group. One's position in the economic and administrative set-up, together with party affiliations and personal qualification, is decisive for one's political power. The new ruling class, by its grip on the state, controls everything it wants to, the general economic plan, foreign policy, rights and duties, life and death of the individual. Its decisions are not restrained by any constitutional guarantees but by a set of rules only, designed for maintaining and expanding its own power. We have seen what control over the general economic plan involves: all the basic decisions on how to distribute the "factors of production" among producer and consumer goods, on the working day, labor condition, on wages and prices. To sum up, control of the general economic plan means control over the standard of living. Antagonisms of interests among the groups within the ruling class might lead to serious difficulties. The class interest of maintaining the new status, however, will probably be strong enough for a long time to overcome these antagonisms before they can turn into a menace to the system. The persons who form the ruling class have been prepared for their task by their position in, or their cooperation with, the monopolistic institutions of private capitalism. There, a rapidly growing number of decisive functions had become invested in a comparatively small group of bureaucrats. The leader-and-follower principle flourished long before it was promulgated as the basic principle of society, since more and more responsibility had been centralized in the top offices of government, business, trade unions, and political parties.

2. Those owners of capital who are "capitalists" without being managers and who could exercise great political influence during the whole era of private capitalism no longer have any necessary social functions. They receive interest on their investments for as long a time and in the measure that the new ruling class may be willing to grant. From the point of view of their social utility, they constitute a surplus population. Under the impact of heavy inheritance taxes, controlled stock markets, and the generally hostile attitude of the new ruling class against the *raffende Kapital,* these "capitalists" will probably disappear. The widespread hatred against them could develop only because the economic laws of capitalism had transformed their social role into that of parasites.

3. A semi-independent group, not belonging to the ruling class but enjoying more privileges than the *Gefolgschaften,* are the free professions and the middle-sized and small businesses under governmental control. Both will disappear wherever a fully developed state capitalism corres-

ponding to our model is reached. The process of concentration which gains unprecedented momentum under state capitalism absorbs the independent small and medium-sized enterprise. The trend towards socialization of medicine, of journalism and other free professions, transforms their members into government employees.

4. The great majority of the people fall into the category of salaried employees of all types. They are subject to the leader principle of command and obedience. All their political rights have been destroyed, and carefully planned atomization has simplified the task of keeping them under strict control. Labor's right to bargain collectively, to strike, to change jobs and residence at will (if its market position permits) is abolished. Work becomes compulsory, wages are fixed by government agencies, the leisure time of the worker and his family is organized from above. In some respects, this is antithetical to the position of labor under private capitalism and revives many traits of feudal conditions.

5. The new state openly appears as an institution in which all earthly power is embodied and which serves the new ruling class as a tool for its power politics. Seemingly independent institutions like party, army, and business form its specialized arms. A complicated relation exists, however, between the means and those who apply them, resulting in some genuine independence for these institutions. Political domination is achieved by organized terror and overwhelming propaganda on the one side, on the other by full employment and adequate standard of living for all key groups, the promise of security and a life of greater abundance for every subject who submits voluntarily and completely. This system is far from being based upon rude force alone. In that it provides many "real" satisfactions for its subjects, it exists partly with the consent of the governed, but this consent cannot change the antagonistic character of a state capitalistic society in which the power interests of the ruling class prevent the people from fully using the productive forces for their own welfare and from having control over the organization and activities of society.

We have referred here and there to what we think are particular traits of the democratic form of state capitalism. Since no approaches to it have so far been made in practice, and since the discussion of its structure is still in a formative stage,[33] no attempt will be made here to construct a model for it.

The trend toward state capitalism is growing, however, in the nontotalitarian states. An increasing number of observers admit, very often reluctantly, that private capitalism is no longer able to handle the new tasks. "All plans for internal post-war reconstruction start with the assumption that more or less permanent government controls will have replaced *laissez-faire* methods both in the national and the international sphere. Thus the choice is not between totalitarian controls and return to 'free enterprise'; the choice is between totalitarian controls and controls voluntarily accepted by the people of each country for the benefit of society as a whole."[34] It is the lesson of all large-scale measures of government interference that they will contribute to the disruption of the market mechanism if they are not coordinated into a general plan. If government is to provide for all the items recognized as mandatory in the more serious postwar reconstruction programs,[35] it must be vested with adequate powers, and these might not stop short of state capitalism.

It is of vital importance for everybody who believes in the values of democracy that an investigation be made as to whether state capitalism can be brought under democratic control. The social as well as the moral problem with which the democracies are confronted has been formulated as follows "How can we get effective use of our resources, yet at the same time preserve the underlying values in our tradition of liberty and democracy? How can we employ our unemployed, how can we use our plant and equipment to the full, how can we take advantage of the best modern technology, yet, in all this make the individual source of value and individual fulfillment in society the basic objective? How can we obtain effective organization of resources, yet at the same time retain the maximum freedom of individual action?"[36] Totalitarian state capitalism offers the solution of economic problems at the price of totalitarian oppression. What measures are necessary to guarantee control of the state by the majority of its people instead of by a small minority? What ways and means can be devised to prevent the abuse of the enormous power vested in state, industrial, and party bureaucracy under state capitalism? How can the loss of economic liberty be rendered compatible with the maintenance of political liberty? How can the disintegrative motive forces of today be replaced by integrative ones? How will the roots from which insurmountable social antagonisms develop be eliminated so that there will not arise a political alliance between dissentient partial interests and the bureaucracy aiming to dominate the majority? Can democratic state capitalism be more than a transitory phase leading either to total oppression or to doing away with the remnants of the capitalistic system?

The main obstacles to the democratic form of state capitalism are of a political nature and can be overcome by political means only. If our thesis proves to be correct, society on its present level can overcome the handicaps of the market system by economic planning. Some of the best brains of this country are studying the problem of how such planning can be done in a democratic way, but a great amount of theoretical work will have to be performed before answers to every question will be forthcoming.

Notes

1. The term *model* is used here in the sense of Max Weber's "ideal type."

2. Here understood simply as absence of technically avoidable "unemployment" of all factors of production. For discussion of this concept, see John Maynard Keynes, *The General Theory of Employment, Interest and Money* (London, 1936).

3. The best short statement on the breakdown of the market mechanism is still appendix A to Senate Document 13 (74th Congress, 1st session, 1935), *Industrial Prices and Their Relative Inflexibility,* by Gardiner C. Means. See also the recent books on the decline of competition by Arthur Robert Burns, Edward H. Chamberlin, and Joan Robinson.

4. They can be defined as those without which even the bare subsistence of society can not be reproduced. The description that follows, however, understands "necessary" functions as those achieving the best results under given historic conditions. This is what liberal theory claims for the market system.

5. In this simple scheme, luxuries are included in the category of consumer goods and defense materials are submerged under machinery.

6. For a discussion of literature on the theory of planning, see Eduard Heimann, "Literature on the Theory of a Socialist Economy," *Social Research,* vol. VI, pp. 87f.; Carl Landauer, "Literature on Economic Planning," ibid., vol. VII, pp. 498f.; and H. D. Dickinson, *Economics of Socialism,* (London, 1939).

    We do not intimate that a general plan exists in Nazi Germany or has ever existed there. In its place stands the goal of arming as speedily and efficiently as possible, with full use of all resources. Some plan-elements have come into being, while the plan principle, used first as a propaganda slogan in Germany, is rapidly spreading there.

7. For an outstanding analysis of the new functions and the performance of the "pseudo-market," see A. Lowe, "Economic Analysis and Social Structure," *The Manchester School,* vol. VII (1936), pp. 30f. Lowe's arguments pertain to "the pricing process under public ownership." Public control over the means of production, however, has the same economic consequences as state ownership.

8. Obviously, the first to bear the brunt of subordinating the private to the "common" interest is the "little man" in all spheres of society.

9. An example of the result is the amazing elasticity and efficiency in building up an enormous war machinery in National Socialist Germany. This, however, should not be interpreted to mean that in Germany private property interests do not endeavor to gain precedence. In motorcar standardization, for instance, the private interests of the big concerns determined all the measures taken. Since a general plan of economic policy was never published in Germany, it is impossible to decide to what extent private interests did obtain preference.

10. It appears that part of the Nazi successes may be better explained as the rational application of the best available methods in all fields (from eliminating important vitamins in the diet of conquered nations to the practical monopoly in international propaganda) than as the result of any innate qualities of a military or organizational character. It is well to recall, in this connection, that German industry originally learned scientific management from America.

11. E.g., new investments no longer flow automatically into those economic fields where the highest profits are made but are directed by the planning board. In consequence, the mechanism known as equalization of the rate of profit no longer works.

12. Frank Munk, *The Economic of Force* (New York, 1940); Lawrence Dennis, *The Dynamics of War and Revolution* (New York, 1940).

13. See Rudolf Hilferding, "State Capitalism or Totalitarian State Economy" (Russian), in *Socialistichesky Vestnik* (Paris, 1940). It should be understood that "production for use" is not intended to mean "for the use of free men in a harmonious society," but simply the contrary of production for the market.

14. For an impressive discussion of this trend in Nazi Germany, see Dal Hitchcock, "The German Financial Revolution," *Harper's Monthly,* Feb. 1941.

15. E. F. M. Durbin, *The Politics of Democratic Socialism* (London, 1940), p. 135.

16. Quoted in the *Report for the Business Executive,* Nov. 28, 1940.

17. See Carl Dreher, "Why Hitler Wins," *Harper's Monthly,* Oct. 1940.

18. So far, the nearest approach to the state capitalist model of distribution has been made in Soviet Russia. See L. E. Hubbard, *Soviet Trade andDistribution* (London, 1938). The trend in Germany shows the same direction.

19. See note 6 above. The latest important publication is that of Durbin, op. cit. Most of those who advocate the superiority of a deliberately "manipulated" market confined "within the straitjacket of planned objectives" have given little attention to the fact that planning is far from being identical with socialism. That is why their work, important as it is, appears even more as a contribution to the theory of state capitalism.

20. L. Robbins, *Economic Planning and International Order* (London, 1937), p. 208.

21. See Gottfried von Haberler, *Prosperity and Depression* (Geneva, 1937).

22. See Carl Landauer,*Planwirtschaft und Verkehrswirtschaft* (Munich, 1931).

23. See, e.g., the "point" system for the distribution of textiles in Germany and England.

24. For this whole set of problems, see Oskar Lange, *On the Economic Theory of Socialism,* ed. E. Lippincott (Minneapolis, 1938).

25. See the studies of the National Resources Planning Board, *Consumer Incomes and Patterns of Resources Use,* reviewed in *Studies in Philosophy and Social Science* 1940, pp. 483–490.

26. The best survey of the history and details of the argument is F. A. von Hayek, ed., *Collectivist Economic Planning* (London, 1935). For a refutation see Lange, op. cit.

27. The German experience shows that probably never in the history of industrialism were new inventions put into application so quickly, or has such an enormous percentage of the national income been used for investments.

28. This also applies to the tendency of the rate of profit to fall which, according to Marxian theory, plays havoc with private capitalism. If expansion of capital is subject to a general plan which is itself approved by the controlling group, the percentage of surplus value in ratio to invested capital could fall close to zero without creating any disturbances. This fall, however, is most effectively counteracted by the enforced maintenance of full employment. We shall not enter upon the discussion of whether state capitalism itself emerges under the pressure of the falling rate of profit, nor how far it makes sense to speak in terms of "value" beyond the limits of market economy.

29. Most of the arguments that follow refer to the totalitarian form of state capitalism only.

30. See Guenter Reimann, *The Vampire Economy: Doing Business under Fascism* (New York, 1939).

31. Julian Gumperz, in *The Expansion of Production and the Totalitarian System* (unpublished), makes the point that after property "becomes a semi-sovereign function of rights, privileges, prerogatives, transactions, that is, more and more dissociated from the active and actual carrying forward of production, this latter function creates a new class and is appropriated by it. . . ." This class "represents a depository of skills, abilities, knowledges, traditions that moves the organization of economic society from one point to another, and organizes the new level of production accomplished. . . . Overproduction from which economic society has been suffering is centered to a large extent in the overproduction of this progressive class . . . and it is therefore not accidental but essential that a totalitarian economy stop, at its source, the production and reproduction of these skills. . . ."

32. This holds true for Germany and Italy, where semifeudal landowners and big business are still in existence and form part of the ruling clique. The situation is different in Soviet Russia, where the old vested interests have been wiped out. Since in Russia property in the means of production has changed hands completely from private owners to the state and no longer exists even in its modified and reduced form discussed above, it is somewhat doubtful whether our model of state capitalism fits the Soviet Union in its present phase.

33. Charles A. Beard, *Public Policy and the General Welfare* (New York, 1941) marks an important step in this discussion.

34. Vera Micheles Dean, "Toward a New World Order," *Foreign Policy Reports,* May 15, 1941, p. 55.

35. A British fact-finding group composed of progressive economists, businessmen, civil servants, and professors, known as PEP (Political and Economic Planning), included the following items in its preliminary program prepared in 1940: "maintenance after the war of full economic activity based on complete use of manpower and resources, regardless of obsolete financial criteria; assurance of a minimum standard of life, based on scientific standards of nutrition and proper provision for dependents; assurance of a minimum standard of housing, based on a socially planned program of housing and social amenities; provision of medical care and a reasonable measure of economic security, covering the hazards of employment, accidents, ill-health, widowhood and old age; the provision of equal opportunities for education in every country and the reestablishment of a European system of higher learning and research open to students of proved ability from all parts of the world; the provision of cultural and recreative activities and the establishment of organizations for the training and leisure of youth on a European scale" (Dean, op. cit., p. 55).

36. National Resources Committee, *The Structure of the American Economy* (Washington, D.C., 1939), p. 3.

8

From Ontology to Technology: Fundamental Tendencies of Industrial Society

Herbert Marcuse

The following pages contain ideas developed during a course held in 1958–1959 at the Ecole Pratique des Hautes Etudes. They are part of a soon-to-be-published book, dedicated to the study of some basic tendencies in the most advanced industrial societies, particularly the United States.[1] These tendencies appear to engender a system of thought and behavior which represses any values, aspirations, or ideas not in conformity with the dominant rationality. An entire dimension of human reality is therefore suppressed: the dimension which permits individuals and classes to develop a theory and technique of transcendence by which they might envisage the "determinate negation" of their society. The radical critique and effective opposition (intellectual as well as political) are now integrated into the status quo; human existence seems to become "one-dimensional." Such an integration cannot be explained by the emergency of *mass culture,* the *organization man,* the *hidden persuaders,* etc. These notions belong to a purely ideological interpretation that neglects the analysis of the most fundamental processes which undermine the base upon which a radical opposition might have developed.

Are this same atrophy of historical transcendence and this neutralization of the negating forces, which appear as the supreme achievement of industrial society, rooted within the same structure of technical civilization, or are they only the work of its repressive institutions? Did these technics so deeply transform capitalism and socialism as to invalidate Marxist and anti-Marxist notions? Is the atrophy of transcendence furthering the absorption of negating forces, announcing the control of its inherent contradiction by both the technological domination of the world and the

Translated by Micheline Ishay

universal administration of society? Or is this process rather inaugurating the phase in which quantitative change is becoming qualitative?

Those are the questions which have guided our analysis. Starting with the political economic transformation of modern technical society, this analysis will examine the different ways that the process of transcendence atrophied in normal behavior, language, traditional culture, as well as in neopositivist and analytical philosophy.

While the new scientific method destroyed the idea that the universe was ordered in relation to a goal, to a teleological structure, it also invalidated a hierarchical social system in which occupations and individual aspirations were predetermined by final causes. The new science, in its neutral form, abstracted itself from an organization of life which deprived the immense majority of human beings of their liberty. In its effort to establish the physical mathematical structure of the universe, this new science also abstracted itself from the concrete individual and its "sensuous body." Such an abstraction was fully validated by its result: a logical system of propositions which guided the use and the methodological transformation of nature and which tended to produce a universe controlled by the power of man.

The reality being reduced (or reducible) to its physical mathematical structure entailed that "truth" became defined by what could be measured or calculated, or by propositions which fulfilled these conditions. This formal reality realizes itself according to its own laws (even though these laws are purely "statistical" in character). Man can understand them, act upon and use them without making them part of his own individual or social existence. For these laws govern human beings insofar as they are purely physical and biological matter. In all other aspects, humans are *eliminated* from nature; or rather the reality aimed at and acknowledged by the scientific method becomes a reality independent of individual and social facticity.

One can justifiably speak of the "metaphysical foundations" of modern science. In this respect, Alexander Koyre recently strongly emphasized the nonempirical and the ontological aspects of Galilean science. The Pythagorean, the Platonic, and the Aristotelian traditions remained, at least up to Newton, powerful enough to provide the scientific method with a "philosophy." One might say that the very notion of physical universal laws, susceptible to unification, from the start preserves a certain version of finality. Soon, however, this idea of finality will become ever more empty—a finality of calculable order, evaluated purely for its ability to predict events. It will become divorced from a *telos* and from a structure tending towards a *telos*. This predictive calculable rationality will define all actions in its terms, relative to what will constitute an "order" based on calculability and predictability (even if only a statistical order).

The density and the opacity of "objects," and of objectivity as well, seem to evaporate. Nature and human reality are no longer considered as a substantial *cosmos.* According to advanced scientific method, thinking is purified of the objects which it opposes: these latter remain only as "convenient intermediaries," as "models" and "invariables" or "obsolete cultural postulates."[2] Or, quoting again another operative formula: Physical matter can no longer provide an objective for "the external and the material world, those are only the results obtained by the achievement of such operations."[3] The totality of objects of thought and practice is now "projected" as *organization:* beyond any perceivable certitude, truth becomes a matter of convention, efficiency, and "internal coherence." The most fundamental experience is no longer concrete experience, overall social practice, but rather the administrative practice organized by technology.

This development reflects the transformation of the natural world into a technical world. It is more than a pun if I say that *technology has replaced ontology.* The new mode of thought annuls the ontological tradition. Hegel summarized the idea which lies at the core of this tradition: Logos, Reason, is the common denominator of the subject and the object and it is perceived as the synthesis of opposites; this synthesis develops and realizes itself in the theoretical and practical struggle to transform the given world into the free and rational world. This is the work of *history.* With that idea, the idealist ontology comprehends the *tension* between subject and object, and the opposition between them. The reality of reason is the tension between different modes of being. Thus, the most resolutely monist system maintained the idea of a substance which deploys itself into subject and object, that is to say, the idea of a dual and antagonistic reality.

The modern transformation from natural to technical reality undermines the very foundation of this dualism. It is true that scientific, modern philosophy begins with the Cartesian notion of two substances: *res cogitans* and *res extensa.* However, since the "matter" of which the latter is constituted is more and more comprehended by mathematical formulas (whose application, in turn, "remolds" this matter), the *res extensa* loses concrete character. While the *res extensa* becomes the world of mathematical structure in itself, the Ego, as the *res cogitans,* even more surely becomes the subject of observation and quantitative computation. A new monism appears, but a monism devoid of substance. The tension between subject and object, the dualist and antagonistic character of reality, tend to disappear and with them the "two-dimensionality" of human existence, the capacity to envisage another mode of human existence within reality, and the ability to transcend facticity towards its real possibilities.

The ability to live in two dimensions was one of the constitutive characteristics of man in pretechnological civilization. The capacity to transcend facticity from the perspective of a *qualitative* change of reality *within* reality was quite different from the belief in religious transcendence which transcended the same reality, and even more so from scientific transcendence, which only transforms the factual in quantitative terms. The ability to comprehend and live historical transcendence is seriously atrophied in the technological world. Man can no longer exist in two dimensions; he has become a one-dimensional man. There is now one dimension of reality which is, in the strict sense of the word, a reality without substance, or rather, a reality in which substance is represented by its technical form which becomes its content, its essence. Every signification, every proposition is validated only within the framework of the behavior of men and things—a one-dimensional context of efficient, theoretical, and practical operations.

At first, it was possible to believe that the "denaturation" of reality is masked by the terrible force through which the technical world resists the will and the thinking of the individual; that the pure and simple power of the matter which man should transform and which transforms him was never so overwhelming. But this power is the very power of man. It is through this same human practice that the technical world has congealed into a "second nature," or a false immediacy, *schlechte Unmittelbarkeit* [bad immediacy], more hostile and destructive than this *original* pretechnical nature. The technical reality does not have any substance other than the subject. But the subject—who would make out of this technical reality the world of his liberty—exists only potentially "in itself" and not "for itself." Consequently, technical reality is deprived of its logos, or, more precisely, that logos appears as deprived of reality, as a logical form without substance. Contemporary positivism, semantics, symbolic logic, and linguistic analysis define and filter the universe of discourse for the use of technicians, specialists, and experts who calculate, adjust, and match without ever asking *for whom* and *for what*. The occupation of these specialists is to *make things work,* but not to give an end to this process. Neither science nor technics have values in themselves; they are "neutral" with respect to values or ends that might have been attributed to them from outside. This neutrality is nonetheless positive: reality is value, and it is *evaluated* precisely as if it were conceived in its pure form (or as pure matter: in this context these two terms, although opposite, converge) and lent itself to all ends. Being assumes the ontological character of *instrumentality;* by its very structure this rationality is susceptible to any use and to any modification.

Are those notions inherent in science? Don't they too easily correspond to the social conditions of experience in which scientific method developed? Demonstrating the link which exists between mathematical and operative science on one hand, and ascending capitalism on the other, does not exhaust the question. This link deserves to be reexamined.

The link existing between science and society is well known. As science was liberating itself, liberating nature from its "external" forces and constituting objectivity as a means in itself, a pure and universal means, an analogous liberation was produced in social relations: man found himself liberated from any individual and "external" dependence. Man entered into the social process as an abstract and universal element, quantifiable in terms of labor power. In the course of this process, the concrete aspect of having different intellectual faculties and individual needs (the secondary qualities!) became reduced to a common denominator, a quantifiable, objective base of exchange, of money, and of means in a universal milieu.

The parallel between social development and scientific development discloses a common principle: efficiency. The scientific method sees in this principle the most certain warranty of its correctness. But there isn't, there couldn't be, efficiency *per se*! In the social process, the end [of efficiency] is the production of consumer goods, which purports to satisfy needs and an exchange value which integrates subjects and objects according to a universal, quantifiable standard. It seems, however, that science wasn't originally indebted to such ends; this is a great illusion. Conceptually speaking, science tended towards a different end. First, science made ends abstract—as processes which appeared themselves incompatible not with "reality," but with the ascending industrial reality in which ends become means in a system of "technicity."[4] In this way, science constructed the universe of intellectual and physical instrumentality, a system truly "hypothetical." Nevertheless, a system of instrumentality depends, as such, on *another* system: on a universe of *ends*. What appears as external, foreign to the terminology of science, is actually part of its structure, its method, and its concepts: of its objectivity.

One should therefore reject the notion of technical neutrality, which offers a perspective on techniques beyond good and evil and which appears as objectivity itself, suspectible to social usage in all its forms. Indeed, a machine, a technical instrument, can be considered as neutral, as pure matter. But the machine, the instrument, does not exist outside an ensemble, a technological totality; it exists only as an element of technicity. This form of technicity is a "state of the world," a way of existing between man and nature. Heidegger stressed that the "project" of an instrumental world precedes (and should precede) the creation of those technologies which serve as the instrument of this ensemble. People should therefore conceive of reality as a technical ensemble (technicity) before attempting to act upon it as a technician. In fact, such "transcendental" knowledge possesses a material base in the needs of society and in the incapacity of society to either satisfy or develop them. I would like to insist on the fact that the abolition of anxiety, the pacification of life, and enjoyment are the essential needs. From the beginning, the technical project contains the requirements of these needs: these requirements are part of the notion of world harmony, of physical laws, and of the mathematician God (the highest idea of universal equality throughout all inequality!). These requirements are intrinsic to the very notion of modern science, which demands the free play of intellectual faculties against repressive powers. If one considers the existential character of technicity, one can speak of a *final technological cause* and the repression of this cause through the social development of technology.

The question is whether neutrality, in relation to values, is a scientific notion, that is to say, a requirement inherent in the structure of modern science. In my opinion, the neutrality of technology (which is a mere manifestation of the neutrality of science) is a political concept. Industrial society clearly developed a notion of technology which undercuts its inherent character. Indeed, as a historical project, technicity has an internal sense of its own: technicity projects instrumentality as a way to release man from labor and anxiety, as a way to pacify the struggle for existence. This is the ultimate purpose for that methodical transformation of the world implied in technicity. Developed as "pure" instrumentality, technology has rendered this concrete purpose into an abstraction. It has ceased to be the goal of technological development. Consequently, pure instrumentality deprived of its ultimate purpose, has become a universal means for *domination*.

Indeed, technicity requires domination: the control of nature as a hostile, destructive, and violent force; the control of man as part of that nature; the exploitation of natural resources for the satisfaction of needs. In these ways, industrial society appropriately exercises its technological domination; but insofar as society has made an abstraction of technology's ultimate purpose, technology itself perpetuates misery, violence, and destruction.

The interdependence of productive and destructive forces, which characterizes technicity as domination, tends to suppress any difference between the "normal" and the abnormal "use" of technology. The difference between the use of "technology" and science by the Nazis and by democracy is dubious. A missile remains a missile whether it destroys London or Moscow, and Mr. von Braun remains Mr. von Braun whether he works for the Brown House or the White House. The absence of an ultimate purpose in technology manifests itself equally in politics, where it becomes open to suspicion and contestation.

If the creation of the technical world did not abolish the domination of man over man, it was because a particular development of technicity—which is more profound and more ancient than technique itself—continued to make out of life merely a means of living. Up to the present, technical progress remains the progress of an alienated labor, of a repressive productivity. Technicity became the most efficient method, the most fruitful way, to subjugate man to his instrument of labor.

Through technicity, society ensures the primitive repression of man by man: enjoyment is sacrificed to the "reality principle." This repression must be exercised most efficiently and intensively, since it is more than ever threatened by technical progress itself. It seems, indeed, that the realization of industrial civilization diminishes the need for repression; confronted with the real possibility for the abolition of labor, however, industrial civilization appears even more irrational. I would like to stress here the immense political impact of Freud's work, as an analysis of the fatal dialectic of progress.

Civilization is man's subjugation to work. In this process, the human organism ceases to exist as an instrument of satisfaction and instead becomes an instrument of work and renunciation: satisfaction is postponed, enjoyment sacrificed. The primary instincts of man naturally tend to immediate satiation and to rest, to tranquility through this appeasement; they oppose themselves to the necessity of work and labor and to the indispensable conditions of satisfaction in a world ruled by starvation and the insufficiency of goods. Society therefore must turn the instincts away from their immediate goal and subjugate them to the "reality principle," which is the very principle of repression.

The human being therefore becomes an instrument of labor; he is productive. But this productivity is always accompanied by suffering and by destruction, which are the marks of the violence done to humans in their biological constitution. The progress of civilization rests therefore upon this essential modification of the "nature" of human beings. Henceforth, individuals make repression their own project and their own enterprise (super-ego, guilt feelings, etc.). Their instincts themselves become repressive; they are the biological and mental bases which sustain and perpetuate political and social repression. To the extent to which the social reorganization of instincts represses spontaneity, eroticism, etc., the instincts of destruction and death become more powerful. Transformed by turn into aggressiveness, which is more or less controlled and useful, these instincts become an inherent force of the progress of civilization. Thus, the progress of civilization is a double process which dialectically intervenes as much in the biological and mental domain as in the domain of political economy; each supports and fortifies the other.

All progress, all growth of productivity, is accompanied by a progressive repression and a productive destruction. The social division of labor engenders this fatal dialectic through which, one could say, all progress of reason contains its own irrationality, every gain of liberty contains a new form of servitude, and all production contains restrictions that are equally efficacious. Now, this dialectic becomes explosive in advanced industrial civilization. To the degree that society masters nature and increases the material and intellectual resources which individuals can put to use, the double repression becomes less necessary as the condition of progress. The realization of technology and the productivity of labor could reduce considerably the gap that exists between needs and their satisfaction. A world truly pacified might emerge, where life would no longer be merely a means for living, but instead become a life in and for itself. Repression continues, however, and so it should continue, since without alienated work it would become impossible to increase that repressive productivity which has become the driving force of society.

A few conclusions, whose speculative character should not be hidden, remain to be suggested.

I admitted that the repressive tendencies in advanced industrial society have resulted from the development of technicity seen as a political project, as a project of domination. That domination implied by technicity is twofold:

- Control of nature: rational exploitation of natural resources, etc.
- Control of man: rational exploitation of natural resources, etc.

According to its own internal logic, the technological project should have been accomplished while annulling itself: the necessity for domination was supposed to disappear. The triumph over misery and the insufficiency of goods should have made it possible to "abolish labor," to put productivity to the service of consumption, and to abandon the struggle of existence in order to enjoy existence. Considerable forces conflict with such a future of technicity: within overall progress and the enhancement of conditions of life, domination and destruction continue. Furthermore: domination and destruction themselves become the conditions of progress. I have stressed that the social organization of instincts plays a major role in this process through which individuals perpetuate their own domination. All social repression rests on a "biological" repression. Consequently, all liberation presupposes a revolution, an upheaval in the order of instincts and needs: a new reality principle. This total transvaluation of values would affect the being of nature as well as the being of man.

Man and nature will always remain the two terms of a dialectical relation, the factors of a dialectical totality. Social organization influences nature as well as man. There can be no liberation, no pacification of human existence, without the liberation and pacification of nature. There is a control over man which is repressive, and there is a control over man which is liberating. There is a control over nature which brings deliverance to nature, as far as its own misery is concerned, and which suppresses violence and destruction. Civilization realized the idea of such a control over nature, in its gardens, parks, and its "protected reserves"; outside the portions limited to the natural environment, it has treated nature as man was treated: as an instrument of repressive reproductivity. "This conquering aggression is characterized by the rape of nature."[5] Yet this sentence is too often perceived as a catch-phrase, as an old image of romanticism and utopia. As a matter of fact, it expresses the essential relation between the destruction of man and the destruction of nature. Man remains master and slave, subject and object of this domination, although domination is transferred to machines and directed against nature. "The machine is only a means; the end is the conquest of nature, the domestication of the natural forces through subjugation: the machine becomes a slave which produces other slaves. Such an inspiration can meet man's desire for liberty. But it is difficult to liberate oneself while transferring servitude to other beings, men, animals, or machines; to rule over an empire of machines which subjugate the entire world is still to rule, and any system of rule presupposes the acceptance of a schema of subjugation."[6]

Notes

1. See also *Hegels Ontology und die Grundlegung einer Theorie des Geschichtlichtkeit* (Frankfurt, 1932); *Reason and Revolution* (London, 1941); *Eros and Civilisation: A Philosophical Inquiry into Freud* (Boston, 1955); *Soviet-Marxism* (New York, 1958).

2. V. Quine, *From a Logical Point of View* (Cambridge, 1953), p. 44

3. H. Dingle "Philosophy of Physics: 1850–1950" *Nature*, vol. 168 (1951), p. 630.

4. Translator's Note: In contrast to the French *technique*, which refers to a particular activity within a particular sociohistorical construct, *technicité* refers to an entire system of technology, including its technical apparatus and scientific knowledge. The word technicity will be kept in the text.

5. Gilbert Simondon, *Du mode d'existence des objets techniques* (Paris, 1958), p. 127.

6. Ibid.

9

The Culture Industry Reconsidered

Theodor W. Adorno

The term *culture industry* was perhaps used for the first time in the book *Dialectic of Enlightenment,* which Horkheimer and I published in Amsterdam in 1947. In our drafts we spoke of "mass culture." We replaced that expression with "culture industry" in order to exclude from the outset the interpretation agreeable to its advocates; that it is a matter of something like a culture that arises spontaneously from the masses themselves, the contemporary form of popular art. From the latter the culture industry must be distinguished in the extreme. The culture industry fuses the old and familiar into a new quality. In all its branches, products which are tailored for consumption by masses, and which to a great extent determine the nature of that consumption, are manufactured more or less according to plan. The individual branches are similar in structure or at least fit into each other, ordering themselves into a system almost without a gap. This is made possible by contemporary technical capabilities as well as by economic and administrative concentration. The culture industry intentionally integrates its consumers from above. To the detriment of both, it forces together the spheres of high and low art, separated for thousands of years. The seriousness of high art is destroyed in speculation about its efficacy; the seriousness of the lower perishes with the civilizational constraints imposed on the rebellious resistance inherent within it as long as social control was not yet total. Thus, although the culture industry undeniably speculates on the conscious and unconscious state of the

---

Translated by Anson G. Rabinbach. This essay was published in Theodor W. Adorno, *Ohne Leitbild* (Frankfurt am Main, 1967). It appears here in English with the permission of Suhrkamp Verlag. An inaccurate and abridged translation appeared in *Cinéaste,* Vol. V. No. 1 (Winter 1971–72).

millions towards which it is directed, the masses are not primary, but secondary; they are an object of calculation, an appendage of the machinery. The customer is not king, as the culture industry would like to have us believe, not its subject but its object. The very term *mass media,* specially honed for the culture industry, already shifts the accent onto harmless terrain. Neither is it a question of primary concern for the masses, nor of the techniques of communication as such, but of the spirit which sufflates them, their master's voice. The culture industry misuses its concern for the masses in order to duplicate, reinforce, and strengthen their mentality, which it presumes is given and unchangeable. How this mentality might be changed is excluded throughout. The masses are not the measure but the ideology of the culture industry, even though the culture industry itself could scarcely exist without adapting to the masses.

The cultural commodities of the industry are governed, as Brecht and Suhrkamp expressed it thirty years ago, by the principle of their realization as value, and not by their own specific content and harmonious formation. The entire practice of the culture industry transfers the profit motive naked onto cultural forms. Ever since these cultural forms first began to earn a living for their creators as commodities in the marketplace, they had already possessed something of this quality. But then they sought after profit only indirectly, over and above their autonomous essence. New on the part of the culture industry is the direct and undisguised primacy of a precisely and thoroughly calculated efficacy in its most typical products. The autonomy of works of art, which of course rarely ever predominated in an entirely pure form, and was always permeated by a constellation of effects, is tendentially eliminated by the culture industry, with or without the conscious will of those in control. The latter include both those who carry out directives as well as those who hold the power. In economic terms they are or were in search of new opportunities for the realization of capital in the most economically developed countries. The old opportunities became increasingly precarious as a result of the same concentration process which alone makes the culture industry possible as an omnipresent phenomenon. Culture, in the true sense, did not simply accommodate itself to human beings; but it always simultaneously raised a protest against the petrified relations under which they lived, thereby honoring them. Insofar as culture becomes wholly assimilated to and integrated in those petrified relations, human beings are once more debased. Cultural entities typical of the culture industry are no longer *also* commodities, they are commodities through and through. This quantitative shift is so great that it calls forth entirely new phenomena. Ultimately, the culture industry no longer even needs to directly pursue everywhere the profit interests from which it originated. These interests have become objectified in its ideology and have even made themselves independent of the compulsion to sell the cultural commodities, which must be swallowed anyway. The culture industry turns into public relations, the manufacturing of "goodwill" *per se,* without regard for particular firms or saleable objects. Brought to bear is a general uncritical consensus, advertisements produced for the world, so that each product of the culture industry becomes its own advertisement.

Nevertheless, those characteristics which originally stamped the transformation of literature into a commodity are maintained in this process. More than anything in the world, the culture industry has its ontology, a scaffolding of rigidly conservative basic categories which can be gleaned, for example, from the commercial English novels of the late seventeenth and early eighteenth centuries. What parades as progress in the culture industry, as the incessantly new which it offers up, remains the disguise for an eternal sameness; everywhere the changes mask a skeleton which has changed just as little as the profit motive itself since the time it first gained its predominance over culture.

Thus, the expression *industry* is not to be taken literally. It refers to the standardization of the thing itself—such as that of the Western, familiar to every moviegoer—and to the rationalization of distribution techniques, but not strictly to the production process. Although in film, the central sector of the culture industry, the production process resembles technical modes of operation in the extensive division of labor, the employment of machines and the separation of the laborers from the means of production—expressed in the perennial conflict between artists active in the culture industry and those who control it—individual forms of production are nevertheless maintained. Each product affects an individual air; individuality itself serves to reinforce ideology, insofar as the illusion is conjured up that the completely reified and mediated is a sanctuary from immediacy and life. Now, as ever, the culture industry exists in the "service" of third persons, maintaining its affinity to the declining circulation process of capital, to the commerce from which it came into being. Its ideology above all makes use of the star system, borrowed from individualistic art and its commercial exploitation. The more dehumanized its methods of operation and content, the more diligently and successfully the culture industry propagates supposedly great personalities and operates with heart-throbs. It is industrial more in a sociological sense, in the incorporation of industrial forms of organization even where nothing is manufactured—as in the rationalization of office work—rather than in the sense of anything really and actually produced by technological rationality. Accordingly, the misinvestments of the culture industry are considerable, throwing those branches rendered obsolete by new techniques into crises, which seldom lead to changes for the better.

The concept of technique in the culture industry is only in name identical with technique in works of art. In the latter, technique is concerned with the internal organization of the object itself, with its inner logic. In contrast, the technique of the culture industry is, from the beginning, one of distribution and mechanical reproduction, and therefore always remains external to its object. The culture industry finds ideological support precisely insofar as it carefully shields itself from the full potential of the techniques contained in its products. It lives parasitically from the extra-artistic technique of the material production of goods, without regard for the obligation to the internal artistic whole implied by its functionality [*Sachlichkeit*], but also without concern for the laws of form demanded by aesthetic autonomy. The result for the physiognomy of the culture industry is essentially a mixture of streamlining, photographic hardness and precision on the one hand, and individualistic residues, sentimentality, and an already rationally disposed and adapted romanticism on the other. Adopting Benjamin's designation of the traditional work of art by the concept of aura, the presence of that which is not present, the culture industry is defined by the fact that it does not strictly counterpose another principle to that of aura, but rather by the fact that it conserves the decaying aura as a foggy mist. By this means the culture industry betrays its own ideological abuses.

It has recently become customary among cultural officials as well as sociologists to warn against underestimating the culture industry while pointing to its great importance for the development of the consciousness of its consumers. It is to be taken seriously, without cultured snobbism. In actuality the culture history is important as a moment of the spirit which dominates today. Whoever ignores its influence out of skepticism for what it stuffs into people would be naive. Yet there is a deceptive glitter about the admonition to take it seriously. Because of its social role, disturbing questions about its quality, about truth or untruth, and about the aesthetic niveau of the culture industry's emissions are repressed, or at least excluded from the so-called sociology of communications. The critic is accused of taking refuge in arrogant esoterica. It would be advisable first to indicate the double meaning of importance that slowly worms its way in unnoticed. Even if it touches the lives of innumerable people, the function of something is no guarantee of its particular quality. The blending of aesthetics with its residual communicative aspects leads art, as a social phenomenon, not to its rightful position in opposition to alleged artistic snobbism, but rather in a variety of ways to the defense of its baneful social consequences. The importance of the culture industry in the spiritual constitution of the masses is no dispensation for reflection on its objective legitimation, its essential being, least of all by a science which thinks itself pragmatic. On the contrary: such reflection becomes necessary precisely for this reason. To take the culture industry as seriously as its unquestioned role demands, means to take it seriously critically, and not to cower in the face of its monopolistic character.

Among those intellectuals anxious to reconcile themselves with the phenomenon and eager to find a common formula to express both their reservations against it and their respect for its power, a tone of ironic toleration prevails unless they have already created a new mythos of the twentieth century from the imposed regression. After all, those intellectuals maintain, everyone knows what pocket novels, films off the rack, family television shows rolled out into serials and hit parades, advice to the lovelorn, and horoscope columns are all about. All of this, however, is harmless and, according to them, even democratic since it responds to a demand, albeit a stimulated one. It also bestows all kinds of blessings, they point out, for example, through the dissemination of information, advice, and stress-reducing patterns of behavior. Of course, as every sociological study measuring something as elementary as how politically informed the public is has proven, the information is meager or indifferent. Moreover, the advice to be gained from manifestations of the culture industry is vacuous, banal, or worse, and the behavior patterns are shamelessly conformist.

The two-faced irony in the relationship of servile intellectuals to the culture industry is not restricted to them alone. It may also be supposed that the consciousness of the consumers themselves is split between the prescribed fun which is supplied to them by the culture industry and a not particularly well-hidden doubt about its blessings. The phrase "the world wants to be deceived" has become truer than had ever been intended. People are not only, as the saying goes, falling for the swindle; if it guarantees them even the most fleeting gratification, they desire a deception which is nonetheless transparent to them. They force their eyes shut and voice approval, in a kind of self-loathing, for what is meted out to them, knowing fully the purpose for which it is manufactured. Without admitting it, they sense that their lives would be completely intolerable as soon as they no longer cling to satisfactions which are none at all.

The most ambitious defense of the culture industry today celebrates its spirit, which might safely be called ideology, as an ordering factor. In a supposedly chaotic world, it provides human beings with something like standards for orientation, and that alone seems worthy of approval. However, what its defenders imagine is preserved by the culture industry is in fact all the more thoroughly destroyed by it. The color film demolishes the genial old tavern to a greater extent than bombs ever could: the film exterminates its *imago*. No homeland can survive being processed by the films which celebrate it, and which thereby turn the unique character on which it thrives into an interchangeable sameness.

That which legitimately could be called culture attempted, as an expression of suffering and contradiction, to maintain a grasp on the idea of the good life. Culture cannot represent either that which merely exists or the conventional and no longer binding categories of order which the culture industry drapes over the idea of the good life as if existing reality were the good life, and as if those categories were its true measure. If the response of the culture industry's representatives is that it does not deliver art at all, this is itself the ideology with which they evade responsibility for that from which the business lives. No misdeed is ever righted by explaining it as such.

The appeal to order alone, without concrete specificity, is futile; the appeal to the dissemination of norms, without these ever proving themselves in reality or before consciousness, is equally futile. The idea of an objectively binding order, huckstered to people because it is so lacking for them, has no claims if it does not prove itself internally and in confrontation with human beings. But this is precisely what no product of the culture industry would engage in. The concepts of order which it hammers into human beings are always those of the status quo. They remain unquestioned, unanalyzed, and undialectically presupposed, even if they no longer have any substance for those who accept them. In contrast to the Kantian, the categorical imperative of the culture industry no longer has anything in common with freedom. It proclaims: You shall conform, without instruction as to what; conform to that which exists anyway, and to that which everyone thinks anyway as a reflex of its power and omnipresence. The power of the culture industry's ideology is such that conformity has replaced consciousness. The order that springs from it is never confronted with what it claims to be or with the real interests of human beings. Order, however, is not good in itself. It would be so only as a good order. The fact that the culture industry is oblivious to this and extols order *in abstracto,* bears witness to the impotence and untruth of the messages it conveys. While it claims to lead the perplexed, it deludes them with false conflicts which they are to exchange for their own. It solves conflicts for them only in appearance, in a way that they can hardly be solved in their real lives. In the products of the culture industry, human beings get into trouble only so that they can be rescued unharmed, usually by representatives of a benevolent collective; and then, in empty harmony, they are reconciled with the general, whose demands they had experienced at the outset as irreconcilable with their interests. For this purpose the culture industry has developed formulas which even reach into such non-conceptual areas as light musical entertainment. Here, too, one gets into a "jam," into rhythmic problems, which can be instantly disentangled by the triumph of the basic beat.

Even its defenders, however, would hardly openly contradict Plato, who maintained that what is objectively and intrinsically untrue cannot also be subjectively good and true for human beings. The concoctions of the culture industry are neither guides for a blissful life, nor a new art of moral responsibility, but rather exhortations to toe the line, behind which stand the most powerful interests. The consensus which it propagates strengthens blind, opaque authority. If the culture industry is measured not by its own substance and logic, but by its efficacy, by its position in reality and its explicit pretentions; if the focus of serious concern is with the efficacy to which it always appeals, the potential of its effect becomes twice as weighty. This potential, however, lies in the promotion and exploitation of the ego-weakness to which the powerless members of contemporary society, with its concentration of power, are condemned. Their consciousness is further developed retrogressively. It is no coincidence that cynical American film producers are heard to say that their pictures must take into consideration the level of eleven-year-olds. In doing so they would very much like to make adults into eleven-year-olds.

It is true that thorough research has not, for the time being, produced an airtight case proving the regressive effects of particular products of the culture industry. No doubt an imaginatively designed experiment could achieve this more successfully than the powerful financial interests concerned would find comfortable. In any case, it can be assumed without hesitation that steady drops hollow the stone, especially since the system of the culture industry that surrounds the masses tolerates hardly any deviation and incessantly drills the same formulas of behavior. Only their deep unconscious mistrust, the last residue of the difference between art and empirical reality in the spiritual make-up of the masses, explains why they have not, to a person, long since perceived and accepted the world as it is constructed for them by the culture industry. Even if its messages were harmless as they are made out to be—on countless occasions they are obviously not harmless, like the movies which chime in with currently popular hate campaigns against intellectuals by portraying them with the usual stereotypes—the attitudes which the culture industry calls forth are anything but harmless. If an astrologer urges his readers to drive carefully on a particular day, that certainly hurts no one; they will, however, be harmed indeed by the stupefaction which lies in the claim that advice which is valid every day, and which is therefore idiotic, needs the approval of the stars.

Human dependence and servitude, the vanishing point of the culture industry, could scarcely be more faithfully described than by the American interviewee who was of the opinion that the dilemmas of the contemporary epoch would end if people would simply follow the lead of prominent personalities. Insofar as the culture industry arouses a feeling of well-being that the world is precisely in that order suggested by the culture industry, the substitute gratification which it prepares for human beings cheats them out of the same happiness which it deceitfully projects. The total effect of the culture industry is one of anti-enlightenment, in which, as Horkheimer and I have noted, enlightenment—that is, the progressive technical domination of nature—becomes mass deception and is turned into a means for fettering consciousness. It impedes the development of autonomous, independent individuals who judge and decide consciously for themselves. These, however, would be the precondition for a democratic society which needs adults who have come of age in order to sustain itself and develop. If the masses have been unjustly reviled from above as masses, the culture industry is not among the least responsible for making them into masses and then despising them, while obstructing the emancipation for which human beings are as ripe as the productive forces of the epoch permit.

10

The Public Sphere:
An Encyclopedia Article

Jürgen Habermas

The Concept. By "the public sphere" we mean first of all a realm of our social life in which something approaching public opinion can be formed. Access is guaranteed to all citizens. A portion of the public sphere comes into being in every conversation in which private individuals assemble to form a public body.[1] They then behave neither like business or professional people transacting private affairs, nor like members of a constitutional order subject to the legal constraints of a state bureaucracy. Citizens behave as a public body when they confer in an unrestricted fashion—that is, with the guarantee of freedom of assembly and association and the freedom to express and publish their opinions—about matters of general interest. In a large public body, this kind of communication requires specific means for transmitting information and influencing those who receive it. Today, newspapers and magazines, radio and television are the media of the public sphere. We speak of the political public sphere in contrast, for instance, to the literary one, when public discussion deals with objects connected to the activity of the state. Although state authority is, so to speak, the executor of the political public sphere, it is not a part of it.[2] To be sure, state authority is usually considered "public" authority, but it derives its task of caring for the well-being of all citizens primarily from this aspect of the public sphere. Only when the exercise of political control is effectively subordinated to the democratic demand that information be accessible to the public, does the political public sphere win an institutionalized influence over the government through the instrument of law-making bodies. The expression *public opinion* refers to the tasks of criticism and control which a public body of citizens informally—and, in periodic elections, formally as well—practices vis-à-vis the ruling structure organized in the form of a state. Regulations demanding that certain

Translated by Sara Lennox and Frank Lennox

proceedings be public [*Publizitätsvorschriften*]—for example, those providing for open court hearings—are also related to this function of public opinion. The public sphere as a sphere which mediates between society and state, in which the public organizes itself as the bearer of public opinion, accords with the principle of the public sphere[3]—that principle of public information which once had to be fought for against the arcane policies of monarchies and which since that time has made possible the democratic control of state activities.

It is no coincidence that these concepts of the public sphere and public opinion arose for the first time only in the eighteenth century. They acquire their specific meaning from a concrete historical situation. It was at that time that the distinction of "opinion" from "opinion publique" and "public opinion" came about. Though mere opinions (cultural assumptions, normative attitudes, collective prejudices and values) seem to persist unchanged in their natural form as a kind of sediment of history, public opinion can by definition come into existence only when a reasoning public is presupposed. Public discussions about the exercise of political power which are both critical in intent and institutionally guaranteed have not always existed—they grew out of a specific phase of bourgeois society and could enter into the order of the bourgeois constitutional state only as a result of a particular constellation of interests.

History. There is no indication that European society of the high Middle Ages possessed a public sphere as a unique realm distinct from the private sphere. Nevertheless, it was not coincidental that during that period symbols of sovereignty, for instance, the princely seal, were deemed "public." At that time there existed a public representation of power. The status of the feudal lord, at whatever level of the feudal pyramid, made it unnecessary to employ the categories "public" and "private." The holder of the position represented it publicly; he showed himself, presented himself as the embodiment of an ever-present "higher" power. The concept of this representation has been maintained up to the most recent constitutional history. Regardless of the degree to which it has loosened itself from the old base, the authority of political power today still demands a representation at the highest level by a head of state. Such elements, however, derive from a prebourgeois social structure. Representation in the sense of a bourgeois public sphere,[4] for instance, the representation of the nation or of particular mandates, has nothing to do with the medieval representative public sphere—a public sphere directly linked to the concrete existence of a ruler. As long as the prince and the estates of the realm still "are" the land, instead of merely functioning as deputies for it, they are able to "represent"; they represent their power "before" the people, instead of for the people.

The feudal authorities (Church, princes, and nobility), to which the representative public sphere was first linked, disintegrated during a long process of polarization. By the end of the eighteenth century they had broken apart into private elements on the one hand, and into public elements on the other. The position of the Church changed with the Reformation: the link to divine authority which the Church represented, that is, religion, became a private matter. So-called religious freedom came to insure what was historically the first area of private autonomy. The Church itself continued its existence as one public and legal body among others. The corresponding polarization within princely authority was visibly manifested in the separation of the public budget from the private household expenses of a ruler. The institutions of public authority, along with the bureaucracy and the military, and in part also with the legal institutions, asserted their independence from the privatized sphere of the princely court. Finally, the feudal estates were transformed as well: the nobility became the organs of public authority, parliament, and the legal institutions; while those occupied in trades and professions, insofar as they had already established urban corporations and territorial organizations, developed into a sphere of bourgeois society which would stand apart from the state as a genuine area of private autonomy.

The representative public sphere yielded to that new sphere of "public authority" which came into being with national and territorial states. Continuous state activity (permanent administration, standing army) now corresponded to the permanence of the relationships which with the stock exchange and the press had developed within the exchange of commodities and information. Public authority consolidated into a concrete opposition for those who were merely subject to it and who at first found only a negative definition of themselves within it. These were the "private individuals" who were excluded from public authority because they held no office. "Public" no longer referred to the "representative" court of a prince endowed with authority, but rather to an institution regulated according to competence, to an apparatus endowed with a monopoly on the legal exertion of authority. Private individuals subsumed in the state at whom public authority was directed now made up the public body.

Society, now a private realm occupying a position in opposition to the state, stood on the one hand as if in clear contrast to the state. On the other hand, that society had become a concern of public interest to the degree that the production of life in the wake of the developing market economy had grown beyond the bounds of private domestic authority. *The bourgeois public sphere* could be understood as the sphere of private individuals assembled into a public body, which almost immediately laid claim to the officially regulated "intellectual newspapers" for use against the public authority itself. In those newspapers, and in moralistic and critical journals, they debated that public authority on the general rules of social intercourse in their fundamentally privatized yet publicly relevant sphere of labor and commodity exchange.

The Liberal Model of the Public Sphere. The medium of this debate—public discussion—was unique and without historical precedent. Hitherto the estates had negotiated agreements with their princes, settling their claims to power from case to case. This development took a different course in England, where the parliament limited royal power, than it did on the Continent, where the monarchies mediatized the estates. The Third Estate then broke with this form of power arrangement, since it could no longer establish itself as a ruling group. A division of power by means of the delineation of the rights of the nobility was no longer possible within an exchange economy—private authority over capitalist property is, after all, unpolitical. Bourgeois individuals are private individuals. As such, they do not "rule." Their claims to power vis-à-vis public authority were thus directed not against the concentration of power, which was to be "shared." Instead, their ideas infiltrated the very principle on which the existing power is based. To the principle of existing power, the bourgeois public opposed the principle of supervision—that very principle which demands that proceedings be made public [*Publizität*]. The principle of supervision is thus a means of transforming the nature of power, not merely one basis of legitimation exchanged for another.

In the first modern constitutions, the catalogues of fundamental rights were a perfect image of the liberal model of the public sphere: they guaranteed the society as a sphere of private autonomy and the restriction of public authority to a few functions. Between these two spheres, the constitutions further insured the existence of a realm of private individuals assembled into a public body who as citizens transmit the needs of bourgeois society to the state, in order, ideally, to transform political into "rational" authority within the medium of this public sphere. The general interest, which was the measure of such rationality, was then guaranteed, according to the presuppositions of a society of free commodity exchange, when the activities of private individuals in the marketplace were freed from social compulsion and from political pressure in the public sphere.

At the same time, daily political newspapers assumed an important role. In the second half of the eighteenth century, literary journalism created serious competition for the earlier news sheets, which were mere compilations of notices. Karl Bücher characterized this great development as follows: "Newspapers changed from mere institutions for the publication of news into bearers and leaders of public opinion—weapons of party politics. This transformed the newspaper business. A new element emerged between the gathering and publication of news: the editorial staff. But for the newspaper publisher it meant that he changed from a vendor of recent news to a dealer in public opinion." The publishers insured the newspapers a commercial basis, yet without commercializing them as such. The press remained an institution of the public itself, effective in the manner of a mediator and intensifier of public discussion, no longer a mere organ for the spreading of news but not yet the medium of a consumer culture.

This type of journalism can be observed above all during periods of revolution, when newspapers of the smallest political groups and organizations spring up—for instance, in Paris in 1789. Even in the Paris of 1848 every half-way eminent politician organized his club, every other his journal: 450 clubs and over 200 journals were established there between February and May alone. Until the permanent legalization of a politically functional public sphere, the appearance of a political newspaper meant joining the struggle for freedom and public opinion, and thus for the public sphere as a principle. Only with the establishment of the bourgeois constitutional state was the intellectual press relieved of the pressure of its convictions. Since then it has been able to abandon its polemical position and take advantage of the earning possibilities of a commercial undertaking. In England, France, and the United States, the transformation from a journalism of conviction to one of commerce began in the 1830s at approximately the same time. In the transition from the literary journalism of private individuals to the public services of the mass media, the public sphere was transformed by the influx of private interests, which received special prominence in the mass media.

The Public Sphere in the Social Welfare State Mass Democracy. Although the liberal model of the public sphere is still instructive today with respect to the normative claim that information be accessible to the public,[5] it cannot be applied to the actual conditions of an industrially advanced mass democracy organized in the form of the social welfare state. In part, the liberal model had always included ideological components, but it is also in part true that the social preconditions, to which the ideological elements could at one time at least be linked, had been fundamentally transformed. The very forms in which the public sphere manifested itself, to which supporters of the liberal model could appeal for evidence, began to change with the Chartist movement in England and the February revolution in France. Because of the diffusion of press and propaganda, the public body expanded beyond the bounds of the bourgeoisie. The public body lost not only its social exclusivity; it lost in addition the coherence created by bourgeois social institutions and a relatively high standard of education. Conflicts hitherto restricted to the private sphere now intrude into the public sphere. Group needs which can expect no satisfaction from a self-regulating market now tend toward a regulation by the state. The public sphere, which must now mediate these demands, becomes a field for the competition of interests, competitions which assume the form of violent conflict. Laws which obviously have come about under the "pressure of the street" can scarcely still be understood as arising from the consensus of private individuals engaged in public discussion. They correspond in a more or less unconcealed manner to the compromise of conflicting private interests. Social organizations which deal with the state act in the political public sphere, whether through the agency of political parties or directly in connection with the public administration. With the interweaving of the public and private realms, not only do the political authorities assume certain functions in the sphere of commodity exchange and social labor, but, conversely, social powers now assume political functions. This leads to a kind of "refeudalization" of the public sphere. Large organizations strive for political compromises with the state and with one another, excluding the public sphere whenever possible. But at the same time the large organizations must assure themselves of at least plebiscitary support from the mass of the population through an apparent display of openness [*demonstrative Publizität*][6].

The political public sphere of the social welfare state is characterized by a peculiar weakening of its critical functions. At one time the process of making proceedings public [*Publizität*] was intended to subject persons or affairs to public reason, and to make political decisions subject to appeal before the court of public opinion. But often enough today the process of making public simply serves the arcane policies of special interests; in the form of "publicity" it wins public prestige for people or affairs, thus making them worthy of acclamation in a climate of nonpublic opinion. The very words "public relations work" [*Öffentlichkeitsarbeit*] betray the fact that a public sphere must first be arduously constructed case by case, a public sphere which earlier grew out of the social structure. Even the central relationship of the public, the parties, and the parliament is affected by this change in function.

Yet this trend towards the weakening of the public sphere as a principle is opposed by the extension of fundamental rights in the social welfare state. The demand that information be accessible to the public is extended from organs of the state to all organizations dealing with the state. To the degree that this is realized, a public body of organized private individuals would take the place of the now-defunct public body of private individuals who relate individually to each other. Only these organized individuals could participate effectively in the process of public communication; only they could use the channels of the public sphere which exist within parties and associations and the process of making proceedings public [*Publizität*] which was established to facilitate the dealings of organizations with the state. Political compromises would have to be legitimized through this process of public communication. The idea of the public sphere, preserved in the social welfare state mass democracy, an idea which calls for a rationalization of power through the medium of public discussion among private individuals, threatens to disintegrate with the structural transformation of the public sphere itself. It could only be realized today, on an altered basis, as a rational reorganization of social and political power under the mutual control of rival organizations committed to the public sphere in their internal structure as well as in their relations with the state and each other.

Notes

1. Habermas's concept of the public sphere is not to be equated with that of "the public," i.e., of the individuals who assemble. His concept is directed instead at the institution, which to be sure only assumes concrete form through the participation of people. It cannot, however, be characterized simply as a crowd. (This and the following notes by Peter Hohendahl.)

2. The state and the public sphere do not overlap, as one might suppose from casual language use. Rather, they confront one another as opponents. Habermas designates that sphere as public which antiquity understood to be private, i.e., the sphere of nongovernmental opinion making.

3. The principle of the public sphere could still be distinguished from an institution which is demonstrable in social history. Habermas thus would mean a model of norms and modes of behavior by means of which the very functioning of public opinion can be guaranteed for the first time. These norms and modes of behavior include: a) general accessibility, b) elimination of all privileges, and c) discovery of general norms and rational legitimations.

4. The expression *represent* is used in a very specific sense in the following section, namely, to "present oneself." The important thing to understand is that the medieval public sphere, if it even deserves this designation, is tied to the *personal*. The feudal lord and estates create the public sphere by means of their very presence.

5. Here it should be understood that Habermas considers the principle behind the bourgeois public sphere, but not its historical form, as indispensable.

6. One must distinguish between Habermas's concept of "making proceedings public" [*Publizität*] and the "public sphere" [*Öffentlichkeit*]. The term *Publizität* describes the degree of public effect generated by a public act. Thus, a situation can arise in which the form of public opinion making is maintained, while the substance of the public sphere has long ago been undermined.

Part III

Cultural Criticism and the Critique of Mass Culture

11

The Mass Ornament

Siegfried Kracauer

> Die Linien des Lebens sind verschieden,
> Wie Wege sind, und wie der Berge Grenzen
> Was hier wir sind, kann dort ein Gott ergänzen
> Mit Harmonien und ewigem Lohn und Frieden.
> —Hölderlin

An analysis of the simple surface manifestations of an epoch can contribute more to determining its place in the historical process than judgments of the epoch about itself. As expressions of the tendencies of a given time, these judgments cannot be considered valid testimonies about its overall situation. On the other hand, the very unconscious nature of surface manifestations allows for direct access to the underlying meaning of existing conditions. Conversely, the interpretation of such manifestations is tied to an understanding of these conditions. The underlying meaning of an epoch and its less obvious pulsations illuminate one another reciprocally.

A change in taste has been taking place quietly in the field of physical culture, always a popular subject in illustrated newspapers. It began with the Tiller Girls. These products of American "distraction factories" are no longer individual girls, but indissoluble female units whose movements are mathematical demonstrations. Even as they crystallize into patterns in the revues of Berlin, performances of the same geometrical exactitude are occurring in similarly packed stadiums in Australia and India, not to mention America. Through weekly newsreels in movie houses they have managed to reach even the tiniest villages. One glance at the screen reveals that the ornaments consist of thousands of bodies, sexless bodies in bathing suits. The regularity of their patterns is acclaimed by the masses, who themselves are arranged in row upon ordered row.

These spectacular pageants, which are brought into existence not only

---

Translated by Barbara Correll and Jack Zipes

by the girls and the spectators at the stadium, have long since taken on an established form. They have achieved an *international* stature and have attracted aesthetic interest.

The bearers of the ornaments are the *masses*. This is not the same as the people, for whenever the people form patterns, these patterns do not hover in mid-air but emerge from community. A current of organic life flows from these communal groups, whose shared destiny connects them with their ornaments. These ornaments appear as a magic force so laden with meaning that they cannot be reduced to a purely linear structure. Even those who have left the community and who are conscious of themselves as individual personalities with unique souls, cannot partake in the forming of new patterns. Should they be included in such a performance, these individuals do not get incorporated into the ornament. For the result would be a colorful composition which could not be worked out to its logical conclusion, since—like prongs of a rake—its points would sink into the remaining vestiges of the spiritual middle layers, weighing it down with its residue. The patterns seen in the stadiums and cabarets reveal nothing of such origins. They are composed of elements which are mere building blocks, nothing more. The construction of an edifice depends on the size of the stones and their number. It is the mass which makes the impact. Only as parts of a mass, not as individuals who believe themselves to be formed from within, are human beings components of a pattern.

The ornament is an *end in itself*. In its early stages the ballet also yielded ornaments which moved kaleidoscopically. But even after they had discarded their ritual meaning, they remained still the plastic formation of the erotic life which gave rise to them and determined their traits. In contrast, the synchronized movement of the girls is devoid of any such connections; it is a linear system which no longer has erotic meaning but at best points to the place where the erotic resides. Nor do the living constellations in the stadiums have the meaning of military demonstrations. No matter how orderly the latter appeared, that order was considered a means to an end; the parade march evolved out of patriotic feelings and in turn aroused them in soldiers and loyal subjects. The constellations of girls, however, have no meaning outside of themselves, and the masses are not a moral unit like a company of soldiers. The patterns cannot even be described as ornamental accessories for gymnastic discipline. The training of the units of girls is intended instead to produce an immense number of parallel lines, and the desired effect is to train the greatest number of people in order to create a pattern of unimaginable dimensions. In the end there is the closed ornament, whose life components have been drained of their substance.

Even though the masses bring it about, they do not participate in conceiving the ornament. And as linear as it may seem, no line juts out of the small segments to determine the whole of the mass pattern. In this it resembles the *aerial photographs* of landscapes and cities, for it does not emerge from the interior of a given reality, but rather appears above it. Similarly, actors are not aware of the stage setting in its totality; yet they consciously take part in its formation, and in the case of ballet dancers, the pattern is still open to the influence of its performers. The more its composition is reduced to linear design, the further it is removed from the immanent consciousness of those forming it. Yet this does not mean that it is observed by a more critical eye. The fact is that nobody would notice the pattern if the crowd of spectators, who have an aesthetic relation to it and do not represent anyone, were not sitting in front of it.

The ornament, detached from its bearers, must be understood *rationally*. It consists of degrees and circles like those found in textbooks of Euclidean geometry. Waves and spirals, the elementary structures of physics, are also included; discarded are the proliferations of organic forms and the radiations of spiritual life. Hereafter, the Tiller Girls can no longer be reassembled as human beings. Their mass gymnastics are never performed by whole, autonomous bodies whose contortions would deny rational understanding. Arms, thighs, and other segments are the smallest components of the composition.

The structure of the mass ornament reflects that of the general contemporary situation. Since the principle of the *capitalist production process* does not stem purely from nature, it must destroy the natural organisms which it regards either as a means or as a force of resistance. Personality and national community [*Volksgemeinschaft*] perish when calculability is demanded; only as a tiny particle of the mass can the individual human being effortlessly clamber up charts and service machines. A system which is indifferent to variations of form leads necessarily to the obliteration of national characteristics and to the fabrication of masses of workers who can be employed and used uniformly throughout the world.

—Like the mass ornament, the capitalist production process is an end in itself. The commodities which it creates are not actually produced to be possessed but to make unlimited profits. Its growth is bound up with that of the factory. The producer does not work for private gains of which he can only make limited use—the surplus profits in America are transferred to cultural accumulation centers such as libraries, universities, etc., in which intellectuals are groomed who through their later activity reimburse with interest the capital advanced to them. The producer works for the expansion of the business; values are not produced for values' sake. Though such work may once have concerned itself with the production and consumption of values, these have now become side effects which serve the production process. The activities which have been invested in the process have divested themselves of their substantial meaning.

—The production process runs its course publicly in secret. Everyone goes through the necessary motions at the conveyor belt, performs a partial function without knowing the entirety. Similar to the pattern in the stadium, the organization hovers above the masses as a monstrous figure whose originator withdraws it from the eyes of its bearers, and who himself hardly reflects upon it.

—It is conceived according to rational principles which the Taylor system only takes to its final conclusion. The hands in the factory correspond to the legs of the Tiller Girls. Psycho-technical aptitude tests seek to compute emotional dispositions above and beyond manual abilities. The mass ornament is the aesthetic reflex of the rationality aspired to by the prevailing economic system.

Certain intellectuals have taken offense at the emergence of the Tiller Girls and the image created by the stadium pageants. Whatever amuses the masses, they judge as a diversion of the masses. Contrary to such opinion, I would argue that the *aesthetic* pleasure gained from the ornamental mass movements is *legitimate*. They belong in fact to the isolated configurations of the time, configurations which imbue a given material with form. The masses which are arranged in them are taken from offices and factories. The structural principle upon which they are modeled determines them in reality as well. When great amounts of reality-content are no longer visible in our world, art must make do with what is left, for an aesthetic presentation is all the more real the less it dispenses with the reality outside the aesthetic sphere. No matter how low one rates the value of the mass ornament, its level of reality is still above that of artistic productions which cultivate obsolete noble sentiments in withered forms—even when they nave no further significance.

The process of history is a battle between weak and distant reason and the *forces of nature,* which in myth ruled over heaven and earth. After the twilight of the gods, the gods did not abdicate; the old nature within and outside of human beings continues to assert itself. The great cultures of humanity have arisen from it, and they must die just like all creatures of nature. The superstructures of *mythological* thinking grow from this source, affirming nature in its omnipotence. With all the differences in its structure, which undergoes transformations from epoch to epoch, mythological thinking stays within the limits which nature has drawn, it acknowledges the organism as the basic model; it adapts itself to existing forms of being [*Gestalthaftigkeit des Seienden*]; it bows to the rule of fate. It reflects the premises of nature in all spheres without rebelling against their existence. Organic sociology, which projects the natural organism as a model for social organization, is no less mythological than is nationalism, which knows no higher unity than that of the nation.

Reason does not move in the circle of natural life. It is concerned with bringing truth into the world. Its realm has already been dreamed of in genuine *folktales* [*Märchen*], which are not stories about miracles but statements about the miraculous arrival of justice. There is a deep historical meaning in the fact that the tales of the Arabian Nights found their way to France during the Enlightenment, and that reason in the eighteenth century recognized the reason of the folktales as its own. In the early periods of history, pure nature was already superseded [*aufgehoben*] by the triumph of truth in the fairy tale. Natural power is defeated by the impotence of good; fidelity triumphs over the art of magic.

In serving the breakthrough of truth, the historical process becomes a *process of demythologizing* and effects a radical dismantling of those positions continually occupied anew by the natural process. The French Enlightenment is a great example of the struggle between reason and the mythological delusions which have encroached upon religious and political areas. This struggle continues, and in the course of historical development nature, increasingly divested of its magic, may become more penetrable by reason.

The *capitalist epoch* is a stage in the process of demystification [*Entzauberung*]. The kind of thinking which is associated with the present economic system has made possible a domination and use of self-contained nature which was not granted to any earlier epoch. The fact that this thinking makes the exploitation of nature possible is not decisive here.

—If human beings were merely exploiters of nature, then nature would have triumphed over nature.

—But what is decisive here is that this process allows for greater independence from natural conditions and in this way makes room for the interjection of reason. We owe the bourgeois revolutions of the last hundred and fifty years precisely to this kind of *rationality* (which emanates partly, though not totally, from the reason of folktales). These revolutions settled scores with the natural powers: the Church, which itself was entangled in worldly affairs, monarchy, and feudalism. The inevitable decomposition of these powers and other mythological ties is the good fortune of reason, since it is only in those places where natural unities collapse that the folktale comes into being.

However, the rationale of the capitalist economic system is not reason itself but obscured reason. From a certain point, it abandons the truth in which it has a stake. *It does not encompass human beings.* The operation of the production process is not set up to take them into consideration, nor is the formation of the socioeconomic organization based on them. There is not one single instance where the system is based on human essences: the question is not whether capitalist thinking should cultivate humanity as a historically nurtured formation, or whether it must let human beings go unchallenged as personalities and satisfy their natural demands. The representatives of this point of view accuse the rationalism of the capitalist system of violating human beings, and in so doing long for the resurrection of a community which will harbor the alleged humanistic element in a way that capitalism cannot. The regressive effect of such involutions aside, they fail to hit upon the central defect of the system. Capitalism does not rationalize too much but *too little*. The thinking it promulgates resists the fulfillment of the reason that is deeply rooted in human nature.

Capitalist thinking can be identified by its *abstractness*. Through its prevalence today, an intellectual framework has been established which encompasses all expressions. The objection raised against this abstract manner of thinking—that it is not capable of grasping the actual substance of life and therefore must give way to concrete observation of phenomena—points clearly to the limits of abstractness. But such an objection is too hasty when it is raised in favor of that false mythological concreteness which sees as its goal organism and form. By returning to this type of concreteness, the ability once acquired to think abstractly would indeed be abandoned; however, the abstractness would not be overcome, for it is the expression of a rationality grown obdurate. The abstract and general determinations of meaning—like the determinations in the area of economics, society, politics, ethics—do not render unto reason that which belongs to reason. In this scheme empiricism is neglected; any kind of utilitarian application can be drawn from abstractions devoid of meaning. Only if we look behind these abstractions which block our way can we find rational insights corresponding to the particularity of a given situation. Despite the substantiality which is to be demanded from them, abstractions are only concrete in one sense. They are not concrete in the vulgar sense which uses the term to designate those ideas which are rooted in natural life.

—The abstractness of contemporary thinking is therefore *ambivalent*. From the point of view of mythological teachings, in which nature naively asserts itself, the process of abstraction as it is practiced in the natural sciences, for example, is a gain in rationality which detracts from the glittering display of natural things. From the perspective of reason, the same process of abstraction appears conditioned by nature; it loses itself in an empty formalism which leaves the natural free rein by not allowing the insights of reason which could penetrate the natural. The prevailing abstractness shows that the process of demythologizing has not been completed. Present-day thinking is confronted with the question of whether it should open itself to reason or remain closed and continue to oppose it. It cannot move beyond its self-imposed boundary unless its base—the economic system—undergoes an essential change. The system's continued existence will support and promote the same type of thinking. In other words, the sustained development of the capitalist system conditions the sustained growth of abstract thinking (or necessitates that it founder in false concreteness). The more abstractness crystallizes, becomes fixed, the greater the tendency for humanity to be left behind, *untouched* by reason. Thus, humanity will once again become subject to the forces of nature, if—when halfway toward abstractness—thinking diverges and rejects a breakthrough to the genuine contents of knowledge. Instead of opposing these forces, muddled thinking itself occasions their rise by ignoring that very process of reason which alone could combat such forces and make them submit. It is only a consequence of capitalism's unhampered expansion of power that the dark forces of nature continue to rise up threateningly, thereby preventing the emergence of a humanity whose essence is reason.

The *mass ornament* is just as ambivalent as abstractness. On the one hand its rationality is a reduction of the natural, which does not give rise to the decay of humanity, but rather, if carried to fruition, would nurture precisely what is most substantial in life. Precisely because the bearer of the ornament does not figure in it as a total personality, as a harmonious union of nature and "intellect" in which the former receives too much and the latter too little, this bearer becomes transparent as a human being, determined by reason. The human figure used in this mass ornament has begun its *exodus* from the organic splendor and individual constituency [*Gestalthaftigkeit*] and entered the realm of anonymity into which it exteriorizes itself when it stands in truth and when the knowledge radiating from its human source dissolves the contours of the visible natural form. Nature is deprived of its substance in the mass ornament, and this indicates the condition under which only those aspects of nature can assert themselves which do not resist illumination through reason. (This is why the trees, ponds, and mountains of old Chinese landscapes were painted as spare ornamental signs.) The organic center is removed and the remaining parts are composed according to laws yielding knowledge about truth, however temporally conditioned such knowledge might be—and not according to laws of nature. Also, only remnants of the human complex enter into the mass ornament. Their selection and compilation in the aesthetic medium result from a principle which represents formbursting reason in a purer way than those other principles which preserve humanity as an organic unity.

Viewed from the perspective of reason, the mass ornament stands revealed as *mythological cult* wrapped in abstractness. The weight granted to reason in the ornament is therefore an illusion which the ornament assumes in contrast to physical presentations of concrete immediacy. In reality, it is the crass manifestation of inferior nature. The more decisively capitalist rationale is cut off from reason and bypasses humanity vanishing into the emptiness of the abstract, the more this primitive nature can make itself felt. The natural in its impenetrability rises up in the mass pattern, despite the rationality of this pattern. Certainly, people as organic beings have disappeared from the ornaments, but that does not bring basic human nature to the fore; rather, the remaining mass particle isolates itself from this essence just as any formal general concept does. Certainly, the legs of the Tiller Girls and not the natural units of their bodies swing in unison with one another; and certainly the thousands in the stadium are also one single star. But this star does not shine, and the legs of the Tiller Girls are the abstract signs of their bodies. Wherever reason breaks down the organic unity and rips open the cultivated natural surface, it speaks out; there it dissects the human form so that undistorted truth itself can model humanity anew. But reason has not permeated the mass ornament, whose patterns are *mute*. The rationale which gives rise to the ornament is strong enough to attract the masses and at the same time to expunge life from the figures. It is too weak to find human beings in the masses or to render the figures of the ornament translucent to knowledge. Since this rationale flees from reasoning into the abstract, uncontrolled nature grows prodigiously under the pretense of rational expression, and uses abstract signs to portray life itself. Nature can no longer convert itself into patterns which are powerful as symbols, as was possible during the times of primitive peoples and religious cults. Such power of symbolic speech has withdrawn from the mass ornament under the influence of the same rationality which keeps the ornament mute. So, in the end, mere nature is all that remains, nature which resists even the statement and formulation of its own meaning. In the mass ornament we see the *rational, empty form* of the cult stripped of any express meaning. As such, it proves itself to be a regression to mythology (a greater regression is scarcely imaginable)—a regression which once again reveals the intransigeance of the capitalist rationale to reason.

That the mass ornament is an offspring of the purely natural is conformed by the role it plays in *social life*. The privileged intellectuals, who do not accept the fact that they are an appendage to the prevailing economic system, have not even understood the mass ornament as a sign of this system. They dismiss the phenomenon while continuing to edify themselves at fine arts events, untouched by the reality present in the stadium pattern. The masses who so spontaneously took to the pattern in openly acknowledging facts in their rough form, are superior to those intellectuals who despise it. With the same rationality that masters them in real life, the bearers of the patterns are swallowed up by the physical nature of the event, thus perpetuating present reality. Songs praising physical culture are sung today not only by the likes of Walter Stolzing.* It is easy to perceive their ideological nature, though the term *physical culture* combines two words which makes sense together. The immense importance attributed to the physical cannot be derived from the limited value which is due to it. Though its supporters are not entirely aware of this, it can only be explained by the alliance [*Bundesgenossenschaft*] that organized physical education maintains with the status quo. Physical training expropriates energies; production and mindless consumption of the ornamental patterns divert from the necessity to change the current order. Reason is impeded when the masses into which it should penetrate yield to emotions provided by the godless mythological cult. Its social meaning is much like that of the Roman *circus games* sponsored by tyrants.

There are numerous attempts being made, which for the sake of reaching a higher sphere, are about to give up the rationality and level of reality reached by the mass ornament. The exertions of physical culture in the field of *rhythmical gymnastics* have set a goal beyond that of personal hygiene—namely, the expression of appealing emotional contents, to which in turn the teachers of physical culture often add worldviews. Even disregarding their aesthetic impossibility, these events seek to recapture precisely what the mass ornament has happily left behind: the organic connection of nature with something that is regarded by overly modest people as soul or spirit. This means that the physical is endowed with meanings which do emanate from it and which may indeed be spiritual, but which do not show the slightest trace of reason. The mass ornament portrays mute nature without any superstructure; rhythmical gymnastics also confiscate even the mythological higher levels and hence strengthen nature all the more in its domination. This is just one example typical of many other hopeless attempts to reach the higher life from mass existence. It is true of the majority of them that they call to mind in a genuinely romantic way the forms and contents which have long since capitulated to the partially justified criticism of the capitalist rationale. They want to link humanity to nature in a much closer fashion than is the case today.

*Walter Stolzing was a famous opera singer of this period, who often had major roles in the operas of Richard Wagner.

12
Lyric Poetry and Society
Theodor W. Adorno

The announcement of a lecture on lyric poetry and society will make a good many of you uncomfortable. You will expect a sociological study of the sort which can take any subject it wants under consideration—just as fifty years ago we had psychologies, thirty years ago phenomenologies of every conceivable thing. You will fear that a discussion of conditions under which works of art have come into being, and their subsequent effects, must impertinently preempt the place belonging to the experience of those works as such; that sociological orderings and relatings will suppress all insight into the truth or falsity of the objects themselves. You will suspect an intellectual of being likely to commit the error Hegel ascribed to the "formal directorate" [*formellen Vorstand*]: that while scanning the whole he will merely stand above the particular existence of which he speaks—that is, he will not see it but merely label it. Such a method becomes most distressing when applied to lyric poetry. The tenderest, most fragile forms must be touched by, even brought together with, precisely that social bustle from which the ideals of our traditional conception of poetry have sought to protect them. A sphere of expression whose very essence lies in defying the power of social organization[1]—either by refusing to see it, or by overcoming it through the pathos of distance, as in Baudelaire or Nietzsche—must be arrogantly made by the sociologist into the opposite of that which it knows itself to be. Can anyone but a philistine, you will ask, talk about lyric poetry and society?

Clearly this suspicion can only be obviated when lyric works are not misused as objects for the demonstration of social theses, when, instead, their relation to social matters exposes something of their essential quality,

Translated by Bruce Mayo

something of the reason for their poetic worth. Such a relation must not lead us away from the works, it must lead us more deeply into them. This is really to be expected, however, as a moment's reflection will show: for the meaning of a poem is not merely the expression of individual experiences and stirrings of emotion. Rather, these become artistic only when, precisely because of their defined aesthetic form, they participate in the generality of things. Of course, what a lyric poem expresses is not necessarily what everyone experiences. Its generality is not a *volonté de tous,* not a generality which arises through an ability to communicate just those things which others are not able to express. Rather, the descent into individuality raises the lyric poem to the realm of the general by virtue of its bringing to light things undistorted, ungrasped, things not yet subsumed—and thus the poem anticipates, in an abstract way, a condition in which no mere generalities (i.e., extreme particularities) can bind and chain that which is human. From a condition of unrestrained individuation, the lyric work strives for, awaits the realm of the general. The peculiar danger of the lyric, however, is that its own principle of individuation never guarantees the creation of compelling authenticity. It is powerless to prevent itself from remaining stuck in the accidentals of naked, isolated existence. The generality of the lyric poem's content is, nevertheless, essentially social in nature. Only he understands what the poem says who perceives in its solitude the voice of humanity; indeed, the loneliness of the lyric expression itself is latent in our individualistic and, ultimately, atomistic society—just as, by contrast, its general binding validity derives from the denseness of its individuation. For this reason the thinking through of a work of art justly requires a concrete inquiry into social content; no proper effort at understanding can satisfy itself with vague feelings of universality and inclusiveness. Such a precisely specifying cast of thought is not at odds with art and does not add merely external commentary—it is in fact required by every linguistic creation. A poem's indigenous material, its patterns and ideas, cannot be exhausted through mere static contemplation. In order to be contemplated aesthetically, they ask to be thought through, and a thought once set into motion by a poem cannot be cut off at the poem's behest.

Nevertheless, such thoughts—which amount to the social interpretation of lyric poetry, as indeed of all art works—cannot lead directly to the so-called social viewpoint or to the social interests represented by the work or held by its author. Their chief task is rather to discover how the entirety of a society, as a unity containing contradictions, appears in a work; in which respects the work remains true to its society, and in which it transcends that society. Such an interpretive procedure must be—as the philosophers would have it—*immanent.* Social ideas should not be brought to works from without but should, instead, be created out of the complete organized view of things present in the works themselves. The sentence in Goethe's *Maxims and Reflections* to the effect that you do not possess what you do not understand, applies not just to our aesthetic attitude toward works of art themselves, but to aesthetic theory as well: nothing but what is in the works, and belongs to their own particular forms, provides a legitimate ground for ascertaining what the content of the works—the things which have been raised into poetry—represents in a social way. This sort of judgment requires knowledge of a work from within, to be sure, and knowledge of the society without. But knowledge has compelling authority only when it rediscovers itself in pure and utter submission to the matter at hand. We must be especially wary of the present insufferable tendency to drag out at every slightest opportunity the concept of ideology. For ideology is untruth —false consciousness, a lie. It manifests itself in the failure of artworks, in their own intrinsic falsehood, and can be uncovered by criticism. To say, however, of great works of art, which fix real existence in determinate forms and thus lend its contradictions a purpose-carrying reconciliation[2]—to say of such works that they are ideological not only belies the truth which they contain: it falsifies the idea of ideology as well. Ideology, as a concept, must not be taken as meaning that all of art and philosophy amount to some particular persons' passing off some particular interests as general ones. The concept of ideology seeks rather to unmask false thought and at the same time to grasp its historical necessity. The greatness of works of art lies solely in their power to let those things be heard which ideology conceals. Whether intended or not, their success transcends false consciousness.

Let me return to your misgivings. You respond to lyric poetry as something set against society, something purely individual. You feel strongly that it should remain this way—that lyric expression, released from the heaviness of material things, should evoke images of a life free of the impositions of the everyday world, of usefulness, of the dumb drive for self-preservation. This demand, however, that of the untouched virgin word, is in itself social in nature. It implies a protest against a social condition which every individual experiences as hostile, distant, cold, and oppressive; and this social condition impresses itself on the poetic form in a negative way: the more heavily social conditions weigh, the more unrelentingly the poem resists, refusing to give in to any heteronomy, and constituting itself purely according to its own particular laws. Its detachment from naked existence becomes the measure of the world's falsity and meanness. Protesting against these conditions, the poem proclaims the dream of a world in which things would be different. The idiosyncrasy of poetic thought, opposing the overpowering force of material things, is a form of reaction against the reification of the world, against the rule of the wares of commerce over people which has been spreading since the beginning of the modern era—which, since the Industrial Revolution, has established itself as the ruling force in life. Even Rilke's "cult of things" belongs to this form of idiosyncrasy, as an attempt to bring the alien objects into subjectively pure expression and dissolve them there—to give their alienness metaphysical credit. The aesthetic weakness of this cult of things, the cryptic gesture, the mixing of religion and decorative handicraft, betrays at once the genuine power of reification that can no longer be painted over with a lyric aura, and can no longer be comprehended.

One only gives another turn to the meaning of such insight into the social nature of lyric poetry when one says that its essential character— as something immediate to us, practically second nature—is thoroughly modern. Landscape painting and its idea of "nature" have, in a similar way, developed independently only in modern times. I know that I exaggerate in saying this and that you could produce many counter-examples for me. The most compelling would be Sappho. Chinese, Japanese, Arabic poetry I leave alone, since I cannot read any of it in the original, and I suspect that translation forces it through a process of accommodation that makes adequate understanding impossible. But the ancient manifestations of what is familiar to us as the specifically lyric spirit are only isolated flashes— just as the backgrounds of older paintings sometimes suggest and anticipate the idea of landscape painting. They do not constitute its form. The great writers of early antiquity who, according to literary notions, must be counted among the lyric poets—Pindar, for one, and Alkaios, but the greater part of Walter von der Vogelweide, as well—are immensely distant from our dominant conceptions about the lyric. They lack the quality of intimacy, of non-materiality which we have justly or unjustly adopted as our criterion of lyric utterance, and only through arduous study can we overcome these conceptions.

Nevertheless, what we mean by lyric—before we stop to elaborate its meaning historically or use it to criticize the forces of individualism—has within it, in its "purest" form, the quality of a break or rupture. The subjective being that makes itself heard in lyric poetry is one which defines and expresses itself as something opposed to the collective and the realm of objectivity. While its expressive gesture is directed toward, it is not intimately at one with nature. It has, so to speak, lost nature and seeks to recreate it through personification and through descent into the subjective being itself. Only after a transformation into human form can nature regain anew that which man's rule over her has taken away. Even lyrical creations which are untouched by conventional, material existence, by the crude world of material objects, owe their high worth to the power the subjective being within them has, in overcoming its alienation, to evoke an image of the natural world. Their pure subjectivity, apparently flawless, without breaks and full of harmony, actually witnesses to the opposite, to a suffering caused by existence foreign to the subject, as much as it shows the subject's love toward that existence. Indeed, the harmony of such creations is nothing other than the mutual correspondence of such suffering and such love. Even the "Warte nur balde, Ruhest du auch"[3] has yet a gesture of consolation; its unfathomable beauty cannot be separated from that which it passes over in silence: the image of a world refusing peace. Solely because the tone of the poem sympathizes with this unstated image does it insist that there is peace nevertheless. One would almost want to take the line "Ach, ich bin des Treibens müde" from the companion poem of the same title as an aid to the interpretation of this *Wanderers Nachtlied*.[4] To be sure, the first poem's greatness moves us as it does because it does not speak of alienated or disturbing things—because no restlessness of objects stands opposed to the speaking subject within the poem; rather, the anxiety is felt as an after-trembling. A second sort of substitute immediacy and wholeness is promised: the human element, language itself, appears as if it were once again the creation, while everything beyond the bounds of the poem fades away in the echo of the soul. The excluded world becomes more than appearance, however; it rises to full truth because, through the spoken expression of benign weariness, a shadow of yearning lingers over its consolation, even the shadow of death. For the "Warte nur balde" all of life is transformed, in an enigmatic, sad smile, to the short moment before falling into sleep. The tone of peace attests that peace itself could not be achieved without the dream's shattering to pieces. The shadow has no power over the image of life returning to itself; but, as a final remembrance of its disfiguration it does lend the dream the ponderous depth which rises under its weightless song. Seeing restful nature, from which the last trace of human form has been erased, the speaking subject becomes aware of its own nothingness. Unnoticeably, silently, irony lightly touches the consolation of this poem: the seconds before the sublime happiness of sleep are the same as those which separate the shortness of life from death. After Goethe, this elevated irony then fell to spitefulness, but it was always bourgeois in character: the elevation of the freed subject always had as its shadow the debasement of the subject to a thing of the marketplace, to that which exists only for others—to the personality of which we ask, "Well now, just what are you?" Within its single moment, however, the "Nachtlied" has its authenticity; the background of disintegration rescues it from triviality, and at the same time the force of disintegration has, as yet, no power over the powerless force of the poem's consolation. It is commonly said that a perfect lyric must possess totality or universality, must comprehend the whole within its bounds, reveal infinitude in its finiteness. If this is to be more than a truism of that sort of aesthetics which subsumes everything under the concept of symbolism, then it signifies that in every lyric poem the historical relation of subject to object, of individual to society within the realm of subjective spirit thrown back on its own resources—this historical relation must have been precipitated in the poem. This precipitation will be more perfect, the more the poem eschews the relation of self to society as an explicit theme and the more it allows this relation to crystallize involuntarily from within the poem.

Now that I have made this formulation, you may reproach me with having so sublimated the relationship between poetry and society—out of fear of sociological crudity—that really nothing remains of the relationship. Precisely that which is not social in a poem should become its social aspect. You might well recall to me that caricature of Gustave Doré's which presents an arch-reactionary politician whose praise of the ancien régime rises to the cry: "And who, my dear sirs, do we have to thank for the Revolution of 1789 if not Louis XIV!" You could apply this to my view of poetry and society: namely, society plays the role of the executed king and poetry that of those who fought against him. Poetry, you would reply, however, may no more be explained in terms of society than the revolution may be construed to the credit of the monarchy which it overthrew—and without whose absurdities it might not have occurred at that time. Whether Doré's politician was really just the stupid, cynical propagandist, as the cartoonist has ridiculed him, is beside the point—or even whether there is more truth to the politician's unintended humor than is plain to common sense (Hegel's *Philosophy of History* would have much to contribute to this politician's vindication).

All the same, there is something wrong with the comparison. Lyric poetry is not to be deduced from society; its social content is precisely its spontaneity, which does not follow from the conditions of the moment. But philosophy (again that of Hegel) knows the speculative proposition that the individual is rendered through the general and vice versa. This can only mean here that resistance to social pressure is not something absolutely individual. Rather, through the individual and his spontaneity, objective historical forces rouse themselves within the poem, forces which are propelling a restricted and restricting social condition beyond itself to a more humane one. These forces, therefore, must belong to an all-embracing configuration and in no case merely to naked individuality, blindly opposing itself to society. Now, assuming that the lyric content has in fact—by virtue of its own subjectivity—such an objective content (and indeed, without this assumption we could hardly explain the simplest feature that makes lyric poetry possible as a genre, namely, its effect on people other than the poet himself speaking in his monologue)—then it has this objectivity only if its withdrawal into itself and away from the social surface is motivated by social forces over and beyond the head of its author. This is accomplished by means of language. The specific paradox belonging to the lyric poem—this subjective, personal element transforming itself into an objective one—is bound to that specific importance which poetry gives to linguistic *form,* an importance from which the primacy of language in all literature (prose forms as well) derives. For language itself has a double aspect. Through its configurations it submits to all possible stirrings of emotion, failing in so little that one might almost think it is language which first produces feeling. On the other hand, language remains the medium of concepts and ideas, and establishes our indispensable relation to generalities and hence to social reality. The most sublime lyric works, therefore, are those in which the subject, without a trace of his material being, intones in language until the voice of language itself is heard. The *subject's* forgetting himself, his abandoning himself to language as if devoting himself completely to an object—this and the direct intimacy and spontaneity of his *expression* are the same. Thus, language begets and joins both poetry and society in their innermost natures. Lyric poetry, therefore, shows itself most thoroughly integrated into society at those points where it does not repeat what society says— where it conveys no pronouncements—but rather where the speaking subject (who succeeds in his expression) comes to full accord with the language itself, i.e., with what language seeks by its own inner tendency.

On the other hand, language cannot be raised to the position of an absolute voice of existence, as some current ontological theories of linguistics would have it. The subject, whose personal expression (in contrast to the mere signification or reporting of objective content) is necessary if that level at which the voice of historical existence may be heard is to be reached—this subject is no mere trimming on the content of language; he is not external to that content. The moment of self-forgetting in which the subject submerges in language is not a sacrifice of himself to Being. It is not a moment of compulsion or of force, not even of force against the speaking subject, but rather a moment of reconciliation; language itself first speaks when it speaks not as something foreign to the subject but as his own voice. When the speaking subject, the "I," forgets himself completely, he is yet entirely present; language (as a sanctified abracadabra) would otherwise submit to the process of reification and disintegrate as it does in everyday speech.

This, however, brings us back to the actual relation between individual and society. Not only is the individual as such brought into being by society, not only are his thoughts and feelings social in nature as well: but looking at things from the other side, society exists only by virtue of its individuals, whose essence it embodies. If in the past the great philosophers professed the truth (rejected, to be sure, by our modern logical positivists) that subject and object are no rigid, isolated poles, but can be identified only within the process in which they interact, then lyric poetry is the experimental test of this philosophical proposition. In the lyric poem the subject negates both his naked, isolated opposition to society as well as his mere functioning within rationally organized society.[5]

But as organized society's ascendancy over the individual grows, the situation of lyric art becomes more precarious. The work of Baudelaire was the first to register this, in refusing to stop at the individual's suffering. Rather (an extreme consequence of European world-weariness), it went beyond the suffering of the individual and accused the entire modern epoch itself of being antilyrical, and by means of heroically stylized language, it hammered out of this accusation the sparks of genuine poetry. With Baudelaire there appears for the first time a note of despair, just delicately balanced on the point of its own paradoxes. As the contradiction of poetic to communicative language grew extreme, all lyric became a precarious and desperate game; not, as narrow-minded, philistine opinion would have it, because poetry had grown incomprehensible, but because— by means of the pure self-awareness of language as a created art-language, and through its effort to attain its own absolute objectivity, without regard for communicating a narrowed, merely historical, ideologically limited objectivity—it removed itself from the objective spirit, i.e., the living language, and replaced it with an antiquated one, a poetically created surrogate. The elevated, poeticizing, subjectively brutal aspect of subsequent weaker poetry is the price that had to be paid for the attempt to keep poetry objectively alive, undisfigured, untarnished. Its false glitter is a counterpart to the demythologized world from which it extricates itself.

Certainly all this requires some qualification if it is not to be misunderstood. It was my assertion that the lyric poem is always the subjective expression of a social antagonism, as well. Since, however, the objective world which produces poetry is in itself antagonistic, the essence of lyric poetry cannot be entirely explained as the expression of a subjectivity to which language lends objectivity. The lyric subject (the more adequately it presents *itself*, the more compellingly) does not merely embody the whole. Rather, it is set apart from the whole in that it owes its existence to special privilege: only the fewest individuals, given the pressures of the necessities of life, are ever allowed to grasp the general truth or shape of things in self-immersion—few, indeed, have been allowed simply to develop themselves as independent individuals, in control of the free expression of their own subjectivities. The others, however, those who not only stand as strangers before the ill-at-ease poet, as if they were only objects—indeed, they have in the most literal sense been reduced to objects, i.e., victims, of the historical process—these others have the same or greater right to grope for the sounds in which suffering and dream are wed. This inalienable right has asserted itself again and again, in ways however impure, deformed, fragmentary, intermittent—in the only ways possible for those who must bear burdens.

All individual lyric poetry is indeed grounded in a collective substratum. If poetry in fact invokes the whole, and not merely the part of luxury, refinement, and tenderness belonging to those who can afford to be tender, then the substantiality even of individual poems derives to a significant degree from their participation in this substratum; in all likelihood it is this substratum that first makes of language the medium in which the subject becomes more than just a subject. The regard which romanticism had for folksong is only the more striking example of this, certainly not the most compelling. For romanticism followed a program of transfusing the collective into the individual—and as a result the individual poem tended to indulge more in a technical illusion of generality than to possess such a generality, one arising out of the poem itself. In place of employing such transfusions, poets who scorn every borrowing from the communal language are often able to participate in the collective substratum because of their historical experience. I name Baudelaire, whose poetry gives a slap in the face to the *juste milieu* and even to every normal, middle-class feeling of social sympathy—who, in poems such as the *Petites vieilles* or the one on the generous-hearted servant girl in the *Tableaux parisiens,* was nevertheless truer to the masses, against whom he turned his tragic-arrogant mask, truer than all the poor-people's poetry.

Because the conception of lyric poetry which I made my starting point—the conception of individual expression—appears today to be shaken to the core by the crisis of the individual, the collective substratum of poetry is thrusting upwards at the most widely various points, first simply as a ferment of individual expression itself, then perhaps also as an anticipation of a condition that transcends naked individuality in a positive way. If the translations don't deceive us, then García Lorca—whom Franco's henchmen murdered, and whom no totalitarian regime could have tolerated—was the bearer of such force; and the name of Brecht suggests itself as that of a poet to whom integrity of expression was granted without his having had to pay the price of being esoteric. I hesitate to judge whether the poetic principle of individuation was in fact transformed into another higher principle here, or whether the cause lies in regression and weakening of the ego. In many cases contemporary poetry may owe its collective force to the linguistic and spiritual rudiments of a not yet completely atomized condition, one which is in every way prebourgeois—that of dialect poetry. Traditional lyric poetry, however, as the strictest aesthetic negation of modern middle-class values, has continued to be bound for just that reason to bourgeois society.

Since reflections about general principles are insufficient, I would like, with the aid of some poems, to make concrete the relation of the poet's subjectivity—which, of course, represents a far more general, collective subjectivity—to its antithetical social reality. The thematic elements (without which noverbal art can express itself, not even *poésie pure*) will need to be interpreted here just as much as the so-called formal elements. Attention must be given especially to the ways in which both interpenetrate, for only by means of such interpenetration does the lyric poem actually capture the historic moment. Incidentally, I would prefer not to take such poems as the one of Goethe, about which I made some remarks without offering analysis. I shall, rather, choose later poems which do not possess the sort of unqualified authenticity one finds in the *Nachtlied*. Undoubtedly, the poems I shall discuss do have something of the collective substratum in them, but I would direct your attention, above all, to ways in which various levels of society's inner contradictory relationships manifest themselves in the poet's speaking. I should repeat that neither the private person of the poet, his psychology, nor his so-called social viewpoint are to come into question here; what matters is the poem itself as a philosophical sundial of history.

First I wish to read to you "Auf einer Wanderung" ("On a Hike") by Mörike.

> In ein freundliches Städtchen tret'ich ein,
> In den Strassen liegt roter Abendschein,
> Aus einem offnenen Fenster eben,
> Ueber den reichsten Blumenflor
> Hinweg, hört man Goldglockentöne schweben,
> Und eine Stimme scheint ein Nachtigallenchor,
> Dass die Blüten beben,
> Dass die Lüfte leben,
> Dass in höherem Rot die Rosen leuchten vor.
>
> Lang' hielt ich staunend, lustbeklommen.
> Wie ich hinaus vors Tor gekommen,
> Ich weiss es wahrlich selber nicht,
> Ach hier, wie liegt die Welt so licht!
> Der Himmel wogt in purpurnem Gewühle,
> Rückwärts die Stadt in goldnem Rauch;
> Wie rauscht der Erlenbach, wie rauscht
> Im Grund die Mühle!
> Ich bin wie trunken, irrgeführt—
> O Muse, du hast mein Herz berührt
> Mit einem Liebeshauch![6]

An image promising that sort of joy which a traveler can still find on the right day in southern German villages, presents itself to the reader, but without the least compromise to the hackneyed idyll of village life, to half-timbered houses and quaint glass-rounded windows. The room evokes a feeling of warmth and coziness in narrow corners, and at the same time it remains a work of elevated style, not disfigured by feelings of mere comfort and *Gemütlichkeit*. It does not sentimentally praise narrow simplicity at the cost of a broader view, nor the bliss of ignorance. Simple story and language help, together, to unite skillfully the heaven of things felt close at hand with that of immense expanses. The story recognizes the village only as a momentary scene, not as a place to be visited at length. The depth of feeling resulting from delight at the girl's voice heard from the window, and the greatness of all nature as well, which hears the chorus—these appear only at a point beyond the confined scene, under the open, crimson sky with its swiftly moving clouds, where golden village and roaring stream fuse into a single ideal image. This image is aided linguistically by an imponderably delicate, hardly definable, ancient and ode-like quality. As if from a great distance, the free rhythms remind us of rhymeless Greek verses, perhaps even the sudden outbreak of pathos in the final line of the first verse, which is nevertheless evoked with the most discreet sort of word placement: "Dass in höherem Rot die Rosen leuchten vor" ("So that in heightened red the roses shine forth").[7]

Decisive is the single word *Muse* at the end. It is as if this word, one of the most abused of German classicism, shines forth for a last time in the light of the setting sun by being conferred on the genius loci, the inner spirit of the friendly village. As something about to disappear, it seems to have mastered all the power delight knows, a power which an invocation of the muse otherwise lacks when, helpless and odd, it is phrased in words of the modern idiom. The inspiration of the poem reveals itself in no other feature quite so perfectly as this: the choice of the most objectionable word at the critical moment, cautiously prepared by the latent Greek poetic gesture dissolves the urgent motion of the whole like a musical cadence. In the briefest of forms, the lyric succeeds in attaining what the German epic vainly sought, even in such conceptions as *Hermann und Dorothea*.[8]

The social significance of this success accords with the stage of historical experience which reveals itself in the poem. German classicism had undertaken in the name of universal humanity to eliminate the accidental elements from subjective feelings, elements which threaten feelings in a society whose interpersonal relationships are no longer direct, but mediated through the market. It strove for an "objectivizing" of the subject, such as Hegel sought in philosophy, and attempted to overcome and reconcile the contradictions of actual living in the ideal realm of spirit. The continuing existence of these contradictions in reality nevertheless had compromised a spiritual solution: compared to the senseless, competitive life of business interests, slaving to outdo one another, without any deeper purpose (what the artist manages to call "prosaic" life); compared to a world in which the fates of individual lives are determined by blind laws, *art*—whose form implies that it speaks for a fulfilled humanity—became a mere empty word. The concept of man envisioned by classicism therefore retreated into the realm of private isolated existence and its images; only here did it seem that the "human" could be preserved. Necessarily, the idea of humanity as something whole, complete, and self-determining was renounced by the middle classes, in politics as much as in aesthetics. The stubborn limiting of oneself to things which are close at hand (which itself obeys an external compulsion) made such ideals as comfort and *Gemütlichkeit* so suspect. Meaning itself became bound to the accidents of individual fortune and happiness; it acquired, or rather usurped, the dignity that it would otherwise attain only in conjunction with the happiness of the whole.

The social force in Mörike's genius, however, consists in the fact that he combined both experiences, that of classical elevated style and that of the romantic, private miniature—and that in doing so he perceived the boundaries of both possibilities with incomparable tact, and skillfully balanced them against each other. No expression of feeling rises beyond what can be attained at the moment. The often-cited organic quality of his work is probably nothing other than this historical-philosophical tact, possessed to such a degree by hardly any other German poet. The presumed pathological traits of Mörike, which psychologists are ready to explain for us, even the failure of the efforts of his later years, are the negative side of his extreme insight into the nature of what is possible. The poems of this hypochondriac pastor of Cleversulzbach, who is counted as one of our naive poets, are virtuoso pieces surpassed by no master of *l'art pour l'art*. The hollow and ideological qualities of the elevated style are as apparent to him as the studied dullness of the petite bourgeoisie—the blindness to all notions of totality characteristic of the Biedermeier period in which the greater part of his poetry appeared. He was inspired to create images which, for one last time, would betray themselves neither in their Biedermeier drapery nor in their homely table scenes, neither in their tones of virile confidence nor in their sloppy table manners. As if perched on a narrow ridge, there appears in him whatever persists of elevated style, echoing as a memory, together with the elements of an unmediated life, promising fulfillment at a time when historical developments had already condemned them. Both aspects of the vanishing era greet the poet on his hike, in their still lingering traces. He already experiences the paradox of lyric poetry in the arriving industrial age. As gently hovering and delicate as these, his first solutions, are the creations of the poets who followed him, even those who appear separated from him by a deep chasm—like Baudelaire, whose style Claudel described as a mixture of

Racine and contemporary journalism. In industrial society the lyric idea of a self-regenerating directness and an immediacy of life—to the extent that it does not merely invoke an impotent romantic past—becomes more and more a condition in which the possible stubbornly flashes its rays over lyric poetry's own impossibility.

The short poem of Stefan George, which I would now like to discuss briefly, appeared in a much later phase of this development. It is one of the famous songs from the *Seventh Ring,* a cycle of extremely compressed poems, poems which, despite their light rhythms, possess an over-heaviness of content, free of all the elements of Art Nouveau. The musical setting by the great composer Anton von Webern first brought this poem and its audacious boldness out of the horrible cultural conservatism of George's circle; with George, ideology and social content fell at widely separated extremes. The song is as follows:

Im windes-weben	Ein glanz entfacht—
War meine frage	Nun drängt der mai
Nur träumerei	Nun muss ich gar
Nur lächeln war	Um dein aug und haar
Was du gegeben	Alle tage
Aus nasser nacht	In sehnen leben.[9]

There is no doubt whatsoever of the poem's elevated style. The joy of things felt close at hand, which Mörike's much older poem still touches briefly, is forbidden here. It is banned by just that Nietzschean sense of "suffering distance" which George knew he was destined to carry on. Between Mörike and him lie only the repellent remains of the Romantics—the idyllic fragments have turned to decayed heart-warmers, hopelessly aged. While George's poetry—that of the splendidly individual—presupposes as a condition of its very possibility an individualistic, bourgeois society, and the individual who exists for himself alone, it nevertheless bans the commonly accepted forms, no less than the themes, of bourgeois poetry. Because this poetry, however, can speak from no other standpoint or configuration than precisely those bourgeois frames of mind which it rejects—not a priori, silently, but with express intention—because of this it is blocked, damned at the source: and so it feigns a feudal condition. This hides itself, socially, behind what is tritely called George's aristocratic stance. It is not the pose which angers the good burgher who cannot fondle these poems in his own accustomed way. Rather, however antisocial this pose appears, it is brought to fruition by the same social dialectic which denies the lyric writer his identification with the existing order of things and its repertoire of forms, while he remains sworn to this order in its every detail: he can speak from no other standpoint than that of a past society, stably ruling itself from within. From this society is taken the ideal of nobility which dictates the choice of every word, image, and sound in the poem; and its form—in some hardly specifiable manner conveyed, as it were, into the linguistic configuration—is medieval. In this sense the poem, like all of George, is in fact neoromantic. It is not, however, real objects, not sounds which are called up, but a buried condition of the soul. The latent force of the ideal, artistically compelled into being, the absence of all crude archaisms, raises the song above the despondent story (which it, nonetheless, offers): it can hardly be mistaken for the cheap decorative imitations of Minnesang and medieval legend, nor for a Sunday-supplement poem of the modern world; its stylization saves it from conformism. There is as little space for the organic reconciliation of conflicts in the poem as George's era granted for the smoothing over of a real one; they are brought under control only by selection, by elimination of the unmanageable.

Wherever "near" things, i.e., things belonging to concrete, immediate experience, are still admitted in George's lyric poetry, they are allowed only at the price of being mythologized. Nothing is allowed to remain as it is. Thus, in one of the landscapes of the *Seventh Ring,* the child who picks berries is transformed into a fairy-tale child, wordlessly, as if with a magic wand, in an act of magic violence. The harmony of the song is wrung from an extreme of dissonance; it rests on what Valéry called *refus,* a stern self-denial of every means by which the convention of lyric poetry pretends to capture the aura of objects. The method retains only the models, the mere formal ideas and schemata of the lyric itself—in discarding every chance element, these forms speak once again, tense with expression. In the Germany of Kaiser Wilhelm the elevated poetic style is allowed to appeal to no tradition, least of all the classical. Elevated style is attained not by pretending to rhetorical figures and rhythms, but by ascetically omitting whatever would lessen the distance from the tainted language of commerce. In order that the subject may truly resist the lonely process of reification, he may not even attempt anymore to retreat to himself—to his private property. He is frightened by the traces of an individualism which has meanwhile sold itself to the literary supplements of the marketplace. The poet must, rather, by denying himself, step out of himself. He must, so to speak, make of himself a vessel for the ideal of a pure language. The great poems of George are dedicated to the preservation of such language. Educated in the Romance languages, but especially in that reduction of lyric poetry to its simplest elements which Verlaine used to create an instrument for the most finely differentiated expression, the ear of George, of this follower of Mallarmé, hears its own language as if it were a foreign tongue. He overcomes his alienation from German by raising it to the alienation of a language which is not spoken any more but imagined, and in whose potential he dimly perceives what might be composed. But his applications of this insight did not quite work out. The four lines "Nun muss ich gar / Um dein aug und harr / Alle tage / In sehnen leben" ("Now must I [gar] / For your eye and hair / Every day / In longing live"), which I count among the most irresistible in German poetry, are like a quotation, but not from another poet. They seem to be, rather, from some corpus neglected by the language, irretrievably lost. The Minnesänger could have created such lines if they, if a tradition—one would almost say, if the German language itself—had succeeded. It was in such a spirit that Borchardt wanted to translate Dante.

The word *gar* has grated on subtle ears; it is probably used in place of *ganz und gar* ["utterly" or "completely," a relatively fixed expression] and, to some extent, on account of the rhyme. One may easily concede that in the way the word has been shoved into the verse, it has no proper meaning at all. But great works of art are those which succeed precisely in the most doubtful places: as, for example, the most sublime musical works are not entirely subsumed by their formal schemes, but radiate beyond them with a few superfluous notes or measures. So it is with this *gar*, a "sediment of the absurd" in Goethe's words, with which language flees the subjective intention which called up the word. Probably it is this word in fact which establishes the rank of the poem, acting with the force of the déjà vu: through it, its linguistic melody reaches out beyond mere signifying. In the age of the decline of language, George grasps in it the idea which the course of history denied language, and constructs lines which sound as if they did come from him but had been present from the very dawn of ages and would always be as they are. Their quixotic qualities, however, the impossibility of such poetic restoration-work, the dangers of mere handicraft, contribute to the content of the poem; the chimerical longing of language for the impossible is made into an expression of the speaker's insatiable erotic longing; he frees himself from himself, relieves himself, in another.

A transformation of such tremendously exaggerated individuality to self-annihilation (and what is the Maximilian-cult of the late George[10] if not a renunciation of individuality desperately trying to interpret itself in a positive way?) was needed to prepare that phantasmagoria for which the German language had vainly grouped in its greatest masters—in folksong. Only by means of a differentiation—which expanded to such a degree that it could no longer endure its own fragmentation, its extreme spread of differences; could endure nothing which failed to show the whole free from the disgrace of individuation, in its particularities—only by means of this extreme differentiation could the lyric Word do the bidding of language's deepest being and oppose its enforced service in the realm of economically organized purposes and goals.[11] And with that the thought of a free humanity is served, even if George's school masked this thought behind a base cult of elevation.[12] George has his truth in his poetry's breaking through the walls of individuality, in its perfection of the particular, in its sensitivity arrayed against the banal as much as, in the end, against the exquisitely choice. If its expression concentrated itself in the individual, completely saturating him with substance and experience garnered from its own loneliness, then precisely this speech becomes the voice of men between whom the barriers have fallen.

Notes

1. "Die Macht der Vergesellschaftung." Adorno implies specifically the forces organizing, rationalizing, "socializing" the structure of society. *Vergesellschaften* in its sociological sense refers to the transition from the organically human communities (*Gemeinschaften*) of earlier historical periods to the rational, purpose-oriented, impersonal *Gesellschaft* characteristic of modern industrial societies.

2. Works of art "die an Gestaltung und allein dadurch an tendenzieller Versöhnung tragender Widersprüche des realen Daseins ihr Wesen haben." This sentence, like many others, is but the tip of an iceberg. I understand it as follows: The artist is forced by the nature of art to render the fluid, evolving world of his experience in static, fixed forms; to do this, he must find common terms in the contradictions of the world which presents itself to him, so that its disparate and contradictory elements can be represented in a single, unified whole. Any discovery of unity in contradictions is necessarily the realization of their human, historical purpose or "Tendenz" (tenor, tendency), since even the simplest acts of perception, such as the recognition of a face in a jumble of lines, require that we impose or discover the human significance in what is otherwise only a confusion of data. And the "timelessness" which we commonly recognize as a quality of great works of art is nothing other than such a discovery of the deeper purpose latent in the historical moment itself to which the work points and out of which it arises.

3. These are the last two lines of a Goethe poem so well known to German readers that it would be superfluous for Adorno to mention the title; in Longfellow's translation (which cannot convey the auditory qualities of the poem) it reads:

    > O'er all the hill-tops
    > Is quiet now,
    > In all the tree-tops
    > Hearest thou
    > Hardly a breath;
    > The birds are asleep in the trees:
    > Wait; soon like these
    > Thou too shalt rest.

4. The other "Wanderer's Night-Song," again in Longfellow's translation:

    > Thou that from the heavens art
    > Every pain and sorrow stillest
    > And the doubly wretched heart
    > Doubly with refreshment fillest,
    > I am wary with contending!
    > Why this rapture and unrest?
    > Peace descending
    > Come, ah, come into my breast!

5. "Vergesellschafteten Gesellschaft." See note 1.

    > I enter a village through the ancient tower,
    > Friendly streets glow in the red evening hour,

In an open window, now, and over
Full beds of flowers ever higher
Golden bell-sounds sweetly hover,
And a single voice seems a nightingale choir:
That the flowers sway,
That breezes play,
And the roses' red to higher hue aspires.

Long stood I joyous, stupefied.
How I left the gate, found the way
Beyond the town, I cannot say;
But here—how bright the world lies!
Above, bright purple billows flow,
Behind, the vaporous town in golden light;
How roars the rushing stream, how roars the mill below!
I reel in bliss, confused, misled—
O Muse! Throughout my heart has spread
A whisper of thy love.

7. Of course, no translation can hope to convey the qualities Adorno refers to here. The preceding two lines of the German poem, one might observe, establish momentarily a somewhat confining, though not strict, iambic diameter ("Dass" suggest a trimeter), which then expands in a "sudden outbreak of pathos" into a vaguely iambic pentameter. Stressing "Dass," one can also read this last line as a sextameter, which subtly echoes the sextameters one can hear in lines 5 and 6.

8. An epic by Goethe depicting events in the life of a rising tavernkeeper's family, in the context of simple German village society, composed in Homeric verse.

9. In weaving winds   A glimmer kindled—
My asking seemed   Now presses May
Merely dreamed   Now must I e'er
What you gave   For your eye and hair
Was merely smiled   Endless days
In glistening night   In longing live.

10. George met the 15-year-old Maximilian Kronberger in Munich in 1902; when the handsome and talented boy died in 1904, George wrote *Maximilian, ein Gedenkbuch* to celebrate his memory. In George's later poetry the youth is raised to a prophet of a rebirth of the Greek spirit.

11. "Economically organized" is, of course, a potentially misleading addition. I mean simply to remind the reader here that the purposes and goals against which the poet's language speaks are not *merely* those which have become fixed in structures of the language he uses, but are indirectly the limited, utilitarian purposes of the social and economic organization in which the language is embedded. The next sentence asserts this relationship on the deeper level of the poem's "timelessness": the true, unerring voice of Language-in-Itself.("das An-sich-Sein der Sprache") is a product—and producer—of the final, unchanging goals, i.e., the *telos* of human history (or history humanely understood).

12. George, like Rilke, lived an austere and "pure" life, and the followers he gathered around him insisted on the corresponding other-worldly purity of the poetic tradition he tried, unsuccessfully, to found.

13

Surrealism: The Last Snapshot of the European Intelligentsia

Walter Benjamin

Intellectual currents can generate a sufficient head of water for the critic to install his power station on them. The necessary gradient, in the case of Surrealism, is produced by the difference in intellectual level between France and Germany. What sprang up in 1919 in France in a small circle of literati—we shall give the most important names at once: André Breton, Louis Aragon, Philippe Soupault, Robert Desnos, Paul Eluard—may have been a meager stream, fed on the damp boredom of postwar Europe and the last trickle of French decadence. The know-alls who even today have not advanced beyond the "authentic origins" of the movement, and even now have nothing to say about it except that yet another clique of literati is here mystifying the honorable public, are a little like a gathering of experts at a spring who, after lengthy deliberation, arrive at the conviction that this paltry stream will never drive turbines.

The German observer is not standing at the head of the stream. That is his opportunity. He is in the valley. He can gauge the energies of the movement. As a German he is long acquainted with the crisis of the intelligentsia, or, more precisely, with that of the humanistic concept of freedom; and he knows how frantic is the determination that has awakened in the movement to go beyond the stage of eternal discussion and, at any price, to reach a decision; he has had direct experience of its highly exposed position between an anarchistic *fronde* and a revolutionary discipline, and so has no excuse for taking the movement for the "artistic," "poetic" one it superficially appears to be. If it was such at the outset, it was, however, precisely at the outset that Breton declared his intention of breaking with a praxis that presents the public with the literary precipitate of a certain

Translated by Edmund Jephcott

form of existence while withholding that existence itself. Stated more briefly and dialectically, this means that the sphere of poetry was here explored from within by a closely knit circle of people pushing the "poetic life" to the utmost limits of possibility. And they can be taken at their word when they assert that Rimbaud's *Saison en enfer* no longer had any secrets for them. For this book is indeed the first document of the movement (in recent times; earlier precursors will be discussed later). Can the point at issue be more definitively and incisively presented than by Rimbaud himself in his personal copy of the book? In the margin, beside the passage "on the silk of the seas and the arctic flowers," he later wrote: "There's no such thing."

In just how inconspicuous and peripheral a substance the dialectical kernel that later grew into Surrealism was originally embedded, was shown by Aragon in 1924—at a time when its development could not yet be foreseen—in his *Vague de rêves*. Today it can be foreseen. For there is no doubt that the heroic phase, whose catalogue of heroes Aragon left us in that work, is over. There is always, in such movements, a moment when the original tension of the secret society must either explode in a matter-of-fact, profane struggle for power and domination, or decay as a public demonstration and be transformed. Surrealism is in this phase of transformation at present. But at the time when it broke over its founders as an inspiring dream wave, it seemed the most integral, conclusive, absolute of movements. Everything with which it came into contact was integrated. Life seemed worth living only where the threshold between waking and sleeping was worn away in everyone as by the steps of multitudinous images flooding back and fourth; language seemed itself only where sound and image, image and sound interpenetrated with automatic precision and such felicity that no chink was left for the penny-in-the-slot called "meaning." Image and language take precedence. Saint-Pol Roux, retiring to bed about daybreak, fixes a notice on his door: "Poet at work." Breton notes: "Quietly. I want to pass where no one yet has passed, quietly!— After you, dearest language." Language takes precedence.

Not only before meaning. Also before the self. In the world's structure, dream loosens individuality like a bad tooth. This loosening of the self by intoxication is, at the same time, precisely the fruitful, living experience that allowed these people to step outside the domain of intoxication. This is not the place to give an exact definition of Surrealist experience. But anyone who has perceived that the writings of this circle are not literature but something else—demonstrations, watchwords, documents, bluffs, forgeries if you will, but at any rate not literature—will also know, for the same reason, that the writings are concerned literally with experiences, not with theories and still less with phantasms. And these experiences are by no means limited to dreams, hours of hashish eating, or opium smoking.

It is a cardinal error to believe that, of "Surrealist experiences," we know only the religious ecstasies or the ecstasies of drugs. The opium of the people, Lenin called religion, and brought the two things closer together than the Surrealists could have liked. I shall refer later to the bitter, passionate revolt against Catholicism in which Rimbaud, Lautréamont, and Apollinaire brought Surrealism into the world. But the true, creative overcoming of religious illumination certainly does not lie in narcotics. It resides in a *profane illumination,* a materialistic, anthropological inspiration, to which hashish, opium, or whatever else can give an introductory lesson. (But a dangerous one; and the religious lesson is stricter.) This profane illumination did not always find the Surrealists equal to it, or to themselves, and the very writings that proclaim it most powerfully, Aragon's incomparable *Paysan de Paris* and Breton's *Nadja,* show very disturbing symptoms of deficiency. For example, there is in *Nadja* an excellent passage on the "delightful days spent looting Paris under tl.e sign of Sacco and Vanzetti"; Breton adds the assurance that in those days Boulevard Bonne-Nouvelle fulfilled the strategic promise of revolt that had always been implicit in its name. But Madame Sacco also appears, not the wife of Fuller's victim but a *voyante,* a fortuneteller who lives at 3 rue des Usines and tells Paul Eluard that he can expect no good from Nadja. Now, I concede that the breakneck career of Surrealism over rooftops, lightning conductors, gutters, verandas, weathercocks, stucco work—all ornaments are grist to the cat burglar's mill—may have taken it also into the humid backroom of spiritualism. But I am not pleased to hear it cautiously tapping on the windowpanes to inquire about its future. Who would not wish to see these adoptive children of revolution most rigorously severed from all the goings-on in the conventicles of down-at-heel dowagers, retired majors, and émigré profiteers?

In other respects Breton's book illustrates well a number of the basic characteristics of this "profane illumination." He calls *Nadja* "a book with a banging door." (In Moscow I lived in a hotel in which almost all the rooms were occupied by Tibetan lamas who had come to Moscow for a congress of Buddhist churches. I was struck by the number of doors in the corridors that were always left ajar. What had at first seemed accidental began to be disturbing. I found out that in these rooms lived members of a sect who had sworn never to occupy closed rooms. The shock I had then must be felt by the reader of *Nadja.*) To live in a glass house is a revolutionary virtue par excellence. It is also an intoxication, a moral exhibitionism, that we badly need. Discretion concerning one's own existence, once an aristocratic virtue, has become more and more an affair of petit-bourgeois parvenus. *Nadja* has achieved the true, creative synthesis between the art novel and the *roman-à-clef.*

Moreover, one need only take love seriously to recognize in it, too—

as *Nadja* also indicates—a "profane illumination." "At just that time" (i.e., when he knew Nadja), the author tells us, "I took a great interest in the epoch of Louis VII, because it was the time of the 'courts of love,' and I tried to picture with great intensity how people saw life then." We have from a recent author quite exact information on Provençal love poetry, which comes surprisingly close to the Surrealist conception of love. "All the poets of the 'new style,' " Erich Auerbach points out in his excellent *Dante: Poet of the Secular World,* "possess a mystical beloved, they all have approximately the same very curious experience of love; to them all Amor bestows or withholds gifts that resemble an illumination more than sensual pleasure; all are subject to a kind of secret bond that determines their inner and perhaps also their outer lives." The dialectics of intoxication are indeed curious. Is not perhaps all ecstasy in one world humiliating sobriety in that complementary to it? What is it that courtly *Minne* seeks—and it, not love, binds Breton to the telepathic girl—if not to make chastity, too, a transport? Into a world that borders not only on tombs of the Sacred Heart or altars to the Virgin, but also on the morning before a battle or after a victory.

The lady, in esoteric love, matters least. So, too, for Breton. He is closer to the things that Nadja is close to than to her. What are these things? Nothing could reveal more about Surrealism than their canon. Where shall I begin? He can boast an extraordinary discovery. He was the first to perceive the revolutionary energies that appear in the "outmoded," in the first iron constructions, the first factory buildings, the earliest photos, the objects that have begun to be extinct, grand pianos, the dresses of five years ago, fashionable restaurants when the vogue has begun to ebb from them. The relation of these things to revolution—no one can have a more exact concept of it than these authors. No one before these visionaries and augurs perceived how destitution—not only social but architectonic, the poverty of interiors, enslaved and enslaving objects—can be suddenly transformed into revolutionary nihilism. Leaving aside Aragon's *Passage de l'Opéra,* Breton and Nadja are the lovers who convert everything that we have experienced on mournful railway journeys (railways are beginning to age), on godforsaken Sunday afternoons in the proletarian quarters of the great cities, in the first glance through the rain-blurred window of a new apartment, into revolutionary experience, if not action. They bring the immense forces of "atmosphere" concealed in these things to the point of explosion. What form do you suppose a life would take that was determined at a decisive moment precisely by the street song last on everyone's lips?

The trick by which this world of things is mastered—it is more proper to speak of a trick than of a method—consists in the substitution of a political for a historical view of the past. "Open, graves, you, the dead of the picture galleries, corpses behind screens, in palaces, castles, and monasteries, here stands the fabulous keeper of keys holding a bunch of the keys to all times, who knows where to press the most artful lock and invites you to step into the midst of the world of today, to mingle with the bearers of burdens, the mechanics whom money ennobles, to make yourself at home in their automobiles, which are beautiful as armor from the age of chivalry, to take your places in the international sleeping cars, and to weld yourself to all the people who today are still proud of their privileges. But civilization will give them short shrift." This speech was attributed to Apollinaire by his friend Henri Hertz. Apollinaire originated this technique. In his volume of novellas, *L'Hérésiarque*, he used it with Machiavellian calculation to blow Catholicism (to which he inwardly clung) to smithereens.

At the center of this world of things stands the most dreamed-of of their objects, the city of Paris itself. But only revolt completely exposes its Surrealist face (deserted streets in which whistles and shots dictate the outcome). And no face is surrealistic in the same degree as the true face of a city. No picture by de Chirico or Max Ernst can match the sharp elevations of the city's inner strongholds, which one must overrun and occupy in order to master their fate and, in their fate, in the fate of their masses, one's own. Nadja is an exponent of these masses and of what inspires them to revolution: "The great living, sonorous unconsciousness that inspires my only convincing acts, in the sense that I always want to prove that it commands forever everything that is mine." Here, therefore, we find the catalogue of these fortifications, from Place Maubert, where as nowhere else dirt has retained all its symbolic power, to the "Théâtre Moderne," which I am inconsolable not to have known. But in Breton's description of the bar on the upper floor —"It is quite dark, with arbors like impenetrable tunnels—a drawing room on the bottom of a lake"— there is something that brings back to my memory that most uncomprehended room in the old Princess Café. It was the back room on the first floor, with couples in the blue light. We called it the "anatomy school"; it was the last restaurant designed for love. In such passages in Breton, photography intervenes in a very strange way. It makes the streets, gates, squares of the city into illustrations of a trashy novel, draws off the banal obviousness of this ancient architecture to inject it with the most pristine intensity toward the events described, to which, as in old chambermaids' books, word-for-word quotations with page numbers refer. And all the parts of Paris that appear here are places where what is between these people turns like a revolving door.

The Surrealists' Paris, too, is a "little universe." That is to say, in the larger one, the cosmos, things look no different. There, too, are crossroads where ghostly signals flash from the traffic, and inconceivable analogies and connections between events are the order of the day. It is the region from which the lyric poetry of Surrealism reports. And this must be noted if only to counter the obligatory misunderstanding of *l'art pour l'art*. For art's sake was scarcely ever to be taken literally; it was almost always a flag under which sailed a cargo that could not be declared because it still lacked a name. This is the moment to embark on a work that would illuminate as has no other the crisis of the arts that we are witnessing: a history of esoteric poetry. Nor is it by any means fortuitous that no such work yet exists. For written as it demands to be written—that is, not as a collection to which particular "specialists" all contribute "what is most worth knowing" from their fields, but as the deeply grounded composition of an individual who, from inner compulsion, portrays less a historical evolution than a constantly renewed, primal upsurge of esoteric poetry— written in such a way it would be one of those scholarly confessions that can be counted in every century. The last page would have to show an X-ray picture of Surrealism. Breton indicates in his *Introduction au discours sur le peu de réalité* how the philosophical realism of the Middle Ages was the basis of poetic experience. This realism, however—that is, the belief in a real, separate existence of concepts whether outside or inside things—has always very quickly crossed over from the logical realm of ideas to the magical realm of words. And it is as magical experiments with words, not as artistic dabbling, that we must understand the passionate phonetic and graphical transformational games that have run through the whole literature of the avant-garde for the past fifteen years, whether it is called Futurism, Dadaism, or Surrealism. How slogans, magic formulas, and concepts are here intermingled is shown by the following words of Apollinaire's from his last manifesto, *L'Esprit nouveau et les poètes*. He says, in 1918: "For the speed and simplicity with which we have all become used to referring by a single word to such complex entities as a crowd, a nation, the universe, there is no modern equivalent in literature. But today's writers fill this gap; their synthetic works create new realities, the plastic manifestations of which are just as complex as those referred to by the words standing for collectives." If, however, Apollinaire and Breton advance even more energetically in the same direction and complete the linkage of Surrealism to the outside world with the declaration "The conquests of science rest far more on a surrealistic than on a logical thinking"—if, in other words, they make mystification, the culmination of which Breton sees in poetry (which is defensible), the foundation of scientific and technical development, too— then such integration is too impetuous. It is very instructive to compare the movement's over-precipitous embrace of the uncomprehended miracle of machines—"The old fables have for the most part been realized; now it is the turn of poets to create new ones that the inventors on their side can than again make real" (Apollinaire)—to compare these overheated fantasies with the well-ventilated utopias of a Scheerbart.

"The thought of all human activity makes me laugh." This utterance of Aragon's shows very clearly the path Surrealism had to follow from its origins to its politicization. In his excellent essay "La révolution et les intellectuels," Pierre Naville, who originally belonged to this group, rightly called this development dialectical. In the transformation of a highly contemplative attitude into revolutionary opposition, the hostility of the bourgeoisie toward every manifestation of radical intellectual freedom played a leading part. This hostility pushed Surrealism to the left. Political events, above all the war in Morocco, accelerated this development. With the manifesto "Intellectuals Against the Moroccan War," which appeared in *L'Humanité,* a fundamentally different platform was gained from that which was characterized by, for example, the famous scandal at the Saint-Pol Roux banquet. At that time, shortly after the war, when the Surrealists, who deemed the celebration for a poet they worshipped compromised by the presence of nationalistic elements, burst out with the cry "Long live Germany," they remained within the boundaries of scandal, toward which, as is known, the bourgeoisie is as thick-skinned as it is sensitive to all action. There is remarkable agreement between the ways in which, under such political auspices, Apollinaire and Aragon saw the future of the poet. The chapters "Persecution" and "Murder" in Apollinaire's *Poète assassiné* contain the famous description of a pogrom against poets. Publishing houses are stormed, books of poems thrown on the fire, poets lynched. And the same scenes are taking place at the same time all over the world. In Aragon, "Imagination," in anticipation of such horrors, calls its company to a last crusade.

To understand such prophecies, and to assess strategically the line arrived at by Surrealism, one must investigate the mode of thought widespread among the so-called well-meaning left-wing bourgeois intelligentsia. It manifests itself clearly enough in the present Russian orientation of these circles. We are not, of course, referring here to Béraud, who pioneered the lie about Russia, or to Fabre-Luce, who trots behind him like a devoted donkey, loaded with every kind of bourgeois ill-will. But how problematic is even the typical mediating book by Duhamel. How difficult to bear is the strained uprightness, the forced animation and sincerity of the Protestant method, dictated by embarrassment and linguistic ignorance, of placing things in some kind of symbolic illumination. How revealing his résumé: "The true, deeper revolution, which could in some sense transform the substance of the Slavonic soul itself, has not yet taken place." It is typical of these left-wing French intellectuals—exactly as it is of their Russian counterparts, too—that their positive function derives entirely from a feeling of obligation, not to the Revolution, but to traditional culture. Their collective achievement, as far as it is positive, approximates conservation. But politically and economically they must always be considered a potential source of sabotage.

Characteristic of this whole left-wing bourgeois position is its irremediable coupling of idealistic morality with political practice. Only in contrast to the helpless compromises of "sentiment" are certain central features of Surrealism, indeed of the Surrealist tradition, to be understood. Little has happened so far to promote this understanding. The seduction was too great to regard the satanism of Rimbaud and a Lautréamont as a pendant to art for art's sake in an inventory of snobbery. If, however, one resolves to open up this romantic dummy, one finds something usable inside. One finds the cult of evil as a political device, however romantic, to disinfect and isolate against all moralizing dilettantism. Convinced of this, and coming across the scenario of a horror play by Breton that centers about a violation of children, one might perhaps go back a few decades. Between 1865 and 1875 a number of great anarchists, without knowing of one another, worked on their infernal machines. And the astonishing thing is that independently of one another they set its clock at exactly the same hour, and forty years later in Western Europe the writings of Dostoyevsky, Rimbaud, and Lautréamont exploded at the same time. One might, to be more exact, select from Dostoyevsky's entire work on the one episode that was actually not published until about 1915, "Stavrogin's Confession" from *The Possessed*. This chapter, which touches very closely on the third canto of the *Chants de Maldoror,* contains a justification of evil in which certain motifs of Surrealism are more powerfully expressed than by any of its present spokesmen. For Stavrogin is a Surrealist *avant la lettre*. No one else understood, as he did, how naïve is the view of the philistines that goodness, for all the manly virtue of those who practice it, is God-inspired; whereas evil stems entirely from our spontaneity, and in it we are independent and self-sufficient beings. No one else saw inspiration, as he did, in even the most ignoble actions, and precisely in them. He considered vileness itself as something preformed, both in the course of the world and also in ourselves, to which we are disposed if not called, as the bourgeois idealist sees virtue. Dostoyevsky's God created not only heaven and earth and man and beast, but also baseness, vengeance, cruelty. And here, too, he gave the devil no opportunity to meddle in his handiwork. That is why all these vices have a pristine vitality in his work; they are perhaps not "splendid," but eternally new, "as on the first day," separated by an infinity from the clichés through which sin is perceived by the philistine.

The pitch of tension that enabled the poets under discussion to achieve at a distance their astonishing effects is documented quite scurrilously in the letter Isidore Ducasse addressed to his publisher on October 23, 1869, in an attempt to make his poetry look acceptable. He places himself in the line of descent from Mickiewicz, Milton, Southey, Alfred de Musset, Baudelaire, and says: "Of course, I somewhat swelled the note to bring something new into this literature that, after all, only sings of despair in order to depress the reader and thus make him long all the more intensely for goodness as a remedy. So that in the end one really sings only of goodness, only the method is more philosophical and less naïve than that of the old school, of which only Victor Hugo and a few others are still alive." But if Lautréamont's erratic book has any lineage at all, or, rather, can be assigned one, it is that of insurrection. Soupault's attempt, in his edition of the complete works in 1927, to write a political curriculum vitae for Isidore Ducasse was therefore a quite understandable and not unperceptive venture. Unfortunately, there is no documentation for it, and that adduced by Soupault rests on a confusion. On the other hand, and happily, a similar attempt in the case of Rimbaud was successful, and it is the achievement of Marcel Coulon to have defended the poet's true image against the Catholic usurpation by Claudel and Berrichon. Rimbaud is indeed a Catholic, but he is one, by his own account, in the most wretched part of himself, which he does not tire of denouncing and consigning to his own and everyone's hatred, his own and everyone's contempt: the part that forces him to confess that he does not understand revolt. But that is the concession of a communard dissatisfied with his own contribution who, by the time he turned his back on poetry, had long since—in his earliest work—taken leave of religion. "Hatred, to you I have entrusted my treasure," he writes in the *Saison en enfer*. This is another dictum around which a poetics of Surrealism might grow like a climbing plant, to sink its roots deeper than the theory of "surprised" creation originated by Apollinaire, to the depth of the insights of Poe.

Since Bakunin, Europe has lacked a radical concept of freedom. The Surrealists have one. They are the first to liquidate the sclerotic liberal-moral-humanistic ideal of freedom, because they are convinced that "freedom, which on this earth can only be bought with a thousand of the hardest sacrifices, must be enjoyed unrestrictedly in its fullness without any kind of pragmatic calculation, as long as its lasts." And this proves to them that "mankind's struggle for liberation in its simplest revolutionary form (which, however, is liberation in every respect), remains the only cause worth serving." But are they successful in welding this experience of freedom to the other revolutionary experience that we have to acknowledge because it has been ours, the constructive, dictatorial side of revolution? In short, have they bound revolt to revolution? How are we to imagine an existence oriented solely toward Boulevard Bonne-Nouvelle, in rooms by Le Corbusier and Oud?

To win the energies of intoxication for the revolution—this is the project about which Surrealism circles in all its books and enterprises. This it may call its most particular task. For them it is not enough that, as we know, an ecstatic component lives in every revolutionary act. This component is identical with the anarchic. But to place the accent exclusively on it would be to subordinate the methodical and disciplinary preparation for revolution entirely to a praxis oscillating between fitness exercises and celebration in advance. Added to this is an inadequate, undialectical conception of the nature of intoxication. The aesthetic of the painter, the poet, *en état de surprise,* of art as the reaction of one surprised, is enmeshed in a number of pernicious romantic prejudices. Any serious exploration of occult, surrealistic, phantasmagoric gifts and phenomena presupposes a dialectical intertwinement to which a romantic turn of mind is impervious. For histrionic or fanatical stress on the mysterious side of the mysterious takes us no further; we penetrate the mystery only to the degree that we recognize it in the everyday world, by virtue of a dialectical optic that perceives the everyday as impenetrable, the impenetrable as everyday. The most passionate investigation of telepathic phenomena, for example, will not teach us half as much about reading (which is an eminently telepathic process) as the profane illumination of reading teaches us about telepathic phenomena. And the most passionate investigation of the hashish trance will not teach us half as much about thinking (which is eminently narcotic) as the profane illumination of thinking teaches us about the hashish trance. The reader, the thinker, the loiterer, the *flâneur,* are types of illuminati just as much as the opium eater, the dreamer, the ecstatic. And more profane. Not to mention that most terrible drug—ourselves—which we take in solitude.

"To win the energies of intoxication for the revolution"—in other words, poetic politics? "We have tried that beverage. Anything, rather than that!" Well, it will interest you all the more how much an excursion into poetry clarifies things. For what is the program of the bourgeois parties? A bad poem on springtime, filled to bursting with metaphors. The socialist sees that "finer future of our children and grandchildren" in a condition in which all act "as if they were angels," and everyone has as much "as if he were rich," and everyone lives "as if he were free." Of angels, wealth, freedom, not a trace. These are mere images. And the stock imagery of these poets of the social-democratic associations? Their *gradus ad Parnassum?* Optimism. A very different air is breathed in the Naville essay that makes the "organization of pessimism" the call of the hour. In the name of his literary friends he delivers an ultimatum in face of which this unprincipled, dilettantish optimism must unfailingly show its true colors: where are the conditions for revolution? In the changing of attitudes or of external circumstances? That is the cardinal question that determines the relation of politics to morality and cannot be glossed over.

Surrealism has come ever closer to the communist answer. And that means pessimism all along the line. Absolutely. Mistrust in the fate of literature, mistrust in the fate of freedom, mistrust in the fate of European humanity, but three times mistrust in all reconciliation: between classes, between nations, between individuals. And unlimited trust only in I. G. Farben and the peaceful perfection of the air force. But what now, what next?

Here due weight must be given to the insight that in the *Traité du style*, Aragon's last book, required a distinction between metaphor and image, a happy insight into questions of style that needs extending. Extension: nowhere do these two—metaphor and image—collide so drastically and so irreconcilably as in politics. For to organize pessimism means nothing other than to expel moral metaphor from politics and to discover in political action a sphere reserved 100 percent for images. This image sphere, however, can no longer be measured out by contemplation. If it is the double task of the revolutionary intelligentsia to overthrow the intellectual predominance of the bourgeoisie and to make contact with the proletarian masses, the intelligentsia has failed almost entirely in the second part of this task because it can no longer be performed contemplatively. And yet this has hindered hardly anybody from approaching it again and again as if it could, and calling for proletarian poets, thinkers, and artists. To counter this, Trotsky had to point out—as early as *Literature and Revolution*—that such artists would only emerge from a victorious revolution. In reality it is far less a matter of making the artist of bourgeois origin into a master of "proletarian art" than of deploying him, even at the expense of his artistic activity, at important points in this sphere of imagery. Indeed, might not perhaps the interruption of his "artistic career" be an essential part of his new function?

The jokes he tells are the better for it. And he tells them better. For in the joke, too, in invective, in misunderstanding, in all cases where an action puts forth its own image and exists, absorbing and consuming it, where nearness looks with its own eyes, the long-sought image sphere is opened, the world of universal and integral actualities, where the "best room" is missing—the sphere, in a word, in which political materialism and physical nature share the inner man, the psyche, the individual, or whatever else we wish to throw to them, with dialectical justice, so that no limb remains unrent. Nevertheless— indeed, precisely after such dialectical annihilation—this will still be a sphere of images and, more concretely, of bodies. For it must in the end be admitted: metaphysical materialism, of the brand of Vogt and Bukharin, as is attested by the experience of the Surrealists, and earlier of Hebel, Georg Büchner, Nietzsche, and Rimbaud, cannot lead without rupture to anthropological materialism. There is a residue. The collective is a body, too. And the *physis* that is being organized for it in technology can, through all its political and factual reality, only be produced in that image sphere to which profane illumination initiates us. Only when in technology body and image so interpenetrate that all revolutionary tension becomes bodily collective innervation, and all the bodily innervations of the collective become revolutionary discharge, has reality transcended itself to the extent demanded by the *Communist Manifesto*. For the moment, only the Surrealists have understood its present commands. They exchange, to a man, the play of human features for the face of an alarm clock that in each minute rings for sixty seconds.

14

Historical Perspectives on Popular Culture

Leo Lowenthal

This chapter was written to be provocative, by one who has been engaged in empirical research for a considerable number of years and who has recently been charged with the administration of a large-scale research program. The author has taken it upon himself to act as the spokesman for an approach to popular culture which some will call "social theory" and others "obsolete, abstract criticism." Specifically, this chapter deals with aspects of the historical and theoretical frame of reference which seem to me to be a basic requirement for the study of mass communications and yet a blindspot in contemporary social science. I know of no better statement with which to highlight this blindspot in contemporary analyses of mass phenomena than De Tocqueville's remarks on the fact-finding obsession of the American mind a century ago:

The practice of Americans leads their minds to fixing the standard of their judgment in themselves alone. As they perceive that they succeed in resolving without assistance all the little difficulties which their practical life presents, they readily conclude that everything in the world may be explained, and that nothing in it transcends the limits of the understanding. Thus they fall to denying what they cannot comprehend; which leaves them but little faith for whatever is extraordinary and an almost insurmountable distaste for whatever is supernatural. As it is on their own testimony that they are accustomed to rely, they like to discern the object which engages their attention with extreme clearness; they therefore strip off as much as possible all that covers it; they rid themselves of whatever separates them from it, they remove whatever conceals it from sight, in order to view it · more closely and in the broad light of day. This disposition of mind soon leads them to condemn forms, which they regard as useless and inconvenient veils placed between them and the truth.[1]

My plea on behalf of these "veils" takes the form of five rather unsystematic groups of observations: (1) I shall indicate that the discussion of popular culture has a century-old tradition in modern history; (2) the historical locus of popular culture today will be fixed; (3) an attempt will be made to evaluate the overall approach of empirical research to the social function of contemporary popular culture; (4) the current philosophical, qualitative, nonresearch analysis of popular culture will be summarized briefly; and (5) some programmatic notes will be offered on the relationship between social criticism and social research.

Popular Culture—an Old Dilemma

In a survey recently undertaken of radio-listening habits in a foreign country, one of the respondents remarked:

> Radio is the companion of the lonely. It has made gigantic strides for almost half a century. Women in particular, especially those with small pensions and without other resources, who are completely isolated, are now in touch with the whole world thanks to the radio. They have undergone a regular transformation; they have found a kind of second youth. They are up-to-date and they know the stars of the headlines, of the theatre, the movies, the world of sports, etc. I have heard village people, discussing the merits of Mozart and Chopin, refer to what the radio had said.

In quite the opposite vein another woman revealed that she did not have a radio set in her home. Asked to explain why, she answered: "Because once there is a set in the house, one cannot resist. Everybody listens idiotically, the kids and the others too. When we stay with my friend G., my husband plays with the radio all the time." Her view was supported by a male respondent, who also refuses to permit a radio in the house. He believes that studies, conversation, and activity around the house provide enough interest, that the indiscriminate outpouring of music and talk over the radio lowers everyone's intellectual level.

These spontaneous remarks reveal two leitmotifs which have run continuously through the modern era: on the one hand, a positive attitude toward all instrumentalities for the socialization of the individual; on the other hand, a deep concern about the inner fate of the individual under the impact of the leveling powers of institutional and other organized forms of leisure activity. This basic dilemma concerning man's existence beyond the requirements of biological and material survival, the vital question of how to live out that stretch of life which is neither sleep nor work, can be said to have found its classic intellectual expression in a philosophical dialogue that never took place. Montaigne in the sixteenth century took stock of the situation of the individual after the breakdown of medieval culture. He was particularly struck by the phenomenon of loneliness in a world without faith, in which tremendous pressures were being exerted on everyone under the conditions of a postfeudal society. To escape destruction by these pressures, to avoid becoming lost in the horrors of isolation, Montaigne suggested distraction as a way out:

> Variety always solaces, dissolves, and scatters. If I cannot combat it, I run away from it; and in running away I double and change my direction. By changing place, occupation, company, I escape into the crowd of other thoughts and diversions, where it loses my trace, and leaves me safe.

> Is it reasonable that even the arts should take advantage of and profit by our natural stupidity and feebleness of mind? The barrister, says Rhetoric, in that farce they call pleading, will be moved by the sound of his own voice and his feigned emotion, and will suffer himself to be cozened by the passion he is acting. He will affect a real and substantial grief in this mummery he is playing, to transmit it to the jury who are still less concerned in the matter than he. Like those men who are hired at funerals to assist in the ceremonial of mourning, who sell their tears and grief by weight and measure; for, although they are stirred by borrowed emotions, it is certain that, through the habit of settling their countenance to suit the occasion, they are often quite carried away and affected with genuine melancholy.[2]

It is significant that quite a few basic concepts which we have been accustomed to regard as very modern emerge as early as the sixteenth century: escape, distraction, entertainment, and, last but not least, vicarious living.

The reply to Montaigne came a century later. Commercial culture had developed in the meantime, and the waning influence of religion, pre- or post-Reformation, had made itself felt much more strongly in the average way of life. Restlessness, the search for relief everywhere and anywhere, had become a major social phenomenon. It was then that Pascal spoke up against the complete surrender of man to self-destroying restlessness:

> Men are entrusted from infancy with the care of their honor, their property, their friends, and even with the property and the honor of their friends. They are overwhelmed with business, with the study of languages, and with physical exercise; and they are made to understand that they cannot be happy unless their health, their honor, their fortune and that of their good friends be in good condition, and that a single thing wanting will make them unhappy. Thus they are given cares and business which make them bustle about from break of day. —It is, you will exclaim, a strange way to make them happy! What more could be done to make them miserable? —Indeed! what could be done? We should only have to relieve them from all these

cares; for then they would see themselves: they would reflect on what they are, whence they came, whither they go, and thus we cannot employ and divert them too much. And this is why, after having given them so much business, we advise them, if they have some time for relaxation, to employ it in amusement, in play, and to be always fully occupied.

How hollow and full of ribaldry is the heart of Man![3]

Again and again he warned against what he called "diversion" as a way of life which could lead only to permanent unhappiness:

When I have occasionally set myself to consider the different distractions of men, the pains and perils to which they expose themselves at court or in war, whence arise so many quarrels, passions, bold and often bad ventures, etc., I have discovered that *all the unhappiness of men arises from one single fact, that they cannot stay quietly in their own chamber*.

They have a secret instinct which impels them to seek amusement and occupation abroad, and which arises from the sense of their constant unhappiness.[4]

Thus, the attitude toward leisure which, for Montaigne, guarantees survival means self-destruction to Pascal. And the controversy is still going on. Each side has its partisans on all intellectual levels in everyday life, as illustrated in the study on radio as well as in learned treatises. On one side there is the benevolent analyst of a mass medium who seems to say that while everything is not yet wonderful, it is getting better every day:

For in the old days the artists and writers and craftsmen were not writing at the behest of the people, but to please small powerful groups, the kings and lords and chieftains, who drew the talent of the time inward towards them and kept it circumscribed within the bounds of their castles and baronies. Much of the fine art of today remains alive only through a similar connection.

Yet, taking civilization as a whole, this ancient process is now in reverse. There is an outward movement. Pictures, entertainment, fun, are beginning to be seen as the rightful possession of all, and the comics join in and reflect this spreading democratization. And if the people's standards are at present lower than those which were set by workers around the seats of the mighty, the people's artists will have the satisfaction of knowing that they are identified with a vast and forward movement, which is giving to everyday folks their right to laugh and flourish under the sun.[5]

On the other hand, we find the nonconformist social critic who connects the loneliness of modern man with his interest in mass media as a setup of utter frustration:

The conditions of earning one's bread in this society create the lonely modern man.

Such conditions help explain the need, sometimes feverish, for an entertainment that so repetitively presents the same reveries, the same daydreams, the same childish fables of success and happiness. So much of the inner life of men is dried up that they tend to become filled with yearnings and to need the consolation of these reveries about people who are happy, healthy, and always successful.

Hence, parallel to the retrogression of consciousness in say, the Hollywood writer, there is a more widespread and also more pernicious retrogression of consciousness in the motion-picture audience. Social and economic conditions have established the basis for this; the motion picture further enforces it.[6]

The differences in the verbalization of the dilemma are obvious. The language of the sixteenth- and seventeenth-century philosophers is still deeply steeped in religious terminology; that of the modern writers in sociological terms; that of the nonprofessional radio listeners or nonlisteners in the ordinary words of everyday life. But beneath these differences in nomenclature the dilemma remains the same: perhaps it could be called a conflict between the psychological and the moral approaches to popular culture.

The Historical Locus of Popular Culture

This section of my discussion will be somewhat dogmatic in character, partly for the sake of brevity but also because it ought to be permissible to pause from time to time in our sociological routine and to speculate about the secular trend in which we, together with our objects of research, find ourselves.

The counterconcept to popular culture is art. Today artistic products are losing the character of spontaneity more and more and are being replaced by the phenomena of popular culture, which are nothing but a manipulated reproduction of reality as it is; and, in so doing, popular culture sanctions and glorifies whatever it finds worth echoing. Schopenhauer remarked that music is "the world once more." This philosophical aphorism throws light on the unbridgeable difference between art and popular culture: it is the difference between an increase in insight through a medium possessing self-sustaining means and mere repetition of given facts with the use of borrowed tools.

A superficial inventory of the contents and motivations in the products of the entertainment and publishing worlds in our Western civilization will include such themes as the nation, the family, religion, free enterprise, individual initiative; and in the Eastern orbit, higher production achievements, national cultures, the moral corruption of the West. The topical differences are not very decisive and, in any case, considerably smaller than the political differences which keep these two worlds apart. Saint-Simon, the great French pre-Marxian socialist philosopher, whose life extended from the *ancien régime* through the Revolution and the Napoleonic era into the days of the reactionary Bourbon restoration, once remarked that while he had experienced the most contradictory political systems, he realized that consistent, deeply rooted social tendencies which were completely impervious to political change made themselves felt in those decades. The very concept of society rests in this insight. Rigidly and consistently different as political systems are from one another today, there is also a complete inconsistency in the content of popular culture within a given political system—and popular culture is an element of society of the first order. The yardstick is expediency, within the total social situation, of course, and particularly the distribution of power.

Nietzsche, who may be called the discoverer and matchless critical analyst of modern popular culture, has formulated its relativism with respect to content:

Modern counterfeit practices in the arts: regarded as necessary—that is to say, as fully in keeping with the needs most proper to the modern soul.

Artists harangue the dark instincts of the dissatisfied, the ambitious, and the self-deceivers of a democratic age: the importance of poses. . . . The procedures of one era are transferred to the realm of another, the object of art is confounded with that of science, with that of the Church, or with that of the interests of the race (nationalism), or with that of philosophy—a man rings all bells at once, and awakens the vague suspicion that he is a god.

Artists flatter women, sufferers, and indignant folk. Narcotics and opiates are made to preponderate in art. The fancy of cultured people, and of readers of poetry and ancient history, is tickled.[7]

What Nietzsche expressed in the general terms of the philosopher of culture has its spokesmen today. In an analysis of cartoon films a modern writer has pointed to the criterion of social expediency in the selection of their materials:

It is just Disney's distinguishing characteristic that he is uncritical of what he reflects. He is quite artless. If the values by which the society lives are still serving, if the prevailing outlook is relatively brightfaced and aggressive, he will improvise from that—and give us Mickey Mouse. If the time is one of crisis, and these values will no longer serve but are in conflict and in question, if the prevailing state of mind is a deep bewilderment, he will improvise with equal lack of inhibition. His particular talent is that he does not embarrass himself. This makes his dreams sometimes monstrous. But it gives them a wide reference.[8]

It may be noted in passing that in the present postwar period disillusionment over the lack of definitive cultural and moral solutions has become prevalent. It finds expression in an artificial permeation of entertainment products with religion. In the average movie the pursuit of love almost invariably means the appearance of the clergyman. Nietzsche had already commented on the artificial respiration administered to religion in an era of decadence and nihilism. When he said, "God is dead," he meant that the frenzied activities of modern life produce popular culture in an attempt to fill a vacuum which cannot be filled. Nietzsche linked the precarious role of religion with the pressure of civilization and its neuroticizing influence on people:

> *In the Neighborhood of Insanity.* —The sum of sensations, knowledge and experiences, the whole burden of culture, therefore, has become so great that an overstraining of nerves and powers of thought is a common danger; indeed the cultivated classes of European countries are throughout neurotic, and almost every one of their great families is on the verge of insanity in one of their branches. True, health is now sought in every possible way; but in the main a diminution of that tension of feeling, of that oppressive burden of culture, is needful, which, even though it might be bought at a heavy sacrifice, would at least give us room for the great hope of a *new Renaissance.*[9]

With this quotation we return to the differences between popular culture and art, between spurious gratification and a genuine experience as a step to greater individual fulfillment (this is the meaning of Aristotle's catharsis). Art lives on the threshold of action. Men free themselves truly from the mythical relation to things by stepping back, so to speak, from that which they once worshiped and which they now discover as the Beautiful. To experience beauty is to be liberated from the overpowering domination of nature over men. In popular culture, men free themselves from mythical powers by discarding everything, even reverence for the Beautiful. They deny anything that transcends the given reality.[10] This is exactly what De Tocqueville meant, I think, in our opening quotation. From the realm of beauty man walks into the realm of entertainment, which is, in turn, integrated with the necessities of society and denies the right to individual fulfillment:

Under the absolute sway of one man the body was attacked in order to subdue the soul; but the soul escaped the blows which were directed against it and rose proudly superior. Such is not the course adopted by tyranny in democratic republics; there the body is left free, and the soul is enslaved. The master no longer says: "You shall think as I do or you shall die"; but he says: "You are free to think differently from me and to retain your life, your property, and all that you possess; but you are henceforth a stranger among your people. You may retain your civil rights, but they will be useless to you, for you will never be chosen by your fellow citizens if you solicit their votes; and they will affect to scorn you if you ask for their esteem. You will remain among men, but you will be deprived of the rights of mankind. Your fellow creatures will shun you like an impure being; and even those who believe in your innocence will abandon you, lest they should be shunned in their turn. Go in peace! I have given you your life, but it is an existence worse than death."[11]

Men no longer surrender to illusions.

Social Research and Popular Culture

The problem is whether, and to what extent, modern social science is equipped to deal with modern social culture. The instruments of research have been brought to a high degree of refinement. But is this enough? Empirical social science has become a kind of applied asceticism. It stands clear of any entanglements with foreign powers and thrives in an atmosphere of rigidly enforced neutrality. It refuses to enter the sphere of meaning. A study of television, for instance, will go to great lengths in analyzing data on the influence of television on family life, but it will leave to poets and dreamers the question of the actual human values of this new institution. Social research takes the phenomena of modern life, including the mass media, at face value. It rejects the task of placing them in a historical and moral context. In the beginning of modern era, social theory had theology as its model, but today the natural sciences have replaced theology. This change in models has far-reaching implications. Theology aims at salvation, natural science at manipulation; the one leads to heaven and hell, the other to technology and machinery. Social science is today defined as an analysis of painstakingly circumscribed, more or less artificially isolated social sectors. It imagines that such horizontal segments constitute its research laboratory, and it seems to forget that the only social research laboratories that are properly admissible are historical situations.

This has not always been the case. Popular culture, particularly as represented by the newspapers, has been a subject of discussion for about 150 years. Before the naturalistic phase of social science set in, the phenomena of popular culture were treated as a social and historical whole. This holds true for religious, philosophical, and political discussions from the time of Napoleon to Hitler. Our contemporary social science literature seems completely void of any knowledge of, or at least of any application of and reference to, the voluminous writings produced on both the left and the right wings of the political and cultural fronts in the nineteenth century. It seems to ignore Catholic social philosophy as well as socialist polemics, Nietzsche as well as the great, but completely unknown, Austrian critic Karl Kraus, who tried to validate the notion of the crisis of modern culture by a critique of popular culture. Kraus focused attention on the analysis of language. The common denominator of his essays is his thesis that it is in the hollowing-out of language that we can see the disintegration, and even the disappearance, of the concept and existence of the autonomous individual, of the personality in its classical sense.

Studies of the role of the press, even of such specialized problems as readership figures, would do well to go back to the nineteenth- and early twentieth-century analyses of the press in Germany. There they would find, in the different political and philosophical camps, illustrations of the fruitfulness of studying social phenomena in context—in the case of the press, the relationship of the modern newspaper to the history of the economic, social, and political emancipation of the middle classes. A study of the modern newspaper is meaningless, in the very exact sense of the word, if it is not aware of the historical framework, which is composed of both critical materials like those of Karl Kraus, writing at the end of an epoch, and optimistic attitudes like the following, from the work of the German publicist Joseph Goerres, at the beginning of the nineteenth century:

What everybody desires and wants shall be expressed in the newspapers; what is depressing and troubling everybody may not remain unexpressed; there must be somebody who is obliged to speak the truth, candid, without reservation, and unfettered. For under a good constitution the right of freedom of expression is not merely tolerated but is a basic requirement; the speaker shall be looked upon as a holy person until he forfeits his right by his own fault and lies. Those who work against such freedom leave themselves open to the charge that the consciousness of their own great faults weighs heavily upon them; those who act justly do not shun free speech—it can in the end lead only to "honor be to whom honor is due"; but those who are dependent on dirt and darkness certainly like secretiveness.[12]

This is not to say that the whole field of sociology has been given over to historical asceticism. Quite a number of leading scholars in social theory and social history have kept alive the conscience of a historical civilization.

It is worth our while to read again the following remarks by Robert E. Park:

> In fact, the reason we have newspapers at all, in the modern sense of the term, is because about one hundred years ago, in 1835 to be exact, a few newspaper publishers in New York City and in London discovered (1) that most human beings, if they could read at all, found it easier to read news than editorial opinion and (2) that the common man would rather be entertained than edified. This, in its day, had the character and importance of a real discovery. It was like the discovery, made late in Hollywood, that gentlemen prefer blonds. At any rate, it is to the consistent application of the principle involved that the modern newspaper owes not merely its present character but its survival as a species.[13]

His point of view finds confirmation in an excellent study in the history of mass culture by Louis B. Wright: "If it is desirable to trace the pedigree of the popular culture of modern America, it is possible to find most of its ideology implicit in the middle-class thought of Elizabethan England. The historian of American culture must look back to the Renaissance and read widely in the forgotten literature of tradesmen."[14]

One of the difficulties which have occasionally arisen in intellectual intercourse between people of American and European backgrounds is perhaps due to the antihistorical allergy of the former and the historical oversensitivity of the latter. I can illustrate this point by a very recent example. When I received the first two volumes of the outstanding work by Samuel A. Stouffer and his staff, *The American Soldier,* I was curious to learn how the authors would place their research within the context of the social theories about the soldier that have been developed from Plato on. To my amazement, I could find no historical reference beyond a solitary quotation from Tolstoy, who wrote somewhere in *War and Peace:* "In warfare the force of armies is a product of the mass multiplied by something else, an unknown x." The authors added the following comment: "Thus for perhaps the first time in military history it is possible to present statistical evidence relating to the factor x described in the quotation from Tolstoy's *War and Peace* at the beginning of this chapter."[15] They seem to have been fascinated by the mathematical symbolism of Tolstoy's sentence, but they successfully resisted the temptation to compare the social situation of armies in the time of Napoleon with modern conditions. In the face of such heroic restraint, it seems appropriate to quote the following flippant remark of a fellow sociologist: "In this respect I speak of the failure of modern psychology. I firmly believe that one can learn more about the *ordre du coeur* from La Rochefoucauld and Pascal (who was the author of this term) than from the most up-to-date textbook on psychology or ethics."[16]

It seems to me that the splendid isolationism of the social researcher is likely to reinforce a common suspicion, namely, that social research is, in the final analysis, nothing but market research, an instrument of expedient manipulation, a tool with which to prepare reluctant customers for enthusiastic spending. Only twenty years ago, social scientists were well aware of the dangers in the mass media, and they did not consider it beyond their duty to concern themselves with the negative, as well as the positive, potentialities of these mass media. In the pioneering article on "The Agencies of Communication" (1933), Malcolm M. Wiley and Stuart A. Rice wrote:

The effects produced may now be quite unpremeditated, although the machinery opens the way for mass impression in keeping with special ends, private or public. The individual, the figures show, increasingly utilizes these media and they inevitably modify his attitudes and behavior. What these modifications are to be depends entirely upon those who control the agencies. Greater possibilities for social manipulation, for ends that are selfish or socially desirable, have never existed. The major problem is to protect the interest and welfare of the individual citizen.[17]

Today, manipulation is taken for granted as an end of social science. A publisher can now dare to praise an outstanding sociological work with the following blurb on the jacket of the book:

For the first time on such a scale an attempt was made to direct human behavior on the basis of scientific evidence, and the results suggest the opening of a new epoch in social studies and in social management.

It is the editor's hope that the value to social science will prove to be as great as to the military, for whom the original research was undertaken.

The problems were Army problems, for the most part peculiar to wartime. But the implications are universal.[18]

Expediency and the lack of a historical or philosophical frame of reference make a sorry marriage of convenience.

Social Criticism of Popular Culture Today

No systematic body of theories is available. The situation has been characterized very aptly by Frederick Laws:

It will hardly be denied that the *condition of criticism today is chaotic,* especially when it is applied to the products of these immense distributing machines, *the new media*. Much reviewing is unselective in its enthusiasm and can with difficulty be distinguished from advertising copy. . . . *There is a lack of clearly expressed and generally recognized standards of value.* We believe that this confusion is partly due to a failure to realize or accept the fact that *the social framework in which works of art are produced and judged has changed fundamentally.* It is nonsense to suppose that the means of distribution or the size of social origin of the audience wholly determines the quality of art or entertainment, but it is stupid to pretend that they do not affect it.[19]

There is a literature on popular culture today which is thoroughly critical. I shall try to summarize the findings of this body of writings in a few brief generalizations. Some direct their critique against the product, but many turn it against the system on which the product depends. In special analyses, as in studies of a purely philosophical and sociological character, most authors concur in their final characterization of the products of popular culture.

The decline of the individual in the mechanized working processes of modern civilization brings about the emergence of mass culture, which replaces folk art or "high" art. A product of popular culture has none of the features of genuine art, but in all its media popular culture proves to have its own genuine characteristics: standardization, stereotypy, conservatism, mendacity, manipulated consumer goods.

There is an interdependence between what the public wants and what the powers of control enforce upon the public in order to remain in power. Most students are of the opinion that the habit of advertisement is the main motivating force in creating receptivity to popular culture and that the products themselves eventually take on the character of advertising. There is no consensus on the taste of the populace. Whereas some have confidence in the people's instinct for the good, the prevailing view seems to be that only the bad and the vulgar are the yardsticks of their aesthetic pleasure.

There is considerable agreement that all media are estranged from values and offer nothing but entertainment and distraction—that, ultimately, they expedite flight from an unbearable reality. Wherever revolutionary tendencies show a timid head, they are mitigated and cut short by a false fulfillment of wish-dreams, like wealth, adventure, passionate love, power, and sensationalism in general.

Prescriptions for improvement run the gamut from naïve proposals to offer aesthetically better merchandise, in order to create in the masses a taste for the valuable in life, in the theory that within the present set-up of social power there is no hope whatsoever for improvement and that better popular culture presupposes a better society.

Finally, there is considerable speculation about the relations between the product of mass culture and real life. The radio, the movies, the newspapers, and the bestsellers are, at the same time, models for the way of life of the masses and an expression of their actual way of life.

Theses on Critical Theory and Empirical Research

In this section, I shall present some of the theoretical motivations which underlie contemporary philosophical speculation about mass media. They comprise some of the ideas which the staff of the Institute of Social Research, under the leadership of Max Horkheimer, has tried to apply in a number of writings.[20]

1. The starting point is not market data. Empirical research, it is argued, is laboring under the false hypothesis that the consumers' choice is the decisive social phenomenon from which one should begin further analysis. We first ask: What are the functions of cultural communication within the total process of a society? Then we ask such specific questions as these: What passes the censorship of the socially powerful agencies? How are things produced under the dicta of formal and informal censorship?

2. We do not conceive such studies to be psychological in the narrow sense. They aim rather at finding out how the objective elements of a social whole are produced and reproduced in the mass media. Thus, we would not accept the taste of the masses as a basic category but would insist on finding out how taste is fed to the consumers as a specific outgrowth of the technological, political, and economic conditions and interests of the masters in the sphere of production. We would want to investigate what "likes" or "dislikes" really mean in social terms. While it is true, for example, that people behave as if there were a large free area of selection according to taste, and while they tend to vote fanatically for or against a specific presentation of popular culture, the question remains as to how such behavior is compatible with the actual elimination of free choice and the institutionalized repetition characteristic of all media. This is probably the theoretical area in which one would have to examine the replacement of taste—a concept of liberalism—by the quest for information.

3. We would question certain more or less tacit assumptions of empirical research, as, for example, the differentiation into "serious" and "nonserious" written, visual, or auditory communications. We would say that the problem of whether we are faced with serious or nonserious literature is two-dimensional. One would first have to furnish an aesthetic analysis of qualities and then investigate whether the aesthetic qualities are not subject to change under the conditions of mass reproduction. We would challenge the assumption that a higher increase in so-called "serious"

programs or products automatically means "progress" in educational and social responsibility, in the understanding of art, and so on. We would say that it is erroneous to assume that one cannot decide what is right and what is wrong in aesthetic matters. A good example of the establishment of aesthetic criteria will be found in the works of Benedetto Croce, who tries to show concretely that works of art have immanent laws which permit decision about their "validity." It is neither necessary nor sufficient to supplement a study of the reaction of respondents by a study of the intentions of art producers in order to find out the nature and quality of the artistic products, or vice versa.

4. We are disturbed by the acceptance at face value of such concepts as "standardization." We want to know what standardization means in industry, in behavior patterns, and in popular culture. We think that the specifically psychological and anthropological character of popular culture is a key to the interpretation of the function of standardization in modern man.

5. In connection with the latter point, we are particularly interested in the phenomenon of psychological regression. We wish to know whether the consumption of popular culture really presupposes a human being with preadult traits or whether modern man has a split personality: half mutilated child and half standardized adult. We want to know the mechanisms of interdependence between the pressures of professional life and the freedom from intellectual and aesthetic tension in which popular culture seems to indulge.

6. As for the problem of the stimulus and its nature, here the connection with European philosophical heritage is particularly noticeable. Our thinking has its roots in the concept of understanding [Verstehen] as it was established philosophically and historically by Dilthey and sociologically by Simmel. We are inclined to think that empirical research conceives the stimulus to be as devoid of content as a color stimulus in a psychological laboratory. We hold that the stimulus in popular culture is itself a historical phenomenon and that the relation between stimulus and response is preformed and prestructured by the historical and social fate of the stimulus as well as of the respondent.

Notes

1. Alexis de Tocqueville, *Democracy in America* (New York: Knopf, 1945), p. 4.

2. *The Essays of Montaigne,* trans. E. J. Trenchmann, (New York: Oxford University Press, 1935), II, p. 291ff.

3. Blaise Pascal, *Pensées* (London and New York: Dent, 1931), p. 44.

4. Ibid., pp. 39–42.

5. Coulton Waugh, *The Comics* (New York: Macmillan, 1947), p. 354.

6. James T. Farrell, *The League of Frightened Philistines* (New York: Vanguard Press, n.d.), pp. 176–77.

7. Friedrich Nietzsche, *The Will to Power,* in *Complete Works,* II (London, 1910), pp. 265–66.

8. Barbara Deming, "The Artlessness of Walt Disney," *Partisan Review* (Spring 1945): 226.

9. Friedrich Nietzsche, *Human, All-Too-Human: A Book for Free Spirits*, in *Complete Works*, VII, p. 227.

10. For a comprehensive theory on myth and art, see Max Horkheimer and Theodor W. Adorno, *Dialektik der Aufklärung* (Amsterdam: Querido Verlag, 1947), passim.

11. De Tocqueville, *Democracy in America*, p. 264.

12. Joseph Goerres, *Rheinischer Merker*, July 1 and 3, 1814.

13. Helen MacGill Hughes, introduction to *News and the Human Interest Story* (Chicago: University of Chicago Press, 1940), pp. xii–xiii.

14. *Middle-Class Culture in Elizabethan England* (Chapel Hill: University of North Carolina Press, 1935), pp. 659–69.

15. Samuel A. Stouffer et al., *The American Soldier: Adjustment during Army Life* (Princeton: Princeton University Press, 1949), p. 8.

16. J. P. Mayer, *Sociology of Film* (London: Faber & Faber, 1945), p. 273.

17. *Recent Social Trends in the United States*, I (New York and London: McGraw-Hill, 1933), p. 215.

18. Stouffer et al., *The American Soldier*, jacket of vols. I and II.

19. Introduction to *Made for Millions: A Critical Study of the New Media of Information and Entertainment* (London: Contact Publishers, 1947), p. xvii.

20. For example, Max Horkheimer, "Art and Mass Culture," *Studies in Philosophy and Social Science*, vol. IX (1941); T. W. Adorno, "On Popular Music," *Studies in Philosophy and Social Science*, vol. IX; Leo Lowenthal, "Biographies in Popular Magazines," *Radio Research, 1942–43*, ed. Paul F. Lazarsfeld and Frank Stanton (New York, 1944).

15

Perennial Fashion—Jazz

Theodor W. Adorno

For almost fifty years, since 1914 when the contagious enthusiasm for it broke out in America, jazz has maintained its place as a mass phenomenon. Its method, all declarations of propagandistic historians notwithstanding, has remained essentially unchanged; its prehistory dates back to certain songs from the first half of the nineteenth century, such as "Turkey in the Straw" and "Old Zip Coon." Jazz is music which fuses the most rudimentary melodic, harmonic, metric, and formal structure with the ostensibly disruptive principle of syncopation, yet without ever really disturbing the crude unity of the basic rhythm, the identically sustained meter, the quarter note. This is not to say that nothing has happened in jazz. The monochromatic piano has been forced to cede the dominant role it played during the ragtime period to small ensembles, generally winds. The wild antics of the first jazz bands from the South, New Orleans above all, and of those from Chicago, have been toned down with the growth of commercialization and the audience, and continued scholarly efforts to recover some of this original animation, whether called "swing" or "be-bop," inexorably succumb to commercial requirements and quickly lose their sting. The syncopation principle, which at first had to call attention to itself by exaggeration, has in the meantime become so self-evident that it no longer needs to accentuate the weak beats as was formally required. Anyone still using such accents today is derided as "corny," as out-of-date as 1927 evening dress. Contrariness has changed into second-degree "smoothness" and the jazz-form of reaction has become so entrenched that an entire generation of youth hears only syncopations without being aware of the original conflict between it and the basic meter. Yet none of this alters the fact that jazz has in its essence remained static, nor does it explain the resulting enigma that millions of people seem never to tire of

Translated by Samuel and Shierry Weber

its monotonous attraction. Winthrop Sargeant, internationally known today as the art editor of *Life* magazine, is responsible for the best, most reliable, and most sensible book on the subject; twenty-five years ago he wrote that jazz was in no way a new musical idiom but rather, "even in its most complex manifestations a very elementary matter of incessantly repeated formulae." This kind of unbiased observation seems possible only in America; in Europe, where jazz has not yet become an everyday phenomenon, there is the tendency, especially among those devotees who have adopted it as *Weltanschauung,* to regard it falsely as a breakthrough of original, untrammeled nature, as a triumph over the musty museum culture. However little doubt there can be regarding the African elements in jazz, it is no less certain that everything unruly in it was from the very beginning integrated into a strict scheme, that its rebellious gestures are accompanied by the tendency to blind obeisance, much like the sado-masochistic type described by analytic psychology, the person who chafes against the father figure while secretly admiring him, who seeks to emulate him and in turn derives enjoyment from the subordination he overtly detests. This propensity accelerates the standardization, commercialization, and rigidification of the medium. It is not as though scurrilous businessmen have corrupted the voice of nature by attacking it from without; jazz takes care of this all by itself. The abuse of jazz is not the external calamity in whose name the puristic defenders of "real," unadulterated jazz furiously protest; such misuse originates in jazz itself. The Negro spirituals, antecedents of the blues, were slave songs and as such combined the lament of unfreedom with its oppressed confirmation. Moreover, it is difficult to isolate the authentic Negro elements in jazz. The white *lumpen proletariat* also participated in its prehistory, during the period preceding its thrust into the spotlight of a society which seemed to be waiting for it and which had long been familiar with its impulses through the cakewalk and tap dancing.

It is precisely this paltry stock of procedures and characteristics, however, the rigorous exclusion of every unregimented impulse, which makes the durability of this "specialty"—one which accepts change only when forced to, and then generally only to suit the demands of advertising—so difficult to grasp. For the fact remains that jazz has established itself for a short eternity in the midst of a phase which is otherwise anything but static, and that it displays not the slightest inclination to relinquish any portion of its monopoly but instead only the tendency to adapt itself to the ear of the listener, no matter whether highly trained or undifferentiated. Yet for all of that it has not become any less fashionable. For almost fifty years the productions of jazz have remained as ephemeral as seasonal styles. Jazz is a form of manneristic interpretation. As with fashions, what is important is show, not the thing itself; instead of jazz itself being composed, "light" music, the most dismal product of the popular-song industry, is dressed up. Jazz fans—short for fanatics—sense this and therefore prefer to emphasize the music's improvisational features. But these are mere frills. Any precocious American teenager knows that the routine today scarcely leaves any room for improvisation, and that what appears as spontaneity is in fact carefully planned out in advance with machinelike precision. But even where there is real improvisation, in oppositional groups which perhaps even today still indulge in such things out of sheer pleasure, the sole material remains popular songs. Thus, the so-called improvisations are actually reduced to the more or less feeble rehashing of basic formulas in which the schema shines through at every moment. Even the improvisations conform largely to norms and recur constantly. The range of the permissible in jazz is as narrowly circum-scribed as in any particular cut of clothes. In view of the wealth of available possibilities for discovering and treating musical material, even in the sphere of entertainment if absolutely necessary, jazz has shown itself to be utterly impoverished. Its use of the existing musical techniques seems to be entirely arbitrary. The ban on changing the basic beat during the course of the music is itself sufficient to constrict composition to the point where what it demands is not aesthetic awareness of style but rather psychological regression. The limitations placed on meter, harmony, and form are not less stifling. Considered as a whole, the perennial sameness of jazz consists not in a basic organization of the material within which the imagination can roam freely and without inhibition, as within an articulate language, but rather in the utilization of certain well-defined tricks, formulas, and clichés to the exclusion of everything else. It is as though one were to cling convulsively to the "latest thing" and deny the image of a particular year by refusing to tear off the page of the calendar. Fashion enthrones itself as something lasting and thus sacrifices the dignity of fashion, its transience.

In order to understand how an entire sphere can be described by a few simple recipes as though nothing else existed, one must first free oneself of the clichés, "vitality" and "rhythm of the time," which are glorified by advertising, by its journalistic appendage, and, in the end, by the victims themselves. The fact is that what jazz has to offer rhythmically is extremely limited. The most striking traits in jazz were all independently produced, developed, and surpassed by serious music since Brahms. And it's "vital-ity" is difficult to take seriously in the face of an assembly-line procedure that is standardized down to its most minute deviations. The jazz ideolo-gists, especially in Europe, mistakenly regard the sum of psycho-techni-cally calculated and tested effects as the expression of an emotional state, the illusion of which jazz evokes in the listener; this attitude is rather like regarding those film stars, whose regular or sorrowful faces are modeled on portraits of famous persons, as being therefore of the same stature as Lucrezia Borgia or Lady Hamilton if, indeed, the latter were not already their own mannequins. What enthusiastically stunted innocence sees as the jungle is actually factory-made through and through, even when, on special occasions, spontaneity is publicized as a featured attraction. The paradoxical immortality of jazz has its roots in the economy. Competition on the culture market has proved the effectiveness of a number of techniques, including syncopation, semi-vocal, semi-instrumental sounds, gliding, impressionistic harmonies, and opulent instrumentation which suggests that "nothing is too good for us." These techniques are then sorted out and kaleidoscopically mixed into ever-new combinations without there taking place even the slightest interaction between the total scheme and the no less schematic details. All that remains is the results of the competition, itself not very "free," and the entire business is then touched up, in particular by the radio. The investments made in "name bands," whose fame is assured by scientifically engineered propaganda, and, even more important, the money used to promote musical bestseller programs like "The Hit Parade" by the firms who buy radio advertising time, make every divergence a risk. Standardization, moreover, means the strengthening of the lasting domination of the listening public and of their conditioned reflexes. They are expected to want only that to which they have become accustomed and to become enraged whenever their expectations are disappointed and fulfillment, which they regard as the customer's inalienable right, is denied. And even if there were attempts to introduce anything really different into light music, they would be doomed from the start by virtue of economic concentration.

The insurmountable character of a phenomenon which is inherently contingent and arbitrarily reflects something of the arbitrary nature of present social controls. The more totally the culture industry roots out all deviations, thus cutting off the medium from its intrinsic possibilities of development, the more the whole blaring dynamic business approaches a standstill. Just as no piece of jazz can, in a musical sense, be said to have a history, just as all its components can be moved about at will, just as no single measure follows from the logic of the musical progression—so the perennial fashion becomes the likeness of a planned, congealed society, not so different from the nightmare vision of Huxley's *Brave New World*. Whether what the ideology here expresses—or exposes—is the tendency of an over-accumulating society to regress to the stage of simple reproduction is for economists to decide. The fear that marked the late writings of a bitterly disappointed Thorstein Veblen, that the play of economic and social forces was coming to rest in a negative, historical state, a kind of higher-potency feudalism, may be highly unlikely, yet it remains the innermost desire of jazz. The image of the technical world possesses an ahistorical aspect that enables it to serve as a mythical mirage of eternity. Planned production seems to purge the life-process of all that is uncontrollable, unpredictable, incalculable in advance and thus to deprive it of what is genuinely new, without which history is hardly conceivable; in addition, the form of the standardized mass-produced article transforms the temporal sequence of objects into more of the same. The fact that a 1950 locomotive looks different from one made in 1850 leaves a paradoxical impression; it is for this reason that the most modern express trains are occasionally decorated with photographs of obsolete models. The surrealists, who have much in common with jazz, have appealed to this level of experience since Apollinaire: "Ici même les automobiles ont l'air d'être anciennes." Traces of this have been unconsciously assimilated by the perennial fashion; jazz, which knows what it is doing when it allies itself with technique, collaborates in the "technological veil" through its rigorously repetitive though objectless cultic ritual, and fosters the illusion that the twentieth century is ancient Egypt, full of slaves and endless dynasties. This remains illusion, however, for although the symbol of technology may be the uniformly revolving wheel, its intrinsic energies develop to an incalculable extent while remaining saddled by a society which is driven forward by its inner tensions, which persists in its irrationality and which grants men far more history than they wish. Timelessness is projected on technology by a world-order which knows that to change would be to collapse. The pseudo-eternity is belied, however, by the bad contingencies and inferiorities that have established themselves as universal principle. The men of the Thousand-Year Reichs of today look like criminals, and the perennial gesture of mass culture is that of the asocial person. The fact that of all the tricks available, syncopation should have been the one to achieve musical dictatorship over the masses recalls the usurpation that characterizes techniques, however rational they may be in themselves, when they are placed at the service of irrational totalitarian control. Mechanisms which in reality are part and parcel of the entire present-day ideology, of the culture industry, are left easily visible in jazz because in the absence of technical knowledge they cannot be as easily identified as, for example, in films. Yet even jazz takes certain precautions. Parallel to standardization is pseudo-individualization. The more strictly the listener is curbed, the less he is permitted to notice it. He is told that jazz is "consumer art," made especially for him. The particular effects with which jazz fills out its schema, syncopation above all, strive to create the appearance of being the outburst of caricature of untrammeled subjectivity—in effect, that of the listener—or perhaps the most subtle nuance dedicated to the greater glory of the audience. But the method becomes trapped in its own net. For while it must constantly promise its listeners something different, excite their attention and keep itself from becoming run-of-the-mill, it is not allowed to leave the beaten path; it must be always new and always the same. Hence, the deviations are just as standardized as the standards and in effect revoke themselves the instant they appear. Jazz, like everything else in the culture industry, gratifies desires only to frustrate them at the same time. However much jazz subjects, representing the music listener in general, may play the nonconformist, in truth they are less and less themselves. Individual features which do not conform to the norm are nevertheless shaped by it, and become marks of mutilation. Terrified, jazz fans identify with the society they dread for having made them what they are. This gives the jazz ritual its affirmative character, that of being accepted into a community of unfree equals. With this in mind, jazz can appeal directly to the mass of listeners in self-justification with a diabolically good conscience. Standard procedures which prevail unquestioned and which have been perfected over long periods of time produce standard reactions. Well-meaning educators, who believe that a change in programming would be enough to bring the violated and oppressed to desire something better, or at least something different, are much too credulous. Even when they do not greatly transcend the ideological realm of the culture industry, serious changes in program policy are angrily rejected in reality. The population is so accustomed to the drivel it gets that it cannot renounce it, even when it sees through it halfway. On the contrary, it feels itself impelled to intensify its enthusiasm in order to convince itself that its ignominy is its good fortune. Jazz sets up schemes of social behavior to which people must in any case conform. Jazz enables them to practice those forms of behavior, and they love it all the more for making the inescapable easier to bear. Jazz reproduces its own mass-basis, without thereby reducing the guilt of those who produce it. The eternity of fashion is a vicious circle.

Jazz fans, as has once again been emphatically shown by David Riesman, can be divided into two clearly distinguishable groups. In the inner circle sit the experts, or those who consider themselves such—for very often the most passionate devotees, those who flaunt the established terminology and differentiate jazz styles with ponderous pretention, are hardly able to give an account, in precise, technical musical concepts, of whatever it is that so moves them. Most of them consider themselves avant-gardistic, thus participating in a confusion that has become ubiquitous today. Among the symptoms of the disintegration of culture and education, not the least is the fact that the distinction between autonomous "high" and commercial "light" art, however questionable it may be, is neither critically reflected nor even noticed any more. And now that certain culturally defeatist intellectuals have pitted the latter against the former, the philistine champions of the culture industry can even take pride in the conviction that they are marching in the vanguard of the Zeitgeist. The organization of culture into "levels" such as the First, Second, and Third Programs, patterned after low, middle and highbrow, is reprehensible. But it cannot be overcome simply by the lowbrow sects declaring themselves to be highbrow. The legitimate discontent with culture provides a pretext but not the slightest justification for the glorification of a highly rationalized section of mass production, one which debases and betrays culture without at all transcending it, as the dawn of a new world sensibility or for confusing it with cubism, Eliot's poetry, and Joyce's prose. Regression is not origin, but origin is the ideology of regression. Anyone who allows the growing respectability of mass culture to seduce him into equating a popular song with modern art because of a few false notes squeaked by a clarinet; anyone who mistakes a triad studded with "dirty notes" for atonality, has already capitulated to barbarism. Art which has degenerated to culture pays the price of being all the more readily confused with its own waste products as its aberrant influence grows. Education, traditionally the privilege of the few, is paid its due by self-conscious illiteracy which proclaims the stupor of tolerated excess to be the realm of freedom. Rebelling feebly, those it affects are always ready to duck, following the lead of jazz, which integrates stumbling and coming-too-soon into the collective march step. There is a striking similarity between this type of jazz enthusiast and many of the young disciples of logical positivism, who throw off philosophical culture with the same zeal as jazz fans dispense with the tradition of serious music. Enthusiasm turns into a matter-of-fact attitude in which all feeling becomes attached to technique, hostile to all meaning. They feel themselves secure within a system so well defined that no mistake could possibly slip by, and the repressed yearning for things outside finds expression as intolerant hatred and in an attitude which combines the superior knowledge of the initiate with the pretentiousness of the person without illusions. Bombastic triviality, superficiality seen as apodictic certitude, transfigures the cowardly defence against every form of self-reflection. All these old accustomed modes of reaction have in recent times lost their innocence, set themselves up as philosophy and thus become truly pernicious.

Gathered around the specialists in a field in which there is little to understand besides rules are the vague, inarticulate followers. In general they are intoxicated by the fame of mass culture, a fame which the latter knows how to manipulate; they could just as well get together in clubs for worshipping film stars or for collecting autographs. What is important to them is the sense of belonging as such, identification, without their paying

206 / Theodor W. Adorno

particular attention to this content. As girls, they have trained themselves to faint upon hearing the voice of a "crooner." Their applause, cued in by a light signal, is transmitted directly on the popular radio programs they are permitted to attend. They call themselves "jitter-bugs," bugs which carry out reflex movements, performers of their own ecstasy. Merely to be carried away by anything at all, to have something of their own, compensates for their impoverished and barren existence. The gesture of adolescence, which raves for this or that on one day with the ever-present possibility of damning it as idiocy on the next, is now socialized. Of course, Europeans tend to overlook the fact that jazz fans on the Continent in no way equal those in America. The element of excess, of insubordination, in jazz, which can still be felt in Europe, is entirely missing today in America. The recollection of anarchic origins which jazz shares with all of today's ready-made mass movements, is fundamentally repressed, however much it may continue to simmer under the surface. Jazz is taken for granted as an institution, house-broken and scrubbed behind the ears. What is common to the jazz enthusiasts of all countries, however, is the moment of compliance, in parodistic exaggeration. In this respect their play recalls the brutal seriousness of the masses of followers in totalitarian states, even though the difference between play and seriousness amounts to that between life and death. The advertisement for a particular song played by a big name band was "Follow your leader, XY." While the leaders in the European dictatorships of both shades raged against the decadence of jazz, the youth of the other countries has long since allowed itself to be electrified, as with marches, by the syncopated dance steps, with bands which do not by accident stem from military music. The division into shock troops and inarticulate following has something of the distinction between party élite and rest of the "people."

The jazz monopoly rests on the exclusiveness of the supply and the economic power behind it. But it would have been broken long ago if the ubiquitous specialty did not contain something universal to which people respond. Jazz must possess a "mass basis," the technique must link up with a moment in the subjects—one which, of course, in turn points back to the social structure and to typical conflicts between the ego and society. What first comes to mind, in quest for that moment, is the eccentric clown or parallels with the early film comics. Individual weakness is proclaimed and revoked in the same breath, stumbling is confirmed as a kind of higher skill. In the process of integrating the asocial, jazz converges with the equally standardized schemas of the detective novel and its offshoots, which regularly distort or unmask the world so that asociality and crime become the everyday norm, but which at the same time charm away the seductive and ominous challenge through the inevitable triumph of order. Psychoanalytic theory alone can provide an adequate explanation of this phenomenon. The aim of jazz is the mechanical reproduction of a regressive moment, a castration symbolism. "Give up your masculinity, let yourself be castrated," the eunuch-like sound of the jazz band both mocks and proclaims, "and you will be rewarded, accepted into a fraternity which shares the mystery of impotence with you, a mystery revealed at the moment of the initiation rite."* If this interpretation of jazz—whose sexual implications are better understood by its shocked opponents than by its apologists—appears arbitrary and far-fetched, the fact remains that it can be substantiated in countless details of the music as well as of the song lyrics. In the book *American Jazz Music,* Wilder Hobson describes an early jazz bandleader Mike Riley, a musical eccentric who must have truly mutilated the instruments. "The band squirted water and tore clothes, and Riley offered perhaps the greatest of trombone comedy acts, an insane rendition of 'Dinah' during which he repeatedly dismembered the horn and reassembled it erratically until the tubing hung down like brass burnishings in a junk shop, with a vaguely harmonic honk still sounding from one or more of the loose ends." Long before, Virgil Thomson had compared the performances of the famed jazz trumpeter Louis Armstrong to those of the great castrati of the eighteenth century. The entire sphere is saturated with terminology which distinguishes between "long-" and "short-haired" musicians. The latter are jazz people who earn money and can afford to appear presentable; the others, the caricature of the Slavic pianist, for instance, whose long mane is exemplary, are grouped under the little esteemed stereotype of the artist who is starving and who flaunts the demands of convention. This is the manifest content of the terminology. What the shorn hair represents hardly requires elaboration. In jazz, the Philistines standing over Samson are permanently transfigured.

In truth, the Philistines. The castration symbolism, deeply buried in the practices of jazz and cut off from consciousness thorough the institutionalization of perennial sameness, is for that very reason probably all the more potent. And sociologically, jazz has the effect of strengthening and extending, down to the very physiology of the subject, the acceptance of a dreamless-realistic world in which all memories of things not wholly integrated have been purged. To comprehend the mass basis of jazz one must take full account of the taboo on artistic expression in America, a taboo which continues unabated despite the official art industry, and which

* This theory is developed in the essay "Jazz," published in 1936 in the *Zeitschrift für Sozialforschung* (p. 252ff.) and elaborated in a review of the books by Sargeant and Hobson in *Studies in Philosophy and Social Science,* 1941, p. 175. ("Jazz" is reprinted in Adorno, *Moments Musicaux* [Frankfurt am Main, 1964], pp. 84–115. Translator's note.)

even affects the expressive impulses of children; progressive education, which seeks to stimulate their faculties of expression as an end in itself, is simply a reaction to this. Although the artist is partially tolerated, partially integrated into the sphere of consumption as an "entertainer," a functionary—like the better-paid waiter subject to the demands of "service"—the stereotype of the artist remains the introvert, the egocentric idiot, frequently the homosexual. While such traits may be tolerated in professional artists—a scandalous private life may even be expected as part of the entertainment—everyone else makes himself immediately suspicious by any spontaneous artistic impulse not ordered in advance by society. A child who prefers to listen to serious music or practice the piano rather than watch a baseball game or television will have to suffer as a "sissy" in his class or in the other groups to which he belongs and which embody far more authority than parents or teacher. The expressive impulse is exposed to the same truth of castration that is symbolized and mechanically and ritually subdued in jazz. Nevertheless, the need for expression, which stands in no necessary relation to the objective quality of art, cannot be entirely eliminated, especially during the years of maturation. Teenagers are not entirely stifled by economic life and its psychological correlative, the reality principle. Their aesthetic impulses are not simply extinguished by suppression but are rather diverted. Jazz is the preferred medium of such diversion. To the masses of young people who, year after year, chase the perennial fashion, presumably to forget it after a few years, it offers a compromise between aesthetic sublimation and social adjustment. The "unrealistic," practically useless, imaginative element is permitted to survive at the price of changing its character; it must tirelessly strive to remake itself in the image of reality, to repeat the latter's commands to itself, to submit to them. Thus, it reintegrates itself into the sphere from which it sought to escape. Art is deprived of its aesthetic dimension, and emerges as part of the very adjustment which it in principle contradicts. Viewed from this standpoint, several unusual features of jazz can be more easily understood. The role played by arrangement, for instance, which cannot be adequately explained in terms of a technical division of labor or of the musical illiteracy of the so-called composers. Nothing is permitted to remain what it intrinsically is. Everything must be fixed up, must bear the traces of a preparation which brings it closer to the sphere of the well-known, thus rendering it more easily comprehensible. At the same time, this process of preparation indicates to the listener that the music is made for him, yet without idealizing him. And finally, arrangement stamps the music with the official seal of approval, which in turn testifies to the absence of all artistic ambitions to achieve distance from reality, to the readiness of the music to swim with the stream; this is music which does not fancy itself any better than it is.

The primacy of adjustment is no less decisive in determining the specific skills which jazz demands from its musicians, to a certain extent from its listeners as well, and certainly from the dancers who strive to imitate the music. Aesthetic technique, in the sense of the quintessence of means employed to objectify an autonomous subject matter, is replaced by the ability to cope with obstacles, to be impervious to disruptive factors like syncopations and yet at the same time to execute cleverly the particular action which underlies the abstract rules. The aesthetic act is made into a sport by means of a system of tricks. To master it is also to demonstrate one's practicality. The achievement of the jazz musician and expert adds up to a sequence of successfully surmounted tests. But expression, the true bearer of aesthetic protest, is ·overtaken by the might against which it protests. Faced by this might it assumes a malicious and miserable tone which barely and momentarily disguises itself as harsh and provocative. The subject which expresses itself expresses precisely this: I am nothing, I am filth, no matter what they do to me, it serves me right. Potentially, this subject has already become one of those Russians accused of a crime who, although innocent, collaborates with the prosecutor from the beginning and is incapable of finding a punishment severe enough. If the aesthetic realm originally emerged as an autonomous sphere from the magic taboo which distinguished the sacred from the everyday, seeking to keep the former pure, the profane now takes its revenge on the descendant of magic, on art. Art is permitted to survive only if it renounces the right to be different, and integrates itself into the omnipotent realm of the profane which finally took over the taboo. Nothing may exist which is not like the world as it is. Jazz is the false liquidation of art—instead of utopia becoming reality, it disappears from the picture.

Part IV

Critical Theory
and Psychology

16

Politics and Psychoanalysis

Erich Fromm

Psychoanalysis has provided the key to an understanding of the often mysterious acting and feeling of the individual personality. It has shown that this irrational acting and feeling are the result of certain instinctual impulses, of which the actor is often unconscious, but which compulsively condition him or her. It therefore seemed to follow that psychoanalysis could also provide the key to an understanding of similarly conditioned *social* action, of similarly irrational *political* events. One correctly proceeded from the fact that society consists of living individuals who are subject to no other laws than those which have been exhibited by the analysis of the individual personality; one could easily see that there was also unreasonable, instinct-determined, compulsive action in social life and soon attempted to analyze religious rituals, dogmas, wars, certain popular customs and a host of other social phenomena obviously tinged with irrationality. Indeed, here and there people went a step further. People believed that social events, like individual neurotic behavior, could not only be *interpreted* in a psychoanalytic manner, but that even the defects and evils of society could be *eliminated,* as is possible with the symptom or character trait of the individual neurotic; that, for instance, eternal peace might be brought about through mass analysis, by "analyzing away" people's blind aggression. Certainly a seductive prospect! Whether it is true, however, and what part the analytical view can play in the understanding of social events, will be briefly illuminated by the following remarks.

Let us recall the method for analytically interpreting the individual personality. It can be reduced to the simple formula: interpretation of the

Translated by Mark Ritter

drive structure from the life-fate [*Lebensschicksal*]; it need only be added that particularly the experiences of early childhood period play a decisive part in the development of the later personality. Furthermore, in this method the constitution of the individual bears a definite relation to the life-fate called the "supplementary series" [*Ergaenzungsreihe*] by Freud, and both factors, constitution and experience, determine the drive structure.

If one is concerned with psychic events, not in the individual but in society, the method must remain the same. Here, too, the task is to interpret the socially relevant psychic attitudes held in common from the common life-fate of the group to be investigated. What is specifically psychoanalytical here is the practice of tracing back many feelings and ideals to physically grounded libidinous strivings, of interpreting concealed and distorted representations of *unconscious* psychic contents, and of connecting emotional attitudes of adults to those that prepared and underpinned them.

What is meant by "common life-fate"? It is those circumstances of life, beyond the individual differences in the lives of individuals, which determine the manner and conditions of life for the members of a social stratum. These are primarily the economic, social, and political circumstances under which a group lives. For society, it is true that *the economy is its fate*.

If we thus reach the conclusion that social psychology must attempt to interpret sociopsychic phenomena from the socioeconomic situation, then the question arises of what relationship a social psychology thus conceived bears to the sociological method of historical materialism.

Historical materialism teaches us to interpret social events from the economic conditions. "The manner in which people produce their means of subsistence depends first of all on the nature of the actual means of subsistence they find in existence and have to reproduce. . . . As individuals express their life, so they are. What they are thus coincides with their production, both with *what* they produce and with *how* they produce. . . . Men are the producers of their conceptions and ideas, etc., but this applies to real, acting men, as they are conditioned by a definite development of their productive forces and of the intercourse corresponding to these, up to its furthest forms. Consciousness can never be anything else than conscious existence and the existence of humanity is its actual process of life."[1] "Life is not determined by consciousness, but consciousness by life."[2]

At first sight, psychoanalysis seems to have many points of contact with historical materialism. Indeed, both theories even seem to say the same thing in one respect, specifically, in their evaluation of the role of consciousness. Both theories depose consciousness from the throne, from which it appeared to direct the actions of people and represent their emotions. But if this question leads one to suspect an agreement of the two points of view, then the further question, namely, that of the forces determining consciousness, soon appears to destroy this lovely agreement. A vulgar conception of both theories comes to the result that there exists an unbridgeable gap between psychoanalysis and historical materialism over the question of the forces determining consciousness. Historical materialism would appear to assume that it is the economic interest, the acquisitive interest, which primarily determines the conscious acting and feeling of people, while psychoanalysis would allocate the corresponding role to sexuality. Even an author like Bertrand Russell compares Marx and Freud with a witty image within the vulgar conception just outlined. He speaks "of the mayfly, which in the larval stage has organs only for eating, while as a fully developed insect (Imago), by contrast, it only has organs for reproduction, but not for nourishment. It does not need the latter, because it only remains alive a few days in this stage. What would happen if the mayfly could think theoretically? 'As a larva it would be a Marxist, as an Imago, a Freudian.' Russell adds that Marx, 'the bookworm of the British Museum,' is the proper representative of the larva philosophy. Russell himself feels more attracted by Freud; that is because, while not unreceptive to the pleasures of love, he knows nothing about making money, or orthodox economics, which was created by dried-up old men."[3]

It is easy to see that this banal conception results from a gross misunderstanding of both psychoanalysis and historical materialism. So far as psychoanalysis is concerned, the misconception arises not primarily because Freud ascribed a major role to the instinct of self preservation, alongside the sexual drives which are understood to go beyond the genital, but above all because, as already explained, he interprets the drive structure of a person from the influence of his/her life-fate on the inherited instincts. It only requires some sustained reflection to realize the fallacy of the vulgar conception of historical materialism sketched out above. Historical materialism is by no means a psychological theory. Its conception has one single psychological presupposition, specifically, that it is people who make history and that people act from the necessity to satisfy their needs. The economy in historical materialism, however, should not be interpreted in psychological categories—i.e., not in terms of individual economic or acquisitive interests—but rather as a purely socioeconomic phenomenon that represents the condition of all human actions. Thus, in historical materialism, one is not at all concerned with economic interests as psychic motives, but rather with the economic *conditions* of all manifestations of human life, including the most sublime cultural achievements.[4] Since people want to live and love, they must be active for the satisfaction of these needs. The *how* of this activity is determined not only by their own physical and mental constitutions, but also by the characteristics of the natural environment, especially the developmental state of the productive forces.

Historical materialism has shown the dependence not only of social and political, but also of ideological, factors on economic conditions. It has, as Engels (in the well-known letter of July 14, 1893) expressly states, "emphasized at first, as it had to do, the derivation of political, juridical and other ideological ideas and the actions mediated by these ideas from the fundamental economic facts." In the process, another problem was "ignored: the manner in which these ideas arise." At this point the research work of psychoanalysis can begin. It can show the way in which certain economic conditions affect the psychic apparatus of a person and produce certain ideological results; it can provide information on *how* ideological facts depend on the economic ones that determine them. Historical materialism moves from the economic condition through the mind and heart of a person to the ideological result, and in the process it proceeds by nothing other than the method it applied in the case of the individual personality: interpretation of the *drive structure* from the life-fate. By *drive structure* one should understand the totality of emotional attitudes which are peculiar to a class, nation, profession, etc., and by *life-fate* the economic, social, and political situation of those same groups. Psychoanalysis will be able to render some important service to sociology because the coherence and stability of a society are by no means formed and guaranteed only by mechanical and rational factors (compulsion by state power, mutual egoistic interests, etc.), but also by a series of libidinous relations within society and particularly among the members of the various classes (for instance, the infantile attachment of the petty bourgeoisie to the ruling class and the related intimidation). Every form of society has not only its own economic and political, but also its specific libidinous structure, and psychoanalysis can finally explain certain deviations from the course of development expected on the basis of the economic preconditions.

It goes without saying that in the analysis of sociopsychological phenomena, equally thorough and extensive knowledge about the life-fate is required as for the analysis of the individual personality. In practical terms, this means the exact knowledge of the economic, social and political situation of the group to be analyzed. It is equally clear that drawing analogies between neurotic symptoms and sociopsychic phenomena, or attempts to explain the latter in terms of the former, are of even less value than interpretations of a person's symptoms, character traits, or dreams which rely purely on analogies to other, previously analyzed cases, without reference to a person's life-fate and life situation.

If the usefulness of analysis, properly applied, for the investigation of sociopsychological phenomena has thus been established, then perhaps it is not so unrealistic to expect that psychoanalysis could also prove useful as a kind of *politico-social therapy*. One might justifiably expect that society would abandon all inappropriate actions, if one could only manage to make it conscious of their unconscious, irrational meanings.

As tempting as this prospect might be, however, it will not withstand a closer scrutiny.

What is the essential aspect of the neurotic response and to what extent is it curable through analysis? The issue is certainly not irrational, instinctive acting and feeling in and of itself, but is rather that type of psychic behavior which contradicts the real needs and necessities of the overall personality, i.e., that behavior which is conditioned by the continuance and persistence of those drive responses that were once adjusted reactions in childhood, but which have long since lost their character of adjustment and functionality. Neurosis may be characterized as a special case of those pathological disturbances which are based upon a faulty ability of the organism to adjust to new living conditions. Analytic therapy attempts to go back to those repressed fixations, make the causes of the fixations once again conscious, and thus enable the now strengthened and mature ego of the personality to overcome those experiences and impressions which the ego previously failed to confront. The goal of analytic therapy is thus the elimination of maladjusted, anachronistic modes of behavior and their replacement by appropriate ones adapted to reality.

Why should the therapy of the masses not be approachable on the same path? The mass is not a neurotic. Certainly it displays strong emotional reactions of various types, such as love, hate, reverence, scorn, joy, sadness, and others. Certainly, also, the emotional attitudes of the mass can be interpreted as a continuation and repetition of certain attitudes formed in childhood. But what emotional attitude is dominant among the members of a group at a particular time, depends on the real living conditions among the masses and the changes in those conditions. Just as the grieving reaction of a person to the death of a beloved relative or the anger of a subordinate to a supervisor who torments him can neither be called "neurotic" nor be "cured" by analysis, it is not neurotic for a repressed class to rise up against its oppressors and actuate strong sadistic impulses in this struggle. Or, to give another example, the emergence of a new religious belief like early Christianity is not a pathological phenomenon, which can be explained in terms of the fixation of certain strivings in the childhoods of the individual members of the group; it is rather an appropriate emotional reaction to the politico-economically conditioned impoverishment of the peasant-proletarian class within the Roman Empire. To emphasize it once again, all phenomena such as religious rites, revolts, wars, etc., are not conceivable without the presence of instinctual psychic reactions, preformed in childhood (just as a war cannot be waged without weapons), though these emotional attitudes are of an omnipresent nature so that the where and when of their emergence is the consequence of social changes; these phenomena are not maladjusted, neurotic reactions attached to infantile fixations in the previously defined sense.

The quasineurotic behavior of the masses, which is an appropriate reaction to current and real, though harmful and unsuitable, living conditions, cannot then be "cured" by "analyzing" them. Instead, it demands the *transformation and elimination of those very living conditions*. To be sure, one can better understand a number of political phenomena with the help of psychoanalysis. Nevertheless, it would be a fateful deception to believe that psychoanalysis can replace politics.

This abrupt rejection of psychoanalysis as a means of changing social conditions requires modification in one point. It is often the case in social life that the changing of certain institutions fails not because the actual conditions prevent change, but because certain illusions of the people hinder them from doing that which is appropriate for them even long after the real conditions which brought about those illusions have disappeared. The ideological superstructure often continues to exist longer than the socioeconomic basis would necessitate. Since psychoanalysis is theoretically suited to explain the genesis of certain socially relevant illusions, it can serve a political function in certain social situations, a function that is also probably the essential cause of its rejection by the official institutions of society, and particularly by its scientific officials.

The theoretical and practical relationship of psychoanalysis and politics contains a multitude of problems not or only barely touched upon here. The purpose of these remarks here is simply to try and correct the crudest misunderstandings and also provide a few hints towards a positive treatment of the problem.

Notes

1. Karl Marx, *The German Ideology,* (Moscow, 1964), p. 37.
2. Ibid., 38.
3. Karl Kautsky, *Die Materialistische Geschichtsauffassung* (Berlin, 1927), vol. I, p. 341.
4. Karl Kautsky has clearly and plainly drawn attention to this difference in the first volume of his *Materialistische Geschichtsauffassung* (1927), but without having always followed this conception in his earlier works, or without even utilizing a more correct conception of psychoanalysis in the work just cited.

17

Introduction to
The Authoritarian Personality

Theodor W. Adorno et al.

This is a book about social discrimination. But its purpose is not simply to add a few more empirical findings to an already extensive body of information. The central theme of the work is a relatively new concept—the rise of an "anthropological" species we call the authoritarian type of man. In contrast to the bigot of the older style, he seems to combine the ideas and skills which are typical of a highly industrialized society with irrational or antirational beliefs. He is at the same time enlightened and superstitious, proud to be an individualist and in constant fear of not being like all the others, jealous of his independence and inclined to submit blindly to power and authority. The character structure which comprises these conflicting trends has already attracted the attention of modern philosophers and political thinkers. This book approaches the problem with the means of sociopsychological research.

The implications and values of the study are practical as well as theoretical. The authors do not believe that there is a short cut to education which will eliminate the long and often circuitous road of painstaking research and theoretical analysis. Nor do they think that such a problem as the position of minorities in modern society, and more specifically the problem of religious and racial hatreds, can be tackled successfully either by the propaganda of tolerance or by apologetic refutation of errors and lies. On the other hand, theoretical activity and practical application are not separated by an unbridgeable gulf. Quite the contrary: the authors are imbued with the conviction that the sincere and systematic scientific elucidation of a phenomenon of such great historical meaning can contribute directly to an amelioration of the cultural atmosphere in which hatred breeds.

This conviction must not be brushed aside as an optimistic illusion. In the history of civilization there have been not a few instances when mass delusions were healed not by focused propaganda but, in the final analysis, because scholars, with their unobtrusive yet insistent work habits, studied what lay at the root of the delusion. Their intellectual contribution, operating within the framework of the development of society as a whole, was decisively effective.

I should like to cite two examples. The superstitious belief in witchcraft was overcome in the seventeenth and eighteenth centuries after men had come more and more under the influence of the results of modern science. The impact of Cartesian rationalism was decisive. This school of philosophers demonstrated—and the natural scientists following them made practical use of their great insight—that the previously accepted belief in the immediate effect of spiritual factors on the realm of the corporal is an illusion. Once this scientifically untenable dogma was eliminated, the foundations of the belief in magic were destroyed.

As a more recent example, we have only to think of the impact of Sigmund Freud's work on modern culture. Its primary importance does not lie in the fact that psychological research and knowledge have been enriched by new findings but in the fact that for some fifty years the intellectual, and especially the educational, world has been made more and more aware of the connection between the suppression of children (both within the home and outside) and society's usually naive ignorance of the psychological dynamics of the life of the child and the adult alike. The permeation of the social consciousness at large with the scientifically acquired experience that the events of early childhood are of prime importance for the happiness and work-potential of the adult has brought about a revolution in the relation between parents and children which would have been deemed impossible a hundred years ago.

The present work, we hope, will find a place in this history of the interdependence between science and the cultural climate. Its ultimate goal is to open new avenues in a research area which can become of immediate practical significance. It seeks to develop and promote an understanding of social-psychological factors which have made it possible for the authoritarian type of man to threaten to replace the individualistic and democratic type prevalent in the past century and a half of our civilization, and of the factors by which this threat may be contained. Progressive analysis of this new "anthropological" type and of its growth conditions, with an ever-increasing scientific differentiation, will enhance the chances of a genuinely educational counterattack.

Confidence in the possibility of a more systematic study of the mechanisms of discrimination and especially of a characterological discrimination-type is not based on the historical experience of the last fifteen years alone, but also on developments within the social sciences themselves during recent decades. Considerable and successful efforts have been made in this country as well as in Europe to raise the various disciplines dealing with man as a social phenomenon at the organizational level of cooperation that has been a tradition in the natural sciences. What I am thinking of are not merely mechanical arrangements for bringing together work done in various fields of study, as in symposia or textbooks, but the mobilization of different methods and skills, developed in distinct fields of theory and empirical investigation, for one common research program.

Such cross-fertilization of different branches of the social sciences and psychology is exactly what has taken place in the present volume. Experts in the fields of social theory and depth psychology, content analysis, clinical psychology, political sociology, and projective testing pooled their experiences and findings. Having worked together in the closest cooperation, they now present as the result of their joint efforts the elements of a theory of the authoritarian type of man in modern society.

They are not unmindful that they were not the first to have studied this phenomenon. They gratefully acknowledge their debt to the remarkable psychological profiles of the prejudiced individual projected by Sigmund Freud, Maurice Samuel, Otto Fenichel, and others. Such brilliant insights were in a sense the indispensable prerequisites for the methodological integration and research organization which the present study has attempted, and we think achieved to a certain degree, on a scale previously unapproached.

The research to be reported in this volume was guided by the following major hypothesis: that the political, economic, and social convictions of an individual often form a broad and coherent pattern, as if bound together by a "mentality" or "spirit," and that this pattern is an expression of deeplying trends in his personality.

The major concern was with the potentially fascistic individual, one whose structure is such as to render him particularly susceptible to antidemocratic propaganda. We say "potential" because we have not studied individuals who were avowedly fascistic or who belonged to known fascist organizations. At the time when most of our data were collected, fascism had just been defeated in war and, hence, we could not expect to find subjects who would openly identify themselves with it; yet there was no difficulty in finding subjects whose outlook was such as to indicate that they would readily accept fascism if it should become a strong or respectable social movement.

In concentrating upon the potential fascist we do not wish to imply that other patterns of personality and ideology might not profitably be studied in the same way. It is our opinion, however, that no politico-social trend imposes a graver threat to our traditional values and institutions than does fascism, and that knowledge of the personality forces that favor its acceptance may ultimately prove useful in combating it. A question may be raised as to why, if we wish to explore new resources for combating fascism, we do not give as much attention to the "potential antifascist." The answer is that we do study trends that stand in opposition to fascism, but we do not conceive that they constitute any single pattern. It is one of the major findings of the present study that individuals who show extreme susceptibility to fascist propaganda have a great deal in common. (They exhibit numerous characteristics that go together to form a "syndrome," although typical variations within this major pattern can be distinguished.) Individuals who are extreme in the opposite direction are much more diverse. The task of diagnosing potential fascism and studying its determinants required techniques especially designed for these purposes; it could not be asked of them that they serve as well for various other patterns. Nevertheless, it was possible to distinguish several types of personality structure that seemed particularly resistant to antidemocratic ideas, and these are given due attention in later chapters.

If a potentially fascistic individual exists, what, precisely, is he like? What goes to make up antidemocratic thought? What are the organizing forces within the person? And if such a person exists, what have been the determinants and what the course of his development?

These are questions upon which the present research was designed to throw some light. Though the notion that the potentially antidemocratic individual is a totality may be accepted as a plausible hypothesis, some analysis is called for at the start. In most approaches to the problem of political types two essential conceptions may be distinguished: the conception of ideology and the conception of underlying needs in the person. Though the two may be thought of as forming an organized whole within the individual, they may nonetheless be studied separately. The same ideological trends may in different individuals have different sources, and the same personal needs may express themselves in different ideological trends.

The term *ideology* is used in this book, in the way that is common in current literature, to stand for an organization of opinions, attitudes, and values—a way of thinking about man and society. We may speak of an individual's total ideology or of his ideology with respect to different areas of social life: politics, economics, religion, minority groups, and so forth. Ideologies have an existence independent of any single individual; and those which exist at a particular time are results both of historical processes and of contemporary social events. These ideologies have different degrees of appeal for different individuals, a matter that depends upon the individual's needs and the degree to which these needs are being satisfied or frustrated.

There are, to be sure, individuals who take unto themselves ideas from more than one existing ideological system and weave them into patterns that are more or less uniquely their own. It can be assumed, however, that when the opinions, attitudes, and values of numerous individuals are examined, common patterns will be discovered. These patterns may not in all cases correspond to the familiar, current ideologies, but they will fulfill the definition of ideology given above and in each case be found to have a function within the overall adjustment of the individual.

The present inquiry into the nature of the potentially fascistic individual began with anti-Semitism in the focus of attention. The authors, in common with most social scientists, hold the view that anti-Semitism is based more largely upon factors in the subject and in his total situation than upon actual characteristics of Jews, and that one place to look for determinants of anti-Semitic opinions and attitudes is within the persons who express them. Since this emphasis on personality required a focusing of attention on psychology rather than on sociology or history—though in the last analysis the three can be separated only artificially—there could be no attempt to account for the existence of anti-Semitic ideas in our society. The question was, rather, Why is it that certain individuals accept these ideas while others do not? And since from the start the research was guided by the hypotheses stated above, it was supposed (1) that anti-Semitism probably is not a specific or isolated phenomenon but a part of a broader ideological framework, and (2) that an individual's susceptibility to this ideology depends primarily upon his psychological needs.

The insights and hypotheses concerning the antidemocratic individual, which are present in our general cultural climate, must be supported by a great deal of painstaking observation, and in many instances by quantification, before they can be regarded as conclusive. How can one say with assurance that the numerous opinions, attitudes, and values expressed by an individual actually constitute a consistent pattern or organized totality? The most intensive investigation of that individual would seem to be necessary. How can one say that opinions, attitudes, and values found in groups of people go together to form patterns, some of which are more common than others? There is no adequate way to proceed other than by actually measuring, in populations, a wide variety of thought contents and determining by means of standard statistical methods which ones go together.

To many social psychologists the scientific study of ideology, as it has been defined, seems a hopeless task. To measure with suitable accuracy a single, specific, isolated attitude is a long and arduous proceeding for both subject and experimenter. (It is frequently argued that unless the attitude is specific and isolated, it cannot properly be measured at all.) How then can we hope to survey within a reasonable period of time the numerous attitudes and ideas that go to make up an ideology? Obviously, some kind of selection is necessary. The investigator must limit himself to what is most significant, and judgments of significance can only be made on the basis of theory.

The theories that have guided the present research will be presented in suitable contexts later. Though theoretical considerations had a role at every stage of the work, a beginning had to be made with the objective study of the most observable and relatively specific opinions, attitudes, and values.

Opinions, attitudes, and values, as we conceive of them, are expressed more or less openly in words. Psychologically they are "on the surface." It must be recognized, however, that when it comes to such affect-laden questions as those concerning minority groups and current political issues, the degree of openness with which a person speaks will depend upon the situation in which he finds himself. There may be a discrepancy between what he says on a particular occasion and what he "really thinks." Let us say that what he really thinks he can express in confidential discussion with his intimates. This much, which is still relatively superficial psychologically, may still be observed directly by the psychologist if he uses appropriate techniques—and this we have attempted to do.

It is to be recognized, however, that the individual may have "secret" thoughts which he will under no circumstances reveal to anyone else if he can help it; he may have thoughts which he cannot admit to himself, and he may have thoughts which he does not express because they are so vague and ill-formed that he cannot put them into words. To gain access to these deeper trends is particularly important, for precisely here may lie the individual's potential for democratic or antidemocratic thought and action in crucial situations.

What people say and, to a lesser degree, what they really think depends very largely upon the climate of opinion in which they are living; but when the climate changes, some individuals adapt themselves much more quickly than others. If there should be a marked increase in antidemocratic propaganda, we should expect some people to accept and repeat it at once, others when it seemed that "everybody believed it," and still others not at all. In other words, individuals differ in their readiness to exhibit antidemocratic tendencies. It seems necessary to study ideology at this "readiness level" in order to gauge the potential for fascism in this country. Observers have noted that the amount of out-spoken anti-Semitism in pre-Hitler Germany was less than that in this country, but this can be known only through intensive investigation, through the detailed survey of what is on the surface and the thorough probing of what lies beneath it.

A question may be raised as to what is the degree of relationship between ideology and action. If an individual is making antidemocratic propaganda or engaging in overt attacks upon minority group members, it is usually assumed that his opinions, attitudes, and values are congruent with his action; but comfort is sometimes found in the thought that though another individual expresses antidemocratic ideas verbally, he does not, and perhaps will not, put them into overt action. Here, once again, there is a question of potentialities. Overt action, like open verbal expression, depends very largely upon the situation of the moment—something that is best described in socioeconomic and political terms—but individuals differ widely with respect to their readiness to be provoked into action. The study of this potential is a part of the study of the individual's overall ideology; to know what kinds and what intensities of belief, attitude, and value are likely to lead to action, and to know what forces' within the individual serve as inhibitions upon action are matters of the greatest practical importance.

There seems little reason to doubt that ideology-in-readiness (ideological receptivity) and ideology-in-words and action are essentially the same stuff. The description of an individual's total ideology must portray not only the organization on each level but organization among levels. What the individual consistently says in public, what he says when he feels safe from criticism, what he thinks but will not say at all, what he thinks but will not admit to himself, what he is disposed to think or to do when various kinds of appeals are made to him—all these phenomena may be conceived of as constituting a single structure. The structure may not be integrated, it may contain contradictions as well as consistencies, but it is organized in the sense that the constituent parts are related in psychologically meaningful ways.

In order to understand such a structure, a theory of the total personality is necessary. According to the theory that has guided the present research, personality is a more or less enduring organization of forces within the individual. These persisting forces of personality help to determine response in various situations, and it is thus largely to them that consistency of behavior—whether verbal or physical—is attributable. But behavior, however consistent, is not the same thing as personality; personality lies behind behavior and within the individual. The forces of personality are not responses but readinesses for response; wheher or not a readiness will issue in overt expression depends not only upon the situation of the moment but upon what other readinesses stand in opposition to it. Personality forces which are inhibited are on a deeper level than those which immediately and consistently express themselves in overt behavior.

What are the forces of personality and what are the processes by which they are organized? For theory as to the structure of personality we have leaned most heavily upon Freud, while for a more or less systematic formulation of the more directly observable and measurable aspects of personality we have been guided primarily by academic psychology. The forces of personality are primarily needs (drives, wishes, emotional impulses) which vary from one individual to another in their quality, their intensity, their mode of gratification, and the objects of their attachment, and which interact with other needs in harmonious or conflicting patterns. There are primitive emotional needs; there are needs to avoid punishment and to keep the goodwill of the social group; there are needs to maintain harmony and integration within the self.

Since it will be granted that opinions, attitudes, and values depend upon human needs, and since personality is essentially an organization of needs, then personality may be regarded as a determinant of ideological preferences. Personality is not, however, to be hypostatized as an ultimate determinant. Far from being something which is given in the beginning, which remains fixed and acts upon the surrounding world, personality evolves under the impact of the social environment and can never be isolated from the social totality within which it occurs. According to the present theory, the effects of environmental forces in moulding the personality are, in general, the more profound the earlier in the life history of the individual they are brought to bear. The major influences upon personality development arise in the course of child training as carried forward in a setting of family life. What happens here is profoundly influenced by economic and social factors. It is not only that each family in trying to rear its children proceeds according to the ways of the social, ethnic, and religious groups in which it has membership, but crude economic factors affect directly the parents' behavior toward the child. This means that broad changes in social conditions and institutions will have a direct bearing upon the kinds of personalities that develop within a society.

The present research seeks to discover correlations between ideology and sociological factors operating in the individual's past—whether or not they continue to operate in his present. In attempting to explain these correlations the relationships between personality and ideology are brought into the picture, the general approach being to consider personality as an agency through which sociological factors are the most crucial ones and in what ways they achieve their effects.

Although personality is a product of the social environment of the past, it is not, once it has developed, a mere object of the contemporary environment. What has developed is a structure within the individual, something which is capable of self-initiated action upon the social environment and of selection with respect to varied impinging stimuli, something which though always modifiable is frequently very resistant to fundamental change. This conception is necessary to explain consistency of behavior in widely varying situations, to explain the persistence of ideological trends in the face of contradicting facts and radically altered social conditions, to explain why people in the same sociological situation have different or even conflicting views on social issues, and why it is that people whose behavior has been changed through psychological manipulation lapse into their old ways as soon as the agencies of manipulation are removed.

The conception of personality structure is the best safeguard against the inclination to attribute persistent trends in the individual to something "innate" or "basic" or "racial" within him. The Nazi allegation that natural, biological traits decide the total being of a person would not have been such a successful political device had it not been possible to point to numerous instances of relative fixity in human behavior and to challenge those who thought to explain them on any basis other than a biological one. Without the conception of personality structure, writers whose approach rests upon the assumption of infinite human flexibility and responsiveness to the social situation of the moment have not helped matters by referring persistent trends which they could not approve to "confusion" or "psychosis" or evil under one name or another. There is, of course, some basis for describing as "pathological" patterns of behavior which do not conform with the most common, and seemingly most lawful, responses to momentary stimuli. But this is to use the term *pathological* in the very narrow sense of deviation from the average found in a particular context and, what is worse, to suggest that everything in the personality structure is to be put under this heading. Actually, personality embraces variables which exist widely in the population and have lawful relations one to another. Personality patterns that have been dismissed as "pathological" because they were not in keeping with the most common manifest trends or the most dominant ideals within a society, have on closer investigation turned out to be but exaggerations of what was almost universal below the surface in that society. What is "pathological" today may with changing social conditions become the dominant trend of tomorrow.

It seems clear then that an adequate approach to the problems before us must take into account both fixity and flexibility; it must regard the two not as mutually exclusive categories but as the extremes of a single continuum along which human characteristics may be placed, and it must provide a basis for understanding the conditions which favor the one extreme or the other. Personality is a concept to account for relative permanence. But it may be emphasized again that personality is mainly a potential; it is a readiness for behavior rather than behavior itself;

228 / T. W. Adorno et. al.

although it consists in dispositions to behave in certain ways, the behavior that actually occurs will always depend upon the objective situation. Where the concern is with antidemocratic trends, a delineation of the conditions for individual expression requires an understanding of the total organization of society.

It has been stated that the personality structure may be such as to render the individual susceptible to antidemocratic propaganda. It may now be asked, what are the conditions under which such propaganda would increase in pitch and volume and come to dominate in press and radio to the exclusion of contrary ideological stimuli, so that what is now potential would become actively manifest. The answer must be sought not in any single personality, not in personality factors found in the mass of people, but in processes at work in society itself. It seems well understood today that whether or not antidemocratic propaganda is to become a dominant force in this country depends primarily upon the situation of the most powerful economic interests, upon whether they, by conscious design or not, make use of this device for maintaining their dominant status. This is a matter about which the great majority of people would have little to say.

The present research, limited as it is to the hitherto largely neglected psychological aspects of fascism, does not concern itself with the production of propaganda. It focuses attention, rather, upon the consumer, the individual for whom the propaganda is designed. In so doing it attempts to take into account not only the psychological structure of the individual but the total objective situation in which he lives. It makes the assumption that people in general tend to accept political and social programs which they believe will serve their economic interests. What these interests are depends in each case upon the individual's position in society as defined in economic and sociological terms. An important part of the present research, therefore, was the attempt to discover what patterns of socioeconomic factors are associated with receptivity, and with resistance, to antidemocratic propaganda.

At the same time, however, it was considered that economic motives in the individual may not have the dominant and crucial role that is often ascribed to them. If economic self-interest were the only determinant of opinion, we should expect people of the same socioeconomic status to have very similar opinions, and we should expect opinion to vary in a meaningful way from one socioeconomic grouping to another. Research has not given very sound support for these expectations. There is only the most general similarity of opinion among people of the same socioeconomic status, and the exceptions are glaring; while variations from one socioeconomic group to another are rarely simple or clear-cut. To explain why it is that people of the same socioeconomic status so frequently have different ideologies, while people of a different status often have very similar ideologies, we must take account of other than purely economic needs.

More than this, it is becoming increasingly plain that people very frequently do not behave in such a way as to further their material interests, even when it is clear to them what these interests are. The resistance of white-collar workers to organization is not due to a belief that the union will not help them economically; the tendency of the small businessman to side with big business in most economic and political matters cannot be due entirely to a belief that this is the way to guarantee his economic independence. In instances such as these the individual seems not only not to consider his material interests, but even to go against them. It is as if he were thinking in terms of a larger group identification, as if his point of view were determined more by his need to support this group and to suppress opposite ones than by rational consideration of his own interests. Indeed, it is with a sense of relief today that one is assured that a group conflict is merely a clash of economic interests—that each side is merely out to "do" the other—and not a struggle in which deep-lying emotional drives have been let loose. When it comes to the ways in which people appraise the social world, irrational trends stand out glaringly. One may conceive of a professional man who opposes the immigration of Jewish refugees on the ground that this will increase the competition with which he has to deal and so decrease his income. However undemocratic this may be, it is at least rational in a limited sense. But for this man to go on, as do most people who oppose Jews on occupational grounds, and accept a wide variety of opinions, many of which are contradictory, about Jews in general, and to attribute various ills of the world to them, is plainly illogical. And it is just as illogical to praise all Jews in accordance with a "good" stereotype of them. Hostility against groups that is based upon real frustration, brought about by members of that group, undoubtedly exists, but such frustrating experiences can hardly account for the fact that prejudice is apt to be generalized. Evidence from the present study confirms what has often been indicated: that a man who is hostile toward one minority group is very likely to be hostile against a wide variety of others. There is no conceivable rational basis for such generalization; and, what is more striking, prejudice against, or totally uncritical acceptance of, a particular group often exists in the absence of any experience with members of that group. The objective situation of the individual seems an unlikely source of such irrationality; rather, we should seek where psychology has already found the sources of dreams, fantasies, and misinterpretations of the world—that is, in the deep-lying needs of the personality.

Another aspect of the individual's situation which we should expect to affect his ideological receptivity is his membership in social groups—

occupational, fraternal, religious, and the like. For historical and sociological reasons, such groups favor and promulgate, whether officially or unofficially, different patterns of ideas. There is reason to believe that individuals, out of their needs to conform and to belong and to believe and through such devices as imitation and conditioning, often take over more or less ready-made the opinions, attitudes, and values that are characteristic of the groups in which they have membership. To the extent that the ideas which prevail in such a group are implicitly or explicitly antidemocratic, the individual group member might be expected to be receptive to propaganda having the same general direction. Accordingly, the present research investigates a variety of groups memberships with a view to what general trends of thought—and how much variability— might be found in each.

It is recognized, however, that a correlation between group membership and ideology may be due to different kinds of determination in different individuals. In some cases it might be that the individual merely repeats opinions which are taken for granted in his social milieu and which he has no reason to question; in other cases it might be that the individual has chosen to join a particular group because it stood for ideals with which he was already in sympathy. In modern society, despite enormous communality in basic culture, it is rare for a person to be subjected to only one pattern of ideas, after he is old enough for ideas to mean something to him. Some selection is usually made, according, it may be supposed, to the needs of his personality. Even when individuals are exposed during their formative years almost exclusively to a single, closely knit pattern of political, economic, social, and religious ideas, it is found that some conform while others rebel, and it seems proper to inquire whether personality factors do not make the difference. The soundest approach, it would seem is to consider that in the determination of ideology, as in the determination of any behavior, there is a situational factor and a personality factor, and that a careful weighing of the role of each will yield the most accurate prediction.

Situational factors, chiefly economic condition and social group memberships, have been studied intensively in recent researches on opinion and attitude, while the more inward, more individualistic factors have not received the attention they deserve. Beyond this, there is still another reason why the present study places particular emphasis upon the personality. Fascism, in order to be successful as a political movement, must have a mass basis. It must secure not only the frightened submission but the active cooperation of the great majority of the people. Since by its very nature it favors the few at the expense of the many, it cannot possibly demonstrate that it will so improve the situation of most people that their real interests will be served. It must therefore make its major appeal, not to rational self-interest, but to emotional needs—often to the most primitive and irrational wishes and fears. If it be argued that fascist propaganda fools people into believing that their lot will be improved, then the question arises: Why are they so easily fooled? Because, it may be supposed, of their personality structure; because of long-established patterns of hopes and aspirations, fears and anxieties that dispose them to certain beliefs and make them resistant to others. The task of fascist propaganda, in other words, is rendered easier to the degree that antidemocratic potentials already exist in the great mass of people. It may be granted that in Germany economic conflicts and dislocations within the society were such that for this reason alone the triumph of fascism was sooner or later inevitable; but the Nazi leaders did not act as if they believed this to be so; instead they acted as if it were necessary at every moment to take into account the psychology of the people—to activate every ounce of their antidemocratic potential, to compromise with them, to stamp out the slightest spark of rebellion. It seems apparent that any attempt to appraise the chances of a fascist triumph in America must reckon with the potential existing in the character of the people. Here lies not only the susceptibility to antidemocratic propaganda but the most dependable sources of resistance to it.

The present writers believe that it is up to the people to decide whether or not this country goes fascist. It is assumed that knowledge of the nature and extent of antidemocratic potentials will indicate programs for democratic action. These programs should not be limited to devices for manipulating people in such a way that they will behave more democratically, but they should be devoted to increasing the kind of self-awareness and self-determination that makes any kind of manipulation impossible. There is one explanation for the existence of an individual's ideology that has not so far been considered: that it is the view of the world which a reasonable man, with some understanding of the role of such determinants as those discussed above, and with complete access to the necessary facts, will organize for himself. This conception, though it has been left to the last, is of crucial importance for a sound approach to ideology. Without it we should have to share the destructive view, which has gained some acceptance in the modern world, that since all ideologies, all philosophies, derive from nonrational sources there is no basis for saying that one has more merit than another.

But the rational system of an objective and thoughtful man is not a thing apart from personality. Such a system is still motivated. What is distinguishing in its sources is mainly the kind of personality organization from which it springs. It might be said that a mature personality (if we may for the moment use this term without defining it) will come closer to achieving a rational system of thought than will an immature one; but a personality is no less dynamic and no less organized for being mature,

18

The Obsolescence of the Freudian Concept of Man

Herbert Marcuse

Some of the basic assumptions of Freudian theory in both their orthodox as well as revisionist development have become obsolescent to the degree to which their object, namely, the "individual" as the embodiment of id, ego, and superego has become obsolescent in the social reality. The evolution of contemporary society has replaced the Freudian model by a social atom whose mental structure no longer exhibits the qualities attributed by Freud to the psychoanalytic object. Psychoanalysis, in its various schools, has continued and spread over large sectors of society, but with the change in its object, the gap between theory and therapy has been widened. Therapy is faced with a situation in which it seems to help the Establishment rather than the individual. The truth of psychoanalysis is thereby not invalidated; on the contrary, the obsolescence of its object reveals the extent to which progress has been in reality regression. Psychoanalysis thus sheds new light on the politics of advanced industrial society.

This essay outlines the contribution of psychoanalysis to political thought by trying to show the social and political content in the basic psychoanalytic concepts themselves. The psychoanalytic categories do not have to be "related" to social and political conditions—they are themselves social and political categories. Psychoanalysis could become an effective social and political instrument, positive as well as negative, in an administrative as well as critical function, because Freud had discovered the mechanisms of social and political control in the depth dimension of instinctual drives and satisfactions.

It has often been said that Freud's theory depended, for much of its validity, on the existence of Viennese middle-class society in the decades preceding the fascist era—from the turn of the century to the interwar period. There is a kernel of truth in this facile correlation, but its geographical and historical limits are false. At the time of its maturity, Freud's theory comprehended the past rather than the present—a vanishing rather than a prevalent image of man, a disappearing form of human existence. Freud describes a dynamic mental structure: the life-and-death struggle between antagonistic forces—id and ego, ego and superego, pleasure principle and reality principle, Eros and Thanatos. This struggle is fought out entirely in and by the individual, in and by his body and mind; the analyst acts as the spokesman (silent spokesman!) of *reason*—in the last analysis the individual's *own* reason. He only activates, articulates what is *in* the patient, his mental faculties and capabilities. "The id shall become ego": here is the rationalist, rational program of psychoanalysis—conquest of the unconscious and its "impossible" drives and objectives. It is by virtue and power of his own reason that the individual abandons the uncompromising claims of the pleasure principle and submits to the dictate of the reality principle, that he learns to maintain the precarious balance between Eros and Thanatos—that he learns to eke out a living in a society (Freud says: "civilization") which is *increasingly* incapable of making him happy, that is to say, of satisfying his instinctual drives.

I wish to emphasize two elements in this conception which indicate its roots in social and political conditions which no longer exist. First, Freud presupposes throughout an irreconcilable conflict between the individual and his society. Second, he presupposes individual awareness of this conflict and, in the case of the patient, the vital need for a settlement— both expressed by the inability to function normally in the given society. The conflict has its roots, not merely in the private case history of the patient but also (and primarily!) in the general, universal fate of the individual under the established reality principle: the ontogenetic case history repeats, in a particular forms, the phylogenetic history of mankind. The dynamic of the Oedipus situation is not only the hidden mode of every father-son relationship but also the secret of the enduring domination of man by man—of the conquests and failures of civilization. In the Oedipus situation are the individual and instinctual roots of the reality principle which governs society. To a considerable extent, therapy depends on the recognition of the internal link between individual and general unhappiness. The successfully analyzed individual remains unhappy, with an unhappy consciousness—but he is cured, "liberated" to the degree to which he recognizes the guilt and the love of the father, the crime and the right of the authorities, his successors, who continue and extend the father's work. Libidinal ties thus continue to insure the individual's submission to his society: he achieves (relative) autonomy within a world of heteronomy.

What are the historical changes that have made this conception obsolete? According to Freud, the fatal conflict between the individual and society is first and foremost experienced and fought out in the confrontation with the father: here, the universal struggle between Eros and Thanatos erupts and determines the development of the individual. And it is the father who enforces the subordination of the pleasure principle to the reality principle; rebellion and the attainment of maturity are stages in the contest with the father. Thus, the primary "socialization" of the individual is the work of the family, as is whatever autonomy the child may achieve—his entire ego develops in a circle and refuge of privacy: becoming oneself with but also *against* the other. The "individual" himself is the living process of *mediation* in which all repression and all liberty are "internalized," made the individual's own doing and undoing.

Now, this situation, in which the ego and superego were formed in the struggle with the father as the paradigmatic representative of the reality principle—this situation is historical: it came to an end with the changes in industrial society which took shape in the interwar period.[1] I enumerate some of the familiar features: transition from free to organized competition, concentration of power in the hands of an omnipresent technical, cultural, and political administration, self-propelling mass production and consumption, subjection of previously private, asocial dimensions of existence to methodical indoctrination, manipulation, control.[2] In order to elucidate the extent to which these changes have undermined the basis of Freudian theory, I wish to emphasize only two interrelated tendencies which affect the social as well as the mental structure.

First, the classical psychoanalytic model, in which the father and the father-dominated family were the agent of mental socialization, is being invalidated by society's direct management of the nascent ego through the mass media, school and sport teams, gangs, etc. Second, this decline in the role of the father follows the decline of the role of private and family enterprise: the son is increasingly less dependent on the father and the family tradition in selecting and finding a job and in earning a living. The socially necessary repressions and the socially necessary behavior are no longer learned—and internalized—in the long struggle with the father*— the ego ideal is rather brought to bear on the ego directly and "from outside," *before* the ego is actually formed as the personal and (relatively) autonomous subject of mediation between him-*self* and others.

These changes reduce the "living space" and the autonomy of the ego and prepare the ground for the formation of *masses*. The mediation between the self and the other gives way to immediate identification. In the social structure, the individual becomes the conscious and unconscious

---

* To be sure, the father continues to enforce the primary diversion of sexuality from the mother, but his authority is no longer fortified and perpetuated by his subsequent education and economic power.

object of administration and obtains his freedom and satisfaction in his role *as* such an object; in the mental structure, the ego shrinks to such an extent that it seems no longer capable of sustaining itself, as a self, in distinction of id and superego. The multidimensional dynamic by which the individual attained and maintained his own balance between autonomy and heteronomy, freedom and repression, pleasure and pain, has given way to a one-dimensional static identification of the individual with the others and with the administered reality principle. In this one-dimensional structure, the space no longer exists in which the mental processes described by Freud can develop; consequently, the object of psychoanalytic therapy is no longer the same, and the social function of psychoanalysis is changed by virtue of the changes in the mental structure—themselves produced and reproduced by the society.

But according to Freud, the basic mental processes and conflicts are not "historical," confined to a specific period and social structure—they are universal, "eternal," and fatal. Then, these processes cannot have disappeared, and these conflicts cannot have been resolved—they must continue to prevail in different forms corresponding to and expressive of the different contents. They do so in the conditions which characterize the new society: in the behavior of the masses and in their relation to their new masters who impose the reality principle, namely, their leaders. The term *leader* here is meant to designate not only the rulers in authoritarian states but also those in totalitarian democracies, and *totalitarian* here is redefined to mean not only terroristic but also pluralistic absorption of all effective opposition by the established society.

Now, Freud himself has applied psychoanalysis to conditions where his classical model of ego formation seemed invalid without essential modifications. In his *Group Psychology and the Analysis of the Ego,* psychoanalysis makes the necessary step from individual to collective psychology, to the analysis of the individual as a member of the masses, the individual mind as collective mind—a necessary step because from the beginning Freudian theory had encountered the universal in the particular, the general in the individual unhappiness. The analysis of the ego turns into *political* analysis where individuals combine in masses, and where the ego ideal, conscience, and responsibility have been "projected," removed from the realm of the individual psyche and embodied in an external agent. This agent, which thus assumes some of the most important functions of the ego (and superego), is the *leader*. As their collective ego ideal he unifies the individuals by the double tie of identification with him, and among the individuals themselves. The complex mental processes involved in the formation of masses must remain outside the scope of this paper; only the points will be emphasized which may show whether the obsolescence of the analysis of the ego also extends to Freud's group psychology. According to Freud's group psychology, the ties which bind the individuals into masses are libidinal relationships. They are in their entirety "aim-inhibited" impulses, and they pertain to a weakened and impoverished ego and thus signify a regression to primitive stages of the development—in the last analysis, to the primal horde.

Freud derives these features from the analysis of two large "artificial" masses which he takes as examples: the Church and the army. The question is whether at least some results of his analysis can be applied to the formation of even larger masses in advanced industrial society. I shall offer a few suggestions in this respect.

The most general and at the same time fundamental element in the formation of masses in developed civilization is, according to Freud, the specific "regression to a primitive mental activity" which relates an advanced civilization back to the prehistoric beginnings—to the primal horde.

Freud enumerates the following features as characteristic of regression in the formation of masses: "dwindling of the conscious individual personality, the focusing of thoughts and feelings into a common direction, the predominance of emotions and of the unconscious mental life, the tendency to the immediate carrying out of intentions as they emerge." These regressive features indicate that the individual has given up his ego ideal and substituted for it the group ideal as embodied in the leader.[3] Now, it seems that the regressive traits noted by Freud are indeed observable in the advanced areas of industrial society. The shrinking of the ego, its reduced resistance to others appears in the ways in which the ego holds itself constantly open to the messages imposed from outside.[4] The antenna on every house, the transistor on every beach, the jukebox in every bar or restaurant are as many cries of desperation—not to be left alone, by himself, not to be separated from the Big Ones, not to be condemned to the emptiness or the hatred or the dreams of oneself. And these cries engulf the others, and even those who still have and want an ego of their own are condemned—a huge captive audience, in which the vast majority enjoys the captor.

But the regression of the ego shows forth in even more fateful forms, above all in the weakening of the "critical" mental faculties: consciousness and conscience. (They are interrelated: no conscience without developed knowledge, without recognition of good and evil.) Conscience and personal responsibility decline "objectively" under conditions of total bureaucratization, where it is most difficult to attribute and to allocate autonomy, and where the functioning of the apparatus determines—and overrides— personal autonomy. However, this familiar notion contains a strong ideological element: the term *bureaucracy* covers (as does the term *administration*) very different and even conflicting realities: the bureaucracy of domination and exploitation is quite another than that of the "administration of things," planfully directed toward the development and satisfaction of vital individual needs. In the advanced industrial societies, the administration of things still proceeds under the bureaucracy of domination: here, the perfectly rational and progressive transfer of individual functions to the apparatus is accompanied by the irrational transfer of conscience and by the repression of consciousness.

The insights of psychoanalysis go a long way to explaining the frightful ease with which the people submit to the exigencies of total administration, which include total preparation for the fatal end. Freed from the authority of the weak father, released form the child-centered family, well equipped with the ideas and facts of life as transmitted by the mass media, the son (and to a still lesser degree, the daughter) enter a ready-made world in which they have to find their way. Paradoxically, the freedom which they had enjoyed in the progressive, child-centered family turns out to be a liability rather than a blessing: the ego that has grown without much struggle appears as a pretty weak entity, ill equipped to become a self with and against others, to offer effective resistance to the powers that now enforce the reality principle, and which are so very different from father (and mother)—but also so very different from the images purveyed by the mass media. (In the context of Freudian theory, the paradox disappears: in a repressive civilization, the weakening of the father's role and his replacement by external authorities must weaken the libidinal energy in the ego and thus weaken its life instincts.)

The more the autonomous ego becomes superfluous, even retarding and disturbing in the functioning of the administered, technified world, the more does the development of the ego depend on its "power of negation," that is to say, on its ability to build and protect a personal, private realm with its own individual needs and faculties. Yet this ability is impaired on two grounds: the immediate, external socialization of the ego, and the control and management of free time—the massification of privacy. Deprived of its power of negation, the ego, striving to "find identity" in the heteronomous world, either spends itself in the numerous mental and emotional diseases which come to psychological treatment, or the ego submits quickly to the required modes of thought and behavior, assimilating its self to the others. But the others, in the role of competitors or superiors, evoke instinctual hostility: identification with their ego ideal activates aggressive energy. The externalized ego ideal guides the spending of this energy: it does not drive the conscience as the moral judge of the ego, but rather directs aggression toward the external enemies of the ego ideal. The individuals are thus mentally and instinctually predisposed to accept and to make their own the political and social necessities which demand the permanent mobilization with and against atomic destruction, the organized familiarity with man-made death and disfiguration.

The member of this society apprehends and evaluates all this, not by himself, in terms of his ego and his own ego ideal (his father and the father's images) but through all others and in terms of their common, externalized ego ideal: the National or Supranational Purpose and its constituted spokesmen. The reality principle speaks en masse: not only through the daily and nightly media which coordinate one privacy with that of all others, but also through the kids, the peer groups, the colleagues, the corporation. The ego conscience is theirs; the rest is deviation, or identity crisis, or personal trouble. But the external ego ideal is not imposed by brute force: there is deep-going harmony between outside and inside, for coordination begins long before the conscious stage: the individuals get from outside what they would want by themselves; identification with the collective ego ideal takes place in the child, although the family is no longer the primary agent of socialization. The conditioning in the family rather is a *negative* one: the child learns that *not* the father but the playmates, the neighbors, the leader of the gang, the sport, the screen are the authorities on appropriate mental and physical behavior. It has been pointed out how this decisive change is connected with the changes in the economic structure: the decline of the individual and family enterprise, of the importance of traditional "inherited" skills and occupations, the need for general education, the increasingly vital and comprehensive function of professional, business, and labor organizations—all this undermined the role of the father—and the psychoanalytic theory of the superego as the heir of the father. In the most advanced sectors of modern society, the citizen is no longer seriously haunted by father images.

These changes seem to invalidate the Freudian interpretation of modern mass society. Freud's conception demands a leader as the unifying agent, and demands transference of the ego ideal to the leader as father image. Moreover, the libidinal ties which bind the members of the masses to the leaders and to each other are supposed to be an "idealistic remodeling of the state of affairs in the primal horde, where all of the sons knew that they were equally persecuted by the primal father, and feared him equally." But the fascist leaders were no "fathers," and the post-fascist and post-Stalinist top leaders do not display the traits of the heirs of the primal father—not by any stretch of "idealizing" imagination. Nor are their citizens all equally persecuted or equally loved: this sort of equality prevails neither in the democratic nor in the authoritarian states. To be sure, Freud envisaged the possibility that "an idea, an abstraction may . . . be substituted for the leader," or that a "common tendency" may serve as substitute, embodied in the figure of a "secondary leader." The National Purpose, or Capitalism, or Communism, or simply Freedom may be such "abstractions"; but they hardly seem to lend themselves to libidinal identification. And we shall certainly be reluctant, in spite of the state of permanent mobilization, to compare contemporary society with an army for which the commander-in-chief would function as the unifying leader. There are, to be sure, enough leaders, and there are top leaders in every state, but none of them seems to fit the image required for Freud's hypothesis. At least in this respect, the attempt at a psychoanalytic theory of the masses appears untenable—here too, the conception is obsolete. We seem to be faced with a reality which was envisaged only at the margin of psychoanalysis—the *vaterlose Gesellschaft* (society without fathers). In such a society, a tremendous release of destructive energy would occur: freed from the instinctual bonds with father as authority and conscience, aggressiveness would be rampant and lead to the collapse of the group. Evidently this is not (or not yet) our historical situation: we may have a society in which the individuals are no longer tamed and guided by the father images, but other and apparently no less effective agents of the reality principle have taken their place. Who are they?

They are no longer identifiable within the conceptual framework of Freud: society has surpassed the stage where psychoanalytic theory could elucidate the ingression of society into the mental structure of the individuals and thus reveal the mechanisms of social control in the individuals. The cornerstone of psychoanalysis is the concept that social controls emerge in the struggle between instinctual and social needs, which is a struggle within the ego and against personal authority. Consequently, even the most complex, the most objective, impersonal social and political control must be "embodied" in a *person*—"embodied" not in the sense of a mere analogy or symbol but in a very literal sense: instinctual ties must bind the master to the slave, the chief to the subordinate, the leader to the led, the sovereign to the people.

Now, nobody would deny that such ties still exist: the election campaigns provide sufficient evidence, and the hucksters know only too well how to play on these instinctual processes. But it is not the image of the father that is here invoked; the stars and starlets of politics, television, and sports are highly fungible (in fact, the question may be raised whether their costly promotion is not already wasteful even in terms of the Establishment—wasteful to the extent to which the choice is narrowed down to one between equivalents in the same class of goods). Their fungibility indicates that we cannot possibly attribute to them as *persons or "personalities"* the vital role which the embodiments of the ego ideal are supposed to play in establishing social cohesion. These star-leaders, together with the innumerable subleaders, are in turn functionaries of a higher authority which is no longer embodied in a person: the authority of the prevailing productive apparatus which, once set in motion and moving efficiently in the set direction, engulfs the leaders and the led—without however, eliminating the radical differences between them, that is, between the masters and the servants. This apparatus includes the whole of the physical plant of production and distribution, the technics, technology, and science applied in this process, and the social division of labor sustaining and propelling the process. Naturally, this apparatus is directed and organized by men, but their ends and the means to attain them are determined by the requirements of maintaining, enlarging, and protecting the apparatus—a loss of autonomy which seems qualitatively different from the dependence on the available "productive forces" characteristic of preceding historical stages. In the corporate system with its vast bureaucracies, individual responsibility is as diffuse and as intertwined with others as is the particular enterprise in the national and international economy. In this diffusion, the ego ideal takes shape which unites the individuals into citizens of the mass-society: overriding the various competing power elites, leaders, and chiefs, it becomes "embodied" in the very tangible laws which move the apparatus and determine the behavior of the material as well as the human object; the technical code, the moral code, and that of profitable productivity are merged into one effective whole.

But while Freud's theory of leadership as heir of the father-superego seems to collapse in the face of a society of total reification, his thesis still stands according to which all lasting civilized association, if it is not sustained by brute terror, must be held together by some sort of libidinal relationships—mutual identification. Now, while an "abstraction" cannot really become the object of libidinal cathexis, a concrete apparatus can become such an object: the example of the automobile may serve as an illustration. But if the automobile (or another machine) is libidinally cathected over and above its use-value as vehicle or place of unsublimated sexual satisfaction, it clearly provides substitute gratification—and a rather poor substitute to boot. Consequently, in Freudian terms, we must assume that the direct, objective enforcement of the reality principle and its imposition on the weakened ego involve weakening of the life instincts (Eros) and growth of instinctual aggression, of destructive energy. And under the social and political conditions prevailing in the coexisting technological societies today, the aggressive energy thus activated finds its very concrete and *personified* object in the common *enemy* outside the group.

For capitalism, communism provides the powerful negation of the ego ideal, of the established reality principle itself, and thus provides the powerful impulse of identification and massification in defense of the established reality principle. The ascendancy of aggressive over libidinal energy appears as an essential factor in this form of social and political cohesion. And in this form, the *personal* cathexis is possible which the reified hierarchy of technological society denies to the individuals—it is the enemy as personified target which becomes the object of instinctual cathexis—the "negative" aggressive cathexis. For in the daily intake of information and propaganda, the images of the enemy are made concrete, immediate—human or rather inhuman: it is not so much communism, a highly complex and "abstract" social system, as the Reds, the Commies, the comrades, Castro, Stalin, the Chinese, who are threatening—a very personalized power against which the masses form and unite. The enemy is thus not only more concrete than the abstraction which is his reality— he is also more flexible and fungible and can assimilate many familiar hated impersonations, such as pinks, intellectuals, beards, foreigners, Jews, in accordance with the level and interest of the respective social group.

This recourse to psychoanalytic concepts for the interpretation of political conditions in no way invalidates or even minimizes the obvious *rational* explanation. Obviously, the very existence and growth of communism presents a clear and present danger to the Western systems; obviously, the latter must mobilize all available resources, mental as well as physical, in its defense; obviously, in the area of atomic and automation technology, such mobilization destroys the more primitive and personal forms of "socialization" characteristic of the preceding stages. No deep psychology is necessary in order to understand these developments. It does seem necessary, however, in view of the massive spread and absorption of the image of the enemy, and in view of the impact on the mental structure of the people. In order words, psychoanalysis may elucidate not the political facts, but what they do to those who suffer these facts.

The danger in mass formation which is perhaps least susceptible to control is the quantum of destructive energy activated by this formation. I see no possibility of denying or even minimizing the prevalence of this danger in advanced industrial society. The arms race, with weapons of total annihilation, with the consent of a large part of the people, is only the most conspicuous sign of this mobilization of destructive energy. To be sure, it is mobilized for the preservation and protection of life—but precisely here, the most provocative propositions of Freud reveal their force: all additional release of destructive energy upsets the precarious balance between Eros and Thanatos and reduces the energy of the life instincts in favor of that of the death instinct. The same thesis applies to the use of destructive energy in the struggle with nature. Technical progress is life-protecting and life-enlarging to the degree to which the destructive energy here at work is "contained" and guided by libidinal energy. This ascendancy of Eros in technical progress would become manifest in the progressive alleviation and pacification of the struggle for existence, in the growth of refined erotic needs and satisfaction. In other words, technical progress would be accompanied by a lasting *desublimation* which, far from reverting mankind to anarchic and primitive stages, would bring about a less repressive yet higher stage of civilization.

Now, there is, in the advanced technological societies of the West, *indeed a large desublimation* (compared with the preceding stages) in sexual mores and behavior, in the better living, in the accessibility of culture (mass culture is desublimated higher culture). Sexual morality has been greatly liberalized; moreover, sexuality is operative as commercial stimulus, business asset, status symbol. But does this mode of desublimation signify the ascendancy of the life-preserving and life-enhancing Eros over its fatal adversary? Freud's concept of sexuality may provide a cue for the answer.

Central in this concept is the conflict between sexuality (as the force of the pleasure principle) and society (the institution of the reality principle) as necessarily repressive of the uncompromised claims of the primary life instincts. By its innermost force, Eros becomes "demonstration against the herd instinct," "rejection of the group's influence."[5] In the technological desublimation today, the all but opposite tendency seems to prevail. The conflict between pleasure and the reality principle is managed by a controlled liberalization which increases satisfaction with the offerings of society. But in this form of release, libidinal energy changes its social function: to the degree to which sexuality is sanctioned and even encouraged by society (not "officially," of course, but by the mores and behavior considered as "regular"), it loses the quality which, according to Freud, is its essentially erotic quality, that of freedom from social control. In this sphere was the surreptitious freedom, the dangerous autonomy of the individual under the pleasure principle; its authoritarian restriction by the society bore witness to the depth of the conflict between individual and society, that is, to the extent of the repression of freedom. Now, with the integration of this sphere into the realm of business and entertainment, the repression itself is repressed: society has enlarged not individual freedom, but its control over the individual. And this growth of social control is achieved not by terror, but by the more or less beneficial productivity and efficiency of the apparatus.

We have here a highly advanced stage of civilization where society subordinates the individuals to its requirements by extending liberty and equality—or, where the reality principle operates through enlarged but controlled *desublimation*. In this new historical form of the reality principle, progress may operate as vehicle of repression. The better and bigger satisfaction is very real, and yet, in Freudian terms, it is *repressive* inasmuch as it diminishes in the individual psyche the sources of the pleasure principle *and* of freedom: the instinctual—and intellectual—resistance against the reality principle. The intellectual resistance too is weakened at its roots: administered satisfaction extends to the realm of higher culture, of the sublimated needs and objectives. One of the essential mechanisms of advanced industrial society is the mass diffusion of art, literature, music, philosophy; they become part of the technical equipment of the daily household and of the daily work world. In this process, they undergo a decisive transformation; they are losing the qualitative difference, namely, the essential dissociation from the established reality principle which was the ground of their liberating function. Now, the images and ideas by virtue of which art, literature, and philosophy once indicated and transcended the given reality are integrated into the society, and the power of the reality principle is greatly extended. These tendencies alone would corroborate Freud's hypothesis that repression increases as industrial society advances and extends its material and cultural benefits to a larger part of the underlying population. The beneficiaries are inextricably tied to the multiplying agencies which produce and distribute the benefits while constantly enlarging the giant apparatus required for the defense of these agencies within and outside the national frontiers; the people turn into the object of administration. As long as peace is maintained, it is a benevolent administration indeed. But the enlarged satisfaction includes and increases the satisfaction of aggressive impulses, and the concentrated mobilization of aggressive energy affects the political process, domestic as well as foreign.

The danger signs are there. The relationship between government and the governed, between the administration and its subjects is changing significantly—without a visible change in the well-functioning democratic institutions. The response of the government to the expressed wants and wishes of the people—essential to any functioning democracy—frequently becomes a response to popular extremism: to demands for more militant, more uncompromising, more risky policies, sometimes blatantly irrational and endangering the very existence of civilization. Thus, the preservation of democracy, and of civilization itself, seems increasingly to depend on the willingness and ability of the government to *withstand* and to curb aggressive impulses "from below."

To summarize, the political implications of Freudian theory as seen in the preceding discussion are:

1. The sweeping changes in advanced industrial society are accompanied by equally basic changes in the primary mental structure. In the society at large, technical progress and the global coexistence of opposed social systems lead to an obsolescence of the role and autonomy of the economic and political subject. The result is ego formation in and by

masses, which depend on the objective, reified leadership of the technical and political administration. In the mental structure, this process is supported by the decline of the father image, the separation of the ego ideal from the ego and its transference to a collective ideal, and a mode of desublimation which intensifies social control of libidinal energy.

2. Shrinkage of the ego, and collectivization of the ego ideal signify a regression to primitive stages of the development, where the accumulated aggression had to be "compensated" by periodic *transgression*. At the present stage, such socially sanctioned transgression seems to be replaced by the normalized social and political use of aggressive energy in the stage of permanent preparedness.

3. In spite of its perfectly rational justification in terms of technology and international politics, the activation of surplus aggressive energy releases instinctual forces which threaten to undermine the established political institutions. The sanctioning of aggressive energy demanded in the prevailing situation makes for a growth of popular extremism in the masses—a rise of irrational forces which confront the leadership with their claims for satisfaction.

4. By virtue of this constellation, the masses determine continuously the policy of the leadership on which they depend, while the leadership sustains and increases its power in response and reaction to the dependent masses. The formation and mobilization of masses engenders authoritarian rule in democratic form. This is the familiar plebiscitarian trend—Freud has uncovered its instinctual roots in the advance of civilization.

5. These are regressive tendencies. The masses are not identical with the "people" on whose sovereign rationality the free society was to be established. Today, the chance of freedom depends to a great extent on the power and willingness to oppose mass opinion, to assert unpopular policies, to alter the direction of progress. Psychoanalysis cannot offer political alternatives, but it can contribute to the restoration of private autonomy and rationality. The politics of mass society begin at home, with the shrinking of the ego and its subjection to the collective ideal. Counteracting this trend may also begin at home: psychoanalysis may help the patient to live with a conscience of his own and with his own ego ideal, which may well mean—to live in refusal and opposition to the Establishment.

Thus, psychoanalysis draws its strength from its obsolescence: from its insistence on individual needs and individual potentialities which have become outdated in the social and political development. That which is obsolete is not, by this token, false. If the advancing industrial society and its politics have invalidated the Freudian model of the individual and his relation to society, if they have undermined the power of the ego to dissociate itself from the others, to become and remain a self, then the

Freudian concepts invoke not only a past left behind but also a future to be recaptured. In his uncompromising denunciation of what a repressive society does to man, in his prediction that, with the progress of civilization, the guilt will grow and death and destruction will ever more effectively threaten the life instincts, Freud has pronounced an indictment which has since been corroborated: by the gas chambers and labor camps, by the torture methods practiced in colonial wars and "police actions," by man's skill and readiness to prepare for "life" underground. It is not the fault of psychoanalysis if it is without power to stem this development. Nor can it buttress its strength by taking in such fads as Zen Buddhism, existentialism, etc. The truth of psychoanalysis lies in its loyalty to its most provocative hypotheses.

Notes

1. These changes have been described and analyzed in *Studien über Autorität und Familie* (Paris: Felix Alcan, 1936), a book edited by Max Horkheimer for the Institut für Sozialforschung. See especially the contributions by Max Horkheimer and Erich Fromm.

2. The trends merely mentioned here are treated at length in my book *One-Dimensional Man: Studies in the Ideology of Advanced Industrial Society* (Boston: Beacon, 1964).

3. Sigmund Freud, *Group Psychology and the Analysis of the Ego* (New York: Liveright, 1949), pp. 91 and 103. All subsequent quotations in this chapter refer to the same work and edition.

4. Ibid., p. 95.

5. Ibid., p. 121. To be sure, according to Freud, Eros strives to unite living cells into ever-larger units, but this unification would mean, for the human being, the strengthening and transcendence of the ego rather than its reduction.

19

The Crisis of Psychoanalysis

Erich Fromm

The last ten years have shown an increasing preoccupation with the problem of psychoanalysis by a number of politically radical philosophers.[1] Jean-Paul Sartre has made some very interesting contributions to psychoanalytic thinking within the framework of his own existentialist philosophy. Apart from Sartre and N. O. Brown, the best known among this group is Herbert Marcuse, who shares this interest in the connection between Marx and Freud with other members of the Frankfurt Institute for Social Research, such as Max Horkheimer and the late Theodor W. Adorno. There are also a number of others, especially Marxists and socialists, who in recent years have shown considerable interest in this problem and have written extensively about it. Unfortunately, this new literature often suffers from the fact that many of the writers are "philosophers of psychoanalysis" with insufficient knowledge of its clinical basis. One does not have to be a psychoanalyst in order to understand Freud's theories, but one must know their clinical basis; otherwise, it is all too easy to misunderstand Freudian concepts and to simply pick out a few vaguely appropriate quotations without sufficient knowledge of the whole system.

Marcuse, having written more extensively about psychoanalysis than any other philosopher, offers a good example of the particular distortion which the "philosophy of psychoanalysis" can inflict upon psychoanalytic theory. He claims that his work "moves exclusively in the field of theory, and keeps outside of the technical discipline which psychoanalysis has become." This is a bewildering statement. It implies that psychoanalysis started as a theoretical system and later became a "technical discipline," whereas Freud's theories were entirely based on clinical observation.

What does Marcuse mean by "technical discipline"? Sometimes it

247

sounds as if he is referring only to problems of therapy; but at other times the word *technical* is used to refer to clinical, empirical data. To make a separation between philosophy and analytic theory, on one hand, and psychoanalytic clinical data, on the other, is untenable in a science whose concepts and theories cannot be understood without reference to the clinical phenomena from which they were developed. To construct a "philosophy of psychoanalysis" which ignores its empirical basis must necessarily lead to serious errors in the understanding of the theory. Let me say again that I am not implying that one must be a psychoanalyst or even that one must have been psychoanalyzed in order to discuss problems of psychoanalysis. But in order to make sense of psychoanalytic concepts, a person must have some interest in and capacity to deal with clinical data, individual or social. Marcuse and others insist on handling concepts like *regression, narcissism, perversions,* etc., while remaining in the world of purely abstract speculation; they are "free" to make fantastic constructions precisely because they have no empirical knowledge against which to check their speculations. Unfortunately, many readers get their information about Freud in this distorted way, not to speak of the serious damage which all muddled thinking inflicts on those exposed to it.

This is not the place to enter into a full discussion of Marcuse's works dealing with psychoanalysis, *Eros and Civilization, One-Dimensional Man,* and *An Essay on Liberation.*[2] I shall restrict myself to a few remarks. First of all, Marcuse, while widely read, makes elementary mistakes in presenting Freudian concepts. Thus, for instance, he misunderstands Freud's "reality principle" and the "pleasure principle" (although at one point he mentions the right quotation), assuming that there are several "reality principles" and asserting that Western civilization is governed by one of them, the "performance principle." Could it be that Marcuse shares the popular misconception that "pleasure principle" refers to the hedonistic norm that the aim of life is pleasure, and "reality principle" to the social norm that man's striving should be directed toward work and duty? Freud, of course, meant nothing of the kind; to him the reality principle was "a modification" of the pleasure principle, not its opponent. Freud's concept of the reality principle is that there is in every human being a capacity to observe reality and a tendency to protect oneself from the damage which the unchecked satisfaction of the instincts could inflict upon one. This reality principle is something quite different from the norms of a given social structure: one society may censor sexual strivings and fantasies very rigidly; hence, the reality principle will tend to protect the person from self-damage by making him repress such fantasies. Another society may do quite the opposite, and hence the reality principle could have no reason to mobilize sexual repression. The "reality principle," in Freud's sense, is the same in both cases; what is different is the social structure and what

I have called the *"social character"* in a given culture or class. (For example, a warrior society will produce a social character in which aggressive drives are fostered, while striving for compassion and love are repressed; in a peaceful, cooperative society the opposite holds true. Or, in nineteenth-century Western middle-class society the strivings for pleasure and spending were repressed, while the anal-hoarding tendencies which result in the restriction of consumption and in pleasure in saving were encouraged; a hundred years later the social character is one that likes to spend and tends to repress the hoarding, stingy tendencies as inappropriate to the demands of society. In every society general human energy is transformed into specific energy which can be used by the society for its own proper functioning. Accordingly, what is repressed depends on the system of the social character, not on different "reality principles.") But the concept of character, in the dynamic sense in which Freud used it, does not appear in Marcuse's writings at all; one would assume that this is because it is not "philosophical" but empirical.

Not less serious is the distortion of Freud's theory in Marcuse's use of the Freudian concept of repression. " 'Repression' and 'repressive' in the non-technical sense," he writes, "are used to designate both conscious and unconscious, external and internal process of restraint, constraint and repression."[3] But the central category of Freud's system is "repression" in the dynamic sense of the repressed being *unconscious*. By using "repression" for both conscious and unconscious data, the whole significance of Freud's concept of repression and unconscious is lost. Indeed, the word *repression* has two meanings: first, the conventional one, namely, to repress in the sense of oppress, or suppress; second, the psychological one used by Freud (although it had been used in this psychological sense before), namely, to remove something from awareness. The two meanings by themselves have nothing to do with each other. By using the concept of repression indiscriminately, Marcuse confuses the central issue of psychoanalysis. He plays on the double meaning of the word *repression,* making it appear as if the two meanings were one, and in this process the meaning of repression in the psychoanalytic sense is lost—although a nice formula is found which unifies a political and a psychological category by the ambiguity of the word.

Another example of Marcuse's treatment of Freud's theories is the theoretical question of the conservative nature of Eros and the life instinct. Marcuse makes much of the "fact" that Freud attributes the same conservative nature (of returning to an earlier stage) to Eros as to the death instinct. He is apparently unaware that after some wavering Freud arrived, in the *Outline of Psychoanalysis,* at the opposite conclusion, namely that Eros does *not* partake of the conservative nature, a position Freud adopted in spite of the great theoretical difficulties it created.

When stripped of much of its verbiage, *Eros and Civilization* presents as the ideal for the new man in the nonrepressive society a reactivation of his pregenital sexuality, especially the sadistic and coprophilic tendencies. In fact, the ideal of Marcuse's "nonrepressive society" seems to be an infantile paradise where all work is play and where there is no serious conflict or tragedy. (He never comes to grips with the problem of the conflict between this ideal and organization of automated industry.) This ideal of the regression to infantile libidinal organization is coupled with an attack against the domination of genital sexuality over the pregenital drives. By some juggling of words, the subordination of oral and anal erotic strivings under the primacy of genitality is identified with monogamous marriage, the bourgeois family, and the principle that genital sexual pleasure is permissible only if it serves procreation. In his attack against genital "domination" Marcuse ignores the obvious fact that genital sexuality is by no means bound to procreation; men and women have always enjoyed sexual pleasure without the intention to procreate, and methods to prevent conception date far back in history. Marcuse seems to imply that because the perversions—like sadism or coprophilia—cannot result in procreation, they are more "free" than genital sexuality. Marcuse's revolutionary rhetoric obscures the irrational and antirevolutionary character of his attitude. Like some avant-garde artists and writers from de Sade and Marinetti to the present, he is attracted by infantile regression, perversions and—as I see it—in a more hidden way by destruction and hate. To express the decay of a society in literature and art and to analyze it scientifically is valid enough, but it is the opposite of revolutionary if the artist or writer shares in and glorifies the morbidity of a society he wants to change.

Closely related to this is Marcuse's glorification of Narcissus and Orpheus, while Prometheus (whom Marx, incidentally, called "the noblest saint and martyr in the philosophical calendar") is degraded to the "archetype hero of the performance principle."[4] The Orphic-Narcissistic images "are committed to the underworld and to death." Orpheus, according to the classical tradition, is "associated with the introduction of homosexuality." But, says Marcuse, "like Narcissus he rejects the normal Eros, not for an ascetic ideal, but for a fuller Eros. Like Narcissus he protests against the repressive order of procreative sexuality. This Orphic and Narcissistic Eros is the negation of this order—the Great Refusal."[5] This Great Refusal is also defined as "refusal to accept separation from the libidinous object (or subject),"[6] in the last analysis, it is the refusal to grow up, to separate fully from mother and soil, and to experience fully sexual pleasure (genital and not anal or sadistic). (Oddly enough, in *One-Dimensional Man* the Great Refusal seems to have changed its meaning completely, though no mention of the change is made; the new meaning is the refusal to bridge the gap between present and future.) That this ideal is precisely the opposite of Freud's concept of human development and corresponds rather to his concept of neurosis and psychosis is well known.

This ideal of liberation from the supremacy of genital sexuality, of course, is also the very opposite of the sexual liberation which Reich proposed, and which is in full swing today.

Whatever the merits of the demand for the revival of these long-practiced perversions, do we really need a revolution to achieve this goal? Marcuse ignores the fact that for Freud the evolution of the libido from primary narcissism to the oral and anal, and then to the genital level, is not primarily a matter of increasing repression, but of the biological process of *maturing,* which leads to the primacy of genital sexuality. For Freud, the healthy person is the one who has reached the genital level and who enjoys sexual intercourse; Freud's whole evolutionary scheme is based upon this idea of genitality as the highest stage of libido development. I am not objecting here to Marcuse's deviation from Freud, but to the confusion created, not only by using Freud's concepts wrongly, but also by giving the impression that he is representing Freud's position, with only minor revisions. In fact, he is constructing a theory that is the opposite of all that is essential in Freud's thinking; this is achieved by quoting sentences out of context, or statements made by Freud and later dropped, or by plain ignorance of Freud's position and/or its meaning. Marcuse does more or less the same with Marx as he does with Freud. While there is some slight criticism of Marx for not having found the whole truth about the new man, he gives the impression of standing, on the whole, for Marx's aims for a socialist society. But he does not comment on the fact that his own ideal of the infantilistic new man is exactly the opposite of Marx's ideal of a productive, self-active man, able to love and to be interested in everything around him. One cannot help feeling that Marcuse uses the popularity of Marx and Freud among the radical young generation to make his anti-Freudian and anti-Marxian concept of the New Man more attractive.

How is it possible that an erudite scholar like Marcuse can have such a distorted picture of psychoanalysis? It seems to me that the answer lies in the particular interest he—as well as some other intellectuals—have in psychoanalysis. For him psychoanalysis is not an empirical method for the uncovering of the unconscious strivings of a person, masked by rationalization, a theory *ad personam,* which deals with the character and demonstrates the various unconscious motivations for apparently "reasonable acts." Psychoanalysis, for Marcuse, is a set of metapsychological speculations about death, the life instinct, infantile sexuality, etc. It was the great achievement of Freud to have taken up a number of problems so far only dealt with abstractly by philosophy and to transform them into the subject matter of empirical investigation. Marcuse seems to be undoing this achievement by retransforming Freud's empirical concepts into the subject matter of philosophical speculation—and a rather muddy speculation, at that.

Notes

1. The French journal *L'Homme et la société* (Editions Anthropos), for instance, published in 1969 a special issue on "Freudo-Marxisme et sociologie de l'alienation."

2. Herbert Marcuse, *Eros and Civilization* (Boston: Beacon Press, 1955); *One-Dimensional Man* (Boston: Beacon Press, 1964); *An Essay on Liberation* (Boston: Beacon Press, 1969). In the *Essay* he has changed some of his former views and adopted others which he had sharply criticized, yet without indicating this explicitly.

3. *Eros and Civilization*, p. 8.

4. Ibid., chap. 8.

5. Ibid., p. 171.

6. Ibid., p. 170.

Part V
Critical Visions

20

Theses on the
Philosophy of History

Walter Benjamin

The story is told of an automaton constructed in such a way that it could play a winning game of chess, answering each move of an opponent with a countermove. A puppet in Turkish attire and with a hookah in its mouth sat before a chessboard placed on a large table. A system of mirrors created the illusion that this table was transparent from all sides. Actually, a little hunchback who was an expert chess player sat inside and guided the puppet's hand by means of strings. One can imagine a philosophical counterpart to this device. The puppet called "historical materialism" is to win all the time. It can easily be a match for anyone if it enlists the services of theology, which today, as we know, is wizened and has to keep out of sight.

"One of the most remarkable characteristics of human nature, writes Lotze, "is, alongside so much selfishness in specific instances, the freedom from envy which the present displays toward the future." Reflection shows us that our image of happiness is thoroughly colored by the time to which the course of our own existence has assigned us. The kind of happiness that could arouse envy in us exists only in the air we have breathed, among people we could have talked to, women who could have given themselves to us. In other words, our image of happiness is undissolubly bound up with the image of redemption. The same applies to our view of the past, which is the concern of history. The past carries with it a temporal index by which it is referred to redemption. There is a secret agreement between past generations and the present one. Our coming was expected on earth. Like every generation that preceded us, we have been endowed with a

Translated by Harry Zohn

weak Messianic power, a power to which the past has a claim. That claim cannot be settled cheaply. Historical materialists are aware of that.

A chronicler who recites events without distinguishing between major and minor ones acts in accordance with the following truth: nothing that has ever happened should be regarded as lost for history. To be sure, only a redeemed mankind receives the fullness of its past—which is to say, only for a redeemed mankind has its past become citable in all its moments. Each moment it has lived becomes a *citation à l'ordre du jour*—and that day is Judgment Day.

Seek for food and clothing first, then the Kingdom of God shall be added unto you. —Hegel, 1807

The class struggle, which is always present to a historian influenced by Marx, is a fight for the crude and material things without which no refined and spiritual things could exist. Nevertheless, it is not in the form of the spoils which fall to the victor that the latter make their presence felt in the class struggle. They manifest themselves in this struggle as courage, humor, cunning, and fortitude. They have retroactive force and will constantly call in question every victory, past and present, of the rulers. As flowers turn toward the sun, by dint of a secret heliotropism the past strives to turn toward that sun which is rising in the sky of history. A historical materialist must be aware of this most inconspicuous of all transformations.

The true picture of the past flits by. The past can be seized only as an image which flashes up at the instant when it can be recognized and is never seen again. "The truth will not run away from us": in the historical outlook of historicism these words of Gottfried Keller mark the exact point where historical materialism cuts through historicism. For every image of the past that is not recognized by the present as one of its own concerns threatens to disappear irretrievably. (The good tidings which the historian of the past brings with throbbing heart may be lost in a void the very moment he opens his mouth.)

To articulate the past historically does not mean to recognize it "the way it really was" (Ranke). It means to seize hold of a memory as it flashes up at a moment of danger. Historical materialism wishes to retain that image of the past which unexpectedly appears to man singled out by history at a moment of danger. The danger affects both the content of the tradition and its receivers. The same threat hangs over both: that of becoming a tool of the ruling classes. In every era the attempt must be made anew to wrest tradition away from a conformism that is about to overpower it. The Messiah comes not only as the redeemer, he comes as the subduer of Antichrist. Only that historian will have the gift of fanning the spark of hope in the past who is firmly convinced that *even the dead* will not be safe from the enemy if he wins. And this enemy has not ceased to be victorious.

> Consider the darkness and the great cold
> In this vale which resounds with misery.
> —Brecht, *The Threepenny Opera*

To historians who wish to relive an era, Fustel de Coulanges recommends that they blot out everything they know about the later course of history. There is no better way of characterizing the method with which historical materialism has broken. It is a process of empathy whose origin is the indolence of the heart, *acedia,* which despairs of grasping and holding the genuine historical image as it flares up briefly. Among medieval theologians it was regarded as the root cause of sadness. Flaubert, who was familiar with it, wrote, "Peu de gens devineront combien il a fallu être triste pour resusciter Carthage."[1] The nature of this sadness stands out more clearly if one asks with whom the adherents of historicism actually empathize. The answer is inevitable: with the victor. And all rulers are the heirs of those who conquered before them. Hence, empathy with the victor invariably benefits the rulers. Historical materialists know what that means. Whoever has emerged victorious participates to this day in the triumphal procession in which the present rulers step over those who are lying prostrate. According to traditional practice, the spoils are carried along in the procession. They are called cultural treasures, and a historical materialist views them with cautious detachment. For without exception the cultural treasures he surveys have an origin which he cannot contemplate without horror. They owe their existence not only to the efforts of the great minds and talents who have created them, but also to the anonymous toil of their contemporaries. There is no document of civilization which is not at the same time a document of barbarism. And just as such a document is not free of barbarism, barbarism taints also the manner in which it was transmitted from one owner to another. A historical materialist therefore dissociates himself from it as far as possible. He regards it as his task to brush history against the grain.

The tradition of the oppressed teaches us that the "state of emergency" in which we live is not the exception but the rule. We must attain to a conception of history that is in keeping with this insight. Then we shall clearly realize that it is our task to bring about a real state of emergency, and this will improve our position in the struggle against fascism. One reason why fascism has a chance is that in the name of progress its opponents treat it as a historical norm. The current amazement that the things we are experiencing are "still" possible in the twentieth century is not philosophical. This amazement is not the beginning of knowledge—unless it is the knowledge that the view of history which gives rise to it is untenable.

> Mein Flügel ist zum Schwung bereit,
> ich kehrte gern zurück,
> denn blieb ich auch lebendige Zeit,
> ich hätte wenig Glück.
> —Gerhard Scholem, "Gruss vom Angelus"[2]

A Klee painting named *Angelus Novus* shows an angel looking as though he is about to move away from something he is fixedly contemplating. His eyes are staring, his mouth is open, his wings are spread. This is how one pictures the angel of history. His face is turned toward the past. Where we perceive a chain of events, he sees one single catastrophe which keeps piling wreckage upon wreckage and hurls it in front of his feet. The angel would like to stay, awaken the dead, and make whole what has been smashed. But a storm is blowing from Paradise; it has got caught in his wings with such violence that the angel can no longer close them. This storm irresistibly propels him into the future to which his back is turned, while the pile of debris before him grows skyward. This storm is what we call progress.

The themes which monastic discipline assigned to friars for meditation were designed to turn them away from the world and its affairs. The thoughts which we are developing here originate from similar considerations. At a moment when the politicians in whom the opponents of fascism had placed their hopes are prostrate and confirm their defeat by betraying their own cause, these observations are intended to disentangle the political worldlings from the snares in which the traitors have entrapped them. Our consideration proceeds from the insight that the politicians' stubborn faith in progress, their confidence in their "mass basis," and, finally, their servile integration in an uncontrollable apparatus have been three aspects of the same thing. It seeks to convey an idea of the high price our accustomed thinking will have to pay for a conception of history that avoids any complicity with the thinking to which these politicians continue to adhere.

The conformism which has been part and parcel of Social Democracy from the beginning attaches not only to its political tactics but to its economic views as well. It is one reason for its later breakdown. Nothing has corrupted the German working class so much as the notion that it was moving with the current. It regarded technological developments as the fall of the stream with which it thought it was moving. From there it was but a step to the illusion that the factory work which was supposed to tend toward technological progress constituted a political achievement. The old Protestant ethic of work was resurrected among German workers in secularized form. The Gotha Program[3] already bears traces of this confusion, defining labor as "the source of all wealth and all culture." Smelling a rat, Marx countered that "the man who possesses no other property than his labor power" must of necessity become "the slave of other men who have made themselves the owners." However, the confusion spread, and soon thereafter Josef Dietzgen proclaimed: "The savior of modern times is called work. The . . . improvement . . . of labor constitutes the wealth which is now able to accomplish what no redeemer has ever been able to do." This vulgar-Marxist conception of the nature of labor bypasses the question of how its products might benefit the workers while still not being at their disposal. It recognizes only the progress in the mastery of nature, not the retrogression of society; it already displays the technocratic features later encountered in fascism. Among these is a conception of nature which differs ominously from the one in the socialist utopias before the 1848 revolution. The new conception of labor amounts to the exploitation of the proletariat. Compared with this positivistic conception, Fourier's fantasies, which have so often been ridiculed, prove to be surprisingly sound. According to Fourier, as a result of efficient cooperative labor, four moons would illuminate the earthly night, the ice would recede from the poles, sea water would no longer taste salty, and beasts of prey would do man's bidding. All this illustrates a kind of labor which, far from exploiting nature, is capable of delivering her of the creations which lie dormant in her womb as potentials. Nature, which, as Dietzgen puts it, "exists gratis," is a complement to the corrupted conception of labor.

We need history, but not the way a spoiled loafer in the garden of knowledge needs it. —Nietzsche, *Of the Use and Abuse of History*

Not man or men but the struggling, oppressed class itself is the depository of historical knowledge. In Marx it appears as the last enslaved class, as the avenger that completes the task of liberation in the name of generation of the downtrodden. This conviction, which had a brief resurgence in the Spartacist group,[4] has always been objectionable to Social Democrats. Within three decades they managed virtually to erase the name of Blanqui, though it had been the rallying sound that had reverberated through the preceding century. Social Democracy thought fit to assign to the working class the role of the redeemer of future generations, in this way cutting the sinews of its greatest strength. This training made the working class forget both its hatred and its spirit of sacrifice, for both are nourished by the image of enslaved ancestors rather than that of liberated grandchildren.

Every day our cause becomes clearer and people get smarter. —Wilhelm Dietzgen, *Die Religion der Sozialdemokratie*

Social Democratic theory, and even more its practice, have been formed by a conception of progress which did not adhere to reality but made dogmatic claims. Progress as pictured in the minds of Social Democrats was, first of all, the progress of mankind itself (and not just advances in men's ability and knowledge). Second, it was something boundless, in keeping with the infinite perfectibility of mankind. Third, progress was regarded as irresistible, something that automatically pursued a straight or spiral course. Each of these predicates is controversial and open to criticism. However, when the chips are down, criticisms must penetrate beyond these predicates and focus on something that they have in common. The concept of the historical progress of mankind cannot be sundered from the concept of its progression through a homogeneous, empty time. A critique of the concept of such a progression must be the basis of any criticism of the concept of progress itself.

Origin is the goal. —Karl Kraus, *Worte in Versen*, vol. I

History is the subject of a structure whose site is not homogeneous, empty time, but time filled by the presence of the now [*Jetztzeit*].[5] Thus, to Robespierre ancient Rome was a past charged with the time of the now which he blasted out of the continuum of history. The French Revolution reviewed itself as Rome reincarnate. It evoked ancient Rome the way fashion evokes costumes of the past. Fashion has a flair for the topical, no matter where it stirs in the thickets of long ago; it is a tiger's leap into the past. This jump, however, takes place in an arena where the ruling class gives the commands. The same leap in the open air of history is the dialectical one, which is how Marx understood the revolution.

The awareness that they are about to make the continuum of history explode is characteristic of the revolutionary classes at the moment of their action. The great revolution introduced a new calendar. The initial day of a calendar serves as a historical time-lapse camera. And, basically, it is the same day that keeps recurring in the guise of holidays, which are days of remembrance. Thus, the calendars do not measure time as clocks do; they are monuments of a historical consciousness of which not the slightest trace has been apparent in Europe in the past hundred years. In the July Revolution an incident occurred which showed this consciousness still alive. On the first evening of fighting it turned out that the clocks in the towers were being fired on simultaneously and independently from several places in Paris. An eyewitness, who may have owed his insight to the rhyme, wrote as follows:

> Qui le croirait! on dit, qu'irrités contre l'heure
> De nouveaux Josués au pied de chaque tour,
> Tiraient sur les cadrans pour arrêter le jour.[6]

A historical materialist cannot do without the notion of a present which is not a transition, but in which time stands still and has come to a stop. For this notion defines the present in which he himself is writing history. Historicism gives the "eternal" image of the past; historical materialism supplies a unique experience with the past. The historical materialist leaves it to others to be drained by the whore called "Once upon a time" in historicism's bordello. He remains in control of his powers, man enough to blast open the continuum of history.

Historicism rightly culminated in universal history. Materialistic historiography differs from it as to method more clearly than from any other kind. Universal history has no theoretical armature. Its method is additive; it musters a mass of data to fill the homogeneous, empty time. Materialistic historiography, on the other hand, is based on a constructive principle. Thinking involves not only the flow of thoughts, but their arrest as well. Where thinking suddenly stops in a configuration pregnant with tensions, it gives that configuration a shock, by which it crystallizes into a monad. A historical materialist approaches a historical subject only where he recognizes the sign of a Messianic cessation of happening, or, put differently, a revolutionary chance in the fight for the oppressed past. He takes cognizance of it in order to blast a specific era out of the homogeneous course of history—blasting a specific life out of the era or a specific work out of the lifework. As a result of this method the lifework is preserved in this work and at the same time canceled;[7] in the lifework, the era; and in the era, the entire course of history. The nourishing fruit of the historically understood contains time as a precious but tasteless seed.

"In relation to the history of organic life on earth," writes a modern biologist, "the paltry fifty millennia of *homo sapiens* constitute something like two seconds at the close of a twenty-four-hour day. On this scale, the history of civilized mankind would fill one-fifth of the last second of the last hour." The present, which, as a model of Messianic time, comprises the entire history of mankind in an enormous abridgment, coincides exactly with the stature which the history of mankind has in the universe.

Historicism contents itself with establishing a causal connection between various moments in history. But no fact that is a cause is for that very reason historical. It became historical posthumously, as it were, through events that may be separated from it by thousands of years. A historian who takes this as his point of departure stops telling the sequence of events like the beads of a rosary. Instead, he grasps the constellation which his own era has formed with a definite earlier one. Thus, he establishes a conception of the present as the "time of the now" which is shot through with chips of Messianic time.

The soothsayers who found out from time what it had in store certainly did not experience time as either homogeneous or empty. Anyone who keeps this in mind will perhaps get an idea of how past times were experienced in remembrance—namely, in just the same way. We know that the Jews were prohibited from investigating the future. The Torah and the prayers instruct them in remembrance, however. This stripped the future of its magic, to which all those succumb who turn to the soothsayers for enlightenment. This does not imply, however, that for the Jews the future turned into homogeneous, empty time. For every second of time was the strait gate through which the Messiah might enter.

Notes

1. "Few will be able to guess how sad one had to be in order to resuscitate Carthage."

2. "My wing is ready for flight, / I would like to turn back. / If I stayed timeless time, / I would have little luck."

3. The Gotha Congress of 1875 united the two German Socialist parties, one led by Ferdinand Lassalle, the other by Karl Marx and Wilhelm Liebknecht. The program, drafted by Liebknecht and Lassalle, was severely attacked by Marx in London. See his "Critique of the Gotha Program."

4. Leftist group, founded by Karl Liebknecht and Rosa Luxemburg at the beginning of World War I in opposition to the pro-war policies of the German Socialist party, later absorbed by the Communist party.

5. Benjamin says *"Jetztzeit"* and indicates by the quotation marks that he does not simply mean an equivalent to *Gegenwart,* that is, present. He clearly is thinking of the mystical *nunc stans*.

6. "Who would have believed it! We are told that new Joshuas at the foot of every tower, as though irritated with time itself, fired at the dials in order to stop the day."

7. The Hegelian term *aufheben* in its threefold meaning: to preserve, to elevate, to cancel.

21

Notes on Institute Activities

Max Horkheimer

The research project summarized below formulates certain problems which the Institute for Social Research intended to investigate about a year ago. General world conditions, however, brought to the fore other social problems more urgently connected with American interests and compelled us to postpone our original intention. The Institute plans, nevertheless, to return to this project in due time.

As published here, the project contains not only research problems but theoretical conceptions which were in part arrived at through previous research and which would in some measure have to be probed through further investigations. It goes without saying that none of these theses will be treated as dogmas once the actual research is carried through.

The publication of the project in the present issue may help further to clarify the conception of critical social research. The prevailing methodological viewpoints of this approach may briefly be characterized as follows.

I. Concepts are historically formed. The categories we intend to use are not generalizations to be attained by a process of abstraction from various individuals and species, nor are they axiomatic definitions and postulates. The process of forming these categories must take into account the historical character of the subject matter to which they pertain, and in such a way that the categories are made to include the actual genesis of that subject matter. This unique character of the relation of the concept to its "material" does not allow of such abstract concepts as "social change," "association," "collective behavior," "masses," unless these are used as mere formalistic classifications of phenomena common to all forms of society. The proper meaning of "masses," for example, cannot be derived through an essentially quantitative analysis or from certain isolated types

264

of "collective behavior," even though such analysis may be an integral part of any attempt at a theoretical interpretation of the term. Proper methodological usage must recognize that the masses are basically different at the different stages of the sociohistorical process and that their function in society is essentially determined by that of other social strata as well as by the peculiar social and economic mechanisms that produce and perpetuate the masses. The category is thus led, by the very nature of its concrete content, to take in other, different sectors of the given social configuration and to follow out the genesis and import of its content within the social totality. The general concept is thus not dissolved into a multitude of empirical facts but is concretized in a theoretical analysis of a given social configuration and related to the whole of the historical process of which it is an indissoluble part. Such analysis is essentially critical in character.

II. Concepts are critically formed. The critical nature of societal concepts may best be elucidated through the problem of value judgments that animates current discussion among social scientists. The latter is much more than a methodological problem today. The totalitarian states are imposing the political values of imperialist power politics upon all scientific, cultural, and economic activities. This engenders all too much readiness in democratic countries to interpret freedom of science (which is held to include freedom from value judgments) as a drawback of the democratic forms of life. Hence derives a positivist and even skeptical attitude. The attempt has been made to overcome this by a return to old metaphysics, such as neo-Thomism. But this proposed return to the supposedly absolute values of past theological and metaphysical systems may facilitate the destruction of individual liberties to an even greater degree than would the conscious and honest skepticism of the positivists. Social theory may be able to circumvent a skeptical spurning of value judgments without succumbing to normative dogmatism. This may be accomplished by relating social institutions and activities to the values they themselves set forth as their standards and ideals. Thus, the activities of a political party may be investigated in the light of the avowed aims and ends of the party without accepting these as valid or evident. If subjected to such an analysis, the social agencies most representative of the present pattern of society will disclose a pervasive discrepancy between what they actually are and the values they accept. To take an example, the media of public communication, radio, press, and film, constantly profess their adherence to the individual's ultimate value and his inalienable freedom, but they operate in such a way that they tend to forswear such values by fettering the individual to prescribed attitudes, thoughts, and buying habits. The ambivalent relation between prevailing values and the social context forces the categories of social theory to become critical and thus to reflect the actual rift between the social reality and the values it posits.

III. Societal concepts are "inductively" formed. Social concepts derive their critical coloring from the fact that the rift between value and reality is typical of the totality of modern culture. This leads to the hypothesis that society is a "system" in the material sense that every single social field or relation contains and reflects, in various ways, the whole itself. Consequently, an intensive analysis of a single relation or institution that is particularly representative of the prevailing pattern of reality may be far better able to develop and grasp the nature of the pattern than would an extensive compilation and description of assorted facts. The "pervasive" character of our society, the fact that it makes its peculiar relations felt in every nook and cranny of the social whole, calls for a methodological conception that will take account of this fact. Categories have to be formed through a process of induction that is the reverse of the traditional inductive method which verified its hypotheses by collecting individual experiences until they attained the weight of universal laws. Induction in social theory, *per contra,* should seek the universal within the particular, not above or beyond it, and, instead of moving from one particular to another and then to the heights of abstraction, should delve deeper and deeper into the particular and discover the universal law therein.

IV. Social concepts are integrative. The peculiar kind of induction we have just outlined makes the formation of social concepts an empirical process and yet distinguishes this from the empirical method employed in the specialized sciences. For example, the concept "youth," denoting a particular entity in present-day society, is not a biological, psychological, or sociological concept, for it takes in the entire social and historical process that influences the mentality and orientation of youth and that constantly transforms these. Consequently, our concept will assume different functions *pari passu* with the changing composition, function, and attitudes of youth within the shifting social pattern. And owing to the fact that the concept is to be formed under the aspect of the historical totality to which it pertains, sociology should be able to develop this changing pattern from the very content of the concept instead of adding specific contents from without.

In this way, the various categories will be integrative ones through their very content and may themselves serve as the basis for combining the experiences and results of the various special sciences without being impeded by their several fixed boundaries.

the very object of knowledge itself. The object meant by the concept *society* is not in itself rationally continuous. Nor is it to its elements as a universal is to particulars; it is not merely a dynamic category, it is a functional one as well. And to this first, still quite abstract approximation, let us add a further qualification, namely, the dependency of all individuals on the totality which they form. In such a totality, everyone is also dependent on everyone else. The whole survives only through the unity of the functions which its members fulfill. Each individual without exception must take some function on himself in order to prolong his existence; indeed, while his function lasts, he is taught to express his gratitude for it.

It is on account of this functional structure that the notion of society cannot be grasped in any immediate fashion, nor is it susceptible of drastic verification, as are the laws of the natural sciences. Positivistic currents in sociology tend therefore to dismiss it as a mere philosophical survival. Yet such realism is itself unrealistic. For while the notion of society may not be deduced from any individual facts, nor on the other hand be apprehended as an individual fact itself, there is nonetheless no social fact which is not determined by society as a whole. Society appears as a whole behind each concrete social situation. Conflicts such as the characteristic ones between manager and employees are not some ultimate reality that is wholly comprehensible without reference to anything outside itself. They are rather the symptoms of deeper antagonisms. Yet one cannot subsume individual conflicts under those larger phenomena as the specific to the general. First and foremost, such antagonisms serve as the laws according to which such conflicts are located in time and space. Thus, for example, the so-called wage satisfaction which is so popular in current management sociology is only apparently related to the conditions in a given factory and in a given branch of production. In reality it depends on the whole price system as it is related to the specific branches; on the parallel forces which result in the price system in the first place and which far exceed the struggles between the various groups of entrepreneurs and workers, inasmuch as the latter have already been built into the system, and represent a voter potential that does not always correspond to their organizational affiliation. What is decisive, in the case of wage satisfaction as well as in all others, is the power structure, whether direct or indirect, the control by the entrepreneurs over the machinery of production. Without a concrete awareness of this fact, it is impossible adequately to understand any given individual situation without assigning to the part what really belongs to the whole. Just as social mediation cannot exist without that which is mediated, without its elements: individual human beings, institutions, situations; in the same way the latter cannot exist without the former's mediation. When details come to seem the strongest reality of all, on account of their tangible immediacy, they blind the eye to genuine perception.

Because society can neither be defined as a concept in the current logical sense, nor empirically demonstrated, while in the meantime social phenomena continue to call out for some kind of conceptualization, the proper organ of the latter is speculative *theory*. Only a thoroughgoing theory of society can tell us what society really is. Recently it has been objected that it is unscientific to insist on concepts such as that of society, inasmuch as truth and falsehood are characteristics of sentences alone, and not of ideas as a whole. Such an objection confuses a self-validation concept such as that of society with a traditional kind of definition. The former must develop as it is being understood, and cannot be fixed in arbitrary terminology to the benefit of some supposed mental tidiness.

The requirement that society must be defined through theory—a requirement which is itself a theory of society—must further address itself to the suspicion that such theory lags far behind the model of the natural sciences, still tacitly assumed to binding on it. In the natural sciences theory represents a clear point of contact between well-defined concepts and repeatable experiments. A self-developing theory of society, however, need not concern itself with this intimidating model, given its enigmatic claim to mediation. For the objection measures the concept of society against the criterion of immediacy and presence, and if society is mediation, then these criteria have no validity for it. The next step is the ideal of knowledge of things from the inside: it is claimed that the theory of society entrenches itself behind such subjectivity. This would only serve to hinder progress in the sciences, so this argument runs, and in the most flourishing ones has been long since eliminated. Yet we must point out that society is both known and not known from the inside. Inasmuch as society remains a product of human activity, its living subjects are still able to recognize themselves in it, as from across a great distance, in a manner radically different than is the case for the objects of chemistry and physics. It is a fact that in middle-class society, rational action is objectively just as "comprehensible" as it is motivated. This was the great lesson of the generation of Max Weber and Dilthey. Yet their ideal of comprehension remained one-sided, insofar as it precluded everything in society that resisted identification by the observer. This was the sense of Durkheim's rule that one should treat social facts like objects, should first and foremost renounce any effort to "understand" them. He was firmly persuaded that society meets each individual primarily as that which is alien and threatening, as constraint. Insofar as that is true, genuine reflection on the nature of society would begin precisely where "comprehension" ceased. The scientific method which Durkheim stands for thus registers that Hegelian "second nature" which society comes to form, against its living members.

This antithesis to Max Weber remains just as partial as the latter's thesis, in that it cannot transcend the idea of society's basic incomprehensibility any more than Weber can transcend that of society's basic comprehensibility. Yet this resistance of society to rational comprehension should be understood first and foremost as the sign of relationships between men which have grown increasingly independent of them, opaque, now standing off against human beings like some different substance. It ought to be the task of sociology today to comprehend the incomprehensible, the advance of human beings into the inhuman.

Besides which, the antitheoretical concepts of that older sociology which had emerged from philosophy are themselves fragments of forgotten or repressed theory. The early twentieth-century German notion of comprehension is a mere secularization of the Hegelian absolute spirit, of the notion of a totality to be grasped; only it limits itself to particular acts, to characteristic images, without any consideration of that totality of society from which the phenomenon to be understood alone derives its meaning. Enthusiasm for the incomprehensible, on the other hand, transforms chronic social antagonisms into *quaestiones facti*. The situation itself, unreconciled, is contemplated without theory, in a kind of mental asceticism, and what is accepted thus ultimately comes to be glorified: society as a mechanism of collective constraint.

In the same way, with equally significant consequences, the dominant categories of contemporary sociology are also fragments of theoretical relationships which it refuses to recognize as such on account of its positivistic leanings. The notion of a "role" has for instance frequently been offered in recent years as one of the keys to sociology and to the understanding of human action in general. This notion is derived from the pure being-for-others of individual men, from that which binds them together with one another in social constraint, unreconciled, each unidentical with himself. Human beings find their "roles" in that structural mechanism of society which trains them to pure self-conservation at the same time that it denies them conservation of their Selves. The all-powerful principle of identity itself, the abstract interchangeability of social tasks, works towards the extinction of their personal identities. It is no accident that the notion of "role" (a notion which claims to be value-free) is derived from the theater, where actors are not in fact the identities they play at being. This divergence is merely an expression of underlying social antagonisms. A genuine theory of society ought to be able to move from such immediate observation of phenomena towards an understanding of their deeper social causes: why human beings today are still sworn to the playing of roles. The Marxist notion of character-masks, which not only anticipates the later category but deduces and founds it socially, was able to account for this implicitly. But if the science of society continues to operate with such concepts, at the same time drawing back in terror from that theory which puts them in perspective and gives them their ultimate meaning, then it merely ends up in the service of ideology. The concept of role, lifted without analysis from the social facade, helps perpetuate the monstrosity of role-playing itself.

A notion of society which was not satisfied to remain at that level would be a *critical* one. It would go far beyond the trivial idea that everything is interrelated. The emptiness and abstractness of this idea is not so much the sign of feeble thinking as it is that of a shabby permanency in the constitution of society itself: that of the market system in modern-day society. The first, objective abstraction takes place, not so much in scientific thought, as in the universal development of the exchange system itself; which happens independently of the qualitative attitudes of producer and consumer, of the mode of production, even of need, which the social mechanism tends to satisfy as a kind of secondary by-product. Profit comes first. A humanity fashioned into a vast network of consumers, the human beings who actually have the needs, have been socially preformed beyond anything which one might naively imagine, and this not only by the level of industrial development but also by the economic relationships themselves into which they enter, even though this is far more difficult to observe empirically. Above and beyond all specific forms of social differentiation, the abstraction implicit in the market system represents the domination of the general over the particular, of society over its captive membership. It is not at all a socially neutral phenomenon, as the logistics of reduction, of uniformity of work time, might suggest. Behind the reduction of men to agents and bearers of exchange value lies the domination of men over men. This remains the basic fact, in spite of the difficulties with which from time to time many of the categories of political science are confronted. The form of the total system requires everyone to respect the law of exchange if he does not wish to be destroyed, irrespective of whether profit is his subjective motivation or not.

This universal law of the market system is not in the least invalidated by the survival of retrograde areas and archaic social forms in various parts of the world. The older theory of imperialism already pointed out the functional relationship between the economies of the advanced capitalistic countries and those of the noncapitalistic areas, as they were then called. The two were not merely juxtaposed; each maintained the other in existence. When old-fashioned colonialism was eliminated, all that was transformed into *political* interests and relationships. In this context, rational economic and developmental aid is scarcely a luxury. Within the exchange society, the precapitalistic remnants and enclaves are by no means something alien, mere relics of the past: they are vital necessities for the market system. Irrational institutions are useful to the stubborn irrationality of a society which is rational in its means but not in its ends. An institution such as the family, which finds its origins in nature and whose binary structure escapes regulation by the equivalency of exchange, owes its relative power of resistance to the fact that without its help, as an irrational component, certain specific modes of existence such as the small peasantry would hardly be able to survive, being themselves impossible to rationalize without the collapse of the entire middle-class edifice.

The process of increasing social rationalization, of universal extension of the market system, is not something that takes place beyond the specific social conflicts and antagonisms, or in spite of them. It works through those antagonisms themselves, the latter at the same time tearing society apart in the process. For in the institution of exchange there is created and reproduced that antagonism which could at any time bring organized society to ultimate catastrophe and destroy it. The whole business keeps creaking and groaning on, at unspeakable human cost, only on account of the profit motive and the interiorization by individuals of the breach torn in society as a whole. Society remains class struggle, today just as in the period when that concept originated; the repression current in the Eastern countries shows that things are no different there either. Although the prediction of increasing pauperization of the proletariat has not proved true over a long period of time, the disappearance of classes as such is mere illusion, epiphenomenon. It is quite possible that subjective class-consciousness has weakened in the advanced countries; in America it was never very strong in the first place. But social theory is not supposed to be predicated on subjective awareness. And as society increasingly controls the very forms of consciousness itself, this is more and more the case. Even the oft-touted equilibrium between habits of consumption and possibilities for education is a subjective phenomenon, part of the consciousness of the individual member of society, rather than an objective social fact. And even from a subjective viewpoint the class relationship is not quite so easy to dismiss as the ruling ideology would have us believe. The most recent empirical sociological investigation has been able to distinguish essential differences in attitude between those assigned in a general statistical way to the upper and the lower classes. The lower classes have fewer illusions, are less "idealistic." The *happy few* hold such "materialism" against them. As in the past, workers today still see society as something split into an upper and a lower. It is well known that the formal possibility of equal education does not correspond in the least to the actual proportion of working class children in the schools and universities.

Screened from subjectivity, the difference between the classes grows objectively with the increasing concentration of capital. This plays a decisive part in the existence of individuals; if it were not so, the notion of class would merely be fetishization. Even though consumers' needs are growing more standardized—for the middle class, in contrast to the older feudality, has always been willing to moderate expenditures over intake, except in the first period of capitalist accumulation—the separation of social power from social helplessness has never been greater than it is now. Almost everyone knows from his own personal experience that his social existence can scarcely be said to have resulted from his own personal initiative; rather he has had to search for gaps, "openings," jobs from which to make a living, irrespective of what seem to him his own human possibilities or talents, should he indeed still have any kind of vague inkling of the latter. The profoundly social-Darwinistic notion of adaptation, borrowed from biology and applied to the so-called sciences of man in a normative manner, expresses this and is indeed its ideology. Not to speak of the degree to which the class situation has been transposed onto the relationship between nations, between the technically developed and underdeveloped countries.

That even so society goes on as successfully as it does is to be attributed to its control over the relationship of basic social forces, which has long since been extended to all the countries of the globe. This control necessarily reinforces the totalitarian tendencies of the social order, and is a political equivalent for and adaptation to the total penetration by the market economy. With this control, however, the very danger increases which such controls are designed to prevent, at least on this side of the Soviet and Chinese empires. It is not the fault of technical development or industrialization as such. The latter is only the image of human productivity itself, cybernetics and computers merely being an extension of the human senses: technical advancement is therefore only a moment in the dialectic between the forces of production and the relationships of production, and not some third thing, demonically self-sufficient. In the established order, industrialization functions in a centralistic way; on its own, it could function differently. Where people think they are closest to things, as with television, delivered into their very living room, nearness is itself mediated through social distance, through great concentration of power. Nothing offers a more striking symbol for the fact that people's lives, what they hold for the closest to them and the greatest reality, personal, maintained in being by them, actually receive their concrete content in large measure from above. Private life is, more than we can even imagine, mere re-privatization; the realities to which men hold have become unreal. "Life itself is a lifeless thing."

A rational and genuinely free society could do without administration as little as it could do without the division of labor itself. But all over the globe, administrations have tended under constraint towards a greater self-sufficiency and independence from their administered subjects, reducing the latter to objects of abstractly normed behavior. As Max Weber saw, such a tendency points back to the ultimate means-ends rationality of the economy itself. Because the latter is indifferent to its end—namely, that of a rational society—and as long as it remains indifferent to such an end, for so long will it be irrational for its own subjects. The Expert is the rational form that such irrationality takes. His rationality is founded on specialization in technical and other processes, but has its ideological side as well. The even smaller units into which the work process is divided begin to resemble each other again, once more losing their need for specialized qualifications.

Inasmuch as these massive social forces and institutions were once human ones, are essentially the reified work of living human beings, this appearance of self-sufficiency and independence in them would seem to be something ideological, a socially necessary mirage which one ought to be able to break through, to change. Yet such pure appearance is the *ens realissimum* in the immediate life of men. The force of gravity of social relationships serves only to strengthen that appearance more and more. In sharp contrast to the period around 1848, when the class struggle revealed itself as a conflict between a group immanent to society, the middle class, and one which was half outside it, the proletariat, Spencer's notion of integration, the very ground law of increasing social rationalization itself, has begun to seize on the very minds of those who are to be integrated into society. Both automatically and deliberately, subjects are hindered from coming to consciousness of themselves as subjects. The supply of goods that floods across them has that result, as does the industry of culture and countless other direct and indirect mechanisms of intellectual control. The culture industry sprang from the profit-making tendency of capital. It developed under the law of the market, the obligation to adapt your consumers to your goods, and then, by a dialectical reversal, ended up having the result of solidifying the existing forms of consciousness and the intellectual status quo. Society needs this tireless intellectual reduplication of everything that is, because without this praise of the monotonously alike and with waning efforts to justify that which exists on the grounds of its mere existence, men would ultimately do away with this state of things in impatience.

Integration goes even further than this. That adaptation of men to social relationships and processes which constitutes history and without which it would have been difficult for the human race to survive has left its mark on them such that the very possibility of breaking free without terrible instinctual conflicts—even breaking free mentally—has come to seem a feeble and a distant one. Men have come to be—triumph of integration!—identified in their innermost behavior patterns with their fate in modern society. In a mockery of all the hopes of philosophy, subject and object have attained ultimate reconciliation. The process is fed by the fact that men owe their life to what is being done to them. The affective rearrangement of industry, the mass appeal of sports, the fetishization of consumer goods, are all symptoms of this trend. The cement which once ideologies supplied is now furnished by these phenomena, which hold the massive social institutions together on the one hand, the psychological constitution of human beings on the other. If we were looking for an ideological justification of a situation in which men are little better than cogs to their own machines, we might claim without much exaggeration that present-day human beings serve as such an ideology in their own existence, for they seek of their own free will to perpetuate what is obviously a perversion of real life. So we come full circle. Men must act in order to change the present petrified conditions of existence, but the latter have left their mark so deeply on people, have deprived them of so much of their life and individuation, that they scarcely seem capable of the spontaneity necessary to do so. From this, apologists for the existing order draw new power for their argument that humanity is not yet ripe. Even to point out the vicious circle breaks a taboo of the integral society. Just as it hardly tolerates anything radically different, so also it keeps an eye out to make sure that anything which is thought or said serves some specific change or has, as they put it, something positive to offer. Thought is subjected to the subtlest censorship of the *terminus ad quem:* whenever it appears critically, it has to indicate the positive steps desired. If such positive goals turn out to be inaccessible to present thinking, why then thought itself ought to come across resigned and tired, as though such obstruction were its own fault and not the signature of the thing itself. That is the point at which society can be recognized as a universal block, both within men and outside them at the same time. Concrete and positive suggestions for change merely strengthen this hindrance, either as ways of administrating the unadministrable, or by calling down repression from the monstrous totality itself. The concept and the theory of society are legitimate only when they do not allow themselves to be attracted by either of these solutions, when they merely hold in negative fashion to the basic possibility inherent in them: that of expressing the fact that such possibility is threatened with suffocation. Such awareness, without any preconceptions as to where it might lead, would be the first condition for an ultimate break in society's omnipotence.

23

Liberation from the Affluent Society

Herbert Marcuse

I am very happy to see so many flowers here and that is why I want to remind you that flowers, by themselves, have no power whatsoever, other than the power of men and women who protect them and take care of them against aggression and destruction.

As a hopeless philosopher for whom philosophy has become inseparable from politics, I am afraid I have to give here today a rather philosophical speech, and I must ask your indulgence. We are dealing with the dialectics of liberation (actually a redundant phrase, because I believe that all dialectic is liberation) and not only liberation in an intellectual sense, but liberation involving the mind and the body, liberation involving entire human existence. Think of Plato: the liberation from the existence in the cave. Think of Hegel: liberation in the sense of progress and freedom on the historical scale. Think of Marx. Now, in what sense is all dialectic liberation? It is liberation from the repressive, from a bad, a false system— be it an organic system, be it a social system, be it a mental or intellectual system: liberation by forces developing within such a system. That is a decisive point. And liberation by virtue of the contradiction generated by the system, precisely because it is a bad, a false system.

I am intentionally using here moral, philosophical terms, values: "bad," "false." For without an objectively justifiable goal of a better, a free human existence, all liberation must remain meaningless—at best, progress in servitude. I believe that in Marx too socialism *ought* to be. This "ought" belongs to the very essence of scientific socialism. It *ought* to be; it is, we may almost say, a biological, sociological, and political necessity. It is a biological necessity inasmuch as a socialist society, according to Marx, would conform with the very *logos* of life, with the essential possibilities

276

of a human existence, not only mentally, not only intellectually, but also organically.

Now, as to today and our own situation. I think we are faced with a novel situation in history, because today we have to be liberated from a relatively well-functioning, rich, powerful society. I am speaking here about liberation from the affluent society, that is to say, the advanced industrial societies. The problem we are facing is the need for liberation not from a poor society, not from a disintegrating society, not even in most cases from a terroristic society, but from a society which develops to a great extent the material and even cultural needs of man—a society which, to use a slogan, delivers the goods to an ever larger part of the population. And that implies, we are facing liberation from a society where liberation is apparently without a mass basis. We know very well the social mechanisms of manipulation, indoctrination, repression which are responsible for this lack of a mass basis, for the integration of the majority of the oppositional forces into the established social system. But I must emphasize again that this is not merely an ideological integration; that it is not merely a social integration; that it takes place precisely on the strong and rich basis which enables the society to develop and satisfy material and cultural needs better than before.

But knowledge of the mechanisms of manipulation or repression, which go down into the very unconscious of man, is not the whole story. I believe that we (and I will use "we" throughout my talk) have been too hesitant, that we have been too ashamed, understandably ashamed, to insist on the integral, radical features of a socialist society, its qualitative difference from all the established societies: the qualitative difference by virtue of which socialism is indeed the negation of the established systems, no matter how productive, no matter how powerful they are or they may appear. In other words—and this is one of the many points where I disagree with Paul Goodman—our fault was not that we have been too immodest, but that we have been too modest. We have, as it were, repressed a great deal of what we should have said and what we should have emphasized.

If today these integral features, these truly radical features which make a socialist society a definite negation of the existing societies, if this qualitative difference today appears as utopian, as idealistic, as metaphysical, this is precisely the form in which these radical features must appear if they are really to be a definite negation of the established society: if socialism is indeed the rupture of history, the radical break, the leap into the realm of freedom—a total rupture.

Let us give one illustration of how this awareness, or half-awareness, of the need for such a total rupture was present in some of the great social struggles of our period. Walter Benjamin quotes reports that during the Paris Commune, in all corners of the city of Paris there were people shooting at the clocks on the towers of the churches, palaces, and so on, thereby consciously or half-consciously expressing the need that somehow time has to be arrested; that at least the prevailing, the established time continuum has to be arrested, and that a new time has to begin—a very strong emphasis on the qualitative difference and on the totality of the rupture between the new society and the old.

ꭗ   In this sense, I should like to discuss here with you the repressed prerequisites of qualitative change. I say intentionally "of qualitative change," not "of revolution," because we know of too many revolutions through which the continuum of repression has been sustained, revolutions which have replaced one system of domination by another. We must become aware of the essentially new features which distinguish a free society as a definite negation of the established societies, and we must begin formulating these features, no matter how metaphysical, no matter how utopian, I would even say no matter how ridiculous we may appear to the normal people in all camps, on the right as well as on the left.

What is the dialectic of liberation with which we here are concerned? It is the construction of a free society, a construction which depends in the first place on the prevalence of the vital need for abolishing the established systems of servitude; and secondly, and this is decisive, it depends on the vital commitment, the striving, conscious as well as sub- and unconscious, for the qualitatively different values of a free human existence. Without the emergence of such new needs and satisfactions, the needs and satisfactions of free men, all change in the social institutions, no matter how great, would only replace one system of servitude by another system of servitude. Nor can the emergence—and I should like to emphasize this—nor can the emergence of such new needs and satisfactions be envisaged as a mere by-product, the mere result, of changed social institutions. We have seen this; it is a fact of experience. The development of the new institutions must already be carried out and carried through by men with the new needs. That, by the way, is the basic idea underlying Marx's own concept of the proletariat as the historical agent of revolution. He saw the industrial proletariat as the historical agent of revolution, not only because it was the basic class in the material process of production, not only because it was at that time the majority of the population, but also because this class was "free" from the repressive and aggressive competitive needs of capitalist society and therefore, at least potentially, the carrier of essentially new needs, goals, and satisfactions.

We can formulate this dialectic of liberation also in a more brutal way, as a vicious circle. The transition from voluntary servitude (as it exists to a great extent in the affluent society) to freedom presupposes the abolition of the institutions and mechanisms of repression. And the abolition of the institutions and mechanisms of repression already presupposes liberation from servitude, prevalence of the need for liberation. As to needs, I think we have to distinguish between the need for changing intolerable conditions of existence, and the need for changing the society as a whole. The two are by no means identical, they are by no means in harmony. *If* the need is for changing intolerable conditions of existence, with at least a reasonable chance that this can be achieved within the established society, with the growth and progress of the established society, then this is merely quantitative change. Qualitative change is a change of the very system as a whole.

I would like to point out that the distinction between quantitative and qualitative change is not identical with the distinction between reform and revolution. Quantitative change can mean and can lead to revolution. Only the conjunction, I suggest, of these two is revolution in the essential sense of the leap from prehistory into the history of man. In other words, the problem with which we are faced is the point where quantity can turn into quality, where the quantitative change in the conditions and institutions can become a qualitative change affecting all human existence.

Today the two potential factors of revolution which I have just mentioned are disjointed. The first is most prevalent in the underdeveloped countries, where quantitative change—that is to say, the creation of human living conditions—is in itself qualitative change, but is not yet freedom. The second potential factor of revolution, the prerequisites of liberation, are potentially there in the advanced industrial countries, but are contained and perverted by the capitalist organization of society.

I think we are faced with a situation in which this advanced capitalist society has reached a point where quantitative change can technically be turned into qualitative change, into authentic liberation. And it is precisely against this truly fatal possibility that the affluent society, advanced capitalism, is mobilized and organized on all fronts, at home as well as abroad.

Before I go on, let me give a brief definition of what I mean by an affluent society. A model, of course, is American society today, although even in the U.S. it is more a tendency, not yet entirely translated into reality. In the first place, it is a capitalist society. It seems to be necessary to remind ourselves of this because there are some people, even on the left, who believe that American society is no longer a class society. I can assure you that it is a class society. It is a capitalist society with a high concentration of economic and political power; with an enlarged and enlarging sector of automation and coordination of production, distribution, and communication; with private ownership in the means of production, which however depends increasingly on ever more active and wide intervention by the government. It is a society in which, as I mentioned, the material as well as cultural needs of the underlying population are satisfied on a scale larger than ever before—but they are satisfied in line with the requirements and interests of the apparatus and of the powers which control the apparatus. And it is a society growing on the condition of accelerating waste, planned obsolescence, and destruction, while the substratum of the population continues to live in poverty and misery.

I believe that these factors are internally interrelated, that they constitute the syndrome of late capitalism: namely, the apparently inseparable unity—inseparable for the system—of productivity and destruction, of satisfaction of needs and repression, of liberty within a system of servitude—that is to say, the subjugation of man to the apparatus, and the inseparable unity of rational and irrational. We can say that the rationality of the society lies in its very insanity, and that the insanity of the society is rational to the degree to which it is efficient, to the degree to which it delivers the goods.

Now the question we must raise is: Why do we need liberation from such a society if it is capable—perhaps in the distant future, but apparently capable—of conquering poverty to a greater degree than ever before, of reducing the toil of labor and the time of labor, and of raising the standard of living? If the price for all goods delivered, the price for this comfortable servitude, for all these achievements, is exacted from people far away from the metropolis and far away from its affluence? If the affluent society itself hardly notices what it is doing, how it is spreading terror and enslavement, how it is fighting liberation in all corners of the globe?

We know the traditional weakness of emotional, moral, and humanitarian arguments in the face of such technological achievement, in the face of the irrational rationality of such a power. These arguments do not seem to carry any weight against the brute facts—we might say brutal facts—of the society and its productivity. And yet, it is only the insistence on the real possibilities of a free society, which is blocked by the affluent society—it is only this insistence in practice as well as in theory, in demonstration as well as in discussion, which still stands in the way of the complete degradation of man to an object, or rather subject/object, of total administration. It is only this insistence which still stands in the way of the progressive brutalization and moronization of man. For—and I should like to emphasize this—the capitalist Welfare State is a Warfare State. It must have an Enemy, with a capital E, a total Enemy; because the perpetuation of servitude, the perpetuation of the miserable struggle for existence in the very face of the new possibilities of freedom, activates and intensifies in this society a primary aggressiveness to a degree, I think, hitherto unknown in history. And this primary aggressiveness must be mobilized in socially useful ways, lest it explode the system itself. Therefore the need for an Enemy, who must be there, and who must be created if he does not exist. Fortunately, I dare say, the Enemy does exist. But his image and his power must, in this society, be inflated beyond all proportions in order to be able to mobilize this aggressiveness of the affluent society in socially useful ways.

The result is a mutilated, crippled, and frustrated human existence: a human existence that is violently defending its own servitude.

We can sum up the fatal situation with which we are confronted. Radical social change is objectively necessary, in the dual sense that it is the only chance to save the possibilities of human freedom and, furthermore, in the sense that the technical and material resources for the realization of freedom are available. But while this objective need is demonstrably there, the subjective need for such a change does not prevail. It does not prevail precisely among those parts of the population that are traditionally considered the agents of historical change. The subjective need is repressed, again on a dual ground: firstly, by virtue of the actual satisfaction of needs, and secondly, by a massive scientific manipulation and administration of needs—that is, by a systematic social control not only of the consciousness, but also of the unconscious of man. This control has been made possible by the very achievements of the greatest liberating sciences of our time, in psychology, mainly psychoanalysis and psychiatry. That they could become and have become at the same time powerful instruments of suppression, one of the most effective engines of suppression, is again one of the terrible aspects of the dialectic of liberation.

This divergence between the objective and the subjective need changes completely, I suggest, the basis, the prospects, and the strategy of liberation. This situation presupposes the emergence of new needs, qualitatively different and even opposed to the prevailing aggressive and repressive needs: the emergence of a new type of man, with a vital, biological drive for liberation, and with a consciousness capable of breaking through the material as well as ideological veil of the affluent society. In other words, liberation seems to be predicated upon the opening and the activation of a depth dimension of human existence, this side of and underneath the traditional material base: not an idealistic dimension, over and above the material base, but a dimension even more material than the material base, a dimension underneath the material base. I will illustrate presently what I mean.

The emphasis on this new dimension does not mean replacing politics by psychology, but rather the other way around. It means finally taking account of the fact that society has invaded even the deepest roots of individual existence, even the unconscious of man. *We* must get at the roots of society in the individuals themselves, the individuals who, because of social engineering, constantly reproduce the continuum of repression even through the great revolution.

This change is, I suggest, not an ideological change. It is dictated by the actual development of an industrial society, which has introduced factors which our theory could formerly correctly neglect. It is dictated by the actual development of industrial society, by the tremendous growth of its material and technical productivity, which has surpassed and rendered obsolete the traditional goals and preconditions of liberation.

Here we are faced with the question: Is liberation from the affluent society identical with the transition from capitalism to socialism? The answer I suggest is: It is not identical, if socialism is defined merely as the planned development of the productive forces and the rationalization of resources (although this remains a precondition for all liberation). It is identical with the transition from capitalism to socialism, if socialism is defined in its most utopian terms: namely, among others, the abolition of labor, the termination of the struggle for existence—that is to say, life as an end in itself and no longer as a means to an end—and the liberation of human sensibility and sensitivity, not as a private factor, but as a force for transformation of human existence and of its environment. To give sensitivity and sensibility their own right is, I think, one of the basic goals of integral socialism. These are the qualitatively different features of a free society. They presuppose, as you may already have seen, a total transvaluation of values, a new anthropology. They presuppose a type of man who rejects the performance principles governing the established societies; a type of man who has rid himself of the aggressiveness and brutality that are inherent in the organization of established society, and in their hypocritical, puritan morality; a type of man who is biologically incapable of fighting wars and creating suffering; a type of man who has a good conscience of joy and pleasure, and who works, collectively and individually, for a social and natural environment in which such an existence becomes possible.

The dialectic of liberation, as turned from quantity into quality, thus involves, I repeat, a break in the continuum of repression which reaches into the depth dimension of the organism itself. Or, we may say that today qualitative change, liberation, involves organic, instinctual, biological changes at the same time as political and social changes.

The new needs and satisfactions have a very material basis, as I have indicated. They are not thought out but are the logical derivation from the technical, material, and intellectual possibilities of advanced, industrial society. They are inherent in, and the expression of, the productivity of advanced industrial society, which has long since made obsolete all kinds of innerworldly asceticism, the entire work discipline on which Judaeo-Christian morality has been based.

Why is this society surpassing and negating this type of man, the traditional type of man, and the forms of his existence, as well as the morality to which it owes much of its origins and foundations? This new, unheard-of, and not anticipated productivity allows the concept of a technology of liberation. Here I can only briefly indicate what I have in mind: such amazing and indeed apparently utopian tendencies as the convergence of technique and art, the convergence of work and play, the convergence of the realm of necessity and the realm of freedom. How? No longer subjected to the dictates of capitalist profitability and of efficiency, no longer to the dictates of scarcity, which today are perpetuated by the capitalist organization of society; socially necessary labor, material production, would and could become (we see the tendency already) increasingly scientific. Technical experimentation, science, and technology would and could become a play with the hitherto hidden—methodically hidden and blocked—potentialities of men and things, of society and nature.

This means one of the oldest dreams of all radical theory and practice. It means that the creative imagination, and not only the rationality of the performance principle, would become a productive force applied to the transformation of the social and natural universe. It would mean the emergence of a form of reality which is the work and the medium of the developing sensibility and sensitivity of man.

And now I throw in the terrible concept: it would mean an "aesthetic" reality—society as a work of art. This is the most utopian, the most radical possibility of liberation today.

What does this mean, in concrete terms? I said, we are not concerned here with private sensitivity and sensibility, but with sensitivity and sensibility, creative imagination and play, becoming forces of transformation. As such they would guide, for example, the total reconstruction of our cities and of the countryside; the restoration of nature after the elimination of the violence and destruction of capitalist industrialization; the creation of internal and external space for privacy, individual autonomy, tranquillity; the elimination of noise, of captive audiences, of enforced togetherness, of pollution, of ugliness. These are not—and I cannot emphasize this strongly enough—snobbish and romantic demands. Biologists today have emphasized that these are organic needs for the human organism, and that their arrest, their perversion and destruction by capitalist society, actually mutilates the human organism, not only in a figurative way but in a very real and literal sense.

I believe that it is only in such a universe that man can be truly free, and truly human relationships between free beings can be established. I believe that the idea of such a universe guided also Marx's concept of socialism, and that these aesthetic needs and goals must from the beginning be present in the reconstruction of society, and not only at the end or in the far future. Otherwise, the needs and satisfactions which reproduce a repressive society would be carried over into the new society. Repressive men would carry over their repression into the new society.

Now, at this farthest point, the question is: How can we possibly envisage the emergence of such qualitatively different needs and goals as organic, biological needs and goals and not as superimposed values? How can we envisage the emergence of these needs and satisfactions within and against the established society—that is to say, prior to liberation? That was the dialectic with which I started, that in a very definite sense we have to be free from in order to create a free society.

Needless to say, the dissolution of the existing system is the precondition for such qualitative change. And the more efficiently the repressive apparatus of the affluent societies operates, the less likely is a gradual transition from servitude to freedom. The fact that today we cannot identify any specific class or any specific group as a revolutionary force—this fact is no excuse for not using any and every possibility and method to arrest the engines of repression in the individual. The diffusion of potential opposition among the entire underlying population corresponds precisely to the total character of our advanced capitalist society. The internal contradictions of the system are as grave as ever before and likely to be aggravated by the violent expansion of capitalist imperialism. Not only the most general contradictions between the tremendous social wealth on the one hand, and the destructive, aggressive, and wasteful use of this wealth on the other; but far more concrete contradictions such as the necessity for the system to automate, the continued reduction of the human base in physical labor-power in the material reproduction of society, and thereby the tendency towards the draining of the sources of surplus profit. Finally, there is the threat of technological unemployment which even the most affluent society may no longer be capable of compensating by the creation of ever more parasitic and unproductive labor: all these contradictions exist. In reaction to them suppression, manipulation and integration are likely to increase.

But fulfillment is there, the ground can and must be prepared. The mutilated consciousness and the mutilated instincts must be broken. The sensitivity and the awareness of the new transcending, antagonistic values—they are there. And they are there, they are here, precisely among the still nonintegrated social groups and among those who, by virtue of their privileged position, can pierce the ideological and material veil of mass communication and indoctrination—namely, the intelligentsia.

We all know the fatal prejudice, practically from the beginning, in the labor movement against the intelligentsia as catalyst of historical change. It is time to ask whether this prejudice against the intellectuals, and the inferiority complex of the intellectuals resulting from it, was not an essential factor in the development of the capitalist as well as the socialist societies: in the development and weakening of the opposition. The intellectuals usually went out to organize the others, to organize in the communities. They certainly did not use the potentiality they had to organize themselves, to organize among themselves not only on a regional, not only on a national, but on an international level. That is, in my view, today one of the most urgent tasks. Can we say that the intelligentsia is the agent of historical change? Can we say that the intelligentsia today is a revolutionary class? The answer I would give is: No, we cannot say that. But we can say, and I think we must say, that the intelligentsia has a decisive preparatory function, not more; and I suggest that this is plenty. By itself it is not and cannot be a revolutionary class, but it can become the catalyst, and it has a preparatory function—certainly not for the first time; that is in fact the way all revolution starts—but more, perhaps, today than ever before. Because—and for this too we have a very material and very concrete basis—it is from this group that the holders of decisive positions in the productive process will be recruited, in the future even more than hitherto. I refer to what we may call the increasingly scientific character of the material process of production, by virtue of which the role of the intelligentsia changes. It is the group from which the decisive holders of decisive positions will be recruited: scientists, researchers, technicians, engineers, even psychologists—because psychology will continue to be a socially necessary instrument, either of servitude or of liberation.

This class, this intelligentsia has been called the new working class. I believe this term is at best premature. They are—and this we should not forget—today the pet beneficiaries of the established system. But they are also at the very source of the glaring contradictions between the liberating capacity of science and its repressive and enslaving use. To activate the repressed and manipulated contradiction, to make it operate as a catalyst of change, that is one of the main tasks of the opposition today. It remains and must remain a political task.

Education is our job, but education in a new sense. Being theory as well as practice, political practice, education today is more than discussion, more than teaching and learning and writing. Unless and until it goes beyond the classroom, until and unless it goes beyond the college, the school, the university, it will remain powerless. Education today must involve the mind *and* the body, reason *and* imagination, the intellectual *and* the instinctual needs, because our entire existence has become the subject/object of politics, of social engineering. I emphasize, it is not a question of making the schools and universities, of making the educational system political. The educational system is political already. I need only remind you of the incredible degree to which (I am speaking of the U.S.) universities are involved in huge research grants (the nature of which you know in many cases) by the government and the various quasi-governmental agencies.

The educational system *is* political, so it is not we who want to politicize the educational system. What we want is a counterpolicy against the established policy. And in this sense we must meet this society on its own ground of total mobilization. We must confront indoctrination in servitude with indoctrination in freedom. We must each of us generate in ourselves, and try to generate in others, the instinctual need for a life without fear, without brutality, and without stupidity. And we must see that we can generate the instinctual and intellectual revulsion against the values of an affluence which spreads aggressiveness and suppression throughout the world.

Before I conclude I would like to say my bit about the Hippies. It seems to me a serious phenomenon. If we are talking of the emergence of an instinctual revulsion against the values of the affluent society, I think here is a place where we should look for it. It seems to me that the Hippies, like any nonconformist movement on the left, are split. That there are two parts, or parties, or tendencies. Much of it is mere masquerade and clownery on the private level, and therefore indeed, as Gerassi suggested, completely harmless, very nice and charming in many cases, but that is all there is to it. But that is not the whole story. There is in the Hippies, and especially in such tendencies in the Hippies as the Diggers and the Provos, an inherent political element—perhaps even more so in the U.S. than here. It is the appearance indeed of new instinctual needs and values. This experience is there. There is a new sensibility against efficient and insane reasonableness. There is the refusal to play by the rules of a rigged game, a game which one knows is rigged from the beginning, and the revolt against the compulsive cleanliness of puritan morality and the aggression bred by this puritan morality as we see it today in Vietnam among other things.

At least this part of the Hippies, in which sexual, moral, and political rebellion are somehow united, is indeed a nonaggressive form of life: a demonstration of an aggressive nonaggressiveness which achieves, at least potentially, the demonstration of qualitatively different values, a transvaluation of values.

All education today is therapy: therapy in the sense of liberating man by all available means from a society in which, sooner or later, he is going to be transformed into a brute, even if he doesn't notice it any more. Education in this sense is therapy, and all therapy today is political theory and practice. What kind of political practice? That depends entirely on the situation. It is hardly imaginable that we should discuss this here in detail. I will only remind you of the various possibilities of demonstrations, of finding out flexible modes of demonstration which can cope with the use of institutionalized violence, of boycott, many other things—anything goes which is such that it indeed has a reasonable chance of strengthening the forces of the opposition.

We can prepare for it as educators, as students. Again, I say, our role is limited. We are no mass movement. I do not believe that in the near future we will see such a mass movement.

I want to add one word about the so-called Third World. I have not spoken of the Third World because my topic was strictly liberation from the affluent society. I agree entirely with Paul Sweezy, that without putting the affluent society in the framework of the Third World it is not understandable. I also believe that here and now our emphasis must be on the advanced industrial societies—not forgetting to do whatever we can and in whatever way we can to support, theoretically and practically, the struggle for liberation in the neocolonial countries which, if again they are not the final force of liberation, at least contribute their share—and it is a considerable share—to the potential weakening and disintegration of the imperialist world system.

Our role as intellectuals is a limited role. On no account should we succumb to any illusions. But even worse than this is to succumb to the widespread defeatism which we witness. The preparatory role today is an indispensable role. I believe I am not being too optimistic—I have not in general the reputation of being too optimistic—when I say that we can already see the signs, not only that *They* are getting frightened and worried but that there are far more concrete, far more tangible manifestations of the essential weakness of the system. Therefore, let us continue with whatever we can—no illusions, but even more, no defeatism.

24

The Reification of the Proletariat

Herbert Marcuse

I will start with a restatement of the reified concept of the proletariat: The proletariat is, by its very existence, a (the) potentially revolutionary force—this quality being definitive of its very existence. Given its existence, its (potential) function in the transformation of society is also given—realization of its existence. Now, I want to defend this reification, which has at least the advantage that it stops the desperate search for the lost revolutionary Subject: a loss held to be due to the prevalent integration of the working class into the capitalist system. The working class still is the "ontological" antagonist of capital, and the potentially revolutionary Subject: but it is a vastly expanded working class, which no longer corresponds directly to the Marxian proletariat.

Late capitalism has redefined the working class: today, in the advanced countries, industrial laborers are no longer the great majority of this class. The "deproletarianization" of the working class is indicated not only in the higher standard of living, in the sphere of consumption; it is a trend rooted in the development of the production process itself, which integrates large strata of nonproletarian workers into the working class: white-collar employees, technicians, engineers, and the steadily growing private and public bureaucracy which assures the creation as well as realization of surplus value. All these have to sell their labor power and are separated from the control of the means of production. In this greatly enlarged working class, the gap between intellectual and material labor is being reduced, knowledge and education are generalized; however, these achievements are invalidated to the degree to which the system reproduces itself through the productivity of *unproductive* labor, which does not increase the social wealth, but rather destroys and abuses it through the production of waste, planned obsolescence, a self-propelling armament industry, management of consciousness and subconsciousness, etc.

The capitalist mode of production, through the increasing mechanization and intellectualization of labor, accumulates an increasing quantity of general ability, skills, knowledge—a human potential which cannot be developed within the established apparatus of production, because it would conflict with the need for full-time dehumanized labor. A large part of it is channeled into unnecessary work, unnecessary in that it is not required for the construction and preservation of a better society but is necessitated only by the requirements of capitalist production.

Under these circumstances, a "counter-consciousness" emerges among the dependent population (today about 90 percent of the total?), an awareness of the ever more blatant obsolescence of the established social division and organization of work. Rudolf Bahro, the militant East German dissident (he was immediately jailed after the publication, in West Germany, of his book *The Alternative*) uses the term *surplus consciousness* to designate this (still largely vague and diffused) awareness. He defines it as "the growing quantity of free mental energy which is no longer tied up in necessary labour and hierarchial knowledge" (*New Left Review,* no. 106, November–December 1977).

"Surplus consciousness" does not describe an ideological entity, signifying a relapse into idealism. Rather, this strange term designates a quality of the mental energy expressed in the actual behavior of men and women under the impact of the mode of production in late capitalism. This energy is "surplus" over and above the energy spent daily in the alienated performances required by the established production relations. Blocked in finding satisfying ways of effective realization, it becomes, among the dependent population, consciousness of frustration, humiliation, and waste. At the same time, capitalist mass production constantly stimulates this consciousness by the display of an ever larger offer of commodities over and above the necessities (and even amenities) of life. The system is thus compelled, by the requirements of enlarged competitive accumulation, to create and to renew constantly the *needs* for "luxuries," which are all but inaccessible to those who lack the necessary purchasing power. Late capitalism invokes the images of an easier, less repressive, less inhuman life, while perpetuating the alienated labor which denies this satisfaction. In short, late capitalism daily demonstrates the fact that the wherewithal for a better society is available, but that the very society which has created these resources of freedom must preclude their use for the enhancement (and today even for the protection) of life.

In this form, the consciousness of the underlying population is penetrated by the inherent contradictions of capitalism. To be sure, their appearance does not correspond to their essence; surplus consciousness does not conceptualize the dynamics of late capitalist production. Nonetheless, surplus consciousness tends to become a material force, not primarily as class consciousness, but rather as the consciousness of an opposition which expresses itself in new (or recaptured) modes of action, initiated not by any specific class, but by a precarious and temporary "alliance" of groups among the dependent population. Such actions include the "citizens' initiatives" (e.g., the organized protest against nuclear energy installations, against capitalist urban renewal), the fight against racism and sexism, the students' protest, etc. At the same time, workers' initiatives transcend the merely economic class struggle in the demands for the self-organization (*autogestion*) of work.

Under the concentrated power of corporate capitalism, its productivity and destructiveness, the opposition is effectively contained. There is no room for a radicalism which would be supported by the people, and the range of movement as well as the demands which result easily appear ideological and reformist. Is this a throwback to previous stages of bourgeois democracy?

In this situation the classical Marxist "timetable" of historical revolutions gains new significance. According to this timetable, a bourgeois-democratic revolution precedes the proletarian-socialist revolution. The former is to create the *preconditions* for the ideological, political, economic, and organizational transition to socialism (assertion and enlargement of civil rights and liberties, reduction of monopoly capital, institutionalization and extension of equality and of public services, emancipation of oppressed racial and national minorities). Today, the subjection of the majority of the bourgeoisie to the hegemony of corporate capital, and the increasingly totalitarian character of the capitalist state threaten to cancel the achievements of the revolutions of the eighteenth and nineteenth centuries; they are to be recaptured and radicalized. The loss of economic power sustained by large sections of the bourgeoisie, and the intensified exploitation of the working class (old and new) make for the formation of a popular base for change. Thus, the "historic compromise," the alliance with bourgeois forces, the rejection of the "dictatorship of the proletariat" in the strategy of Eurocommunism has roots in the very structure of late capitalism. "Eurocommunism" does not aim at replacing the revolution by the vote, nor does it necessarily project features of the revolution itself. It rather claims to be a theory and praxis responding to a whole (and probably long) period during which capitalism mobilizes its entire economic, technological, and military power to make the world—its world—safe for enlarged accumulation. This implies, on the part of capital, the need to contain the class struggle within economic forms, to obtain and maintain the collaboration of the working class by dividing it into a privileged population in the advanced capitalist countries, and an underprivileged population both in these countries and abroad. Within the global system, the multinational corporations keep the competitive conflicts from becoming explosive.

This overall capitalist policy is largely successful. The subjection of the petty and middle bourgeoisie to monopoly capital has not led to their "proletarianization." The material achievements of capitalism, its life-and-death power, and the apparent absence of a better alternative stabilize the system. Within the global framework, however, a vast reservoir of anticapitalist sentiment is built up. In the developed capitalist countries, it does not result in a revolutionary movement, if by "revolutionary" we understand commitment to the mass struggle for the overthrow of the established social system.

Eurocommunism aims at articulating and winning over this large anti-capitalist (but not yet socialist) opposition outside the "proletariat." The changes are promising. One reason: the "surplus consciousness" has negated the *reification* which veiled the real mechanism of domination behind the facade of free, objective exchange relationships. Can there still be any mystification of who is governing and in whose interests, of what is the base of their power? Not only is the ideology of capitalism wearing thin (inalienable human rights? the "invisible" hand of free competition? private enterprise? equality?)—the very reality of the system no longer conceals its utter destructiveness (the proliferation of nuclear energy, the poisoning of the life environment, chronic unemployment and inflation, perfected control of the population, etc.).

To conclude: The tendency is to the right. It meets an enlarged opposition, qualitatively weakened by internal division, and by the lack of an organization adapted to the conditions of corporate capitalism. At the same time, the global conflicts between the capitalist powers and with the Third World tend to weaken the stabilization of the system, without, however, posing a serious threat. The life-and-death question for the Left is: Can the transformation of the corporate State into a neofascist State be prevented? The question, as well as the possible answers, do not arise from a *revision* of Marxian theory; they are posed by Marxian theory itself!

25

The Tasks of a Critical Theory of Society

Jürgen Habermas

A.—The work of the Institute for Social Research was essentially dominated by six themes until the early 1940s, when the circle of collaborators that had gathered in New York began to break up. These research interests are reflected in the lead theoretical articles that appeared in the main part of the *Zeitschrift für Sozialforschung*. They have to do with (a) the forms of integration in postliberal societies, (b) family socialization and ego development, (c) mass media and mass culture, (d) the social psychology behind the cessation of protest, (e) the theory of art, and (f) the critique of positivism and science.[1] This spectrum of themes reflects Horkheimer's conception of an interdisciplinary social science.[2] In this phase the central line of inquiry, which I characterized with the catchphrase "rationalization as reification," was to be worked out with the differentiated means of various disciplines.[3] Before the "critique of instrumental reason" contracted the process of reification into a topic for the philosophy of history again, Horkheimer and his circle had made "real abstractions" the object of empirical inquiry. From this theoretical standpoint it is not difficult to see the unity in the multiplicity of themes enumerated above.

(a) To begin with, after the far-reaching changes in liberal capitalism the concept of reification needed to be specified.[4] National Socialism, above all, proved an incentive to examine the altered relationship between the economy and the state, to tackle the question of whether a new principle of social organization had arisen with the transition from the Weimar Republic to the authoritarian state, of whether fascism evinced stronger similarities to the capitalist societies of the West or, given the totalitarian features of its political system, had more in common with Stalinism. Pollock and Horkheimer were inclined to the view that the Nazi regime was like the Soviet regime, in that a state-capitalist order had been estab-

Translated by Thomas McCarthy

lished in which private ownership of the means of production retained only a formal character, while the steering of general economic processes passed from the market to planning bureaucracies; in the process the management of large concerns seemed to merge with party and administrative elites. In this view, corresponding to the authoritarian state we have a totally administered society. The form of societal integration is determined by a purposive, rational—at least in intention—exercise of centrally steered, administrative domination.

Neumann and Kirchheimer opposed to this theory the thesis that the authoritarian state represented only the totalitarian husk of a monopoly capitalism that remained intact, in that the market mechanism functioned the same as before. On this view, even a developed fascism did not displace the primacy of economic imperatives in relation to the state. The compromises among the elites of economy, party, and administration came about *on the basis* of an economic system of private capitalism. From this standpoint, the structural analogies between developed capitalist societies—whether in the political form of a totalitarian regime or of a mass democracy—stood out clearly. Since the totalitarian state was not seen as the center of power, societal integration did not take place exclusively in the forms of technocratically generalized, administrative rationality.[5]

(b and c) The relation between the economic and administrative systems of action determined how society was integrated, which forms of rationality the life-contexts of individuals were subjected to. However, the subsumption of sociated individuals under the dominant pattern of social control, the process of reification itself, had to be studied elsewhere: in the family, which, as the agency of socialization, prepared coming generations for the imperatives of the occupational system; and in the political-cultural public sphere, where, via the mass media, mass culture produced compliance in relation to political institutions. The theory of state capitalism could only explain the *type* of societal integration. The analytical social psychology that Fromm,[6] in the tradition of left Freudianism,[7] linked with questions from Marxist social theory was supposed, on the other hand, to explain the *processes* through which individual consciousness was adjusted to the functional requirements of the system, in which a monopolistic economy and an authoritarian state had coalesced.

Institute co-workers investigated the structural change of the bourgeois nuclear family, which had led to a loss of function and a weakening of the authoritarian position of the father, and which had at the same time mediatized the familial haven and left coming generations more and more in the socializing grip of extrafamilial forces. They also investigated the development of a culture industry that desublimated culture, robbed it of its rational content, and functionalized it for purposes of the manipulative control of consciousness. Meanwhile, reification remained, as it was in Lukacs, a category of the philosophy of consciousness; it was discerned in the attitudes and modes of behavior of individuals. The phenomena of reified consciousness were to be explained empirically, with the help of psychoanalytic personality theory. The authoritarian, easily manipulable character with a weak ego appeared in forms typical of the times; the corresponding superego formations were traced back to a complicated interplay of social structure and instinctual vicissitudes.

Again there were two lines of interpretation. Horkheimer, Adorno, and Marcuse held on to Freudian instinct theory and invoked the dynamics of an inner nature that, while it did react to societal pressure, nevertheless remained in its core resistant to the violence of socialization.[8] Fromm, on the other hand, took up ideas from ego psychology and shifted the process of ego development into the medium of social interaction, which permeated and structured the natural substratum of instinctual impulses.[9] Another front formed around the question of the ideological character of mass culture, with Adorno on one side and Benjamin on the other. Whereas Adorno (along with Lowenthal and Marcuse) implacably opposed the experiential content of authentic art to consumerized culture, Benjamin steadfastly placed his hopes in the secular illuminations that were to come from a mass art stripped of its aura.

(d) Thus in the course of the 1930s the narrower circle of members of the institute developed a consistent position in regard to all these themes. A monolithic picture of a totally administered society emerged; corresponding to it was a repressive mode of socialization that shut out inner nature and an omnipresent social control exercised through the channels of mass communication. Over against this, the positions of Neumann and Kirchheimer, Fromm and Benjamin are not easily reduced to a common denominator. They share a more differentiated assessment of the complex and contradictory character both of forms of integration in postliberal societies and of family socialization and mass culture. These competing approaches might have provided starting points for an analysis of potentials still resistant to the reification of consciousness. But the experiences of the German émigrés in the contemporary horizon of the 1930s motivated them rather to investigate the mechanisms that might explain the suspension of protest potentials. This was also the direction of their studies of the political consciousness of workers and employees, and especially of the studies of anti-Semitism begun by the institute in Germany and continued in America up to the late 1940s.[10]

(e and f) Processes of the reification of consciousness could be made the object of a wide-ranging program of empirical research only after the theory of value had lost its foundational role. With this, of course, also went the normative content of rational natural law theory that was preserved in value theory.[11] As we have seen, its place was then occupied by the theory of societal rationalization stemming from Lukacs. The normative content of the concept of reification now had to be gotten from the rational potential of modern culture. For this reason, in its classical period critical theory maintained an emphatically affirmative relation to the art and philosophy of the bourgeois era. The arts—for Lowenthal and Marcuse, classical German literature above all; for Benjamin and Adorno, the literary and musical avant-garde—were the preferred object of an ideology critique aimed at separating the transcendent contents of authentic art—whether utopian or critical—from the affirmative, ideologically worn-out components of bourgeois ideals. As a result, philosophy retained central importance as the keeper of those bourgeois ideals. "Reason," Marcuse wrote in the essay that complemented Horkheimer's programmatic demarcation of critical theory from traditional theory, "is the fundamental category of philosophical thought, the only one by means of which it has bound itself to human destiny."[12] And further on: "Reason, mind, morality, knowledge, and happiness are not only categories of bourgeois philosophy, but concerns of mankind. As such they must be preserved, if not derived anew. When critical theory examines the philosophical doctrines in which it was still possible to speak of man, it deals first with the camouflage and misinterpretation that characterized the discussion of man in the bourgeois period."[13]

This confrontation with the tradition through the critique of ideology could aim at the truth content of philosophical concepts and problems, at appropriating their systematic content, only because critique was guided by theoretical assumptions. At that time critical theory was still based on the Marxist philosophy of history, that is, on the conviction that the forces of production were developing on objectively explosive power. Only on this presupposition could critique be restricted to "bringing to consciousness potentialities that have emerged within the maturing historical situation itself."[14] Without a *theory of history* there could be no immanent critique that applied to the manifestations of objective spirit and distinguished what things and human beings could be from what they actually were.[15] Critique would be delivered up to the reigning standards in any given historical epoch. The research program of the 1930s stood and fell with its historical-philosophical trust in the rational potential of bourgeois culture—a potential that would be released in social movements under the pressure of developed forces of production. Ironically, however, the critiques of ideology carried out by Horkheimer, Marcuse, and Adorno confirmed them in the belief that culture was losing its autonomy in postliberal societies and was being incorporated into the machinery of the economic-administrative system. The development of productive forces, and even critical thought itself, was moving more and more into a perspecuve of bleak assimilation to their opposites. In the totally administered society only instrumental reason, expanded into a totality, found embodiment; everything that existed was transformed into a real abstraction. In that case, however, what was taken hold of and deformed by these abstractions escaped the grasp of empirical inquiry.

The fragility of the Marxist philosophy of history that implicitly serves as the foundation of this attempt to develop critical theory in interdisciplinary form makes it clear why it had to fail and why Horkheimer and Adorno scaled down this program to the speculative observations of the *Dialectic of Enlightenment*. Historical-materialist assumptions regarding the dialectical relation between productive forces and productive relations had been transformed into pseudonormative propositions concerning an objective teleology in history. This was the motor force behind the realization of a reason that had been given ambiguous expression in bourgeois ideals. Critical theory could secure its normative foundations only in a philosophy of history. But this foundation was not able to support an empirical research program.

This was also evident in the lack of a clearly demarcated object domain like the communicative practice of the everyday lifeworld in which rationality structures are embodied and processes of reification can be traced. The basic concepts of critical theory placed the consciousness of individuals directly vis-à-vis economic and administrative mechanisms of integration, which were only extended inward, intrapsychically. In contrast to this, the theory of communicative action can ascertain for itself the rational content of anthropologically deep-seated structures by means of an analysis that, *to begin with,* proceeds reconstructively, that is, unhistorically. It describes structures of action and structures of mutual understanding that are found in the intuitive knowledge of competent members of modern societies. There is no way back from them to a theory of history that does not distinguish between problems of developmental logic and problems of developmental dynamics.

In this way I have attempted to free historical materialism from its philosophical ballast.[16] Two abstractions are required for this: (i) abstracting the development of cognitive structures from the historical dynamic of events, and (ii) abstracting the evolution of society from the historical concretion of forms of life. Both help in getting beyond the confusion of basic categories to which the philosophy of history owes its existence.

A theory developed in this way can no longer start by examining concrete ideals immanent in traditional forms of life. It must orient itself to the range of learning processes that is opened up at a given time by a historically attained level of learning. It must refrain from critically evaluating and normatively ordering totalities, forms of life and cultures, and life-contexts and epochs *as a whole*. And yet it can take up some of the intentions for which the interdisciplinary research program of earlier critical theory remains instructive.

B.—Coming at the end of a complicated study of the main features of a theory of communicative action, this suggestion cannot count even as a "promissory note." It is less a promise than a conjecture. So as not to leave it entirely ungrounded, in what follows I will comment briefly on the theses mentioned above, and in the same order. With these illustrative remarks I also intend to emphasize the fully open character and the flexibility of an approach to social theory whose fruitfulness can be confirmed only in the ramifications of social and philosophical research. As to what social theory can accomplish in and of itself—it resembles the focusing power of a magnifying glass. Only when the social sciences no longer sparked a single thought would the time for social theory be past.

(a) *On the forms of integration in postliberal societies.* Occidental rationalism arose within the framework of bourgeois capitalist societies. For this reason, following Marx and Weber I have examined the initial conditions of modernization in connection with societies of this type and have traced the capitalist path of development. In postliberal societies there is a fork in this path: modernization pushes forward in one direction through endogenously produced problems of economic accumulation, in the other through problems arising from the state's efforts at rationalization. Along the developmental path of organized capitalism, a political order of welfare-state mass democracy took shape. In some places, however, under the pressure of economic crises, the mode of production, threatened by social disintegration, could be maintained for a time only in the political form of authoritarian or fascist orders. Along the developmental path of bureaucratic socialism a political order of dictatorship by state parties took shape. In recent years Stalinist domination by force has given way to more moderate, post-Stalinist regimes; the beginnings of a democratic workers' movement and of democratic decision-making processes within the Party are for the time visible only in Poland. Both the fascist and the democratic deviations from the two dominant patterns depend rather strongly, it seems, on national peculiarities, particularly on the political culture of the countries in question. At any rate, these branchings make historical specifications necessary even at the most general level of types of societal integration and of corresponding social pathologies. If we permit ourselves to simplify in an ideal-typical manner and limit ourselves to the two dominant variants of postliberal societies, and if we start from the assumption that alienation phenomena arise as systemically induced deformations of the lifeworld, then we can take a few steps toward a comparative analysis of principles of societal organizations, kinds of crisis tendencies, and forms of social pathology.

On our assumption, a considerably rationalized lifeworld is one of the initial conditions for modernization processes. It must be possible to anchor money and power in the lifeworld as media, that is, to institutionalize them by means of positive law. If these conditions are met, economic and administrative systems can be differentiated out, systems that have a complementary relation to one another and enter into interchanges with their environments via steering media. At this level of system differentiation modern societies arise, first capitalist societies, and later—setting themselves off from those—bureaucratic-socialist societies. A capitalist path of modernization opens up as soon as the economic system develops its own intrinsic dynamic of growth and, with its endogenously produced problems, takes the lead, that is, the evolutionary primacy, for society as a whole. The path of modernization runs in another direction when, on the basis of state ownership of most of the means of production and an institutionalized one-party rule, the administrative action system gains a like autonomy in relation to the economic system.

To the extent that these organizational principles are established, there arise interchange relations between the two functionally interlocked subsystems and the societal components of the lifeworld in locked subsystems and the societal components of the lifeworld in which the media are anchored. The lifeworld, more or less relieved of tasks of material reproduction, can in turn become more differentiated in its symbolic structures and can set free the inner logic of development of cultural modernity. At the same time, the private and public spheres are now set off as the environments of the system. According to whether the economic system or the state apparatus attains evolutionary primacy, either private households or politically relevant memberships are the point of entry for crises that are shifted from the subsystems to the lifeworld. In modernized societies disturbances in the material reproduction of the lifeworld take the form of stubborn systemic disequilibria; the latter either take effect directly as *crises* or they call forth *pathologies* in the lifeworld.

Steering crises were first studied in connection with the business cycle of market economies. In bureaucratic socialism, crisis tendencies spring from self-blocking mechanisms in planning administrations, as they do on the other side from endogenous interruptions of accumulation processes. Like the paradoxes of exchange rationality, the paradoxes of planning rationality can be explained by the fact that rational action orientations come into contradiction with themselves through unintended systemic effects. These crisis tendencies are worked through not only in the subsystem in which they arise, but also in the complementary action system into which they can be shifted. Just as the capitalist economy relies on organizational performances of the state, the socialist planning bureaucracy has to rely on self-steering performances of the economy. Developed capitalism swings between the contrary policies of "the market's self-healing powers" and state interventionism.[17] The structural dilemma is even clearer on the other side, where policy oscillates hopelessly between increased central planning and decentralization, between orienting economic programs toward investment and toward consumption.

These *systemic disequilibria* become *crises* only when the performances of economy and state remain manifestly below an established level of aspiration and harm the symbolic reproduction of the lifeworld by calling forth conflicts and reactions of resistance there. It is the societal components of the lifeworld that are directly affected by this. Before such conflicts threaten core domains of social integration, they are pushed to the periphery—before anomic conditions arise there are appearances of withdrawal of legitimation or motivation. But when steering crises—that is, perceived disturbances of material reproduction—are successfully intercepted by having recourse to lifeworld resources, pathologies arise in the lifeworld. These resources appear as contributions to cultural reproduction, social integration, and socialization. For the continued existence of the economy and the state, it is the resources listed in the middle column as contributing to the maintenance of society that are relevant, for it is here, in the institutional orders of the lifeworld, that subsystems are anchored.

We can represent the replacement of steering crises with lifeworld pathologies as follows: anomic conditions are avoided, and legitimations and motivations important for maintaining institutional orders are secured, at the expense of, and through the ruthless exploitation of, other resources. Culture and personality come under attack for the sake of warding off crises and stabilizing society. Instead of manifestations of anomic (and instead of the withdrawal of legitimation and motivation in place of anomie), phenomena of alienation and the unsettling of collective identity emerge. I have traced such phenomena back to a colonization of the lifeworld and characterized them as a reification of the communicative practice of everyday life.

However, deformations of the lifeworld take the form of a reification of communicative relations only in capitalist societies, that is, only where the private household is the point of incursion for the displacement of crises into the lifeworld. This is not a question of the overextension of a single medium but of the monetarization and bureaucratization of the spheres of action of employees and of consumers, of citizens and of clients of state bureaucracies. Deformations of the lifeworld take a different form in societies in which the points of incursion for the penetration of crises into the lifeworld are politically relevant memberships. There too, in bureaucratic-socialist societies, domains of action that are dependent on social integration are switched over to mechanisms of system integration. But instead of the reification of communicative relations we find the shamming of communicative relations in bureaucratically desiccated, forcibly "humanized" domains of pseudopolitical intercourse in an overextended and administered public sphere. This pseudopoliticization is symmetrical to reifying privatization in certain respects. The lifeworld is not directly assimilated to the system, that is, to legally regulated, formally organized domains of action; rather, systemically self-sufficient organizations are fictively put back into a simulated horizon of the lifeworld. While the system is draped out as the lifeworld, the lifeworld is absorbed by the system.[18]

(b) *Family socialization and ego development*. The diagnosis of an uncoupling of system and lifeworld also offers a different perspective for judging the structural change in family, education, and personality development. For a psychoanalysis viewed from a Marxist standpoint, the theory of the Oedipus complex, interpreted sociologically, was pivotal for explaining how the functional imperatives of the economic system could establish themselves in the superego structures of the dominant social character. Thus, for example, Löwenthal's studies of drama and fiction in the nineteenth century served to show in detail that the constraints of the economic system—concentrated in status hierarchies, occupational roles, and gender stereotypes—penetrated into the inner-most aspects of life history via intrafamilial dependencies and patterns of socialization.[19] The intimacy of highly personalized relations merely concealed the blind force of economic interdependencies that had become autonomous in relation to the private sphere—a force that was experienced as "fate."

Thus the family was viewed as the agency through which systemic imperatives influenced our instinctual vicissitudes; its communicative internal structure was not taken seriously. Because the family was always viewed only from functionalist standpoints and was never given its own weight from structuralist points of view, the epochal changes in the bourgeois family could be misunderstood; in particular, the results of the leveling out of paternal authority could be interpreted wrongly. It seemed as if systemic imperatives now had the chance—by way of a mediatized family—to take hold directly of intrapsychic events, a process that the soft medium of mass culture could at most slow down. If, by contrast, we *also* recognize in the structural transformation of the bourgeois family the inherent rationalization of the lifeworld; if we see that, in egalitarian patterns of relationship, in individuated forms of intercourse, and in liberalized child-rearing practices, some of the potential for rationality ingrained in communicative action is *also* released; then the changed conditions of socialization in the middle-class nuclear family appear in a different light.

Empirical indicators suggest the growing autonomy of a nuclear family in which socialization processes take place through the medium of largely deinstitutionalized communicative action. Communicative infrastructures are developing that have freed themselves from latent entanglements in systemic dependencies. The contrast between the *homme* who is educated to freedom and humanity in the intimate sphere and the *citoyen* who obeys functional necessities in the sphere of social labor was always an ideology. But it has now taken on a different meaning. Familiar lifeworlds see the imperatives of the economic and administrative systems coming at them from outside, instead of being mediatized by them from behind. In the families and their environments we can observe a polarization between communicatively structured and formally organized domains of action; this places socialization processes under different conditions and exposes them to a different type of danger. This view is supported by two rough sociopsychological clues: the diminishing significance of the Oedipal problematic and the growing significance of adolescent crises.

For some time now, psychoanalytically trained physicians have observed a symptomatic change in the typical manifestations of illness. Classical hysterias have almost died out; the number of compulsion neuroses is drastically reduced; on the other hand, narcissistic disturbances are on the increase.[20] Christopher Lasch has taken this symptomatic change as the occasion for a diagnosis of the times that goes beyond the clinical domain.[21] It confirms the fact that the significant changes in the present escape sociopsychological explanations that start from the Oedipal problematic, from an internalization of societal repression which is simply masked by parental authority. The better explanations start from the premise that the communication structures that have been set free in the family provide conditions for socialization that are as demanding as they are vulnerable. The potential for irritability grows, and with it the probability that instabilities in parental behavior will have a comparatively strong effect—a subtle neglect.

The other phenomenon, a sharpening of the adolescence problematic, also speaks for the socializatory significance of the uncoupling of system and lifeworld.[22] Systemic imperatives do not so much insinuate themselves into the family, establish themselves in systematically distorted communication, and inconspicuously intervene in the formation of the self as, rather, openly come at the family from outside. As a result, there is a tendency toward disparities between competences, attitudes, and motives, on the one hand, and the functional requirements of adult roles on the other. The problem of detaching oneself from the family and forming one's own identity have in any case turned adolescent development (which is scarcely safeguarded by institutions anymore) into a critical test for the ability of the coming generation to connect up with the preceding one. When the conditions of socialization in the family are no longer functionally in tune with the organizational membership conditions that the growing child will one day have to meet, the problems that young people have to solve in their adolescence become insoluble for more and more of them. One indication of this is the social and even political significance that youth protest and withdrawal cultures have gained since the end of the 1960s.[23]

This new problem situation cannot be handled with the old theoretical means. If we connect the epochal changes in family socialization with the rationalization of the lifeworld, socializatory interaction becomes the point of reference for the analysis of ego development, and systematically distorted communication—the reification of interpersonal relations—the point of reference for investigating pathogenesis. The theory of communicative action provides a framework within which the structural model of ego, id, and superego can be recast.[24] Instead of an instinct theory that represents the relation of ego to inner nature in terms of a philosophy of consciousness—on the model of relations between subject and object—we have a theory of socialization that connects Freud with Mead, gives structures of intersubjectivity their due, and replaces hypotheses about instinctual vicissitudes with assumptions about identity formation.[25] This approach can (i) appropriate more recent developments in psychoanalytic research, particularly the theory of object relations[26] and ego psychology,[27] (ii) take up the theory of defense mechanisms[28] in such a way that the interconnections between intra-psychic communication barriers and communication disturbances at the interpersonal level become comprehensible,[29] and (iii) use the assumptions about mechanisms of conscious and unconscious mastery to establish a connection between orthogenesis and pathogenesis. The cognitive and sociomoral development studied in the Piagetian tradition[30] takes place in accord with structural patterns that provide a reliable foil for intuitively recorded clinical deviations.

(c) *Mass media and mass culture.* With its distinction between system and lifeworld, the theory of communicative action brings out the independent logic of socializatory interaction; the corresponding distinction between two contrary types of communication media makes us sensitive to the ambivalent potential of mass communications. The theory makes us skeptical of the thesis that the essence of the public sphere has been liquidated in postliberal societies. According to Horkheimer and Adorno, the communication flows steered via mass media *take the place of* those communication structures that had once made possible public discussion and self-understanding by citizens and private individuals. With the shift from writing to images and sounds, the electronic media—first film and radio, later television—present themselves as an apparatus that completely permeates and dominates the language of everyday communication. On the one hand, it transforms the authentic content of modern culture into the sterilized and ideologically effective stereotypes of a mass culture that merely replicates what exists; on the other hand, it uses up a culture cleansed of all subversive and transcending elements for an encompassing system of social controls, which is spread over individuals, in part reinforcing their weakened internal behavioral controls, in part replacing them. The mode of functioning of the culture industry is said to be a mirror image of the psychic apparatus, which, as long as the internalization of paternal authority was still functioning, had subjected instinctual nature to the control of the superego in the way that technology had subjected outer nature to its domination.

Against this theory we can raise the empirical objections that can always be brought against stylizing oversimplifications—that it proceeds ahistorically and does not take into consideration the structural change in the bourgeois public sphere; that it is not complex enough to take account of the marked national differences—from differences between private, public-legal, and state-controlled organizational structures of broadcasting agencies, to differences in programming, viewing practices, political culture, and so forth. But there is an even more serious objection, an objection in principle, that can be derived from the dualism of media discussed above.[31]

I distinguished two sorts of media that can ease the burden of the (risky and demanding) coordinating mechanism of reaching understanding: on the one hand, steering media, via which subsystems are differentiated out of the lifeworld; on the other hand, generalized forms of communication, which do not replace reaching agreement in language but merely condense it, and thus remain tied to lifeworld contexts. Steering media uncouple the coordination of action from building consensus in language altogether and neutralize it in regard to the alternative of coming to an agreement or failing to do so. In the other case we are dealing with a specialization of linguistic processes of consensus formation that remains dependent on recourse to the resources of the lifeworld background. The mass media belong to these generalized forms of communication. They free communication processes from the provinciality of spatiotemporally restricted contexts and permit public spheres to emerge, through establishing the abstract simultaneity of a virtually present network of communication contents far removed in space and time and through keeping messages available for manifold contexts.

These media publics hierarchize and at the same time remove restrictions on the horizon of possible communication. The one aspect cannot be separated from the other—and therein lies their ambivalent potential. Insofar as mass media one-sidedly channel communication flows in a centralized network—from the center to the periphery or from above to below—they considerably strengthen the efficacy of social controls. But tapping this authoritarian potential is always precarious because there is a counterweight of emancipatory potential built into communication structures themselves. Mass media can simultaneously contextualize and concentrate processes of reaching understanding, but it is only in the first instance that they relieve interaction from yes/no responses to criticizable validity claims. Abstracted and clustered though they are, these communications cannot be reliably shielded from the possibility of opposition by responsible actors.

When communications research is not abridged in an empiricist manner and allows for dimensions of reification in communicative everyday practice,[32] it confirms this ambivalence. Again and again reception research and program analysis have provided illustrations of theses in culture criticism that Adorno, above all, developed with a certain overstatement. In the meantime, the same energy has been put into working out the contradictions resulting from the facts that

- the broadcasting networks are exposed to competing interests; they are not able to smoothly integrate economic, political and ideological, professional and aesthetic viewpoints;[33]
- normally the mass media cannot, without generating conflict, avoid the obligations that accrue to them from their journalistic mission and the professional code of journalism;[34]
- the programs do not only, or even for the most part, reflect the standards of mass culture;[35] even when they take the trivial forms of popular entertainment, they may contain critical messages—"popular culture as popular revenge";[36]
- ideological messages miss their audience because the intended meaning is turned into its opposite under conditions of being received against a certain subcultural background;[37]
- the inner logic of everyday communicative practice sets up defenses against the direct manipulative intervention of the mass media;[38] and
- the technical development of electronic media does not necessarily move in the direction of centralizing networks, even though "video pluralism" and "television democracy" are at the moment not much more than anarchist visions.[39]

(d) *Potentials for protest.* My thesis concerning the colonization of the lifeworld, for which Weber's theory of societal rationalization served as a point of departure, is based on a critique of functionalist reason, which agrees with the critique of instrumental reason only in its intention and in its ironic use of the word *reason*. One major difference is that the theory of communicative action conceives of the lifeworld as a sphere in which processes of reification do not appear as mere reflexes—as manifestations of a repressive integration emanating from an oligopolistic economy and an authoritarian state. In this respect, the earlier critical theory merely repeated the errors of Marxist functionalism.[40] My references to the socializatory relevance of the uncoupling of system and lifeworld and my remarks on the ambivalent potentials of mass media and mass culture show the private and public spheres in the light of a rationalized lifeworld in which system imperatives *clash with* independent communication structures. The transposition of communicative action to media-steered interactions and the deformation of the structures of a damaged intersubjectivity are by no means predecided processes that might be distilled from a few global concepts. The analysis of lifeworld pathologies calls for an (unbiased) investigation of tendencies *and* contradictions. The fact that in welfare-state mass democracies class conflict has been institutionalized and thereby pacified does not mean that protest potential has been altogether laid to rest. But the potentials for protest emerge now along different lines of conflict—just where we would expect them to emerge if the thesis of the colonization of the lifeworld were correct.

In the past decade or two, conflicts have developed in advanced Western societies that deviate in various ways from the welfare-state pattern of institutionalized conflict over distribution. They no longer flare up in domains of material reproduction; they are no longer channeled through parties and associations; and they can no longer be allayed by compensations. Rather, these new conflicts arise in domains of cultural reproduction, social integration, and socialization; they are carried out in subinstitutional—or at least extraparliamentary—forms of protest; and the underlying deficits reflect a reification of communicatively structured domains of action that will not respond to the media of money and power. The issue is not primarily one of compensations that the welfare state can provide, but of defending and restoring endangered ways of life. In short, the new conflicts are not ignited by distribution problems but by questions having to do with the grammar of forms of life.

This new type of conflict is an expression of the "silent revolution" in values and attitudes that R. Inglehart has observed in entire populations.[41] Studies by Hildebrandt and Dalton, and by Barnes and Kaase, confirm the change in themes from the "old politics" (which turns on questions of economic and social security, internal and military security) to a "new politics."[42] The new problems have to do with quality of life, equal rights, individual self-realization, participation, and human rights. In terms of social statistics, the "old politics" is more strongly supported by employers, workers, and middle-class tradesmen, whereas the new politics finds stronger support in the new middle classes, among the younger generation, and in groups with more formal education. These phenomena tally with my thesis regarding internal colonization.

If we take the view that the growth of the economic-administrative complex sets off processes of erosion in the lifeworld, then we would expect old conflicts to be overlaid with new ones. A line of conflict forms between, on the one hand, a center composed of strata *directly* involved in the production process and interested in maintaining capitalist growth as the basis of the welfare-state compromise, and, on the other hand, a periphery composed of a variegated array of groups that are lumped together. Among the latter are those groups that are further removed from the "productivist core of performance" in late capitalist societies,[43] that have been more strongly sensitized to the self-destructive consequences of the growth in complexity or have been more strongly affected by them.[44] The bond that unites these heterogeneous groups is the critique of growth. Neither the bourgeois emancipation movements nor the struggles of the organized labor movement can serve as a model for this protest. Historical parallels are more likely to be found in the social-romantic movements of the early industrial period, which were supported by craftsmen, plebians, and workers, in the defensive movements of the populist middle class, in the escapist movements (nourished by bourgeois critiques of civilization) undertaken by reformers, the *Wandervögel*, and the like.

The current potentials for protest are very difficult to classify, because scenes, groupings, and topics change very rapidly. To the extent that organizational nuclei are formed at the level of parties or associations, members are recruited from the same diffuse reservoir.[45] The following catchphrases serve at the moment to identify the various currents in the Federal Republic of Germany: the antinuclear and environmental movements; the peace movement (including the theme of north-south conflict); single-issue and local movements; the alternative movement (which encompasses the urban "scene," with its squatters and alternative projects, as well as the rural communes); the minorities (the elderly, gays, handicapped, and so forth); the psychoscene, with support groups and youth sects; religious fundamentalism; the tax-protest movement, school protest by parents' associations, resistance to "modernist" reforms; and, finally, the women's movement. Of international significance are the autonomy movements struggling for regional, linguistic, cultural, and also religious independence.

In this spectrum I will differentiate emancipatory potentials from potentials for resistance and withdrawal. After the American civil rights movement—which has since issued in a particularistic self-affirmation of black subcultures—only the feminist movement stands in the tradition of bourgeois-socialist liberation movements. The struggle against patriarchal oppression and for the redemption of a promise that has long been anchored in the acknowledged universalistic foundations of morality and law gives feminism the impetus of an offensive movement, whereas the other movements have a more defensive character. The resistance and withdrawal movements aim at stemming formally organized domains of action for the sake of communicatively structured domains, and not at conquering new territory. There is an element of particularism that connects feminism with these movements; the emancipation of women means not only establishing formal equality and eliminating male privilege, but overturning concrete forms of life marked by male monopolies. Furthermore, the historical legacy of the sexual division of labor to which women were subjected in the bourgeois nuclear family has given them access to contrasting virtues, to a register of values complementary to those of the male world and opposed to a one-sidedly rationalized everyday practice.

Within resistance movements we can distinguish further between the defense of traditional and social rank (based on property) and a defense that already operates on the basis of a rationalized lifeworld and tries out new ways of cooperating and living together. This criterion makes it possible to demarcate the protest of the traditional middle classes against threats to neighborhoods by large technical projects, the protest of parents against comprehensive schools, the protest against taxes (patterned after the movement in support of Proposition 13 in California), and most of the movements for autonomy, on the one side, from the core of a new conflict potential, on the other: youth and alternative movements for which a critique of growth sparked by themes of ecology and peace is the common focus. It is possible to conceive of these conflicts in terms of resistance to tendencies toward a colonization of the lifeworld, as I hope now to indicate, at least in a cursory way.[46] The objectives, attitudes, and ways of acting prevalent in youth protest groups can be understood, to begin with, as reactions to certain problem situations that are perceived with great sensitivity.

"Green" problems. The intervention of large-scale industry into ecological balances, the growing scarcity of nonrenewable natural resources, as well as demographic developments present industrially developed societies with major problems; but these challenges are abstract at first and call for technical and economic solutions, which must in turn be globally planned and implemented by administrative means. What sets off the protest is rather the tangible destruction of the urban environment; the despoliation of the countryside through housing developments, industrialization, and pollution; the impairment of health through the ravages of civilization, pharmaceutical side effects, and the like—that is, developments that noticeably affect the organic foundations of the lifeworld and make us drastically aware of standards of liability, of inflexible limits to the deprivation of sensual-aesthetic background needs.

Problems of excessive complexity. There are certainly good reasons to fear military potentials for destruction, nuclear power plants, atomic waste, genetic engineering, the storage and central utilization of private data, and the like. These real anxieties are combined, however, with the terror of a new category of risks that are literally invisible and are comprehensible only from the perspective of the system. These risks invade the lifeworld and at the same time burst its dimensions. The anxieties function as catalysts for a feeling of being overwhelmed in view of the possible consequences of processes for which we are morally accountable—since we do set them in motion technically and politically—and yet for which we can no longer take moral responsibility—since their scale has put them beyond our control. Here resistance is directed against abstractions that are forced upon the lifeworld, although they go beyond the spatial, temporal, and social limits of complexity of even highly differentiated lifeworlds, centered as these are around the senses.

Overburdening the communicative infrastructure. Something that is expressed rather blatantly in the manifestations of the psychomovement and renewed religious fundamentalism is also a motivating force behind most alternative projects and many citizens' action groups—the painful manifestations of deprivation in a culturally impoverished and one-sidedly rationalized practice of everyday life. For this reason, ascriptive characteristics such as gender, age, skin color, neighborhood or locality, and religious affiliation serve to build up and separate communities, to establish subculturally protected communities supportive of the search for personal and collective identity. The revaluation of the particular, the natural, the provincial, of social spaces that are small enough to be familiar, of decentralized forms of commerce and despecialized activities, of segmented pubs, simple interactions and dedifferentiated public spheres—all this is meant to foster the revitalization of possibilities for expression and communication that have been buried alive. Resistance to reformist interventions that turn into their opposite, because the means by which they are implemented run counter to the declared aims of social integration, also belongs in this context.

The new conflicts arise along the seams between system and lifeworld. Earlier I described how the interchange between the private and public spheres, on the one hand, and the economic and administrative action systems, on the other, takes place via the media of money and power, and how it is institutionalized in the roles of employees and consumers, citizens and clients of the state. It is just these roles that are the targets of protest. Alternative practice is directed against the profit-dependent instrumentalization of work in one's vocation, the market-dependent mobilization of labor power, against the extension of pressures of competition and performance all the way down into elementary school. It also takes aim at the monetarization of services, relationships, and time, at the consumerist redefinition of private spheres of life and personal lifestyles. Furthermore, the relation of clients to public-service agencies is to be opened up and reorganized in a participatory mode, along the lines of self-help organizations. It is above all in the domains of social policy and health policy (e.g., in connection with psychiatric care) that models of reform point in this direction. Finally, certain forms of protest negate the definitions of the role of citizen and the routines for pursuing interests in a purposive-rational manner—forms ranging from the undirected explosion of disturbances by youth ("Zurich is burning!"), through calculated or surrealistic violations of rules (after the pattern of the American civil rights movement and student protests), to violent provocation and intimidation.

According to the programmatic conceptions of some theoreticians, a partial disintegration of the social roles of employees and consumers, of clients and citizens of the state, is supposed to clear the way for counterinstitutions that develop from within the lifeworld in order to set limits to the inner dynamics of the economic and political-administrative action systems. These institutions are supposed, on the one hand, to divert out of the economic system a second, informal sector that is no longer oriented to profit and, on the other hand, to oppose to the party system new forms of a "politics in the first person," a politics that is expressive and at the same time has a democratic base.[47] Such institutions would reverse just those abstractions and neutralizations by which in modern societies labor and political will-formation have been tied to media-steered interaction. The capitalist enterprise and the mass party (as an "ideology-neutral organization for acquiring power") generalize their points of social entry via labor markets and manufactured public spheres; they treat their employees and voters as abstract labor power and voting subjects; and they keep at a distance—as environments of the system—those spheres in which personal and collective identities can alone take shape. By contrast, the counterinstitutions are intended to dedifferentiate some parts of the formally organized domains of action, remove them from the clutches of the steering media, and return these "liberated areas" to the action-coordinating mechanism of reaching understanding.

However unrealistic these ideas may be, they are important for the polemical significance of the new resistance and withdrawal movements reacting to the colonization of the lifeworld. This significance is obscured, both in the self-understanding of those involved and in the ideological imputations of their opponents, if the communicative rationality of cultural modernity is rashly equated with the functionalist rationality of self-maintaining economic and administrative action systems—that is, whenever the rationalization of the lifeworld is not carefully distinguished from the increasing complexity of the social system. This confusion explains the fronts—which are out of place and obscure the real political oppositions—between the antimodernism of the Young Conservatives[48] and the neoconservative defense of postmodernity[49] that robs a modernity at variance with itself of its rational content and its perspectives on the future.[50]

Notes

1. See the nine-volume reprint of *Zeitschrift für Sozialforschung* by Kösel Verlag (Munich, 1979).

2. The state of the program is discussed in W. Bonss and A. Honneth, eds., *Sozialforschung als Kritik* (Frankfurt, 1982).

3. H. Dubiel, *Theory and Politics: Studies in the Development of Critical Theory* (Cambridge, Mass., 1985), pt. 2.

4. On what follows, see H. Dubiel and A. Söllner, "Die Nationalsozialismusforschung des Instituts für Sozialforchung," in Dubiel and Söllner, eds., *Recht und Staat im Nationalsozialismus* (Frankfurt, 1981), pp. 7ff.

5. As Marcuse presented it even then: "Social Implications of Modern Technology," *Zeitschrift für Sozialforschung* 9 (1941): 414ff.

6. E. Fromm. "Über Methode and Aufgabe einer analytischen Sozialpsychologie," *Zeitschrift für Sozialforschung* 1 (1932): 28ff. English translation in E. Fromm, *The Crisis of Psychoanalysis* (Greenwich, Conn., 1971).

7. H. Dahmer, *Libido und Gessellschaft* (Frankfurt, 1973); H. Dahmer, ed., *Analytische Sozialpsychologie* (Frankfurt, 1980).

8. They did not change their position. See. T. W. Adorno, "Sociology and Psychology," *New Left Review* 46 (1967): 67–80, and 47 (1968): 79–90; H. Marcuse, *Eros and Civilization* (Boston, 1955); and idem, *Five Lectures* (Boston, 1970).

9. E. Fromm, *Escape from Freedom* (New York, 1942).

10. E. Fromm, *Arbeiter und Angestellte am Vorabend des Dritten Reiches: Eine sozialpsychologische Untersuchung,* ed. W. Bonss (Stuttgart, 1980).

11. E. M. Lange, "Wertformanalyse, Geldkritik und die Konstruktion des Fetischismus bei Marx," *Neue philosophische Hefte* 13 (1978): 1 ff.

12. H. Marcuse, "Philosophy and Critical Theory," in *Negations* (Boston, 1968), p. 135.

13. Ibid., p. 147.

14. Ibid., p. 158.

15. Ibid.

16. See J. Habermas, *Communication and the Evolution of Society* (Boston, 1979), esp. chaps. 3 and 4.

17. On the discussion of the breakdown of Keynesian economic policy in the West, see P. C. Roberts, "The Breakdown of the Keynesian Model," *Public Interest* (1978): 20ff; J. A. Kregel, "From Post-Keynes to Pre-Keynes," *Social Research* 46 (1979): 212ff.; J. D. Wisman, "Legitimation, Ideology-Critique and Economics," *Social Research* 46 (1979): 291ff; P. Davidson, "Post Keynesian Economics," *Public Interest* (1980): 151ff.

18. A. Arato, "Critical Sociology and Authoritarian State Socialism," in D. Held and J. Thompson, eds., *Habermas: Critical Debates* (Cambridge, Mass., 1982), pp. 196–218.

19. L. Löwenthal, *Gesammelte Schriften,* vol. 2 (Frankfurt, 1981).

20. H. Kohut, *Narzissmus: Eine Theorie der Behandlung narzistischer Persön-lichkeitsstörungen* (Frankfurt, 1973); and idem, *Die Heilung des Selbst* (Frankfurt, 1979).

21. Christopher Lasch, *The Culture of Narcissism* (New York, 1978).

22. P. Blos, *On Adolescence* (New York, 1962); Erik Erikson, *Identity and the Life Cycle* (New York, 1959).

23. See R. Döbert and G. Nunner-Winkler, *Adoleszenzkrise und Identitätsbildung* (Frankfurt, 1975); T. Ziehe, *Pubertät und Narzissmus* (Frankfurt, 1975); R. M. Merelman, "Moral Development

and Potential Radicalism in Adolescence," *Youth and Society* 9 (1977): 29ff.; C. A. Rootes, "Politics of Moral Protest and Legitimation Problems of the Modern Capitalist State," *Theory and Society* 9 (1980): 473ff.

24. See J. Habermas, *Knowledge and Human Interests* (Boston, 1971), esp. chaps. 10–12; A. Lorenzer, *Sprachzerstörung und Rekonstruktion* (Frankfurt, 1970); K. Menne, M. Looser, A. Osterland, K. Brede, and E. Moersch, *Sprache, Handlung und Unbewusstes* (Frankfurt, 1976).

25. J. Habermas, "Moral Development and Ego Identity," in *Communication and the Evolution of Society*, pp. 69–94; R. Keagan, *The Evolving Self* (Cambridge, Mass., 1981).

26. W. R. D. Fairbane, *An Object Relations Theory of Personality* (London, 1952); D. W. Winnicott, *The Maturational Process and the Facilitating Environment* (New York, 1965).

27. See E. Jacobson, *The Self and the Object World* (New York, 1964); M. Mahler, *Symbiose und Individuation*, 2 vols. (Stuttgart, 1972); Kohut, *Narzissmus;* H. Kohut, *Introspektion, Empathie und Psychoanalyse* (Frankfurt, 1976); O. Kernberg, *Borderline-Störungen und pathologischer Narzissmus* (Frankfurt, 1978).

28. A. Freud, *The Ego and the Mechanisms of Defense* (New York, 1946); D. R. Miller and G. E. Swanson, *Inner Conflict and Defense* (New York, 1966); L. B. Murphy, "The Problem of Defense and the Concept of Coping," in E. Antony and C. Koipernik, eds., *The Child in His Family* (New York, 1970); N. Haan, "A Tripartite Model of Ego-Functioning," *Journal of Neurological Mental Disease* 148 (1969): 14ff.

29. R. Dobert, G. Nunner-Winkler, and J. Habermas, eds., *Entwicklung des Ichs* (Cologne, 1977); R. L. Selman, *The Growth of Interpersonal Understanding* (New York, 1980).

30. W. Damon, ed., *New Directions for Child Development*, 2 vols. (San Francisco, 1978); H. Furth, *Piaget and Knowledge* (Chicago, 1981).

31. See pp. 277ff., J. Habermas, *Theory of Communicative Action*, Vol. II (Boston: Beacon Press, 1987).

32. C. W. Mills, *Politics, Power and People* (New York, 1963); B. Rosenberg and D. White, eds., *Mass Culture* (Glencoe, Ill., 1957): A. Gouldner, *The Dialectics of Ideology and Technology* (New York, 1976): E. Barnouw, *The Sponser* (New York, 1977); D. Smythe, "Communications: Blind Spot of Western Marxism," *Canadian Journal of Political and Social Theory* 1 (1977); T. Gitlin, "Media Sociology: The Dominant Paradigm," *Theory and Society* 6 (1978); 205ff.

33. D. Kellner, "Network Television and American Society: Introduction to a Critical Theory of Television," *Theory and Society* 10 (1981); 31ff.

34. Ibid., pp. 38ff.

35. A. Singlewood, *The Myth of Mass Culture* (London, 1977).

36. D. Kellner, "TV, Ideology and Emancipatory Popular Culture," *Socialist Review* 45 (1979); 13ff.

37. D. Kellner, "Kulturindustrie und Massenkommunikation: Die kritische Theorie und ihre Folgen," in W. Bonss and A. Honneth, eds., *Sozialforschung als Kritik* (Frankfurt, 1982), pp. 482–515.

38. From Lazarsfeld's early radio studies on the dual character of communication flows and the role of opinion leaders, the independent weight of everyday communication in relations to mass communication has been confirmed again and again: "In the last analysis it is people talking with people more than people listening to, or reading, or looking at the mass media that really causes opinions to change" (Mills, *Power, Politics and People*, p. 590). See P. Lazarsfeld, B. Berelson, and H. Gaudet, *The People's Choice* (New York, 1948); P. Lazarsfeld and E. Katz, *Personal Influence* (New York, 1955). Compare O. Negt and A. Kluge, *Öffentlichkeit und Erfahrung* (Frankfurt, 1970), and, by the same authors, *Geschichte und Eigensinn* (Munich, 1981).

39. H. M. Ensensberger, "Baukasten zu einer Theorie der Meiden," in *Palaver* (Frankfurt, 1974), pp. 91ff.

40. S. Benhabib, "Modernity and the Aporias of Critical Theory," *Telos* 49 (1981): 38–60.

41. R. Inglehart, "Wertwandel und politisches Verhalten," in J. Matthes, ed., *Sozialer Wandel in Westeuropa* (Frankfurt, 1979).

42. K. Hilderbrandt and R. J. Dalton, "Die neue Politik," *Politische Vierteljahresschrift* 18 (1977): 230ff; S. H. Barnes, M. Kaase et al., *Political Action* (Beverly Hills and London, 1979).

43. J. Hirsch, "Alternativbewegung: Eine politische Alternative," in R. Roth, ed., *Parlamentarisches Ritual und politische Alternativen* (Frankfurt, 1980).

44. On this point I found a manuscript by K. W. Brand very helpful: "Zur Diskussion um Entstehung, Funktion und Perspektive der Ökologie- und Alternativbewegung" (Munich, 1980).

45. Hirsch, "Alternativbewegung"; J. Huber, *Wer soll das alles ändern?* (Berlin, 1980).

46. J. Rraschke, "Politik und Wertwandel in den westlichen Demokratien," supplement to the weekly paper *Das Parlament,* September 1980, pp. 23ff.

47. On the dual economy, see A. Gorz, *Abschied vom Proletariat* (Frankfurt, 1980); J. Huber, *Wer soll das alles ändern?* Concerning the effects of democratic mass parties on the lifeworld contexts of voters, see Claus Offe, "Konkurrenzpartei und kollektive politische Identität," in Roth, *Parlamentarisches Ritual.*

48. See, for example, B. Guggenberger, *Bürgerinitiativen in der Parteindemokratie* (Stuttgart, 1980).

49. See, for example, P. Berger, B. Berger, and H. Kellner, *Das Unbehagen in der Modernität* (Frankfurt, 1975).

50. J. Habermas, "Modernity versus Postmodernity," *New German Critique* 22 (1981): 3–14; L. Baier, "Wer unsere Köpfe kolonisiert," in *Literaturmagazin* 9 (1978).

Annotated Bibliography

By Douglas MacKay Kellner

Those who read German should consult Rolf Wiggershaus, *Die Frankfurter Schule* (Munich: Hanser, 1986), which is the most comprehensive and incisive account of the genesis and history of Critical Theory yet produced. An excellent history in English of the Institute for Social Research, which provides a good introduction to Critical Theory, is provided in Martin Jay, *The Dialectical Imagination* (Boston, Little, Brown, 1973). See also Jay's studies in *Marxism and Totality* (Berkeley: University of California Press, 1984) and *Permanent Exiles: Essays on the Intellectual Migration from Germany to America* (New York: Columbia University Press, 1986).

Other introductions in English include Albrecht Wellmer, *The Critical Theory of Society* (New York: Seabury, 1974); Phil Slater, *Origin and Significance of the Frankfurt School* (London: Routledge & Kegan Paul, 1977); Zoltan Tar, *The Frankfurt School* (New York and London: John Wiley & Sons, 1977); David Held, *Introduction to Critical Theory* (Berkeley: University of California Press, 1980); Paul Connerton, *The Tragedy of Enlightenment* (Cambridge: Cambridge University Press, 1980); George Friedman, *The Political Philosophy of the Frankfurt School* (Ithaca: Cornell University Press, 1981); Tom Bottomore, *The Frankfurt School* (London and New York: Tavistock Publications, 1984); Helmut Dubiel, *Theory and Politics* (Cambridge: MIT Press, 1985); and Douglas Kellner, *Critical Theory, Marxism, and Modernity* (Cambridge: Polity Press, 1989). Slater, Tar, and Bottomore attack Critical Theory from the standpoint of orthodox Marxism and sociology, while Friedman criticizes it from a neoconservative position influenced by Leo Strauss. Wellmer, Held, Connerton, Dubiel, and Kellner provide more immanent critiques of the tradition.

Collections of essays on Critical Theory include John O'Neill, ed., *On

Critical Theory (New York: Seabury, 1976); Judith Marcus and Zoltan Tar, eds., *Foundations of the Frankfurt School of Social Research* (New Brunswick: Transaction Books, 1984); and, for German readers, Wolfgang Bonss and Axel Honneth, eds., *Sozialforschung als Kritik* (Frankfurt: Suhrkamp, 1982). On the application of Critical Theory to contemporary issues, see John Forester, ed., *Critical Theory and Public Life* (Cambridge: MIT Press, 1985). For an overview of literature on Critical Theory, see Douglas Kellner and Rick Roderick, "Recent Literature on Critical Theory," *New German Critique* 23 (Spring–Summer 1981): 141–177.

An excellent analysis of the roots of Critical Theory is provided by Andrew Feenberg, *Lukács, Marx and the Sources of Critical Theory* (Totowa, N.J.: Rowan and Littlefield, 1981). Feenberg points to the particular importance of Lukács's *History and Class Consciousness* (Cambridge: MIT Press, 1971) in the genesis of this tradition. On the synthesis of Marxism and psychoanalysis, see Russell Jacoby, *Social Amnesia* (Boston: Beacon Press, 1976). William Leiss, *Domination of Nature* (Boston: Beacon Press, 1972) applies Critical Theory to ecological issues; its relevance to issues of community and the decline of public life is emphasized by John Keane, *Public Life and Late Capitalism* (Cambridge: Cambridge University Press, 1984). An analysis of the epistemological and moral foundations of Critical Theory appears in Seyla Benhabib, *Critique, Norm, and Utopia* (New York: Columbia University Press, 1986). For discussions of the critique of modern philosophy by Habermas and recent critical theorists, see Kenneth Baynes et al., *The End of Philosophy* (Cambridge: MIT Press, 1987). Patricia Mills provides an excellent discussion of Critical Theory and feminism in *Woman, Nature and Psyche* (New Haven: Yale University Press, 1987). The role of Critical Theory in the debate over postmodernism is elaborated by Douglas Kellner, "Postmodernism as Social Theory: Some Problems and Challenges," *Theory, Culture and Society* 5, no. 2/3 (1988).

The major works of T. W. Adorno available in English include (with Max Horkheimer) *Dialectic of Enlightenment* (New York: Herder and Herder, 1972); *Minima Moralia* (London: New Left Books, 1974); *Prisms* (London: Neville Spearman, 1967); *Jargon of Authenticity* (Evanston: Northwestern University Press, 1973); *Negative Dialectics* (London: Routledge & Kegan Paul, 1973); *Against Epistemology: A Metacritique* (Cambridge: MIT Press, 1982); and *Aesthetic Theory* (London: Routledge & Kegan Paul, 1984). Works on Adorno include Susan Buck-Morss, *The Origin of Negative Dialectics* (New York: The Free Press, 1977); Gillian Rose, *The Melancholy Science* (London: Macmillan, 1981); and Martin Jay, *Adorno* (Cambridge: Harvard University Press, 1984).

The most important works of Erich Fromm include *Escape from Freedom* (New York: Holt, Rinehart and Winston, 1941); *Man for Himself*

(New York: Holt, Rinehart and Winston, 1947); *The Sane Society* (New York: Holt, Rinehart and Winston, 1955); *The Crisis of Psychoanalysis* (New York: Holt, Rinehart, Winston, 1970); and *The Working Class in Weimar Germany* (Cambridge: Harvard University Press, 1984). On Fromm and Critical Theory, see Rainer Funk, *Erich Fromm: The Courage to Be Human* (New York: Continuum, 1982) and John Rickert, "The Fromm-Marcuse Debate Revisited," *Theory and Society* 15 (1986): 351–400.

Crucial works of Jürgen Habermas include *Structural Changes of the Public Sphere* (Cambridge: MIT Press, 1989); *Knowledge and Human Interests* (Boston: Beacon Press, 1972); *Theory and Practice* (Boston: Beacon Press, 1973); *Towards a Rational Society* (Boston: Beacon Press, 1970); *Legitimation Crisis* (Boston: Beacon Press, 1975); *Theory of Communicative Action*, 2 vols. (Boston: Beacon Press, 1983 and 1987); Peter Dews, ed., *Habermas: Autonomy and Solidarity* (London: New Left Books, 1986); and *The Philosophical Discourse of Modernity* (Cambridge: MIT Press, 1987). Major critical studies of Habermas include Thomas McCarthy, *The Critical Theory of Jürgen Habermas* (Cambridge: MIT Press, 1978) and Rick Roderick, *Habermas and the Foundations of Critical Theory* (New York: St. Martin's, 1986).

Max Horkheimer's most important works include *Dammerung* (Zurich: Verlag Oprecht & Helbling, 1934) [written under the pseudonym Heinrich Regius]; selections translated by Michael Shaw in *Dawn and Decline: Notes, 1926–1931 and 1950–1969* (New York: Seabury, 1978); *Critical Theory* (New York: Seabury, 1972); *Eclipse of Reason* (New York: Oxford University Press, 1974); and *Critique of Instrumental Reason* (New York: Seabury, 1974). On Horkheimer, see the critical studies in Alfred Schmidt and Norbert Altwicker, eds., *Max Horkheimer heute: Werk und Wirkung* (Frankfurt: Fisher, 1986).

Leo Lowenthal's major works include *Literature, Popular Culture and Society* (Englewood Cliffs, N.J.: Prentice-Hall, 1961); *Literature and the Image of Man* (Boston: Beacon Press, 1957); as well as the collection of his works published in *Literature and Mass Culture: Communication in Society*, vol. 1 (New Brunswick, N.J.: Transaction Books, 1984). On Lowenthal, see the essays collected in *Telos* 45 (Fall 1980).

The most influential writings of Herbert Marcuse include *Reason and Revolution* (Boston: Beacon Press, 1960); *Eros and Civilization* (Boston: Beacon Press, 1955); *One-Dimensional Man* (Boston: Beacon Press, 1964); *Negations* (Boston: Beacon Press, 1968); *An Essay on Liberation* (Boston: Beacon Press, 1969); *Counterrevolution and Revolt* (Boston: Beacon Press, 1972); and *The Aesthetic Dimension* (Boston: Beacon Press, 1978). Critical studies include Douglas Kellner, *Herbert Marcuse and the Crisis of Marxism* (London and Berkeley: Macmillan and University of

California Press, 1984) and Robert Pippin et al., eds., *Marcuse: Critical Theory and the Promise of Utopia* (South Hadley, Mass.: Bergin & Garvey, 1988).

Works by others associated with the Frankfurt School include Walter Benjamin, *Illuminations* (New York: Schocken, 1969) and *Reflections* (New York: Harcourt, Brace, Jovanovich, 1979); Friedrich Pollock, ed., *Gruppenexperiment* (Frankfurt: Institut für Sozialforschung, 1955); Pollock, *The Economic and Social Consequences of Automation* (Oxford: Basil Blackwell, 1957); Franz Neumann, *Behemoth* (New York: Oxford University Press, 1944); and the Frankfurt Institute for Social Research, *Aspects of Sociology* (Boston: Beacon Press, 1973). See also the excellent collection of essays in Andrew Arato and Eike Gebhardt, eds., *The Essential Frankfurt School Reader* (New York: Continuum, 1982) and the essays in T. W. Adorno et al., *The Positivist Dispute in German Sociology* (New York: Harper and Row, 1976).

Works by members of the second generation of Critical Theory include Alfred Schmidt, *The Concept of Nature in Marx* (London: New Left Books, 1971); Oskar Negt, *Politik als Protest* (Frankfurt: Agit-buch, 1971) and *Keine Demokratie ohne Sozialismus: Über den Zusammenhang von Politik, Geschichte und Moral* (Frankfurt: Suhrkamp, 1976; Negt and Alexander Kluge, *Öffentlichkeit und Erfahrung* (Frankfurt: Suhrkamp, 1972); Claus Offe, *Contradictions of the Welfare State* (London: Hutchinson, 1984) and *Disorganized Capitalism* (London: Polity Press, 1985). On Offe, see John Keane, "The Legacy of Political Economy: Thinking with and against Claus Offe," *Canadian Journal of Political and Social Theory* Vol. 2, No. 3 (Fall, 1978), pgs 49–92; Albrecht Wellmer, *Modernität und Post-modernität* (Frankfurt: Suhrkamp, 1985).